THE BEAUTIFUL, THE SUBLIME,
AND THE PICTURESQUE
IN
EIGHTEENTH-CENTURY
BRITISH AESTHETIC THEORY

WALTER JOHN HIPPLE, *Jr.*

The Beautiful, The Sublime, & The Picturesque

In

Eighteenth-Century British Aesthetic Theory

Carbondale

THE SOUTHERN ILLINOIS UNIVERSITY PRESS

1957

CONTENTS

v

THE BEAUTIFUL, THE SUBLIME,

AND THE PICTURESQUE

IN

EIGHTEENTH-CENTURY

BRITISH AESTHETIC THEORY

Philosophers, who find
Some favorite system to their mind,
In every point to make it fit,
Will force all nature to submit.

—SWIFT

INTRODUCTION

THIS STUDY is both more and less than its title suggests: more in that the writings on aesthetics of the authors treated are discussed without close restriction to arguments on beauty, sublimity, and picturesqueness; less in that numerous eighteenth-century writers on the beautiful, the sublime, and the picturesque, writers even of some intrinsic or historical importance, are omitted.

I

THE METHOD of my inquiry has dictated the first deviation from the subject as narrowly conceived. It is my opinion that previous reviews of the several aspects of eighteenth-century aesthetic theory —of sublimity, of the picturesque, of taste, or of still more limited topics—have been in some measure vitiated by this very limitation. Since sublimity and picturesqueness are usually defined by distinction from beauty and from one another, and since the principles, bases, and functions of these distinctions are ordinarily different in different writers, no adequate and accurate account of any one such character, divorced from the others, is possible. All three must be seen at once, for the philosophic problem consists partly in their interrelations.

The view of these aesthetic characters adopted by a writer is ordinarily a consequence of, or is at any rate referred to, a set of psychological (or metaphysical) principles, and is further determined by the devices of argumentation employed. Treatment of beauty, sublimity, and picturesqueness requires, therefore, some examination of the philosophic and methodological principles of the aestheticians surveyed. There is in all aesthetic phenomena, moreover, an interaction of subject and object—of the faculties of the percipient with the properties and relations of the aesthetic object—which makes it impossible to define either variable independently of the other: taste cannot be discussed in abstraction from the nature of beauty, nor is beauty definable apart from the nature of the mind apprehending it. Taste, therefore—and those faculties into which taste may be resolved, or with which it may be connected—must be treated conjointly with beauty. Very often, too, the solution of critical problems in the arts—of the paradox, for instance, that imitations of unpleasant originals may be aesthetically agreeable—is so closely connected with the view taken of the nature of beauty, or of taste, that such problems must be included as well.

II

EACH SYSTEM of aesthetics, then, is presented as an integral whole, and presented, moreover, in its own terms; and I have intended hereby to avoid two great evils of scholarly surveys. There is first (as I hope) no distortion of doctrine consequent upon wrenching fragments out of their systematic contexts to be incorporated into an historical or dialectical account organized on principles different from those of the systems analyzed. For most of the authors I have studied, there exist no accurate accounts of their positions; and this defect I hope that I have in some measure supplied.

A more subtle undermining of the logical integrity of texts results, it seems to me, from the almost universal practice of treating a "topic" as it appears in one or several authors. When a writer's pronouncements on the picturesque, or the use of figurative language, or the cultivation of taste, or the relation of judgment to genius (or whatever it may be) are picked out of his books and ranged alongside the pronouncements of his predecessors and successors, not only is the precise meaning lost, but the opinions usually come to seem shallow and witless. One comes away from articles or books about writers who were, in their day, reckoned as impressive thinkers convinced that *tous les hommes sont fous.* The opinions even of Aristotle and Hume, so reported, are such as any sophomore would reject with scorn. The great difference between the judgments of a good writer and those of everyman lies in the circumstance that in one case the opinions are supported by arguments and have a systematic connection with opinions on other topics. The philosophic value of a thought is a function of its context, and can be estimated only in its context. A major difference, then, between this study and many others of the same period, is—that I take the period, its writers, and its books seriously, and try to make the doctrines reported seem as plausible as I can by outlining their logical bases.

It will strike the reader of this study, that it does not seem to be a history. It is not a history; it is a philosophical survey of a series of aestheticians, a survey in which the writers are arranged chronologically chiefly for the reason that the later ones had read the earlier, and argue with them—arguments which are not fully intelligible unless one is familiar with the positions canvassed. My interest has been in systems considered as logical structures, not in the changing tastes, suppositions, and approaches of the men who create the systems; and I have wished to keep the two questions distinct.

The historical problem seems to me, moreover, exceptionally difficult of solution: what are those narrative propositions about eighteenth-century British aesthetics which will neither conflict with the data nor be so vaguely general as to be nugatory? The existing histories (books and articles) seem to me to fall into the two classes which R. S. Crane has described: philological and dialectical.[1] In a history of philosophy, or of some branch or problem of philosophy, handled as a philological inquiry, the influence of philosophical and methodological principles is minimized. The intellectual causes determining the propositions enunciated by theorists are ignored in favor of a technique of comparison of passages in the work treated with passages in other works exhibiting similarity in terms, distinctions, organization, or doctrine. This procedure does have the merit of focussing attention upon the text, and the more dubious advantage that the historian need have no special philosophic competence, and, indeed, need not even have read continuously or entire the texts he discusses. In its common form, the philological method produces source-and-influence studies; in its extreme form, scholars may be led to attempt solution of philosophical problems by merely linguistic considerations.

The other common mode of intellectual history is dialectical: the historian endeavors to cope with the diversity of terms, principles, and arguments in the writers he treats by arranging them under a set of organizing ideas which he himself supplies. These organizing ideas or terms must clearly be larger in scope—vaguer—than those used by the authors discussed; and very commonly they are ordered in pairs of general contraries—reason and feeling, objective and subjective, classical and romantic, Faustian and Apollonian, and so forth. The attitudes of authors, as inferred from or read into their statements, are ranged under such heads without much regard to the arguments by which the statements were supported; and lines of persistence and change are traced within or between these sets of attitudes. Such analogical history produces, in its more pedestrian mode, the studies of literary or philosophical problems which analyze the struggles of authors with the dilemmas and inconsistencies that appear when their texts are interpreted in the light of the historian's schematism; and in its more ambitious mode, studies in the evolution of the *Zeitgeist*.

III

NOT FINDING a history in the subject, and not desiring to superimpose one, I confine this book to the analysis of texts, interposing historical conjectures only where clear-cut intellectual causes appear to me. This analysis of texts is not intended to be précis-writing. There is summary of doctrine here, fuller, in the case of many of these writers, than is available elsewhere; but the summary is accompanied by commentary pointing out philosophic principles, methods of argument, interconnections of parts within systems, interrelations between systems. In particular, the disputes conducted so vigorously among the eighteenth-century aestheticians—most notably that three-cornered argument of Price, Knight, and Repton over the picturesque —are treated with the intention of showing how far translation from the language of one system into that of another can solve the differences, and how far they are real; and if real, how far they arise from the fundamental suppositions and argumentative techniques of the disputants. I have not hesitated to engage in criticism of my authors; but this criticism is not usually based only on difference of opinion. I have intended to discover the coherence and adequacy of each system. But the author of a system may through some prejudice or passion lose sight of or contravene his own principles; he may fail to carry them out to their full reach and scope; he may introduce dogmas logically unconnected with the system; and, of course, his principles may be from the first unequal to explanation of the phenomena. In confuting the opinions of predecessors or antagonists, moreover, authors characteristically misconceive and misstate the positions they attack; and the analyst must set these misconstructions right.

Before entering upon exposition of the several systems, it may be proper to hazard a few generalizations about the entire group of writers treated. All are concerned with a subject—beauty, or beauty and sublimity, or beauty and sublimity and picturesqueness—which transcends the boundaries between nature and art. The principles of aesthetics and criticism, accordingly, are sought not in the peculiar nature of art, but in what is common to nature and art—and this common element, since the Cartesian revolution in philosophy, is of course the mind which apprehends both realms. At the beginning of the century, Addison proclaimed that "Musick, Architecture and Painting, as well as Poetry and Oratory, are to deduce their Laws and Rules from the general Sense and Taste of Mankind, and not from the Principles of those Arts themselves; or, in other Words, the Taste is not to conform to the Art, but the Art to the Taste." [2] A host of writers during the century iterate and reiterate like opinions, and towards its close Alison echoes the thought once more, quoting the very passage from *The Spectator*.[3] All these aestheticians (again), whether philosophers, artists, or amateurs, are concerned with the response of the mind to the qualities and relations of objects in nature and art, and there are in every case three problems: the nature of the effects on the mind—beauty and sublimity and picturesqueness as feelings; the nature of the causes of those effects in objects—beauty and sublimity and picturesqueness as traits of the objects of perception and consciousness; and the nature of the connection between causes and effects—the mechanism of efficiency. The way in which these three problems are formulated and solved is, of course, in some measure unique in each writer, and the isolation of this uniqueness is the chief problem of the scholar.

In the first place, a distinction can be drawn between literal and dialectical writers—between, that is, those writers who employ terms univocally, who keep aesthetic questions separate (except for causal connections) from ethical and scientific questions, and who are concerned with discovering literal cause-and-effect sequences; and those writers who employ terms analogically (ordinarily arranged as contraries), who tend to bring aesthetics, ethics, and science under the same principles, and who argue less by cause-and-effect than by distinguishing "levels" of thought and reality. Of the writers here treated, Reynolds alone is dialectical. The great majority are literal, and seek literal causes of aesthetic sensibility; further differentiation can be effected by considering the kinds of causes discovered. The mechanism through which the objective properties and relations produce their subjective responses may be either physiological or psychological: that is, feelings of beauty (or of sublimity or picturesqueness) may be taken to be the direct consequence of organic and nervous responses, or (instead) they may be held to be the consequence of purely mental operations subsequent to perception or consciousness of their objects. No writer finds these aesthetic feelings *wholly* dependent on physiological agency, but physiological causes play a controlling role in the theory of Burke, a substantial role in that of Uvedale Price, and no inconsiderable part in the theory of Payne Knight.[4]

Those writers who emphasize mental faculties and operations as the essential mechanism producing our feelings of beauty may either postulate special faculties appropriated to this purpose—the internal senses of Hutcheson and Lord Kames—or may emphasize special modes of operation of faculties appropriated to other functions—notably the association of ideas. If internal senses are appealed to, a further distinction can be based on the number of such senses: whether various modes of beauty are analogically reduced to perceptions of one such sense (as in Hutcheson) or whether the number of senses is multiplied to match the different classes or material causes of beauty (as in Lord Kames).

If no extraordinary sense is discovered, and beauty is attributed to the ordinary faculties functioning in some special way, the case is more complex. If the term "association of ideas" is taken in a sense sufficiently loose, all of these mental phenomena can be so designated: thus Alison can be said to trace all aesthetic effect to "association." But if the term be taken this broadly (to which some writers make objection), then various kinds of association need to be discriminated. Associations among atomic impressions and ideas must be distinguished from habits and tendencies of the faculties. Comprised among atomic associations are associations between impressions of the external senses, as in the improved perceptions of sight. There are direct associations between sense impressions and passions. There are associations between the ideas of the qualities and relations of sensible objects and those of human personality. There are associations involving the ideas of external objects as wholes (i.e., in distinction from their qualities and relations severally), and these of two kinds: the ideas of the objects may be associated as such (the idea of a tree *qua* tree) with ideas of human life and activity, or with other affecting ideas; or they may be associated as signs or symbols (Matthew Arnold's Signal Elm, for instance) of historical, social, artistic, or other phenomena. The bent of a writer in attending more to one or more to another type of these associations is of great, indeed of crucial, influence in determining the kind of aesthetic system he will devise. Convinced of the importance of such differences in efficient causes for explaining the aesthetic doctrine, and the taste, of my writers, I have throughout noted with care the mechanisms they postulate or infer; and where there is enough of a general system to admit of such reduction, I have attempted to trace these positions to still more fundamental divergences.

IV

I HAVE REMARKED that this study is not only, in one sense, more, but in another, less than it seems to promise. It is less, since not all writers, perhaps not even all important writers, on beauty, sublimity, and picturesqueness, are included in the survey. Among the authors not treated (unless by allusion) are Shaftesbury, Richardson, Akenside, Harris, Spence, Webb, Lowth, Adam Smith, James Usher, Thomas Whately, Beattie, Priestley, John Stedman, William Greenfield,[5] Jeffrey, and Brown. Some apology will be demanded for the inclusion of *this,* and the exclusion of *that* author—perhaps for the exclusion of any. It was my feeling, that any writer treated at all should be treated fully, and a necessary limitation of scale prevented this full treatment of *all* pertinent writers. A selection being necessary, I have dwelt, first, upon those writers who appear to me to be of greatest intrinsic interest, and, second, upon those who are necessary antecedents to the former. This second criterion accounts for the exclusion of philosophers like Shaftesbury and Adam Smith in favor of amateurs and gardeners like Gilpin and Repton. The inclusion of Addison needs, I suppose, no apology, since (though by no means a profound thinker) Addison far more than any other writer initiated and directed the aesthetic speculation of the century. Gilpin plays a rather similar role in the discussion of the picturesque late in the century. Repton is so inextricably intertwined in controversy with Price and Knight that he could not well be omitted (and it was an additional incentive that there exists no comprehensive study of Repton's theory). Hume and Blair and Reid are not of signal importance as aestheticians, but the cogency of Hume's brief observations, and his standing as a philosopher, alike demand his inclusion; Blair's role as the leading rhetorician, and Reid's as the leading philosopher of the latter part of the century, dictated a study of their views. The works of Hutcheson and Hogarth, Gerard and Burke, Kames and Reynolds, Alison, Price, and Knight, and of Dugald

Stewart make defense of their inclusion unnecessary, for these are the major works of the century.

One final note may be proper to this Introduction. I am aware that the words "aesthetic," "aesthetics," were not used in the eighteenth century; the study now termed "aesthetics" was then most often called "philosophical criticism." But this term, besides being cumbersome, seems to imply, because of the ordinary connection of "criticism" with art, a particular theory of aesthetics, and one very foreign to the British writers of the eighteenth century. I have, therefore, indulged the anachronism of employing the modern term.

I

Beautiful and Sublime

CHAPTER 1

Joseph Addison

ఘ

ALTHOUGH writers like John Dennis and Lord Shaftesbury had been discussing the sublime, or the sublime and the beautiful, for some years, it was Addison's "Essay on the Pleasures of the Imagination" which formulated the problems of aesthetics in such a fashion as to initiate that long discussion of beauty and sublimity—and later of the picturesque—which attracted the interest and exercised the talents of philosophers, men of letters, artists, and amateurs until well into the nineteenth century.

When Addison announced his forthcoming essay—comprised in *The Spectator* papers of June 21 through July 3, 1712 (Nos. 411–21)—he spoke of it as an undertaking "intirely new." [1] Doubtless nothing is entirely new under the sun, and much ink has been shed in tracing out faint anticipations of Addison's thoughts; Longinus, and the commentators on Longinus, have been raked through, philosophers from the time of Descartes and Hobbes have been searched, French critics and English poets have been examined—yet after all, Addison's claim to originality seems sound enough. In any event, I propose to rest in the conviction shared by most of the eighteenth-century aestheticians, that their science began with Addison.

The papers on the pleasures of imagination were intended by Addison to be ancillary to an inquiry into the nature and acquisition of a "fine Taste of Writing," an inquiry broached in *Spectator* No. 409, which announces the forthcoming series. The last five papers of the "Essay" itself are devoted to this application, although it is the more purely aesthetic portion of the series which was chiefly influential on Addison's successors. The account of taste is slender enough, yet Addison contrives to suggest many of the avenues of inquiry which later writers explored more thoroughly. The analogy of mental with physical taste suggests that taste consists in a discriminating perception which can discern "not only the general Beauties and Imperfections of an Author, but discover the several Ways of thinking and expressing himself, which diversify him from all other Authors, with the several Foreign Infusions of Thought and Language, and the particular Authors from whom they were borrowed." [2] It is not difficult to see in this view of taste, or in the definition of it as *"that Faculty of the Soul, which discerns the Beauties of an Author with Pleasure, and the Imperfections with Dislike,"* [3] the sensibility, the acute perception or "refinement," and the correctness which Gerard was later to elucidate and analyze. The examination for taste which Addison provides supposes these same characteristics of the faculty: one should be delighted by admired authors (sensibility), should be able to isolate the peculiar virtue of an author (refinement), and should see the difference between the expression of a thought by a great writer and a mediocre (correctness). Addison's taste in criticism is Longinian; he wishes for critics who will go beyond formulation of architectonic rules to isolate that more essential excellence which "elevates and astonishes the Fancy, and gives a Greatness of Mind to the Reader. . . ." [4] He proposes himself to supply this defect, and his "Essay" enters upon this criticism of qualities more essential than the formal traits of literary kinds.

By "Pleasures of the Imagination," Addison means "such as arise from visible Objects, either when we have them actually in our View, or when we call up their Ideas into our Minds by Paintings, Statues, Descriptions, or any the like Occasion." [5] Although Addison complains of the "loose and uncircumscribed" use of the term "imagination," and announces that he will "fix and determine" its meaning, he really employs it to designate a conglomerate faculty of presentation, of memory, of conception, and of association both controlled and undirected: the "noble Writer," Addison remarks, "should be born with this Faculty in its full Strength and Vigour, so as to be able to receive lively Ideas from outward Objects, to retain them long, and to range them together, upon occasion, in such Figures and Representations as are most likely to hit the Fancy of the Reader." [6] Yet despite this broad notion of imagination, Addison restricts it to ideas of sight: "We cannot indeed have a single Image in the Fancy that did not make its first Entrance through the Sight. . . ." [7] Now, putting aside the objection that *mere* sight does not perceive even distance and size, it is clear that images or ideas of the other senses are retained and used by the fancy, though not retained so vividly nor used so freely as those of sight; Addison himself later instances the associated pleasures drawn from other senses in actual perception, and it is not easy to see how he is to explain the "blending" of sounds and smells and sights if qualities of sight are perceived by "imagination" and those of the other senses by some other and unspecified faculty. Still more grave in its consequences is the exclusion from imagination of all the objects of consciousness, the operations of mind. Are not passions, volitions, deliberations, all remembered and conceived reflectively? and separated, modified, and compounded? By excluding such objects from the imagination, Addison is led to ignore the manifold interconnections of the mental and material worlds, and therefore also all the beauty and sublimity flowing from the cognition of mental traits either directly or through their material expressions and analogues.

The distinction Addison draws between primary pleasures of the imagination, which "entirely proceed from such Objects as are before our Eyes," and secondary pleasures, "which flow from the Ideas of visible Objects, when the Objects are not actually before the Eye, but are called up into our Memories, or formed into agreeable Visions of Things that are either Absent or Fictitious," [8] has been often misconceived. Some commentators have thought that this division somehow follows out Locke's distinction of primary and secondary qualities of matter—with which it appears to me to have nothing in common but the words "primary" and "secondary," used in a sense different from Locke's.[9] Nor are Addison's primary and secondary pleasures correspondent with Hutcheson's absolute and relative beauty; for relative beauty is the beauty of imitation, whereas Addison's secondary pleasures, though they may proceed from imitation, do not essentially do so—there is no pleasure from recognition of imitation in the mere conception of an absent object. The secondary pleasures do not necessarily involve art: mere conceptions of memory afford them. They arise, in short, from objects "that once entered in at our Eyes, and are afterwards called up into the Mind *either* barely by its own Operations, *or* on occasion of something without us, as Statues, or Descriptions." [10]

Addison concludes his first paper with those observations on the advantages of the pleasures of imagination which were to be copied and enlarged upon throughout the following century—that the pleasures of imagination are intermediate between those of sense and of intellect, since they "do not require such a Bent of Thought as is necessary to our more serious Employments, nor, at the same Time, suffer the Mind to sink into that Negligence and Remissness, which are apt to accompany our more sensual Delights, but, like a gentle Exercise to the Faculties, awaken them from Sloth and Idleness, without putting them upon any Labour or Difficulty." [11]

Returning to the primary pleasures, Addison makes his most signal advance in aesthetic theory by distinguishing three sources for them: the great, the uncommon, the beautiful. The differentiation of the great, or sublime, and the beautiful is the most striking feature of eighteenth-century aesthetic theory, and even Addison's threefold division—although obnoxious to objection for making novelty (which is a relation) co-ordinate with the qualities of beauty and sublimity—shows a remarkable persistence. Akenside employed it in his celebrated didactic poem, *The Pleasures of Imagination*.[12] Forty years after Addison wrote, Joseph Warton declared that "greatness, novelty, and beauty, are usually and justly reckoned the three principal sources of the pleasures that strike the imagination." [13] Still later Daniel Webb was to write that "the Jupiter and Minerva of Phidias were subjects of astonishment in the most enlightened ages. It should seem, that the wonderful effect of these statues, proceeded from an union of the beautiful, with the great and uncommon; thus combining the whole influence of visible objects on the imagination." [14] And even Thomas Reid, though pointing out the fault of the categorization, and striking out novelty in the course of his argument, still adopts the division as a tentative arrangement.[15]

Some partial anticipations of Addison's distinction have been noted by Monk and others who have traced the development of Longinian sublimity, yet there appears to remain an irreducible surd of originality in the clear differentiation of beauty and sublimity. Monk has observed that Addison does not, in his "Essay on the Pleasures of the Imagination," use the term "sublimity," presumably because of its association with rhetoric and purely critical writing.[16] Addison's critique of *Paradise Lost* is perhaps the best place to study his use of "sublimity"; it is noteworthy that throughout this entire series, Addison speaks of actions and characters and objects as being "great," "noble," "majestic," "magnificent," "marvellous," and so forth—but never as being "sublime." Addison does speak, to be sure, of Milton's "sublime Genius," "sublime imagination," and "sublime manner of thinking," but this is a mere grammatical shorthand—"sublime genius" means, not genius which is itself sublime as an object, but a genius for turning out sublime images and taxemes.[17] The term "sublimity" is really confined in its application to images, to sentiments, and to certain devices of language; Addison uses the word, in short, precisely as Longinus does.

Attention to the nature of those Miltonic descriptions the greatness (or the sublimity) of which Addison especially admires illumines his conception of greatness, for numbers of them are images of those stupendous prospects which, in the "Pleasures of the Imagination" papers, typify greatness. Thus, Satan's sitting on the brink of the causeway from Heaven to Earth, "and taking a Survey of the whole Face of Nature, that appeared to him new and fresh in all its Beauties, with the Simile illustrating this Circumstance, fills the Mind of the Reader with as surprising and glorious an Idea as any that arises in the whole Poem." [18] The scene, in Addison's terminology, is great, the simile sublime. Again, Satan's "Roaming upon the Frontiers of the Creation, between that Mass of Matter, which was wrought into a World, and that shapeless unformed Heap of Materials, which still lay in *Chaos* and Confusion, strikes the Imagination with something astonishingly great and wild." [19] Here is the same taste, the same delight in spatial magnitude, especially when wild and "rude," that determines the illustrations in the "Pleasures of the Imagination": "By *Greatness* [Addison declares], I do not only mean the Bulk of any single Object, but the Largeness of a whole View, considered as one entire Piece. Such are the Prospects of an open Champian Country, a vast uncultivated Desart, of huge Heaps of Mountains, high Rocks and Precipices, or a wide Expanse of Waters, where we are not struck with the Novelty or Beauty of the Sight, but with that rude kind of Magnificence which appears in many of these stupendous Works of Nature." [20] Theodore Moore calls this emphasis on magnitude "Addison's confusion of external size of form with an aesthetic sublime." [21] It is unquestionable that Addison sees an "aesthetic sublime" in physical magnitude—but why is this a confusion? Vast objects tease the imagination, which "loves to be filled with an Object, or to grasp at any thing that is too big for its Capacity," and "we are flung into a pleasing Astonishment at such unbounded Views, and feel a delightful Stilness and Amazement in the Soul at the Apprehension of them." The delight in vastness arises also (which I take to be a distinct cause) from the circumstance that "the Mind of Man naturally hates every thing that looks like a Restraint upon it, and is apt to fancy it self under a sort of Confinement, when the Sight is pent up in a narrow Compass, and shortened on every side by the Neighborhood of Walls or Moun-

tains." [22] The last phrase is interesting, for it suggests very strongly
Addison's preference of open prospects to, say, mountain passes, or
his preference of the Pantheon to a Gothic cathedral, his preference
(in brief) of horizontal extent as against elevation. In any event,
vastness causes a feeling resembling that with which we are struck
by the rhetorical sublime, and the transition is natural and obvious.
It is usual to remark that Longinus himself compares the sublime
with physical greatness:

> [Nature] has from the start implanted in our souls an irresistible love
> of whatever is great and stands to us as the more divine to the less.
> Wherefore not even the whole of the universe suffices for man's con-
> templation or scope of thought, but human speculations frequently exceed
> its compass. . . . Hence indeed it is that moved by some natural im-
> pulse we do not marvel at small streams . . . but at the Nile, the
> Danube, or the Rhine, and much more at the Ocean; nor yet are we
> more stirred by this flamelet that we kindle . . . than by the fires
> in heaven . . . or consider it more wondrous than the craters of
> Aetna. . . .[23]

This identification of the sublime with physical vastness was in
part a consequence of the adjustment philosophers and theologians
had made to the Copernican cosmology: the infinity of deity was
conceived by men like More and Burnet as extending through unbounded space, and the spatial immensity was seen as an image of
the divine nature.[24] The sublime thus became an aid to enthusiastic
devotion, and Addison judged this to be its final cause. But there
is also a purely systematic reason why Addison should stress magnitude: the sublime must depend on visual images, in consequence of
Addison's limitation upon the scope of imagination—and the only
trait of visible objects which astonishes the mind without operating
clearly as a sign or by engaging the passions, is magnitude.

There is in Addison no complicated discussion of the comparative
greatness of height, depth, and horizontal extent, or of the sublimity
of time, or of the multitudinous other causes of the sublime which
so occupy the attention of Gerard, of Burke, and of later writers.
Nor is the psychological mechanism of sublimity traced beyond the
apparently instinctive love of the imagination to expand and yet be
baffled, or its instinctive hatred of circumscription. This is no more
than a hint towards a theory of sublimity.

The new or uncommon, Addison affirms, "Raises a Pleasure in
the Imagination because it fills the Soul with an agreeable Surprise,
gratifies its Curiosity, and gives it an Idea of which it was not

before possest." [25] Addison's conception of novelty is very general: though the new and the singular are separately named, their effects are not differentiated; there is no discussion of unexpectedness; nor any distinction of immediate from subsequent response; nor any treatment of the commingling of novelty with feelings other than the sublime and beautiful. Addison's novelty, indeed, includes variety and even motion and change generally.[26] The very generality of the notion makes source-hunting equally easy and inconclusive: for in what writer can we look without discovering some of these topics?

"But there is nothing," Addison continues, "that makes its way more directly to the Soul than *Beauty,* which immediately diffuses a secret Satisfaction and Complacency through the Imagination, and gives a Finishing to any thing that is Great or Uncommon." The gaiety of the emotion of beauty is insisted upon by numerous writers throughout the century, partly, no doubt, in consequence of the desire to distinguish it from the graver emotion of sublimity; as Addison puts it, "the very first Discovery of it [Beauty] strikes the Mind with an inward Joy, and spreads a Chearfulness and Delight through all its Faculties." [27] The beautiful and sublime, though different and distinguishable, are nowise incompatible for Addison, the two pleasures being even heightened by their conjunction. In certain contexts the sublime is made a species of the beautiful, as when Addison speaks loosely of the "beauties" (i.e., the excellences) of writing: he has endeavored to show, he says, that some passages of *Paradise Lost* "are beautifull by being Sublime, others by being Soft, others by being Natural. . . ." [28] Observing that different species of animals appear to have different notions of sexual beauty, Addison concludes that beauty is a function of our nature, not a property inherent in objects absolutely. He takes no pains (as Burke and later writers were quick to point out [29]) to show that the sexual attractions are based upon the perception of a beauty bearing any analogy to that more general beauty "in the several Products of Art and Nature" which consists "either in the Gaiety or Variety of Colours, in the Symmetry and Proportion of Parts, in the Arrangement and Disposition of Bodies, or in a just Mixture and Concurrence of all together." [30]

In treating both beauty and sublimity, Addison has limited himself strictly to the visual-tactile properties, and even these are not exhausted, for there is no study of the beauty or sublimity of motion. The fashion in which sound becomes beautiful or sublime is given no study beyond the observation that agreeable sounds conjoined with sights in particular scenes may reinforce the visual delights. There is no hint of the sublimity of the terrific, or of power or energy, or of moral grandeur or intellectual force, and none of the beauty of the softer moral traits and their expressions.

Nor, in the discussion of beauty, do we find even those hints of the efficient mechanism which Addison presented in his discussion of sublimity and novelty. He tells us, indeed, that "it is impossible for us to assign the necessary Cause of this [aesthetic] Pleasure, because we know neither the Nature of an Idea, nor the Substance of a Human Soul, which might help us to discover the Conformity or Disagreeableness of the one to the other; and therefore, for want of such a Light, all that we can do in Speculations of this kind, is to reflect on those Operations of the Soul that are most agreeable, and to range, under their proper Heads, what is pleasing or displeasing to the Mind, without being able to trace out the several necessary and efficient Causes from whence the Pleasure or Displeasure arises." [31] It is true that efficient causes in the sense of ultimate ties between matter and mind or antecedents and consequents, are undiscoverable; but a phenomenological account of the invariant sequences of sense perception, mental operation, and feeling is still possible; and Addison shirks the chief problem and difficulty when he gives up the search for efficient causes in favor of final causes which "lie more bare and open to our Observation" and "are generally more useful than the other, as they give us greater Occasion of admiring the Goodness and Wisdom of the first Contriver." [32] The final causes which Addison postulates are that delight in the great leads us to the contemplation of Deity, that pleasure in the novel stimulates our study of the creation, that attraction to our own species prevents the production of infertile monsters, that general beauty makes the creation gay and agreeable. Such insights as these seem hardly a sufficient recompense for the efficient causes we are denied; but Addison's merit is, after all, rather to initiate various lines of inquiry than to arrive at conclusive results.

Addison's aesthetic analysis is complicated by the overlapping of various distinctions he employs: since the distinction of primary and secondary pleasures does not correspond to a distinction between art and nature, we find art affording primary pleasures and nature secondary. [33] Nature alone can exhibit true vastness, "but tho' there are several of these wild Scenes, that are more delightful than any artificial Shows; yet we find the Works of Nature still more pleasant, the more they resemble those of Art: For in this case our Pleasure rises from a double Principle; from the Agreeableness of the Objects to the Eye, and from their Similitude to other Objects: We are pleased as well with comparing their Beauties, as with surveying them, and can represent them to our Minds, either as Copies or Originals." [34] Here Nature yields a secondary pleasure through its resemblance to art works which it suggests: and here, I take it, is a hint of William Gilpin's *picturesque*—the natural scene suitable for pictorial representation because composed *like* a picture. Addison, as always, throws out only hints: he does not distinguish the feelings evoked by a natural scene which is merely composed *as if* by design, and by one which calls to mind particular works of art, or the manner of particular masters or schools. The converse principle, *ars est celare artem*, is more a commonplace; but Addison's application of it to gardening theory betrays an advanced taste. Not only does Addison regard parterres and topiary work with some contempt; he envisions the *ferme ornée*. In a later *Spectator*, Addison (disguised as a correspondent) writes with pride that "if a Foreigner who had seen nothing of our Country should be conveyed into my Garden at his first landing, he would look upon it as a natural Wilderness, and one of the uncultivated Parts of our Country." [35] In this same paper Addison recommends a winter garden of plants which are not deciduous—the first such suggestion (I believe) in English garden literature. And he concludes with a rhapsody which (like the proposal for a winter garden) anticipates in little Lord Kames's enthusiasm for the art: "I look upon the Pleasure which we take in a Garden, as one of the most innocent Delights in humane Life. A Garden was the Habitation of our first Parents before the Fall. It is naturally apt to fill the Mind with Calmness and Tranquility, and to lay all its turbulent Passions at Rest. It gives us a great Insight into the Contrivance and Wisdom of Providence, and suggests innumerable Subjects for Meditation." [36]

But to return—there are not only secondary pleasures in nature, but primary pleasures in art. The art which beyond others yields primary pleasures is, of course, architecture. Greatness is the distinguishing excellence of architecture, greatness not only of absolute dimension, but of manner, "which has such force upon the Imagination, that a small Building, where *it* appears, shall give the Mind nobler Ideas than one of twenty times the Bulk, where the Manner is ordinary or little." [37] That there is a greatness of manner in which major parts are few and imposing, unperplexed by minute divisions and ornaments, is evident;[38] that on this account the interior of the Pantheon fills the imagination "with something Great and Amazing," while that of a Gothic cathedral affects but little, "which can arise from nothing else but the Greatness of the Manner in the one, and the Meanness in the other," [39] is less certain. Addison was insensitive to the sublimity of Gothic, and his account of greatness lacks the elements which could correct his prejudice. The Gothic sublimity depends in great measure on the height of the roof, greater than that of the Pantheon in actuality and still greater in appearance because of the relative narrowness; but Addison's treatment of greatness does not remark the peculiar effects of height, or the influence of the terrific, or the element of wonder, or the impression made by dim light, or indeed anything which might contribute to an appreciation of the greatness of Gothic. The greatness of the Pantheon consists, according to Addison's analysis, chiefly in the circumstance of the rotunda's being perceived in one *coup d'oeil;* Burke later brings the sublimity of a rotunda under what he terms the artificial infinite, the succession of uniform parts which gives the imagination no rest. [40] There is no reason why Addison could not admit Burke's principle (though he could not subscribe to the physiological explanation which Burke hazards); if he had employed Burke's principle, he would have been led by the same reasoning to appreciate the effect of the Gothic nave.

Many, perhaps most, of the pleasures of art are secondary, proceeding from "that Action of the Mind, which compares the Ideas arising from the Original Objects, with the Ideas we receive from the Statue, Picture, Description, or Sound that represents them." [41] As with the primary pleasures, Addison does not seek the efficient cause, and he supplies this defect with a final cause, the encouraging of search after truth, which depends upon comparing ideas together to observe their congruity and disagreement.

The mimetic arts (all, that is, save gardening and architecture) are enumerated in order of degree of resemblance to their originals: sculpture, painting, verbal description, music. Description in words of visible objects may produce more lively ideas (Addison maintains) than the things themselves, because of the poet's powers of selection and combination; and no doubt the same observation is true in lesser degree of the other arts. Indeed, "because the Mind of Man requires something more perfect in Matter, than what it finds there, and can never meet with any Sight in Nature which sufficiently answers its highest Ideas of Pleasantness; or, in other Words, because the Imagination can fancy to it self Things more Great, Strange, or Beautiful, than the Eye ever saw, and is still sensible of some Defect in what it has seen; on this account it is the part of a Poet to humour the Imagination in its own Notions, by mending and perfecting Nature where he describes a Reality, and by adding greater Beauties than are put together in nature, where he describes a Fiction," provided only that he does not, by reforming nature too much, "run into Absurdities, by endeavouring to excel." [42]

The secondary pleasures are distinguished further by the circumstance—one of the persistent problems of the century—that disagreeable originals may please "in an apt description," or, no doubt, in a skilful painting or even in a statue. Addison's explanation is of the simplest: the pleasure of comparing "the Ideas that arise from Words [or from the plastic medium], with the Ideas that arise from the Objects themselves." [43] Since the pleasure of comparison is, by this account, simply reckoned off against the unpleasantness of the image, a pleasant subject, *caeteris paribus*, is preferable: "But if the Description of what is Little, Common, or Deformed, be acceptable to the Imagination, the Description of what is Great, Surprising, or Beautiful, is much more so; because here we are not only delighted with *comparing* the Representation with the Original, but are highly pleased with the Original it self." [44] Another recommendation of description is that it may represent to us "such Objects as are apt to raise a secret Ferment in the Mind of the Reader, and to work, with Violence, upon his Passions." [45] This principle introduces that special case of the imitation of unpleasant originals which is most often treated of—the pity and fear of tragedy. Beyond the recognition of just imitation in this case, is the agreeable consciousness of our own security from the perils and sufferings represented, a consciousness permitted by the comparative detachment with which we view imitations.[46]

In the final paper of the series, Addison appears to approach to the beauty and sublimity of mind by treating of the similitudes and allegories drawn from "the visible Parts of Nature," by means of which allusions a truth of understanding is reflected in an image of imagination. But although this subject might have led into the realm of the associations and expressions by which mental and material beauty and sublimity are fused, Addison has nothing more in mind than the ornamental function which such figures may serve in writing, and his observations are mere critical points about the subjects and uses of such ornaments. Addison remains a sort of materialist, sticking close to the visual properties of external objects; he seems to see in the objects of consciousness, in the operations of the mind itself, little that is pertinent to aesthetics. He is the only British aesthetician who so limits the province of imagination and the range of qualities which provide its pleasures.

The various phenomena of association could have bridged the gap between mind and matter for Addison, and he was not unaware of the influence of association—yet he makes little enough of it. He treats briefly of association among the impressions of the different senses,[47] and briefly also of the associations of ideas, especially of those associations based upon contiguity (". . . a particular Smell or Colour is able to fill the Mind, on a sudden, with the Picture of the Fields or Gardens where we first met with it, and to bring up into View all the Variety of Images that once attended it" [48]). This phenomenon, as also the heightened delightfulness of pleasant scenes reviewed reflectively, Addison explains by a "Cartesian" associationism, involving a hypothetical physiology of brain traces and animal spirits. Yet I think it clear from Addison's denial of the possibility of finding efficient causes when "we know neither the Nature of an Idea, nor the Substance of a Human Soul," that he cannot subscribe to these Cartesian explanations in all earnestness.[49]

Addison's aesthetic theory is valuable not for its systematic rigor or its psychological profundity, for these merits it has in very ordinary measure, but for its clear and simple formulation of a set of problems which were to exercise many of the keenest minds for the following century and more, and which established as well a vogue in popular taste and a pattern for practicing artists. The problems were the nature of our sentiments of beauty and like aesthetic feelings, the material causes of these responses, the function of the aesthetic feelings, and—though this last problem Addison himself shirked—the mechanism through which the feelings are generated.[50] But this estimate of Addison's accomplishment is not new: it is that of the eighteenth century. As Hugh Blair put it, "Mr. Addison was the first who attempted a regular inquiry [into the pleasures of taste], in his Essay on the Pleasures of the Imagination. . . . He has reduced these Pleasures under three heads; Beauty, Grandeur, and Novelty. His speculations on this subject, if not exceedingly profound, are, however, very beautiful and entertaining; and he has the merit of having opened a track, which was before unbeaten." [51]

CHAPTER 2

Francis Hutcheson

THE FIRST treatise to follow the path of aesthetic inquiry which Addison had opened up—the first philosophical document in modern aesthetics—was *An Inquiry into the Original of Our Ideas of Beauty and Virtue*.[1] Issued anonymously in 1725, this work was the first important performance by Francis Hutcheson, Presbyterian teacher and later professor of moral philosophy at Glasgow. The *Inquiry* was followed three years later by *An Essay on the Nature and Conduct of the Passions and Affections. With Illustrations of the Moral Sense. By the Author of the Inquiry into the Original of Our Ideas of Beauty and Virtue*,[2] and the two works constitute a kind of unity. Hutcheson's theory has attracted some attention in the past few decades, though it has not been accorded any very persuasive exposition. The major study is W. R. Scott's *Francis Hutcheson: His Life, Teaching and Position in the History of Philosophy*, and Scott's attitude is belittling: "To foster the taste for Philosophy was Hutcheson's main work. It would be unreasonable to expect that he also created a Philosophy." [3] Expecting not much in the way of systematic thought, Scott does not find much. He discerns three stages in Hutcheson's development—represented by the *Inquiry*, the *Essay*, and the *System of Moral Philosophy* together with the fourth edition of the *Inquiry*. Hutcheson himself, however, had never thought the *System* ready for the press; and in the two earlier works he speaks with entire unconsciousness of any shift in his position. Indeed, throughout the *Essay* volume, he refers to his four treatises by number, as if they constituted parts of a single system: "An Inquiry concerning Beauty, Order, &c." becomes Treatise I; "An Inquiry concerning the Original of Our Ideas of Virtue or Moral Good," Treatise II; "An Essay on the Nature and Conduct of the Passions," Treatise III; and "Illustrations upon the Moral Sense," Treatise IV.

Scott's entire study is weakened by his adoption of an arbitrarily genetic approach; some recent studies, while avoiding this fault, have been too slight to be very valuable; an adequate treatment of Hutcheson's thought remains to be written.[4]

Hutcheson's method is partly differential, partly integral. Less of a Platonist than Shaftesbury, Hutcheson separates beauty from morality (for though the moral may be beautiful, its morality is distinct from its beauty); beauty and morality spring from different causes and appeal to different faculties. Yet the beauty of which Hutcheson is in search is found in physical objects, in the theorems of science, in the acts of rational agents: clearly this beauty is analogical, a universal appearing in similar but not literally identical manifestations in these radically different subjects. It is possible to see how the problem which Hutcheson had engaged, together with his chosen method, would lead naturally to such a result. Hutcheson's interest was primarily ethical; his metaphysics and aesthetics are ancillary to the ethical speculations in which his major contributions were made. As a half-way disciple of Shaftesbury, Hutcheson was concerned to vindicate human nature against the selfish theories of ethics, the Hobbesian and Mandevillian, which engrossed the attention of disputants at this time, and also to correct the errors of those anti-Hobbists who injudiciously traced the springs of virtue to divine reward and punishment or to the natural self-gratulatory pleasure of virtue. The line which Hutcheson took as a guide through the labyrinthine maze of error was the notion of internal senses; by "sense" Hutcheson means, "a *Determination of the Mind, to receive any Idea from the Presence of an Object, Which occurs to us, independently on our Will.*"[5] Reacting against strained reduction of apparently clear perceptions to remote (and sometimes discreditable) principles, he tends always to assert the originality of the perceptions. The slightness and generality of his metaphysics facilitated the proliferation of original principles which this approach involved.

Hutcheson's spontaneous interest in aesthetics was probably slight. He displays little familiarity with works of art and a pretty casual appreciation of external nature; his aesthetics is coldly schematic. The principal design of the inquiries into beauty and virtue is to show, "*That* human Nature *was not left quite indifferent in the affair of* Virtue, *to form to it self Observations concerning the* Advantage *or* Disadvantage *of Actions, and accordingly to regulate its Conduct.*"[6] The sense of beauty is taken up first, however, because, "*If the Reader is convinc'd of such Determinations of the Mind to be pleas'd with* Forms, Proportions, Resemblances, Theorems, *it will be no difficult matter to apprehend another* superior Sense natural *to Men, determining them to be pleas'd with* Actions, Characters, Affections." [7]

"Beauty," Hutcheson remarks as he begins his analysis, "is taken for the Idea rais'd in us, and a Sense of Beauty for our Power of receiving this Idea," and the object of the inquiry is "to discover what is the immediate Occasion of these pleasant Ideas, or what real Quality in the Objects ordinarily excites them." [8] The ideas of beauty are either original and absolute or comparative and relative—in both cases ideal, but in the latter imitative or resemblant. "All *Beauty*," Hutcheson declares, "is relative to the Sense of some Mind perceiving it; but what we call *relative* is that which is apprehended in any *Object*, commonly consider'd as an *Imitation* of some Original: And this *Beauty* is founded on a *Conformity*, or a kind of *Unity* between the Original and the Copy." [9] The investigation of original beauty is concise; Hutcheson turns first to its simpler kinds, as in regular figures. "The Figures that excite in us the Ideas of Beauty, seem to be those in which there is *Uniformity amidst Variety*. There are many Conceptions of Objects that are agreeable upon other accounts, such as Grandeur, Novelty, Sanctity, and some others. . . . But what we call Beautiful in Objects, to speak in the Mathematical Style, seems to be in a compound Ratio of Uniformity and Variety. . . ." [10] The internal sense, consequently, is *"a passive Power of receiving Ideas of Beauty from all Objects in which there is Uniformity amidst Variety."* [11] The question should be raised, why Hutcheson takes the beauty of figure as simplest, when he acknowledges that the eye of itself perceives only color. The answer is, I suppose, that study of the beauty of color leads directly to no important results universally applicable, whereas the principle of uniformity in variety is applicable (analogically, at least) to pretty nearly any subject. Intellectual comprehension of the variety in uniformity is of course not prerequisite to the perception of beauty; the internal sense is immediately affected by that compound ratio. It is true, however, that the greatest variety in uniformity is to be found in the realm of intellect—a theorem of science may contain an infinity of infinites, as the theory of tangents applies to infinite species of curves, each of which contains an infinity of sizes, each of which in turn comprises an infinity of individuals. Again, a principle may be deductively fertile, like the Newtonian laws or the theory of natural rights; the desire of reducing to system is stimulated by the aesthetic sense independently of any notion of utility.

Scott finds that in the later phases of Hutcheson's thought uniformity tends to displace variety in the formula.[12] I believe, however, that Scott takes mere rhetorical changes for changes in doctrine, and does so because he misconceives the formula in the first instance. Scott understands that the discovery of new uniformities *ipso facto* reduces variety; this is not true. Variety is the number and kind of parts, units, aspects, or whatever that make up the whole; and uniformity is the relations (of resemblance, causation, illation, or what not) obtaining among them. Uniformity can, accordingly, vary in some part independently of variety; the properties of a regular plane figure are very numerous, but the discovery of new ones does not reduce its variety, for the number of sides and angles is unchanged. A number of modern aestheticians are concerned with this very relation of uniformity and variety. George D. Birkhoff, for instance, finds the formula for beauty to be the ratio of uniformity ("order," as he terms it) to variety ("complexity"), whereas Hutcheson had found it to be the *compound* ratio—i.e., the product. This difference arises from Birkhoff's premise that all mental effort (as in perceiving variety) is painful, and that recognition of order is a kind of reward for the effort; for a given uniformity, then, the more variety the less satisfaction.[13] Hutcheson, like other writers of his century, supposes instead that the mind finds vacuity painful, so that variety is inherently pleasurable up to a certain rate of perception; for a given uniformity, the more variety tied together by it the better. Hutcheson's position seems to me the only defensible one on this point.

The more complex problems of beauty are found in relative beauty. The beauty of imitations of the unattractive is explained in this system merely in terms of the pleasure of imitation as such. But the notion of "imitation" is given some breadth by the possibility that imitation is of intention or idea rather than of a natural object. Artists, accordingly, may "not form their Works so as to attain the highest Perfection of *original Beauty* separately consider'd; because a Composition of this *relative Beauty*, along with some degree of the *original* Kind, may give more Pleasure, than a more *perfect original Beauty* separately. Thus we can see that *Regularity* in laying out of Gardens in *Parterres, Vista's, parallel Walks,* is often neglected to obtain an Imitation of Nature even in some of its *Wildnesses.*" [14] This account has the paradoxical consequence that *irregularity* is enjoyable because indicative of *design*—an unnecessary finesse, for the beauty of irregular gardens would be well accounted for merely as imitation of Nature.

Quite generally, perception of fitness and design is a principal source of beauty, and treatment of the topic leads Hutcheson into a rather intricate argument, "Concerning our Reasonings about Design and Wisdom in the Cause, from the Beauty or Regularity of Effects"—or, to put it plainly, natural theology. It is a misreading of Hutcheson to see natural theology either as an unwarranted intrusion into the realm of aesthetics or (at the other extreme) as the underlying basis of his aesthetic system;[15] it is true that to a reflective and devout mind all beauty, even original beauty, is relative to a Design—but it is not *only* relative.

Although the sense of beauty is subjective, ideal, and connected arbitrarily with the nature of things by the "Author of our Nature," there is nonetheless a standard of taste. This standard is consistent with the observed discrepancies of taste among men. For the internal sense spontaneously yields pleasures only; aesthetic pain arises from disappointment (setting aside the function of appearances as natural or arbitrary signs of something painful). Men differ in their experience, and thus in the cultivation of the sense: what gives unfeigned pleasure to the untutored may (through comparison) be excruciating to the cultivated. Diversity of fancies arises also from casual associations which may make men "have an aversion of Objects of *Beauty*, and a liking to others void of it, but under different Conceptions than those of *Beauty* or *Deformity*."[16] The term "association" is employed by Hutcheson in a rather pejorative sense, to suggest confusions which falsify the perceptions of sense, distort the passions, or mislead the reason. This use of the term (derived from Locke) is found also in Lord Kames and in Alison, even though this latter bases his entire aesthetics on what Hume would call "association." These writers confine the term "association" to the accidental aspect of the associative process, and attribute the universal aspect to other causes (as in Hutcheson) or discuss it in different terms (as in Alison). But even taking the concept of association as Hume understood it, it is still of no signal importance in Hutcheson (and of little more in Kames), for when original perceptions constitute the bulk of aesthetic experience, there is no need for explanations. Setting aside, then, differences in taste resulting from the various degrees of cultivation of the mind and from the casual associations which color our perceptions, the principles of aesthetic judgment are universal. Nor does "The Power of Custom, Education, and Example, as to Our

Internal Senses" contradict this truth; for neither custom, nor education, nor example can create a species of sensation *de novo*—all must
presuppose a natural basis of aesthetic perception.

The first inquiry concludes—appropriately, in view of the emphasis
the theory throws upon design—with illustration of the final causes.
Why should Deity have established the arbitrary connection between
regular objects and our pleasure in them? Why should He have
created so regular a universe? Limited beings find regularity useful,
for the economy of life depends upon the uniformity of nature; and
we owe it to Divine benevolence that interest and utility coincide with
pleasure. Pleasure, accordingly, is conjoined with regular objects,
fruitful actions, enlarging theorems, and the universe was created
regular to satisfy the implanted sense and give scope to virtue.[17]

The "Inquiry concerning Beauty" contains little discussion of moral
beauty. But the second treatise, and major portions of the third and
fourth, treat of moral beauty, for virtue is beautiful. Some explication
of Hutcheson's ethics is requisite to make this clear. Hutcheson's purpose is to show that some actions and affections are immediately good,
that by a superior moral sense we have pleasure in contemplating
them without any view of natural advantage; and that the incitement
to virtue is not the intention of securing this pleasure of approbation
or any other natural good, but a principle entirely different from
self-love or interest.[18] His analysis uncovers the existence of three
senses distinct both from the external senses and from the aesthetic
sense. These are the *Publick Sense,* "our Determination to be pleased
with the *Happiness* of others, and to be uneasy at their *Misery*"; the
Moral Sense, by which "we perceive *Virtue,* or *Vice* in our selves or
others"; and a *Sense of Honour* "which makes the *Approbation,* or
Gratitude of others, for any good Actions we have done, the necessary
occasion of Pleasure; and their *Dislike, Condemnation,* or *Resentment* of Injuries done by us, the occasion of that uneasy Sensation
called *Shame,* even when we fear no further evil from them." [19]
There is also a *Sense of Dignity* or suitableness to human nature, but
this may reduce to a modification of the moral sense.[20] Answering to
each of these senses is a set of desires and aversions: the public sense
produces a desire of the happiness, and an aversion from the misery,
of others; the moral sense gives us a desire of virtue and an aversion
from vice; and the sense of honor produces a noble ambition for
praise and a shrinking from blame.[21]

This apparatus of senses and their correspondent desires enables
Hutcheson to answer the two leading questions of ethics: What is

virtue? Why should I be virtuous? Abstracting from particular habits or prejudices, "every one is so constituted as to approve every *particular kind Affection* toward any one, which argues no *want of Affection* towards others. And constantly to approve that Temper which desires, and those Actions which tend to procure the greatest Moment of Good in the Power of the Agent toward the most extensive System to which it can reach . . . [and consequently] the Perfection of Virtue consists in 'having the *universal calm Benevolence,* the prevalent Affection of the Mind, so as to limit and counteract not only the *selfish Passions,* but even the *particular kind Affections.*' " [22] And why should I be virtuous? For three reasons—derived from three senses. Primarily because my public sense causes me to desire the welfare of others, because I feel a calm yet active benevolence extending to all mankind. Partly because I wish to be virtuous and thus enjoy the pleasurable consciousness of my own merit; although this self-approval follows in any particular instance only if it was not sought, reflection on it may lead me to form my character along the lines of virtue. Lastly because I desire the praise and gratitude of my fellow men, and to be secure of the approbation of Deity.

It is remarkable that Hutcheson reduces *all* virtue to benevolence. The various internal senses are determinations to feel it or approve it or appreciate its reflection from others. All moral affections become modifications of love and hatred; talents, abilities, and the cardinal virtues of the ancients become instruments, participating in virtue when applied benevolently. Hutcheson makes very subtle use, however, of so monolithic a system. He argues, for instance, that it is better to aid the good than the evil, for we thereby assist in a more extensive scheme of benevolence; and he postulates a regularly graduated diminution of love as its objects are progressively more remote from us, an inverse variation analogous with gravitation and equally necessary to the order of the universe. The most virtuous acts, in consequence of all this, "have the most universal, unlimited Tendency to the *greatest* and *most extensive Happiness* of all the *rational Agents* to whom our Influence can extend." [23] This truth is represented symbolically in Hutcheson's well-known mathematical calculus of virtue:

$$B = \frac{M - I}{A}$$

wherein "B" is benevolence, "M" the total moment of public good accomplished, "I" the moment of personal good, and "A" the abilities of the agent.[24] Thomas Reid was provoked by this formula to write his first work, "An Essay on Quantity, Occasioned by Reading a

Treatise in Which Simple and Compound Ratios Are Applied to Virtue and Merit" (1748). Reid argues that motives and happiness are not susceptible of mensuration, so that no mathematical reasoning on such subjects can ever advance a step. This is obvious; but Hutcheson was not really attempting to reason mathematically—only to use a symbolic notation which would represent his argument more vividly.

In ethics as in aesthetics, Hutcheson stops short in his analysis, resting his system upon perceptions and determinations presumed to be original. Hume subsequently placed these moral questions within a comprehensive system grounded on a precise metaphysics and unified by a flexible but consistent philosophic method, and in so doing he was led to analyze further the apparently original principles which Hutcheson had invoked. By introducing sympathy—itself susceptible of metaphysical analysis—as the first principle of his ethics, Hume was able to resolve all of Hutcheson's ethical senses into more elemental principles and at the same time to escape the exclusive benevolism of the Hutchesonian ethic.[25]

This conspectus of Hutcheson's ethical theory has been preliminary to explication of the beauty of virtue, and to this topic I return. The beauty of virtue consists in the relation of virtuous dispositions, intentions, and actions to the system of sensitive beings. Virtue is the cement of the macrocosm, and because it does unite the rational or sensitive creation into a system of mutual dependence and complicated interrelationship, it is beautiful: uniformity in variety. It must be granted, to be sure, that this is stretching the flexibility of an analogical term pretty far.

But there is another and more special way in which the beauty of the physical and intellectual worlds is united with that of the moral: habitual dispositions form the countenance, and the natural form of the countenance may also resemble the expression of passion—in these ways moral beauty is seen as physical beauty, the attributes of the significatum being transferred by association to the sign.

THERE is a further Consideration which must not be pass'd over, concerning the EXTERNAL BEAUTY of Persons, which all allow to have great Power over human Minds. Now it is some apprehended *Morality*, some natural or imagin'd indication of *concomitant Virtue*, which gives it this powerful Charm above all other kinds of *Beauty*. Let us consider the Characters of *Beauty*, which are commonly admir'd in Countenances, and we shall find them to be *Sweetness, Mildness, Majesty, Dignity, Vivacity, Humility, Tenderness, Good-nature;* that is, that certain

Airs, Proportions, je ne scai quoy's, are natural Indications of such Virtues, or of Abilitys or Dispositions toward them.[26]

The same is true of air and motion, which represent such moral qualities as roughness, gentleness, and so forth. These latter signs, however, Hutcheson regards as conventional (unlike Kames and Alison, who treat them as for the most part natural). All of these beauties are to be distinguished from the moral beauty proper on which they ultimately depend—that is a question of uniformity in variety.

It is these moral beauties which play a principal role in literature and painting.

> We shall find the same *moral Sense* to be the Foundation of the chief Pleasures of Poetry. We hinted, in the former Treatise, at the Foundation of Delight in the *Numbers, Measures, Metaphors, Similitudes*. But as the Contemplation of *moral Objects*, either of *Vice* or *Virtue*, affects us more strongly, and moves our Passions in a quite different and more powerful manner than *natural Beauty*, or (what we commonly call) *Deformity;* so the most moving Beautys bear a Relation to our *moral Sense*, and affect us more vehemently than the Representation of *natural Objects* in the liveliest Descriptions. *Dramatic*, and *Epic* poetry are entirely addressed to this *Sense*, and raise our Passions by the Fortunes of *Characters*, distinctly represented as *morally good*, or *evil*. . . . Where we are studying to raise any *Desire*, or *Admiration* of an Object *really beautiful*, we are not content with a *bare Narration*, but endeavour, if we can, to present the *Object* it self, or the most *lively Image* of it. And hence it is that the *Epic Poem*, or *Tragedy*, give a vastly greater Pleasure than the Writings of *Philosophers*, tho both aim at recommending *Virtue*.[27]

Lord Kames's notion of "ideal presence" is here projected, though not developed, by Hutcheson; the notion is, indeed, almost certain to occur in the psychological analysis of taste. Much, in fact, of Kames's theory of tragedy is scattered through the ethical treatises of Hutcheson. The "sympathetic emotion of virtue" appears: "When we form the Idea of a *morally good Action*, or see it represented in the *Drama*, or read it in *Epicks* or *Romance*, we feel a *Desire* arising of doing the like." [28] The compulsive attraction of pity is remarked, and used (together with delight in moral beauty) to account for the enjoyment in tragedy:

> . . . we are not immediately excited by *Compassion* to desire the *Removal* of our own Pain; we think it just to be so affected upon the Occasion, and dislike those who are not so: but we are excited directly to desire

the *Relief* of the Miserable; and if we see this impossible, we may by *Reflection* discern it to be vain for us to indulge our *Compassion* any further; and then from *Self-love* we retire from the Object which occasions our Pain, and study to divert our Thoughts. But where there is no such *Reflection,* People are hurry'd by a *natural, kind Instinct,* to see Objects of *Compassion.* . . .

THIS same Principle leads men to *Tragedys;* only we are to observe, that another strong reason of this, is the *moral Beauty* of the *Characters* and *Actions* which we love to behold: for I doubt, whether any Audience would be pleas'd, barely to see fictitious Scenes of Misery, if they were kept strangers to the *moral Qualitys* of the Sufferers, or their *Characters* and *Actions.*[29]

It should be remarked also, that Kames's distinction of pleasant (in immediate feeling) and agreeable (in objective survey) is made use of by Hutcheson: many virtues and passions are painful, yet provide a reflex pleasure of self-approval.[30]

But beauty, even though so broadly and loosely understood by Hutcheson, does not embrace all aesthetic pleasure: "GRANDEUR and *Novelty* are two ideas different from *Beauty,* which often recommend Objects to us. The Reason of this is foreign to the present Subject. See *Spectator,* No. 412." [31] This acquiescence in the slight treatment which Addison accords grandeur and novelty is surprising. Thorpe has observed truly that Hutcheson's aesthetics might be expected to agree more with Addison's than with Shaftesbury's, since Hutcheson, like Addison, is writing in the tradition of Locke. But Thorpe exaggerates in saying that the treatise on beauty is "the most important gloss to Addison's essay that had yet been made." [32] Hutcheson's beauty extends through the physical, moral, and intellectual realms, whereas Addison's is physical only (albeit he may speak figuratively of moral beauty); Addison implies internal senses which apprehend beauty, grandeur, and novelty, but provides no philosophic justification of this position; Addison's beauty appears most vividly in color, whereas Hutcheson's is a beauty of form; in short, Hutcheson's theory is part and parcel of a philosophic system, Addison's an expression of the taste of an amateur and essayist.

The real question on Hutcheson's use of Addison is: Why, in supplanting Addison's simple notion of beauty with his own more philosophical conception, did Hutcheson leave Addison's grandeur and novelty untransformed? Certainly grandeur could be treated so as to pervade not only the physical but also the intellectual and moral worlds. The explanation presumably is, that grandeur and novelty do not share with beauty that peculiarly intimate connection with morality, and Hutcheson's chief concern was always morals. Certain virtues are of course sublime; the lack of connection I point to is methodological rather than substantive. Beauty emerges from the relations of part and part, part and whole, and so, as Hutcheson conceives it, does morality; the senses appropriated to beauty and morality are concerned, therefore, with analogous relationships. Grandeur, however, is not susceptible of this kind of analysis, nor does investigation of its influence on the mind have any analogy with that mode of ethical speculation in which Hutcheson engaged.

It is conceivable, however, that if Hutcheson's aesthetic thought had been more spontaneous and self-dependent, it might in turn have shaped his position on ethics. Construction of an aesthetics of sublimity alongside that of beauty might well have meant dissolution of the exclusive benevolism of Hutchesonian ethics. Qualities noble in themselves might have found place alongside those contributing to humanity: courage, intellectual power, and force of will would have become virtues rather than instruments. Something of this sort appears to have occurred in the thought of Lord Kames: Hutcheson's aesthetic sense is fractured into many, each natural and original, and the moral senses of Hutcheson are still further divided, with virtue no longer confined to benevolence.

One contemporary of Hutcheson, Charles Louis De Villette, desired a shift of the theory in the contrary direction—towards a still closer dependence of beauty on virtue. De Villette's "Essay Philosophique sur le Beau, & sur le Goût," brought to light by A. O. Aldridge,[33] demands a beauty more obviously identical than Hutcheson's in physical and moral subjects. As De Villette thinks,

> *1.* Un objet est Beau à proportion du degré de *Sagesse,* c'est à dire de Sagacité, de genie, d'habileté, qui se montre dans les moyens necessaries à l-execution du Dessein, comme sont les combinaisons, les rapports.
>
> *2.* En second lieu, & principalement, un objet est Beau à proportion du degré de Bienfaisance (de cette Bienfaisance qui concerne, non une exemption de Mal, mais un Plaisir actuel, & *Positif,* un Plaisir tel que je l'ai indiqué) à proportion, dis-je, du degré de Bienfaisance que le Dessein etale au Spectateur.[34]

He conceives of beauty as (*1*) providing a pleasing sensation, physical or moral, (*2*) permitting the patient to see design and benevolence in the provision of the pleasure, and therefore (*3*) awakening a feeling of love and gratitude, which, together with the other feelings, constitutes the sentiment of beauty. The tendency of this doctrine is to subsume the aesthetic sense under other faculties: physical and moral sensation, and intellection, and a mode of piety. The feeling of beauty is neither simple nor original, and requires no special sense appropriated to it.[35]

The path marked out by Hutcheson himself, no more than that I have indicated as a variant not incompatible with Hutcheson's system as a whole, was not followed by any disciple. Almost all later writers acknowledge the beauty of uniformity in variety, but all subsume this beauty in a more comprehensive conception of which it forms but a part or aspect; and such transformation is possible only because the philosophic basis of aesthetics is shifted or its analytical method altered.

CHAPTER 3

David Hume

❀

AS THE MOST original, systematic, and subtle thinker of the century, David Hume might have commanded a great influence over British aesthetic speculation. In formulating an associational psychology which could be turned to account in aesthetic investigation, indeed, his influence was profound; the systems of Gerard and Alison, and important aspects of the work of the picturesque school, derive in great measure from Humeian psychology. Most modern scholars, to be sure, agree in declaring that Hartley's psychology carried the day for associationism in aesthetics;[1] there is, however, no external evidence for any decisive influence of Hartley on British aestheticians before James Mill, and the internal evidence of such systems as Gerard's and Alison's points to Hume instead. Yet though these later aestheticians occasionally borrow from or quote him, Hume had little direct effect upon aesthetic discussion. The slightness of his impact is readily explicable: save for cogent and probing analyses of certain special problems, Hume's aesthetics is slender. The essay, "Of the Standard of Taste," is the only extended piece of Hume's work which is strictly aesthetical in character; the essay, "Of Tragedy," and certain sections of *A Treatise of Human Nature* have important aesthetic implications, yet the first is really a critical problem the more general aesthetic implications of which were not developed by Hume, and the treatment of beauty and sublimity in the *Treatise* is always ancillary to other discussions.[2] The other works contain little of importance. What is attempted here, accordingly, is a concise adumbration of Hume's aesthetic position, so far as this can be inferred from his writings, together with analyses of the two essays, "Of the Standard of Taste" and "Of Tragedy."[3]

A Treatise of Human Nature is an effort to apply inductive techniques, through observation and introspective experiment, to psychology, from which all other sciences depend: the science of "human nature" is Hume's metaphysics. Mathematics, natural philosophy, and natural religion do not come, except by way of analogy and illustration, within the scope of Hume's study; for though they are ultimately dependent on human nature, deriving from psychology their fundamental principles and concepts (space, time, causality, &c.), their immediate reference is to external reality. But logic, morals, politics, and criticism are branches of the science of human nature itself:

> The sole end of logic is to explain the principles and operations of our reasoning faculty, and the nature of our ideas: morals and criticism regard our tastes and sentiments: and politics consider men as united in society and dependent on each other. In these four sciences of *Logic,* *Morals, Criticism,* and *Politics,* is comprehended almost everything, which it can any way import us to be acquainted with, or which can tend either to the improvement or ornament of the human mind.[4]

But though Hume treats of logic, morals, and politics at length in his essays and treatises, criticism (and this term comprehends, of course, the "philosophical criticism" now termed aesthetics) receives slight attention, entering the *Treatise* only incidentally.

The first principles of Hume's metaphysics are: that the immediate objects of knowledge are perceptions of the mind, rather than the external world itself; that these perceptions are distinguishable into impressions and ideas, according as they are more or less vivid and lively, and into simple and complex; "that all our simple ideas in their first appearance are deriv'd from simple impressions, which are correspondent to them, and which they exactly represent";[5] that there is a "liberty of the imagination to transpose and change its ideas"[6] in accordance with the laws which Hume discovers. These comprehensive principles are supplemented in the course of discussion with subordinate, or at any rate more confined, principles.

The aesthetic sentiments, like the moral, are, of course, impressions —lively originals, not fainter derivatives. They are, moreover, secondary and reflexive impressions, arising in consequence of sensations (primary impressions) or ideas. And they are distinguished from the passions by their comparative calmness: "The reflective impressions may be divided into two kinds, *viz.* the *calm* and the *violent.* Of the first kind is the sense of beauty and deformity in action, composition, and external objects. Of the second are the passions of love and hatred, grief and joy, pride and humility."[7] This "beauty and deformity in action" is not the visual beauty of motion, but the moral beauty of behavior: in the fashion of his age, Hume speaks often of the "beauty" of character and behavior, a locution justified for him by the important analogy between aesthetic and moral feeling; Hume does not, however, intend to identify the two species of emotion: "Now there is nothing common to natural and moral beauty . . . but this power of producing pleasure. . . ."[8]

The chief treatment of beauty in the *Treatise* is ancillary to the analysis of the passions of pride and humility. Hume is concerned to demonstrate that those passions arise from a double relation of impressions and ideas: a relation between the idea of the object of the passion (self) and that of the cause of it (some trait related to self), together with a similarity between the passion excited by the cause and that of pride or humility, as the case may be. "That cause, which excites the passion, is related to the object, which nature has attributed to the passion; the sensation, which the cause separately produces, is related to the sensation of the passion: From this double relation of ideas and impressions, the passion is deriv'd."[9] Thus, the idea of personal beauty may be connected with the idea of self through contiguity and cause-and-effect, as being *our* beauty, and the emotion of beauty is pleasant, as is the emotion of pride; accordingly, beauty excites pride in its possessor.

This analysis requires that beauty be pleasurable; and such is, indeed, so far the case that "pleasure and pain . . . are not only necessary attendants of beauty and deformity, but constitute their very essence."[10] If we examine theories "to explain the difference betwixt beauty and deformity," Hume declares, "we shall find that all of them resolve into this, that beauty is such an order and construction of parts, as either by the *primary constitution* of our nature, by *custom,* or by *caprice,* is fitted to give a pleasure and satisfaction to the soul."[11] The three origins of beauty here suggested are really only those which Hutcheson had already considered, and those which one might expect to find in a psychology employing association as a principal analytical device: there must be some things originally beautiful, others beautiful through customary association, others beautiful owing to peculiar and arbitrary associations.

Of the beauties which are such by nature, a further differentiation is possible: Hume distinguishes here, as in the case of the virtues, between properties which are useful and those which are inherently pleasurable. In his moral theory, Hume discovers four classes of virtues, classes formed by the intersection of two distinctions—that between useful and immediately pleasurable, that between agent and patient. The virtues are useful or agreeable to ourselves or to others; moral sentiments, as Hume puts it, "may arise either from the mere species or appearance of characters and passions, or from reflections on their tendency to the happiness of mankind, and of particular persons. My opinion is, that both these causes are intermix'd in our judgments of morals; after the same manner as they are in our decisions concerning most kinds of external beauty: Tho' I am also of opinion, that reflections on the tendencies of actions have by far the greatest influence, and determine all the great lines of our duty." [12] In the aesthetic realm, where qualities rather than actions and traits of character are in consideration, there is no distinction of agent and patient, of ourselves and others, and in consequence there are only two modes of beauty: the *utile* and the *dulce*. And in aesthetics as in morals, Hume lays greatest stress on utility: "Most of the works of art," he declares, "are esteem'd beautiful, in proportion to their fitness for the use of man, and even many of the productions of nature derive their beauty from that source. Handsome and beautiful, on most occasions, is not an absolute but a relative quality, and pleases us by nothing but its tendency to produce an end that is agreeable." [13]

Hume insists upon the influence of utility on our ideas of beauty more, perhaps, than would be readily justifiable, were it not that his discussions of beauty usually occur in contexts which make such emphasis appropriate; Hume never has occasion to treat of the beauty of color and figure as such, but is always considering beauty relative to some other circumstance. He remarks, for instance, that "nothing renders a field more agreeable than its fertility, and . . . scarce any advantages of ornament or situation will be able to equal this beauty. . . . I know not but a plain, overgrown with furze and broom, may be, in itself, as beautiful as a hill cover'd with vines or olive-trees; tho' it will never appear so to one, who is acquainted with the value of each. But this is a beauty merely of imagination, and has no foundation in what appears to the senses." [14] But this passage occurs as an illustration of the force of sympathy, a discussion in its turn contributory to the analysis of love and hatred. Hume always concedes, though he has never occasion to treat, a beauty inherently pleasurable without reference to utility: "Some species of beauty," he observes on one occasion, "especially the natural kinds, on their first appearance, command our affection and approbation; and where they fail of this effect, it is impossible for any reasoning to redress their influence, or adapt them better to our taste and sentiment." [15]

Monk is led to the conclusion that beauty, for Hume, is "an impersonal recognition of the functional perfection of an object, the knowledge that it is complete and at least latently purposive." [16] This judgment errs in two particulars: it ignores immediate beauty, and it confuses utility with fitness. An instrument of torture is purposive, yet not beautiful by Hume's criteria. Hume nowhere speaks of the beauty of fitness except as conducive to utility and human happiness. McCosh, too, overlooks the importance of immediate beauty for Hume; troubled by Hume's utilitarianism, he remarks that "the aesthetic tastes of one satisfied with such a theory could not have been keen, and we do not wonder to find that in the letters written during his travels, he never makes a single allusion to a fine statue or painting." [17] Hume's insensitivity to the visual arts (to which Brunius also testifies) is, perhaps, responsible for some of the limitations of his theory of beauty. The broad sense in which Hume understands "utility" must, however, be recalled; whatever is instrumental to happiness is useful—the whole train of social virtues are useful— and the expressions of countenance imaging them would no doubt be ranked by Hume as among the beauties of *utility*.

The beauty of utility affects us chiefly—indeed, wholly—by sympathy; even when the beautiful object is useful to and being used by the judge himself, his appreciation of it is universalized—it is not his selfish interest which makes the object beautiful, but his detached view of the object as useful to the employer (who chances to be himself). In such a case one appreciates *qua* spectator the feelings one has *qua* user, and it is the former sentiment, not the latter, which is aesthetic. "In every judgement of beauty, the feelings of the person affected enter into consideration, and communicate to the spectator similar touches of pain or pleasure," [18] and this would be true even if the person affected and the spectator were the same. Monk observes this disinterestedness of aesthetic judgment and connects it with an alleged subjectivity, remarking that Hume, like Kant, referred beauty and sublimity to the perceiving mind alone,[19] in contrast with an earlier "tendency to regard the sublime [I suppose also the beautiful] as a quality residing in objects, having objective reality like the primary characteristics of matter." [20] It appears to me, however, that Hume is in accord with both previous and subsequent writers of the century in finding the sentiment of beauty within the perceiving mind and the causes of it without; there is no historical progression in this viewpoint.

Hume's treatment of beauty goes no further than this; there is little subtlety of differentiation (of design from fitness from utility, for instance), little analysis of the various classes of associations which influence judgments of beauty, no treatment of the mechanisms by which the immediate beauties operate. Hume's aesthetics is formed of hints—and one of the most important of these suggests an analysis of sublimity. Following a discussion of the influence of imagination on the passions, Hume treats "Of Contiguity and Distance in Space and Time." [21] The treatment is conducted in terms of the vivacity of ideas and of habits of the imagination and the passions. Ideas of objects remote in time or space are faint in proportion to their remoteness, not only because they lose the association to self (through which ideas acquire a vicarious vivacity), but because the fancy proceeds to their conception through the conception of the intermediate objects, a process interrupted by repeated recalling of the fancy to the present self. Removal in time, moreover, renders ideas feebler than distance in space, for the parts of extension, being united to the senses, "acquire an union in the fancy." [22] And thirdly, future time has a lesser effect than past, because the fancy tends to run in the direction of the passage of time. On this last point it could easily be objected, I think, that since ideas of future objects are only fancies, while those of objects past may be memories or beliefs, removal into the future might weaken our ideas more than remoteness in the past.

The weakening of conceptions in any of these ways of course weakens correspondingly all those practical passions which arise from the conceptions: we do not fear what is remote, and so forth. But curiously, there is a set of aesthetic emotions—admiration and esteem as Hume terms them, sublimity as they are usually designated when more than usually elevated and intense—which run counter to the tendency of the imagination, which wax as the conception wanes. In accounting for this circumstance, Hume repeats the conventional observation that "the mere view and contemplation of any greatness, whether successive or extended, enlarges the soul, and gives it a sensible delight and pleasure. A wide plain, the ocean, eternity, a succession of several ages; all these are entertaining objects, and excel every thing, however beautiful, which accompanies not its beauty with a suitable greatness." [23] In conceiving a remote object, the fancy proceeds through conception of the intervening distance, the greatness of which excites admiration, which admiration is transferred to the associated object.

A further principle is requisite to explain the superior effect of temporal over spatial distance, and of future time to past. This principle is a property of human nature: both the passions and the imagination tend to exert their force by opposing obstacles.

> 'Tis a quality very observable in human nature, that any opposition which does not entirely discourage and intimidate us, has rather a contrary effect, and inspires us with a more than ordinary grandeur and magnanimity. In collecting our force to overcome the opposition, we invigorate the soul, and give it an elevation with which otherwise it wou'd never have been acquainted. . . .
>
> This is also true in the inverse. Opposition not only enlarges the soul; but the soul, when full of courage and magnanimity, in a manner seeks opposition. . . .
>
> Whatever supports and fills the passions is agreeable to us; as on the contrary, what weakens and infeebles them is uneasy. As opposition has the first effect, and facility the second, no wonder the mind, in certain dispositions, desires the former, and is averse to the latter.[24]

The notion of vacuity being painful to the mind is, of course, a commonplace; Du Bos, Lord Kames, and other writers had based aesthetic theorems upon it. To Hume the idea is especially congenial, since his entire system rests upon distinctions in force or vivacity of perception. The tendency of the mind to oppose obstacles appears to depend upon this principle: the force of an idea or impression is more sensibly felt when resistance is overcome, and forcible perceptions are *ipso facto* pleasurable.[25]

The natural tendency of imagination is, through association with the phenomena of gravitation, to pursue objects downward; and in accordance with the present principle, it counteracts its own tendency and rises in aspiration, elevation, and sublimity.[26] In like manner, the greater difficulty of forming a conception across an interval of time makes temporal distance more impressive than spatial; and the superior resistance of the past makes antiquity more admirable than futurity. More precisely, a short remove in time or space weakens our emotion by enfeebling the conception without arousing us to overcome the difficulty; whereas, a greater remove engages our powers and excites admiration. It must be noted that there are other possible causes for the sublimity of the past; Dugald Stewart suggests a series of associations between antiquity and elevation, associations systematically attractive to Stewart, but which could also be adapted to Hume's position without inconsistency, and which would enable Hume to avoid the difficulties attending his view of the relative difficulty of conceiving past and future.[27]

All this is but a fragment of a theory of sublimity, but Hume has nonetheless grasped a clue which could have been followed out into its ramifying consequences to yield a theory of sublimity systematically integrated with a metaphysical psychology. Hume's investigation of the faculty which apprehends aesthetic quality is less truncated: "Of the Standard of Taste," though brief, is pithy. "The great variety of Taste, as well as of opinion, which prevails in the world," he observes, "is too obvious not to have fallen under every one's observation"; and this evident variety will "be found, on examination, to be still greater in reality than in appearance." [28] For since the very terms employed in discussing matters of taste signify praise and blame, men necessarily agree, for the most part, on the general propositions formed with these terms; while the application of them to concrete instances may be radically different: "when critics come to particulars, this seeming unanimity vanishes; and it is found, that they had affixed a very different meaning to their expressions." [29] All this is opposite to the case in matters of opinion and science: "The difference among men is there oftener found to lie in generals than in particulars; and to be less in reality than in appearance. An explanation of the terms commonly ends the controversy; and the disputants are surprized to find, that they had been quarreling, while at bottom they agreed in their judgment." [30] Hume employs in this contrast one of the fundamental distinctions in his system: the opposition of matters of sentiment and taste to matters of opinion and science is founded on the distinction of impressions and ideas, and Hume has tacitly taken it for granted that feelings of beauty and the reverse are essentially impressions, emotions—rather than ideas, judgments.

Parallel to the situation in criticism is that in morals, where again all agree as to names—that virtue, like beauty, is good—but may yet disagree on the extension of the names to actual conduct and character; this analogy is itself a kind of proof. Amidst such diversities, "it is natural for us to seek a *Standard of Taste;* a rule, by which the various sentiments of men may be reconciled; at least, a decision, afforded, confirming one sentiment, and condemning another." [31] The problem of the essay is thus defined. And the direction in which the solution is to be found is discovered by meeting the objection, that in matters of judgment there is a standard (to wit, "real matter of fact"), to which disputes may be referred, whereas all sentiments are "right," since they are not representative of something outside the mind. "Beauty," it is urged, "is no quality in things themselves: It exists merely in the mind which contemplates them; and each mind perceives a different beauty. One person may even perceive deformity, where another is sensible of beauty; and every individual ought to acquiesce in his own sentiment, without pretending to regulate those of others." [32]

Hume observes very justly that no one really applies this principle in its full latitude, that in practice all admit of a standard even while subscribing to the proverb which denies one. It is true that the rules of composition (Hume throughout has literature in mind, though analogous reasonings would be applicable to the beauties of nature or of the other arts) do not depend on *relations of ideas*, and are not susceptible of demonstrative reasoning; they depend upon *experience*. Sentiments do not *resemble* external objects and relations (and to this extent the point that all sentiments are equally right is just); they are *caused* by the properties and relations of external objects, and causation is a relation discovery of which depends upon experience.[33] The experience here in question is simply the pleasure and pain yielded by the different modes and devices of composition; the "rules" are nothing but "general observations, concerning what has been universally found to please in all countries and in all ages." [34] If authors appear to please while abrogating the rules, either the rules involved are false, or the authors please despite these licences in virtue of other beauties conformable to rule. But please whom? one may ask. For "though all the general rules of art are founded only on experience and on the observation of the common sentiments of human nature, we must not imagine, that, on every occasion, the feelings of men will be conformable to these rules. Those finer emotions of the mind are of a very tender and delicate nature, and require the concurrence of many favourable circumstances to make them play with facility and exactness, according to their general and established principles." [35] There *is* a "relation, which nature has placed between the form and the sentiment"—a relation of cause and effect—but the effect, as always, may be obstructed by contrary causes. For the object to make its due impression, there must be a "perfect serenity of mind, a recollection of thought, a due attention to the object; if any of these circumstances be wanting, our experiment will be fallacious, and we shall be unable to judge of the catholic and universal beauty." [36]

The natural tendency of objective beauties to produce agreeable sentiments may in any given case be frustrated; but the tendency can still be determined "from the durable admiration, which attends those works, that have survived all the caprices of mode and fashion, all the mistakes of ignorance and envy"—*quod semper, quod ubique.* From this test we learn that

> some particular forms or qualities, from the original structure of the internal fabric, are calculated to please, and others to displease; and if they fail of their effect in any particular instance, it is from some apparent defect or imperfection in the organ. . . . If, in the sound state of the organ, there be an entire or a considerable uniformity of sentiment among men, we may thence derive an idea of the perfect beauty; in like manner as the appearance of objects in the day-light, to the eye of a man in health, is denominated their true and real colour, even while colour is allowed to be merely a phantasm of the senses.[37]

This step concludes the demonstration that there is a standard which, though subjective in the sense that it depends upon a certain adaptation of human nature to the objects of its perceptions, is *not* subjective in the sense that it depends upon individual preference. The next stage in the inquiry is to determine what those defects are which may deform the taste of individuals. There is first "the want of that *delicacy* of imagination, which is requisite to convey a sensibility of those finer emotions," [38] a delicacy illustrated by that well-worn story of Sancho Panza's wine-tasting kinsmen. The delicacy of mental taste comprises the two abilities this story suggests: sensibility to every beauty, and refinement in isolating the various beauties. "Where the organs are so fine, as to allow nothing to escape them; and at the same time so exact as to perceive every ingredient in the composition: This we call delicacy of taste, whether we employ these terms in the literal or metaphorical sense." [39] The rules of composition are like the key and thong of the story—they justify the delicacy of the true critic. And the false critic can be confounded by the production of these rules, for "when we show him an avowed principle of art; when we illustrate this principle by examples, whose operation, from his own particular taste, he acknowledges to be conformable to the principle; when we prove, that the same principle may be applied to the present case, where he did not perceive or feel its influence: He must conclude, upon the whole, that the fault lies in himself, and that he wants the delicacy, which is requisite to make him sensible of every beauty and every blemish, in any composition or discourse." [40]

But delicacy is not all; practice is requisite to improve vague and hesitant responses into "clear and distinct sentiments" wherewith the critic "discerns that very degree and kind of approbation or displeasure, which each part is naturally fitted to produce." [41] Practice, moreover, leads inevitably to "*comparisons* between the several species and degrees of excellence," and it is only by comparison that the merit of a performance can be assessed. Hume makes the point which Hutcheson had made before him, that the coarsest daubing or most vulgar ballad is in itself pleasing, and becomes painful only to those accustomed to higher merits—comparison having its usual influence of exaggerating differences. The critic must divest himself, Hume continues, of prejudice, setting aside his individual being and peculiar circumstances and considering himself as "a man in general." [42] The aesthetic attitude thus assumed is very like the attitude Hume supposes for moral judgment, where we readily distinguish our personal interest and response from that universalized response we feel as generalized spectator. In the case of criticism, indeed, we must even assume the point of view which the performance, though designed for a different age and nation, requires. It is *good sense* which enables us to correct, or set aside temporarily, our prejudices—and, Hume remarks, "in this respect, as well as in many others, reason, if not an essential part of taste, is at least requisite to the operations of this latter faculty." [43] A competent reason is requisite to judge of the interrelations of parts in a work, and of their subordinacy to an end. Poetry, moreover, "is nothing but a chain of propositions and reasonings; not always, indeed, the justest and most exact, but still plausible and specious, however disguised by the colouring of the imagination." [44]

In short, few are qualified to establish their own sentiment as the standard of beauty. "Strong sense, united to delicate sentiment, improved by practice, perfected by comparison, and cleared of all prejudice, can alone entitle critics to this valuable character; and the joint verdict of such, wherever they are to be found, is the true standard of taste and beauty." [45] The difficulty remaining is to ascertain the criteria by which such judges may be recognized. This question, however, is not perplexed by the difficulties which embarrassed the original issue, the existence of a standard. For we are no longer discussing sentiments, with all their subjectivity; *this* is a matter of fact, a question of ideas rather than impressions. Doubt and dispute may persist, but the doubts and disputes are of the kind which attend questions submitted to the understanding, and the remedy is the usual one of argumentation. Indeed, these aesthetic questions are decided much more readily than scientific, and the authority of literary classics is more durable than that of scientific systems. Men of taste, though few, acquire an ascendancy which makes their preferences prevail.

The possibility of determining the standard established, Hume concludes by conceding two limitations on the universality of the standard: "The one is the different humours of particular men; the other, the particular manners and opinions of our age and country." [46] All diversities in the internal frame of men are not indicative of defect or perversion: "It is plainly an error in a critic," Hume declares, "to confine his approbation to one species or style of writing, and condemn all the rest. But it is almost impossible not to feel a predilection for that which suits our particular turn and disposition. Such preferences are innocent and unavoidable, and can never reasonably be the object of dispute, because there is no standard, by which they can be decided." [47] In like manner, we are inevitably more touched by representations of life which resembles that of our own age and country. Where the disconformity consists only in customs or in speculative opinions, full allowance should be made, and we should accommodate our judgments to the work; but where the principles of morality and decency alter from age to age, though we may excuse the poet we cannot relish the composition.

The drift of Hume's argument, taken as a whole, is contrary to the purpose of Hutcheson. Hutcheson's effort was to establish a distinct sense of beauty, whereas Hume endeavors to get the issue out of the realm of impressions and into that of judgment and ideas. So little, however, has the import of Hume's argument been grasped, that Scott could pronounce Hume's discussion "almost a reproduction of Hutcheson's early work," [48] and Wilson O. Clough could say that "Hume, thorough-going rationalist, tried to bring taste and the arts under reason and good sense, but had finally to accept the subjective criteria of feeling and sensibility." [49] No philosophical critic of the eighteenth century was an antinomian in taste; all establish a standard, and the only problem is to determine how the standard is established within the context of each system.

The essay "Of Tragedy" is devoted to explanation of the apparently "unaccountable pleasure, which the spectators of a well-written tragedy receive from sorrow, terror, anxiety, and other passions, that are in themselves disagreeable and uneasy." [50] Solution of this crux, a part of the more general aesthetic problem of imitations of displeasing originals, was repeatedly attempted by critics and aestheticians of the eighteenth century; no explanation of the narrower problem, the pleasure from tragedy, was more ingenious and systematic than Hume's. Hume makes subtle use of the principles of inductive reasoning developed in the *Treatise of Human Nature*; much artful logic is concealed in an apparently casually structured essay.[51]

It is a paradox that painful passions should be the cause of pleasure in a tragedy; but that they are so is incontestable, since the more keenly we are afflicted by them, the greater is our enjoyment. Hume's solution comprises three steps: determination of the conditions which a solution must meet, development of an hypothesis conforming to those requirements, and inductive verification of the hypothesis.

The Abbé Du Bos had attacked the enigma by noting that a certain enjoyment accompanies any action or passion which occupies the mind and prevents disagreeable vacuity;[52] Hume himself had recourse to this principle in the *Treatise*, and "Of Tragedy" confirms the account. But Hume suggests a difficulty "in applying to the present subject, in its full extent, this solution"—for the theory does not account for the very fact here to be explained, that what is displeasing in reality may be pleasurable in imitation.[53] The solution must, in short, be found in something differentiating art from life. The theory of Fontenelle attempts just that.[54] Arguing that pleasure and pain, so different as effects, may proceed from related causes (moderated pain, e.g., yields pleasure), Fontenelle is able to show why the excitement of the mind is still pleasing in the theater even when the passions would be painful in real life. For the half-awareness of fiction moderates the pain, reducing the affliction to a point where the emotion is pleasurable; in real life, however, no reflection (even, I presume, on our comparative security) can render grief agreeable. This reasoning is much like arguments employed by Hume at several points in the *Treatise*. " 'Tis only in dramatic performances and in religious discourses," he declares ironically, "that [fear and terror] ever give pleasure. In these latter cases the imagination reposes itself indolently on the idea; and the passion, being soften'd by the want of belief in the subject, has no more than the agreeable effect of enlivening the mind, and fixing the attention."[55] But the theory appealing to the nature of poetical belief fails of full explanation, for it rests the difference in effect on the degree of belief accorded the affecting scenes, whereas, Hume argues, events of a really distressing nature may be pleasantly exciting in oratorical presentation which is fully believed—the more vividly the rhetorician puts before us the afflict-ing circumstances, the less we are aware of their remoteness, the more we are pleasurably stirred.

The evidence thus far adduced indicates that the cause of the para-doxical pleasure of tragedy must be something common to rhetoric and poetic, and some common differentia of both from reality. This statement of the problem precludes not only the solutions traditional before Hume but also most of those developed after or in opposition to his own. The hypothesis that tragedy pleases by suggesting our own comparative security has a history reaching back to Lucretius and had in modern times the authority of Hobbes;[56] yet Hume does not con-descend to refute it. Given Hume's problem, the theory is irrelevant, for (in its unelaborated form, at least) it does not entail any differen-tiation of art from life; indeed, consciousness of our security would be yet greater in real than in imitated distress. Had Hume taken up this notion, I presume that he would have argued that a satisfaction stemming from *comparison* of our state with that which we observe would disappear as *sympathy* becomes more acute; the influence of comparison runs always counter to that of sympathy.[57] Yet our pleas-ure in tragic representations increases with the degree of sympathy felt—a circumstance which is a conclusive refutation of the theory in question. Nor could Hume assent to an explanation grounding our enjoyment on an instinctive delight in compassion—a notion advanced by Burke, Adam Smith, Blair, Lord Kames, Bishop Hurd, Campbell, and a host of lesser lights; all the variants of this theory have a com-mon failing: without further development, they do not account for any difference in our reactions to tragedy and to real situations. As Hume observed dryly in a letter to Adam Smith, "It is always thought a difficult Problem to account for the Pleasure, receivd from the Tears & Grief & Sympathy of Tragedy; which woud not be the Case, if all Sympathy was agreeable. An Hospital woud be a more entertaining Place than a Ball." [58] In the same fashion, the various moral feelings aroused—admiration of courageous resistance to mis-fortune, &c.—are not pertinent to this problem.

What, then, is to resolve the paradox? Hume notes that in a rhetor-ical description of a melancholy or terrifying episode we find pleasure in (1) apprehension of the talents and faculties of the rhetorician—his art in assembling details, his judgment in combining, his genius in presenting them—and in (2) the beauties of the rhetoric itself—the language and force of expression. These pleasures of art exceed the pain of the melancholy passions suggested by the subject (which, though believed in perhaps, is not before our senses), and by this predominance "convert" the excitement of the distressful emotions to their own aggrandizement.

> The impulse or vehemence, arising from sorrow, compassion, indignation, receives a new direction from the sentiments of beauty. The latter, being the predominant emotion, seize the whole mind, and convert the former into themselves, at least tincture them so strongly as totally to alter their nature. And the soul, being, at the same time, rouzed by passion, and charmed by eloquence, feels on the whole a strong movement, which is altogether delightful.[59]

This account will *a fortiori* explain the effects of tragedy, wherein the pleasure arising from detection of imitation is added to the sources of pleasure common to rhetoric and poetic. The weakened belief in tragedy may also have its influence; but it is necessary in any case to combine the charms of genius with the excitements of the subject.

Conversion of the passions, this change of a passion into another, even an opposite, passion under the influence of a predominating emotion, is not a notion developed *ad hoc* by Hume for the sake of constructing an ingenious theory of tragedy. The *Treatise* discusses conversion in three passages. It is mentioned rather incidentally in the explanation of unnatural malice against oneself: a man enjoying a pleasure while a friend suffers is made uneasy by the contrast and surrenders his pleasure; such comparison would ordinarily lead to self-gratulation and an accession of pleasure, save that "as grief is here suppos'd to be the predominant passion, every addition falls to that side, and is swallow'd up in it, without operating in the least upon the contrary affection." [60] A more general account of conversion is found in the section treating "Of the Causes of the Violent Passions": "'Tis a remarkable property of human nature," Hume observes, "that any emotion, which attends a passion, is easily converted into it, tho' in their natures they be originally different from, and even contrary to each other"; and he distinguishes this process from the production of one passion out of another through the double relation of impressions and ideas.[61] Hume discriminates finally, in treating "Of the Direct Passions," three other modes of rencounter between passions: alternation when they arise from different objects, cancellation when the same object provokes opposite passions, mixture in a new passion when the same object produces different emotions

but is of uncertain probability. Conversion into the predominant passion, Hume observes, commonly arises at the first shock of conflicting
passions.[62]

The conversion of painful feelings by artistry and beauty satisfies
the two conditions for a solution to the problem "Of Tragedy": it is
common to art and rhetoric, and differentiates both from actuality.
Adducing the effects of artistry, imitation, and beauty is, of course, no
novelty in the theory of tragedy; what is new is that Hume conceives
these elements not as merely counterbalancing the disturbing passions of pity and fear, but as transforming those passions into a new
pleasure. Conversion explains the effect of tragedy "by an infusion
of a new feeling, not merely by weakening or diminishing the sorrow." [63] It must be stressed that Hume's hypothesis does not intellec-
tualize art: the influence of artistry need not be consciously recognized; these are pleasures of the imagination, felt intuitively, not
calculations of judgment (though of course judgment may make us
aware of circumstances which permit our taste to respond). Refutations of Hume's theory, both in the eighteenth century and today,
commonly overthrow a view which Hume did not advance.[64]

Hume's analysis, traced this far, is only an hypothesis; confirmation is requisite, and the confirmation Hume finds is appropriate to
his system. "To explain the ultimate causes of our mental actions is
impossible," he remarks early in the *Treatise;* " 'tis sufficient if we
can give any satisfactory account of them from experience and analogy." [65] Finding analogies to the cause-effect sequence here being
studied is, then, the most efficient confirmation. The instances Hume
brings forward to "afford us some insight into the analogy of nature"
are carefully selected and arranged to constitute a complete induction.
The first group of instances includes the effects of novelty, of curiosity and impatience, of the encountering of difficulties, all which
tend to enhance whatever predominant passion they accompany,
whether agreeable or distressing. Painful feelings are converted into
pleasurable more strikingly in another set of instances—when anxiety
for a sickly child increases affection for it, when death of a friend enhances appreciation of him, when loneliness in absence, or jealousy,
reinforces love. Next the cases in which the principle operates contrariwise, so that, aesthetic pleasures being subordinated to painful
passions, the pleasure is converted to augmentation of the painful
feelings: as (in tragedy) when excess of horror or mere passive suffering convert the pleasures of imagination into augmentation of
horror or disturbing compassion. In one of his infrequent discussions

of painting, Hume here observes that painters have been "very un-happy in their subjects"—having chosen either the "ghastly mythol-ogy" of Christianity or the implausible fictions of Ovid. Hume rates the power of light, color, and form perhaps too low; the visual beauty of painting can convert more disagreeable feelings than Hume con-cedes. Hume does not attempt application of the theory of conversion to imitations of the ugly and disgusting; I am inclined to think, that, in painting at least, imitation of ugly or disgusting originals does not yield a conversion, the mind not being stirred as by the terrific or pathetic, and the unpleasantness of the original being simply sub-ducted from the beauty of the representation.[66]

Conversion is reversed when the subordinate passion becomes the predominant: "Too much jealousy extinguishes love: Too much dif-ficulty renders us indifferent: Too much sickness and infirmity dis-gusts a selfish and unkind parent." [67] Hume's final instance presents the common-life equivalent of a tragedy—a gloomy story unadorned with the embellishments of art and genius, and conveying only a disturbing uneasiness. Investigation of the inadequate conjectures of other writers had enabled Hume to present his own more complete and adequate hypothesis; he had established the reality of conversion of the passions, and by close analogies had given strong support to his conjecture; what remained was to suggest that the addition of im-agination, art, and judgment, expressive force and numbers, and imi-tative verisimilitude to a subject dismal and unpleasant, does in fact convert uneasiness to enjoyment.

CHAPTER 4

William Hogarth

⟨❀⟩

THE ONLY aesthetic treatise of the quarter-century between Hutcheson's *Inquiry* (1725) and Burke's *Sublime and Beautiful* (1757) fame of which has survived into the twentieth century is William Hogarth's *The Analysis of Beauty*. The story behind the publication of the *Analysis* in 1753—of the curiosity aroused by Hogarth's self-portrait of 1745 with "The LINE of BEAUTY And GRACE," wiry and golden, resting on his palette, curiosity kept up by a print of the portrait in 1749 and whetted by the subscription ticket for the *Analysis* in 1752, which featured an engraving of "Columbus Breaking the Egg," cleverly apposite to Hogarth's solution of the enigma of beauty—all this has been told before.[1] But though Columbus, in setting the broken egg on end, might confound the sceptic and humble the proud, Hogarth met with no such luck. Ridicule as well as applause greeted his theory; in several of a maliciously witty series of prints from the hand of Paul Sandby, Hogarth was represented as Painter Pugg—in mockery of the bellicose insularity Hogarth had displayed in his own satirical attacks on the vogue for Italian art and which led him to set his British pug beside his own likeness in the picture of 1745, that likeness itself resting on volumes of Shakespeare, Milton, and Swift. Pugg's studio windows are closed by shutters labeled "Pour Raphael," "Pour Rubens," "Pour Rembrandt"—to exclude any gleam from the genius of those masters; the imp of vanity whispers in his ear; he draws from hideously grotesque models whose curves caricature the line of grace; a bust of Raphael is desecrated as his wig block; and more of the same.[2]

But among the major aestheticians of the next half-century Hogarth's theory was accorded the same sort of recognition as Hutcheson's: it was taken, that is, as true of a limited class of aesthetic phenomena, but subsumed into theories represented as more comprehensive. Such subsumption in the hands of Burke and Gerard, Reynolds and Alison was accomplished, however, only by shifting the surviving parts of Hogarth's doctrine onto new philosophic bases different from, and indeed incompatible with, those which for Hogarth himself had justified his as a complete theory of beauty.

Until quite recently the *Analysis* has been curiously ignored in modern scholarship on the eighteenth century. Lives and critiques of Hogarth fill a library shelf, yet none has offered more than cursory remarks about the *Analysis;* and the learned journals, though they bulge with articles on Hogarth the artist, ignore Hogarth the aesthetician.[3] Typical of the prevailing attitude, perhaps, is Marjorie Bowen's remark that the *Analysis* "is a very curious production, now no more than a literary curiosity. . . . That so great a painter could really have seriously concerned himself with the odd theories put forward in this book is not to be believed." [4] A new and elaborate edition by Joseph Burke has, however, supplied this defect; Peter Quennell's study of Hogarth attends seriously to Hogarth's theory; and it is unlikely that commentators can in future ignore it.

The Preface to *The Analysis of Beauty,* indeed, may seem to deserve some of the ridicule which has been heaped upon the book. Hogarth recites at length, as saving him "the trouble of collecting an historical account of these arts among the ancients," [5] Le Blon's fabulous notion that the Greeks possessed a secret and mysterious rule or "analogy" brought by Pythagoras from Chaldea or Egypt. Though a commonplace of Hogarth's age, and even pretty good art history for the period, this notion gives the Preface an air of buncombe for the modern ahistorical reader. But the treatise itself is free of such crotchets, and ought to be considered even by hostile critics as a serious and significant theory, unique in important respects among the British systems of the eighteenth century.

"I now offer to the public," Hogarth declares, "a short essay, accompanied with two explanatory prints, in which I shall endeavour to shew what the principles are in nature, by which we are directed to call the forms of some bodies beautiful, others ugly; some graceful, and others the reverse; by considering more minutely than has hitherto been done, the nature of those lines, and their different combinations, which serve to raise in the mind the ideas of all the variety of forms imaginable." [6] He appeals to a disinterested audience, neither of fashionable connoisseurs nor of painters; those, he concludes, "who have no bias of any kind, either from their own practice, or the lessons of others, are fittest to examine into the truth of the principles laid down in the following pages." [7] Such appeal is not merely an expression of Hogarth's pique at a fashionable cant of criticism; it implies a philosophic standpoint. Implicit in Hogarth's statements is the priority of nature to art as an object of aesthetic analysis; the fault with painters and connoisseurs is that by having "espoused and adopted their first notions from nothing but *imitations,* and becoming too often as bigotted to their faults, as their beauties, they at length, in a manner, totally neglect, or at least disregard the works of nature, merely because they do not tally with what their minds are so strongly prepossess'd with." [8] The beginning with nature, or with what is common to nature and art, is characteristic of an analytic philosophy; the peculiarities of art can then be accounted for by a study of the effects of imitation. The approach always strives to separate the different elements contributing to aesthetic effect, and to relate them individually to the powers or sensibilities of the mind with which they react.

And so with the linear analysis which Hogarth promises. The element of which wholes are composed is for Hogarth the line; accordingly, the Introduction to the *Analysis* explains at some length the fashion in which volume can be seen lineally:

> In order to my being well understood, let every object under our consideration, be imagined to have its inward contents scoop'd out so nicely, as to have nothing of it left but a thin shell, exactly corresponding both in its inner and outer surface, to the shape of the object itself: and let us likewise suppose this thin shell to be made up of very fine threads, closely connected together, and equally perceptible, whether the eye is supposed to observe them from without, or within; and we shall find the ideas of the two surfaces of this shell will naturally coincide. . . . [The] oftner we think of objects in this shell-like manner, we shall facilitate and strengthen our conception of any particular part of the surface of an object we are viewing, by acquiring thereby a more perfect knowledge of the whole, to which it belongs: because the imagination will naturally enter into the vacant space within this shell, and there at once, as from a center, view the whole form within, and mark the opposite corresponding parts so strongly, as to retain the idea of the whole, and make us masters of the meaning of every view of the object, as we walk round it, and view it from without. [9]

This is manifestly a highly artificial technique, for it does away with all conception of solidity, and reduces perception of surface to a strange complication of perceptions of line. Hogarth conceives a sphere as "an infinite number of straight rays of equal lengths, issuing from the center . . . and circumscribed or wound about at their other extremities with close connected circular threads, or lines, forming a true spherical shell." [10] Actually (as I think) a sphere is conceived as a surface of which the lighting varies in a certain fashion or which provides certain tactile sensations; the reduction of this comparatively simple impression to a multitude of ideas of lines requires a positive effort of imagination. Nevertheless, this forced way of regarding objects does have the advantage which interests Hogarth—of permitting evolution of all possible views from a single image. The artist thus "arrives at the knack of recalling [even the most irregular figures] . . . into his mind when the objects themselves are not before him." [11] This technique, then, duly elaborated, is part of the technical memory or visual grammar of which Hogarth speaks in his autobiographical fragments; the reduction of figures, attitudes, and actions to combinations of elementary lines is another part of this system.

With this hint of his linear analysis by way of introduction, Hogarth enters upon his main subject by undertaking to consider

> the fundamental principles, which are generally allowed to give elegance and beauty, when duly blended together, to compositions of all kinds whatever; and point out to my readers, the particular force of each, in those compositions in nature and art, which seem most to *please and entertain the eye,* and give that grace and beauty, which is the subject of this enquiry. The principles I mean, are FITNESS, VARIETY, UNIFORMITY, SIMPLICITY, INTRICACY, AND QUANTITY;—*all which co-operate in the production of beauty, mutually correcting and restraining each other occasionally.*[12]

Fitness is first both as prior in nature and as indispensable. It has been remarked by Joseph Burke that Hogarth drew on Xenophon's *Memorabilia* for some of his remarks on fitness, and perhaps conceived his idea for the print, "The Statuary's Yard," from Socrates' visit to the sculptor Cleiton.[13] The debt is likely; but, in general, it must be affirmed that Socrates' discussion is undertaken for a different purpose, rests on different presuppositions, employs a different method, and evolves a doctrine with only partial or accidental similarities to Hogarth's. Socrates, for instance, declares that "all things are good and beautiful in relation to those purposes for which they are well adapted, bad and ugly in relation to those for which they are ill adapted," an identification of beauty and fitness which Hogarth could by no means accept; or, in his visit to Parrhasius, Socrates argues for imitation of the soul, not merely of the physical form, and repeats this demand in talking with Cleiton—but this is an aspect of beauty which only indirectly and accidentally enters Hogarth's theory.[14] There is at any rate nothing Socratic in the development Hogarth gives to his ideas, and the theory into which they are fitted is wholly unlike any classical theory. Fitness, for Hogarth, is not the whole of beauty but a material cause of it—necessary, but sufficient of itself for only a very moderate degree of beauty. Its principal influence, in fact, is in modifying unqualified beauty into "characteristic" beauties adapted to particular circumstances. It must be noted that beauty of fitness does not depend on appreciation of the concord between part and function considered *qua* concord in the manner of Hutcheson, who reduced fitness analogically to a special instance of uniformity in variety; rather, it is a pleasure transferred by association from the "mind" (i.e., from the cognition of fitness) to the "eye" (the apparently simple perception of the object).

Variety yields a more positive beauty than does fitness:

> All the senses delight in it, and equally are averse to sameness. The ear is as much offended with one even continued note, as the eye is with being fix'd to a point, or to the view of a dead wall.
>
> Yet when the eye is glutted with a succession of variety, it finds relief in a certain degree of sameness; and even plain space becomes agreeable, and properly introduced, and contrasted with variety, adds to it more variety.
>
> I mean here, and every where indeed, a composed variety; for variety uncomposed, and without design, is confusion and deformity.[15]

The psychology supposed here, that the sense, or the attention, delights in a moderate degree of exertion, a mean between vacuity and distraction, is pretty generally assumed among eighteenth-century aestheticians, and is a truism comparatively independent of philosophic system.

Hogarth's statements about variety have sometimes a paradoxical air because he tends to include much of regularity in variety: his variety is "composed." *Regularity* considered in itself, rather than as a relief to or as the composition of variety, is pleasing only as suggestive of fitness: "If the uniformity of figures, parts, or lines were truly the chief cause of beauty, the more exactly uniform their appearances were kept, the more pleasure the eye would receive: but this is so far from being the case, that when the mind has once been satisfied, that the parts answer one another, with so exact an uniformity, as to preserve to the whole the character of fitness to stand, to move, to sink, to swim, to fly, &c. without losing the balance: the eye is rejoiced to see the object turn'd, and shifted, so as to vary these uniform appearances." [16] Regularity often pleases, to be sure, in forms merely decorative, as in a molding; but as Hogarth does not usually distinguish design from fitness from utility such regularities are still comprehended in what he terms fitness. Apart from fitness, he declares, "regularity and sameness . . . is want of elegance and true taste." [17]

Uniformity and variety are not, properly speaking, contraries for Hogarth, for although they vary in inverse proportion, the problem is not to strike a mean but to secure the maximum "composed variety," given as prerequisite that kind and degree of regularity needed to fit an object for its end. The "uniformity" of Hutcheson's theory is found in Hogarth fractured into the composition of variety, the symmetry or regularity indicative of fitness, and simplicity, fourth of Hogarth's principles. There is for Hogarth no peculiar sense adapted to perceiving uniformity in variety, for the different modes of that union are pleasing from different principles.

Simplicity is agreeable because of its influence in facilitating perception: "Simplicity, without variety, is wholly insipid, and at best does only not displease; but when variety is join'd to it, then it pleases, because it enhances the pleasure of variety, by giving the eye the power of enjoying it with ease." [18]

The pleasure of *intricacy* arises from the instinctive love of pursuit, from the delight in moderate exertion: "The active mind is ever bent to be employ'd. Pursuing is the business of our lives; and even abstracted from any other view, gives pleasure. Every arising difficulty, that for a while attends and interrupts the pursuit, gives a sort of spring to the mind, enhances the pleasure, and makes what would else be toil and labour, become sport and recreation." [19] Intricacy of form is defined, accordingly, as "that peculiarity in the lines, which compose it, that *leads the eye a wanton kind of chace*, and from the pleasure that gives the mind, intitles it to the name of beautiful: and it may be justly said, that the cause of the idea of grace more immediately resides in this principle, than in the other five, except variety; which indeed includes this, and all the others." [20] Variety includes the others only in that they are insufficient to produce beauty without it, and serve as prerequisites or limits or reliefs to it; intricacy, of course, is only a special mode of variety.

Although Hogarth constantly speaks of "the eye" finding pleasure in this or that, it is doubtful whether he always intends these locutions quite literally. The pleasure of intricacy is not, properly speaking, a pleasure of the sense; it stems from satisfaction of a natural appetite through use of the eye, and the pleasure only appears to pertain to the organ of sight. It does seem evident, however, that Hogarth thought that the eye followed a line with a movement duplicating the course of the line: "we shall always suppose some such principal ray moving along with the eye, and tracing out the parts of every form we mean to examine in the most perfect manner . . ." and so forth.[21] He speaks also of "pleasing vibrations of the optic nerves" produced by light and shadow,[22] and has other curious physiological notions, most noteworthy the anatomy he devises in explaining the color of the skin.[23] Eye movements are really staccato, but the attention—the mind's eye—is not conscious of the discrete movements of the organ, and Hogarth's view will stand if we conventionally interpret it to refer to the attention rather than to the organic eye.[24]

Quantity, last of the principles of beauty, is of course associated with sublimity. And Hogarth concedes a sublimity independent of beauty: "Forms of magnitude, although ill-shaped, will however, on account of their vastness, draw our attention and raise our admiration. . . . [But] when forms of beauty are presented to the eye in large quantities, the pleasure increases on the mind, and horror is soften'd into reverence." [25] The moral associations of sublimity are not analyzed by Hogarth; the independence from moral feeling is in fact one of the striking traits of Hogarth's aesthetic. Even the sublimity of the human form is treated formally; true greatness (Hogarth does not use the term "sublimity") stems from proportion rather than from quantity merely. Elucidation of the peculiar excellence of the Apollo Belvedere demonstrates that "*greatness* of proportion must be considered, as depending on the application of *quantity* to those parts of the body where it can give more scope to its grace in movement, as to the neck for the larger and more swan-like turns of the head, and to the legs and thighs, for the more ample sway of all the upper parts together." [26] This analysis thus reduces greatness to the same principles from which beauty depends, and which are discussed below. Curiously, Hogarth digresses into an account of the ridiculous in the midst of his treatment of quantity—the transition hinging upon the circumstance that exaggerated quantity may become absurd. The ridiculous depends partly on the conception of impropriety and incongruity (which in Hogarth's loose and general way of speaking are modes of unfitness), partly on merely linear factors: "When improper, or *incompatible* excesses meet, they always excite laughter; more especially when the forms of those excesses are inelegant, that is, when they are composed of unvaried lines." [27] It is characteristic of Hogarth's aesthetic that he should not trace out the associations which render regular curves and unvaried lines ridiculous in the human face and figure.[28]

These six principles are the substructure of the theory: fitness is a prior condition, quantity a supervening excellence, and the rest are all modifications of variety—intricacy being a mode, and uniformity and simplicity limits, of variety. That variety in which Hogarth is interested is linear. Line is progressively more various as we advance from straight and "circular" lines through those partly straight and partly circular, through the waving line with its reverse curve, to the serpentine line, which, varying in three dimensions, "hath the power of super-adding grace to beauty." [29] It is the waving line alone which is properly entitled "the line of beauty"; the serpentine line is "the line of grace," and is of a higher order.

Analysis of beauty in terms of the waving or serpentine line naturally arises with the Baroque, and is found, without systematic elaboration, in Lomazzo and various other writers before Hogarth.[30] Hogarth's theory affords a rationale for baroque, or, as Joseph Burke has well argued, especially for rococo art. Nonetheless, it would be an error to suppose that the theory is merely a rationalization for a style fashionable in Hogarth's age. Not so; the serpentine line is not (or not primarily) a grand compositional line, dictating the sweep and order of an entire canvas—it is a line found in the parts, in a fold of drapery or a curl of hair, in the gesture of a hand or the stance of a figure. It is not confined (I use Wölfflin's terminology) to the Baroque but is found, too, in the Renaissance style, even in that of the quattrocento—in Botticelli as in Rembrandt, in Fra Angelico as in Velasquez. And no style has more of Hogarthian beauty and grace than Raphael's—a style quintessentially Renaissance. It is true, as Burke has argued,[31] that Hogarth neither much approved in theory nor much followed in practice the linear manner, the closed form, the clear presentation, the planar composition of the Renaissance style; but the serpentine line can still be found in a picture symmetrical, frontal, and planar.

The problem of composition is (fitness apart) one of employing various kinds of lines in various relations one to another, yet without destroying simplicity: "In a word, it may be said, the art of composing well, is the art of varying well." [32] What is remarkable in Hogarth's treatment of composition is that whether he is discussing a candlestick or St. Paul's, he handles the problem in terms of his simple linear analysis. The connotative aspects of composition, the various classes of associations which qualify our reactions to objects and their qualities and relations, are scarcely mentioned—and the occasional reference to such associations seems an intrusion unwarranted by any systematic necessity. Hogarth has properly no place for such judgments except through elaboration of his notion of "fitness," and this consideration alone is not adequate to the whole range of moral association. We see distinctly what is left out in Hogarth when we think of Ruskin, whose emphasis is almost wholly on the kinds of considerations excluded from Hogarth's system. Yet the intrusion of moral association is nonetheless discernible even in Hogarth's purely formal criteria. The precise line of beauty, for instance, is distinguished from those lines which, insufficiently curving, are "mean and poor," and from those of excessive curvature, which are "gross and clumsy." [33] "Mean" and "gross" are terms not literally applicable to the influence of variety on the sense or the attention: they suggest, alongside this physiological effect, moral associations. Attitude and action exhibit the same fusion of moral and formal qualities, for the graceful is found to be also the genteel. Some writers later in the century, most notably and systematically Alison, reduce *all* the influence of Hogarth's formal properties to moral association, though even for Alison the associations with formal qualities remain distinguishable in their aesthetic effect from associations with concrete wholes.

Hogarth's effort to abstract beauty from moral association implies no preference for abstract art: "Subject[s] of most consequence," he declares, "are those that most entertain and Improve the mind and are of public utility." [34] It is simply that *this* excellence is an excellence distinct from beauty.

In his first manuscript draft of the *Analysis,* Hogarth categorized the "inherent quallity of objects & the motions they excite in us" by analogy with moral and other feelings:

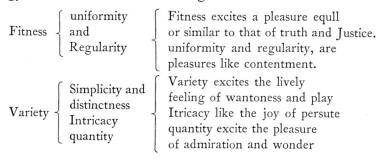

Fitness { uniformity and Regularity } { Fitness excites a pleasure equll or similar to that of truth and Justice. uniformity and regularity, are pleasures like contentment.

Variety { Simplicity and distinctness Intricacy quantity } { Variety excites the lively feeling of wantoness and play Itricacy like the joy of persute quantity excite the pleasure of admiration and wonder

all which Joyning in their precise degrees in the human
have the power of creating esteem love Honour
Simplicity and distinctness in like the pleasure of easy attainment.

This analysis, however, is not quite a reduction of aesthetic feeling to moral. Fitness excites a pleasure like that of truth and Justice (I presume) because cognition of it is intellectual (even though through experience it may come to be judged of at sight), not a matter of direct feeling. Again, justice is a virtue violation of which excites antipathy, but satisfaction of which ordinarily causes only calm approbation—and so with fitness. Variety and the properties associated with it in Hogarth's table yield a pleasure which is both immediately felt and of positive character, a pleasure which, when its cause is a human being, is a mode of love. This interpretation of Hogarth's sketch is confessedly conjectural; but I am in any event not persuaded that Hogarth was here attempting to escape the thorny tangle of aesthetic analysis by turning into "the broad, and more beaten path of moral beauty." [35]

It is unnecessary to trace Hogarth's application, sometimes a little fanciful, of the serpentine line to analysis of the human figure. All this is part of what he terms "the first general idea of form"—determined by "the nature of variety, and . . . its effects on the mind; with the manner how such impressions are made by means of the different feelings given to the eye, from its movements in tracing and coursing over surfaces of all kinds." [36] But there is a second "general idea of form" arising from fitness, an idea involving not only the surfaces of objects considered as shells, but the motion and function of the objects and hence their solidity and contents. It is this second conception which gives rise to judgments of fit proportion, "which is one part of beauty to the mind tho' not always so to the eye." [37] Hogarth heaps ridicule upon theories of proportion which pretend an absolute merit in certain ratios, especially ratios proper to harmony: "Albert Durer, Lamozzo . . . and some others, have not only puzzled mankind with a heap of minute unnecessary divisions, but also with a strange *notion* that those divisions are govern'd by the laws of music; which mistake they seem to have been led into, by having seen certain uniform and consonant divisions upon one string produce harmony to the ear, and by persuading themselves, that similar distances in lines belonging to form, would, in like manner, delight the eye." [38] Hogarth is inclined, indeed, to run the analogy the other way, to reduce sound under the laws of visual beauty.[39] But the true beauty or "gentility" of proportion in the figure depends only upon such general proportions of length, breadth, and thickness as give maximum variety consistent with "character," and similarly for the smaller parts of figures.[40] This "character" depends "on a figure being remarkable as to its form, either in some particular part, or altogether," provided that this singularity can be attributed to "some remarkable circumstance or cause"—as the "tuscan" legs of chairmen and the broad shoulders and spindle shanks of Thames watermen clearly arise from their professions. Although Hogarth treats the greatness of the Apollo Belvedere alongside these characteristic beauties, it must be noted that greatness is not comparable with the rugged strength of a Hercules or the softness of an Antinous; for although the proportions of the Apollo suggest dignity and fleetness, the traits of a sun-god, this greatness is pleasing also without regard to specific function, from its general connection with graceful motion.

Hogarth's psychology naturally leads him to reduce all phenomena analogically to modifications of line. The beauties of color are treated, accordingly, not in terms of the effects of colors as such, but as gradations of shading. The beauty both of prime tints which serve as shades to one another and of "retiring shades" (variations in brilliance) is linear: it arises from the variety of the shading, and four species of variation are distinguished, corresponding to straight, curved, waving, and serpentine lines. Composition with shades is treated in terms of opposition, simplicity, and breadth—really variety and simplicity again—but there is only the slightest ramification of these principles into subordinate rules and criteria. The handling of the entire subject of coloring is hampered by the reduction to linear analysis.

Associative factors of course intrude into discussion of the lines and coloring of the face; yet Hogarth's system is inimical to elaboration of such factors, and the analysis remains on the level of shrewd common-sense generalizations; there is no treatment comparable to the complex study Alison subsequently makes of facial beauty. Attitude and action, topics of the two final chapters of the *Analysis,* admit of lineal definition more readily than do light and color, and Hogarth's observations are accordingly more rewarding. Illustrated by the print, "The Country Dance," the analysis fuses formal and connotative factors, for the graceful turns out to be also the genteel, and the regular the ridiculous. The fusion of line with expression or character is not analyzed by Hogarth; insofar as his treatment of expression is systematic at all, it is so by virtue of his tendency to describe expression by his principles of variety, uniformity, and the rest, and especially in terms of lines. Recognition of the expressiveness of form has been remarked by almost every aesthetician since antiquity; the novelty in Hogarth is that the beauty of form does not derive from the expression but from independent causes, the expressiveness being superadded and coincidental. Hogarth's distinction of fitness or utility from ornamental beauty also plays through his discussion of motion; he notes that "all useful habitual motions, such as are readiest to serve the necessary purposes of life, are those made up of plain lines, i.e. straight and circular lines," whereas "graceful movements in serpentine lines, are used but occasionally, and rather at times of leisure, than constantly applied to every action we make . . . they being properly speaking, only the ornamental part of gesture. . . ."[41]

Two persistent misconceptions which have obstructed sympathetic understanding of the *Analysis* should perhaps be dispatched here. First is the notion that Hogarth tossed off the theories of the *Analysis* as a *jeu d'esprit* or as a device to escape from the position into which his controversy with the connoisseurs had thrust him. Ranged against this view is not only the coherence of the argument itself, but positive external evidence of Hogarth's continued adherence to its principles. Only three years before his death Hogarth affirmed his intention of publishing a supplement.[42] And his last work (1764), "THE BATHOS, *or Manner of Sinking, in Sublime Paintings, inscribed to the Dealers in Dark Pictures*," refers to the line of beauty. A band beneath the engraving depicts on one side a pyramidal spiral shell—"*The Conic Form in wch the Goddess of Beauty was worship^d by the Ancients at Paphos in ye Island of* CYPRUS"—and on the other, the serpentine line twisted about a cone—"*A Copy of the precise Line of Beauty* [really the line of grace], *as it is represented on the 1st explanatory Plate* [Plate 1, fig. 26] *of the Analysis of Beauty. Note, the similarity of these two Conic Figures, did not occur to the Author, till two or three Years after his publication of the Analysis, in 1754* [1753]." This detail demonstrates, if demonstration is needed, Hogarth's devotion to his theory as long as he lived.

A second false issue arises over the relation of Hogarth's own practice to his theory. Detractors point with contempt to the discrepancy between Hogarth's painting and his aesthetic, while admirers may seek to find the theory exemplified in the paintings. It is of course obvious that Hogarth is best and best known as a comic painter, whereas the *Analysis* is devoted almost wholly to the beautiful. But

Hogarth nowhere insists that the beautiful is the only end of art; of other possible ends, the ridiculous is a subordinate theme in the *Analysis* and the principal object of Hogarth's art. There is a true correspondence between theory and practice: "Hogarth's earliest works are conceived on a formal pattern exactly in accordance with his later theories. That is to say, idealized or romantic figures are serpentine, comic ones angular or round." [43] Even in so trifling an effort as the engraving of "Columbus Breaking the Egg" this distinction can be seen: the figure of Columbus—the hair, the gesture of the right hand, &c.—is, in this context, graceful and genteel; those figures expressing vulgar astonishment, chagrin, or annoyance are not. But it is enthusiasm for Charles Holmes to declare that in the *Analysis* Hogarth attempted "to explain that vital principle, whereby his art was different from that of all his contemporaries," or for Hesketh Hubbard to apply this idea by detecting the line of beauty in such a painting as "Calais Gate." [44] The line of grace is clearly inappropriate to the satirical works and is rarely found in them unless to point up some contrast or irony. The high-comedy and conversation pieces are not devoid of grace—"The Lady's Last Stake" might be instanced—but it is in the history paintings that grace and beauty are to be sought, in "The Pool of Bethesda" and "The Good Samaritan," or twenty years later and less strikingly in "The Ascension" (for St. Mary Redcliffe's). Better than in Hogarth's own works, however, Hogarthian grace and beauty are seen in Raphael and Annibale Caracci—with some exaggeration in Guido Reni. But in any event, the merit of an aesthetic theory is a function of its analytical acuity and its fruitfulness in application, not of its pertinence to the works of its author, which is a mere *argumentum ad hominem*.

CHAPTER 5

Alexander Gerard

IN 1756, Alexander Gerard, then professor of moral philosophy and logic at Marischal College, submitted *An Essay on Taste* for a prize offered by the Edinburgh Society for the Encouragement of Arts, Sciences, Manufactures, and Agriculture. This essay, published in 1759,[1] is the most elaborate investigation of the faculty of taste during the eighteenth century, and, indeed, treated the subject with such elaborateness as to discourage subsequent inquiries of comparable detail. A second edition was called for in 1764; and the third edition, 1780, added an important analysis of the standard of taste.[2] Gerard's other important aesthetic treatise, *An Essay on Genius,* appeared in London and Edinburgh in 1774, although Gerard observes that "the first part [was] composed, and some progress made in the second part, so long ago as the year 1758."[3] The later book is the more impressive analytically, but its principal subject is foreign to the present study and it will be considered only incidentally.

"Taste," observes Gerard,

consists chiefly in the improvement of those principles, which are commonly called *the powers of imagination,* and are considered by modern philosophers as *internal* or *reflex* senses. . . . These are reducible to the following principles; the senses of novelty, of sublimity, of beauty, of imitation, of harmony, of ridicule, and of virtue. With the explication of these, we must, therefore, begin our enquiry into the nature of *taste.* We shall next endeavour to discover, how these senses co-operate in forming *taste,* what other powers of the mind are combined with them in their exertions, what constitutes that refinement and perfection of them, which we term *good taste,* and by what means it is obtained. And last of all, we shall, by a review of the principles, operation, and subjects of *taste,* determine its genuine rank among our faculties, its proper province, and real importance.[4]

67

This statement is the rationale for the three parts of the *Essay:* the component faculties; their conjunction; and the relations between the taste thus constituted and other faculties and principles.

The seven internal senses are not ultimate principles of human nature: they are compound and derivative faculties. They are termed senses because they share with the external senses independence of volition, and immediacy and simplicity of perception; for though they are compound in principle, they are simple in feeling and their perceptions are inconceivable prior to experience. "Those who are unacquainted with philosophy," Gerard remarks,

> reckon all our powers ultimate qualities of the mind. But nature delights in simplicity, and produces numerous effects, by a few causes of extensive influence; and it is the business of philosophy to investigate these causes, and to explain the phaenomena from them. On enquiry it appears that the internal senses are not ultimate principles, because all their phaenomena can be accounted for, by simpler qualities of the mind. Thus the pleasure we receive from beautiful forms is resolvible into the pleasure of facility and that of moderate exertion . . . but the sentiment of beauty arises, without our reflecting on this mixture. This sentiment is compound in its *principles,* but perfectly simple in its *feeling.* . . .[5]

And in general, the phenomena of taste "proceed, either from the general laws of *sensation,* or from certain operations of the *imagination.* Taste, though itself a species of sensation, is, in respect of its principles, justly reduced to imagination."[6] Gerard can wield Occam's razor.

A general principle of sensation, subsuming the notion that moderate activity is pleasurable, is that

> when an object is presented to any of our senses, the mind conforms it self to its nature and appearance, feels an emotion, and is put in a frame suitable and analogous; of which we have a perception by consciousness or reflection. Thus difficulty produces a consciousness of a grateful exertion of energy: facility of an even and regular flow of spirits: excellence, perfection, or sublimity, begets an enlargement of mind and conscious pride; deficience or imperfection, a depression of soul, and painful humility. This adapting of the mind to its present object is the *immediate* cause of many of the pleasures and pains of taste; and, by its *consequences,* it augments or diminishes many others.[7]

This is not, however, the sole such principle; association and sympathy ("which enlivens our *ideas* of the passions infused by it to such a pitch, as in a manner converts them into the passions themselves"[8]) modify our sensations.

The fundamental faculties for Gerard are the usual: external sense, memory, imagination, judgment. Gerard's view of these faculties is essentially that of Hume, though Gerard is an eclectic writer and on occasion imitates Reid or Hutcheson instead. But the Hutchesonian element in Gerard can be overestimated: Gerard analyzes senses or faculties which for Hutcheson were simple and original, and he does not attempt to reduce beauty to a single species.

Of the various internal senses, the only one which need be treated before proceeding to the more strictly aesthetic problems is the sense of virtue. Since Gerard is only incidentally concerned with morals, he does not proliferate distinctions, and comprehends under the "sense or taste of virtue" perceptions of the "beauty" of virtue, of its fitness to human nature, of its obligatory character, of its good desert—all which perceptions might perhaps be referred to separate senses. There is, furthermore, nothing systematic in Gerard's treatment of this sense. When Hutcheson speaks of the "beauty" of virtue, his language conveys not a vague and figurative meaning but a significance systematically connected with the whole of his thought—that virtue is so related to the economy of the universe as to present a picture of uniformity in variety. Gerard means, in contrast, only that certain traits of character yield pleasurable perceptions in onlookers, perceptions vaguely like those caused by visible beauty. The connection between ethics and aesthetics in this system, beyond the fact that virtue is in some sense "beautiful" or "sublime," is causal. Both character and taste arise in large part from similar operations of the imagination: "By being compounded with one another, or with other original qualities of human nature, they ["operations of imagination," "energies of fancy"] generate most of our compounded powers. In particular, they produce *affection* and *taste* of every kind; the former, by operating in conjunction with those qualities of the mind, which fit us for action; the latter, by being combined with the general laws of sensation." [9] The prevailing passions influence the turn of taste, and taste reciprocally modifies the bent of the passions. On the whole, taste is favorable to virtue, since it minimizes sensual pleasure, produces an agreeable cast of mind conducive to the gentler affections, and imparts a "peculiar sensibility to all the other powers of the soul." [10] But although taste is naturally more favorable to virtue than to vice, "it is necessary to remember that many different causes concur in forming the characters of men. Taste is but one of these causes; and not one of the most powerful. It is not therefore to be expected that the character should be, in every instance, perfectly analogous to the taste." [11] These differentiations and causal connections clearly mark Gerard's approach as literal and differential, in contrast with Hutcheson's more analogical and organic treatment.

The phenomena of memory, though surprisingly varied in Gerard's analysis,[12] present no peculiar problem, and it is possible to pass directly to the treatment of imagination and judgment. The analysis of imagination is roughly similar to that of Hume; there is a comparable treatment of association and of the Humeian distinction between natural relations (by which the imagination associates spontaneously) and philosophical relations (by which the judgment may connect reflexively).[13] And other operations of the imagination besides association follow Hume pretty closely. The contrariety of the influence of sympathy with that of comparison is remarked upon; for though simply associated perceptions transmit their qualities to one another, yet if the connected ideas have such a degree of relation as invites comparison, the effect is opposite, and a pleasant idea will appear less so by comparison with a more pleasant.[14] The influence of the passions on association is given an extraordinarily rich treatment; [15] as in much of the *Essay on Genius*, Gerard goes far beyond Hume in the evolution of a detailed associational psychology, though often at some cost in systematic rigor.

The study of judgment is more different from orthodox Humeianism. Judgment is either of truth or of beauty, which latter kind is taste. Gerard is rather quick in accepting a variety of intellectual faculties concerned with truth as original and unanalyzable, borrowing eclectically from Reid, from Beattie, and from Campbell. But the question of judgment as it pertains to beauty will take its proper place hereafter.

The "sense or taste of novelty" is included by Gerard among the internal senses because of the tradition established by Addison. His explanation of the love of novelty is rather surprisingly complicated. Five principles can be distinguished: the elevation and pleasurable exertion of the mind in conceiving the new phenomenon; surprise; composition with other passions or emotions; reflection on success in surmounting difficulty, or self-gratulation on acquisition of the new perception; sympathy with the original genius displayed in inventive works of science and art.[16] The pleasing sentiment arising from novelty blends readily with other agreeable passions an object happens to produce; but what is of interest is that such composition may become a conversion: "The exercise of mind, which the conception of new objects occasions, though it be pleasant in its own nature, ren-

ders a disagreeable object more disagreeable at first: for the most opposite sensations produced by the same cause, and existing in the mind
at once, are easily transfused into one another, and, by their composition form one more violent, which always follows the nature of the
ingredient that was most intense." [17] Gerard makes use of this Humeian theory of conversion not only in accounting for the effects of
novelty, but also in treating of the ridiculous and in discussing
tragedy.

The internal senses of chief importance for this study are, of
course, those of sublimity and beauty. "GRANDEUR or sublimity,"
Gerard declares, "gives us a still higher and nobler pleasure [than
novelty], by means of a sense appropriated to the perception of it;
while meanness renders any object, to which it adheres, disagreeable
and distasteful. Objects are sublime, which possess *quantity* or amplitude, and *simplicity* in conjunction." [18] The emotion of sublimity is
produced by such objects because we

> contemplate objects and ideas with a disposition similar to their nature.
> When a large object is presented, the mind expands itself to the extent
> of that object, and is filled with one grand sensation, which totally
> possessing it, composes it into a solemn sedateness, and strikes it with deep
> silent wonder and admiration: it finds such a difficulty in spreading itself
> to the dimensions of its object, as enlivens and invigorates its frame: and
> having overcome the opposition which this occasions, it sometimes imag-
> ines itself present in every part of the scene, which it contemplates; and,
> from the sense of this immensity, feels a noble pride, and entertains a
> lofty conception of its own capacity.[19]

Each part of this analysis—greatness, simplicity conjoined therewith,
the enlargement of the mind to match the scene, and its conscious
pride—each part was to be found in *An Essay on the Sublime* by Dr.
[John] Baillie, which had appeared posthumously in 1747.[20] Similar
ideas, of course, appear as commonplaces in classical authors; and
Hume, too, notes that "the mere view and contemplation of any
greatness, whether successive or extended, enlarges the soul, and
gives it a sensible delight and pleasure," and that (contrariwise) the
mind "spreads itself" on objects, seeing its own traits existing in the
object of perception.[21] Both notions are more intimately connected
with a general theory of the mind in Hume than in Gerard, and
there is actually loss of content as well as of systematic connection in
Gerard's formulation; for Gerard, following Baillie, emphasizes extent as principal cause of the sensation of sublimity, whereas elevation and temporal distance were found by Hume to be still more

sublime. The sublimity of duration and that of great number are traced by Gerard to their participation in quantity.

Sublimity of the passions and affections is explained by association with their causes, objects, or effects: "as these always enter into our conception of the passion, and are often connected with quantity, they naturally render the passion sublime." [22] Here again Gerard has followed Baillie, and it is interesting to note that both find universal benevolence sublime, whereas to writers who distinguish the sublime and beautiful on a basis other than quantity, benevolence is more usually felt to be beautiful. The sublime of science, for Gerard as for Baillie, is found to consist in "universal principles and general theorems, from which, as from an inexhaustible source, flow multitudes of corollaries and subordinate truths"; [23] thus, the very reason which makes science beautiful for Hutcheson makes it sublime for Gerard.

An object which is not in itself sublime by its quantity may become so not only by association of ideas (as with the sublimity of passions and affections) but by association of impressions and feelings: "It must also be remarked, that whatever excites in the mind a sensation or emotion similar to what is excited by vast objects is on this account denominated sublime. . . ." [24] Terrific objects are termed sublime because of the likeness of the awful sedateness they inspire to sublimity. And in the same way, we admire as sublime pre-eminence in strength, power, genius, magnanimity which enables a man to despise honors, riches, or death, and other excellences: "Such degrees of excellence, by an original principle of the mind, excite wonder and astonishment, the same emotion which is produced by amplitude. A great degree of *quality* has here the same effect upon the mind, as vastness of *quantity*, and it produces this effect in the same manner, by stretching and elevating the mind in the conception of it." [25] Baillie had attempted to show, by a strained reduction, that these excellences were sublime only because they implied quantity in the objects upon which they were exerted—worlds, multitudes, nothingness, &c. Although Gerard's assertion that we admire such traits by an *original* property of the mind may be mooted, his introduction of the principle of association of impressions, of like feelings, is of signal importance.

Gerard does not himself apply the term "association" to this commingling of like emotions, nor does he apply it to the relation whereby passions become sublime through connection with their causes, objects, or effects. He confines the term to a narrower range of phenomena. The sublime of diction is traced to "association" with the ideas presented or the character of the speaker, and the grandeur of elevated, distant, and temporally remote objects is referred to association, with due acknowledgement of Hume's explanation. This ascription of the greatness of such objects to association is not in contradiction with the analysis of the sublimity of duration and extent already mentioned; in the earlier context, it was the extent and time *per se* which were inherently sublime from their participation in quantity, while here it is the objects removed *in* time or space which are, by association with the intervals, sublime. It is puzzling why the relation of sign to significatum should be "association" and not that of cause to effect, of which it is but a special case. Most of the Scottish philosophers use the term "association" in a somewhat pejorative sense; Hutcheson, for instance, calls by this name only accidental, personal, idiosyncratic associations—a usage derived, perhaps, from Locke. Gerard's associations, however, are universal, not personal; he must consider that these relations are less close than those other relations through which objects may become sublime.

Sublimity in the arts rarely arises directly. Even in architecture, it is chiefly the suggestion of strength or durability or magnificence which is the cause of our emotion. In painting, the sublimity of the objects of imitation—scenes of grandeur or sublime passions—may be supplemented by "an artful kind of disproportion, which assigns to some well chosen member a greater degree of *quantity* than it commonly has" [26]—a point drawn, of course, from Hogarth. Gerard's discussion of the visual arts is largely based upon Baillie, but brief though his treatment is, he supplements Baillie by insisting on the importance of comparative magnitude, which affects the mind much as absolute magnitude does. In poetry, sublimity must arise largely from the subject, though it may be artfully heightened by compositional devices. Here Gerard is supplementing Baillie (who scarcely touches upon the arts of language) by rhetorical theory, yet he takes pains to point out that Longinus uses "sublimity" metaphorically to describe any superlative excellence of composition, whereas he is confining the term to its precise significance; the nervous, vehement, pathetic, and elegant are not sublime for Gerard unless they are applied to a subject which is naturally sublime. Baillie and Gerard are wholly inadequate in treating of the sublime of music, observing only that the length (quantity) and gravity of the notes contribute to sublimity, ignoring even so obvious a consideration as volume; Gerard adds, that music may inspire passions which are sublime, and through this association would itself become sublime. In all this, Gerard has done no more than indicate the lines along which explanations must be sought; not until Alison is the real content of an aesthetic of the sublime and beautiful worked out, and then it is a content evolved by rigorously systematic method, radically in contrast with Gerard's eclectic patchwork. It is Gerard's *Essay on Genius* rather than the early *Essay on Taste* which approaches Alison's work in proliferation of detail, rigor of system, and insight into associational mechanism.

Baillie had denied vigorously that terror could be sublime, although the two feelings could co-exist or oscillate in the mind when stimulated by the same object; in their own nature, indeed, terror and sublimity are opposite: "The *Sublime* dilates and elevates the Soul, *Fear* sinks and contracts it. . . ." [27] "There ever enters in the Description of *Storms*," Baillie observes, ". . . some small degree of *Dread*, and this *Dread* may be so heighten'd (when a Person is actually in one) as intirely to destroy the *Sublime*." [28] Gerard, in contrast, urges that terror is similar in its feeling to the sublime: "objects exciting terror . . . are in general sublime; for terror always implies astonishment, occupies the whole soul, and suspends all its motions." [29] With the theory of Burke and the strictures on it of Payne Knight, the terrific was to become a focus of controversy among theorists of the sublime; and even this early difference between Baillie and Gerard manifests the influence of system in the statement and solution of problems. Baillie, sticking very close to magnitude as the one intrinsic sublimity, is led necessarily to separate the sublime from the pathetic. Passions may be sublime as objects of perception, if they are connected with vastness by their causes or results; but the passion felt subjectively is not sublimity, nor is its cause sublime in the same respect as it is pathetic.

> The *Sublime*, when it exists *simple* and unmixed, by filling the *Mind* with one *vast and uniform Idea*, affects it with a solemn *Sedateness;* by this means the Soul itself becomes, as it were, one *simple grand Sensation*. Thus the Sublime not hurrying us from *Object* to *Object*, rather *composes* than *agitates*, whilst the very *Essence* of the *Pathetick* consists in an *Agitation* of the *Passions*, which is ever effected by crouding into the Thoughts a thousand different Objects, and hurrying the Mind into various Scenes.[30]

Doubtless Gerard would concede that real practical fear is in itself depressing and opposite to sublimity; but terrific objects are sublime when we can regard them detachedly. It might even be argued that a certain degree of fearful agitation can be converted to sublimity. Admitting as he does that like feelings may become practically indistinguishable and may properly be called by the same name, Gerard is under no compulsion to distinguish the terrific or the admirable from the sublime, or to explain away their apparent sublimity by finding some connection with physical greatness.

"BEAUTIFUL objects," Gerard premises, "are of different kinds, and produce pleasure by means of different principles of human nature." [31] Beauty, indeed, is an *omnium-gatherum* of all aesthetic effects not especially appropriated to some other sense:

> THERE is perhaps no term used in a looser sense than beauty, which is applied to almost every thing that pleases us. Though this usage is doubtless too indefinite, we may, without a faulty deviation from precision, apply this epithet to every pleasure which is conveyed to the eye, and which has not got a proper and peculiar name; to the pleasure we receive, either when an object of sight suggests pleasant ideas of other senses; or when the ideas suggested are agreeable ones formed from the sensations of sight; or when both these circumstances concur. In all these cases, beauty is, at least in part, resolvable into association.[32]

The several classes of beauty, though distinct in their principles, are reduced to the same genus by the similarity of their feeling—by association of impressions.

Beauty of figure is traced, though without any remarkable subtlety, to uniformity (and simplicity), variety (and intricacy), and proportion. Uniformity ensures facility of perception; variety gratifies the love of novelty; [33] uniformity and variety together—Hutcheson's formula set on a different basis—please because they conform to the nature of the perceiving mind, "giving the mind at once the opposite gratifications of facility and active exertion, mixed with, and mellowing one another." [34] Proportion too may depend upon the nature of perception, the principle being Aristotle's rule of magnitude: a size discernible but not incomprehensible. But for the most part, for Gerard as for Hogarth, proportion depends upon fitness. This fit proportion is not the beauty of utility itself, but a generalized association based only ultimately on utility. Utility itself is of course also pleasing, both directly as being useful and indirectly through the inferences it may afford of art and skill in the causes. Since considerations of utility determine the laws of the various arts which propose various ends, most of the beauties of belles-lettres would be reduced under this rubric, although the beauties of the visual arts would fall primarily under the heads of figure and color.

The beauty of color is partly original and partly associative. By being "less hurtful to the organs of sight," [35] some colors afford a mechanical pleasure which all the associationists concede, though all do not, with Gerard, consider it beauty. The splendor of other colors produces a mood cheerful and vivacious, and though Gerard does not term this "association," it clearly *is* association of impressions based on the resemblance of sensation to emotion. When Gerard observes that "the beauty of colors is, in most instances, resolvable into *association*," [36] he is using that term in the more confined sense discussed above. This association appears in the suggestion of mental dispositions by the colors of the countenance; Gerard's plan, however, does not require him to analyze this commonplace, and no searching study of the beauty of the face was made until the second edition of Alison's *Essays on Taste* in 1811.

It can not properly be said that Gerard's treatment of beauty derives from Hogarth, as Monk has suggested.[37] Gerard handles his subject wholly in terms of ideas, impressions, and the habits of association, whereas Hogarth hankers after an untenable physiological theory and in any case does not employ association as a principle unless incidentally and implicitly. Hogarth, furthermore, tends to reduce the varieties of beauty to the model of the waving line, whereas Gerard's effort is rather to analyze and separate the kinds of beauty and the faculties which discriminate them. Sublimity for Hogarth is simply an excellence supervening to beauty, whereas Gerard finds independent roots for it in the mind. Monk remarks, on this point, that for Gerard "beauty is said to be largely intellectual, sublimity largely emotional"; [38] but all aesthetic feelings are "emotional"— are, that is, impressions—and some of the modes of beauty are perceptions making as direct and immediate impact upon the mind as those of sublimity.

Gerard's discrimination of aesthetic categories leads him to treat imitation as appealing to a separate sense or taste. His analysis of this sense is pretty subtle:

> Similitude is a very powerful principle of association, which, by continually connecting the ideas in which it is found, and leading our thoughts from one of them to the other, produces in mankind a strong tendency to comparison. As comparison implies in the very act a gentle exertion of the mind, it is on that account agreeable. As a farther energy is requisite for discovering the original by the copy; and as this discovery produces a grateful consciousness of our own discernment and sagacity,

and includes the pleasant feeling of success; the recognizing resemblance, in consequence of comparison, augments our pleasure. And when the imitation is intended, our admiration of the skill and ingenuity of the artist diffuses itself over the effect from which that skill is inferred, and compleats the delight which the work inspires.[39]

It is this complex pleasure of imitation which, in the case of unpleasant originals, "converts into delight even the *uneasy* impressions, which spring from the objects imitated." It is thus that the suspense, anxiety, and terror of tragedy afford a more serious and intense satisfaction than the gaiety of comedy. "When thus secondarily produced," those feelings "agitate and employ the mind, and rouse and give scope to its greatest activity; while at the same time our implicit knowledge that the occasion is remote or fictitious, enables the pleasure of imitation to relieve the pure torment which would attend their primary operation." [40] Gerard makes ingenious use of the theory of conversion in his subsequent discussion of the sense or taste of ridicule, a discussion otherwise undistinguished. Wit, humor, and ridicule please partly by imitation, which pleasure is serious; but it is converted to gaiety by the ludicrousness of the subject. Here the primary feeling of the original converts the feeling from the imitation, whereas in tragedy the converse is true.

Imitation to Gerard is always a resemblance of copy and original, but his conception of this resemblance is flexible. Painting and sculpture are strictly imitative, but the medium of poetry (setting dialogue aside) has no resemblance to the sensible and intelligible objects signified. A poem is an imitation not of its particular subject but of Nature: the real subject is a conception of the poet, a conception which resembles, but is never identical with, existing things.

> In a word, poetry is called an imitation, not because it produces a lively idea of its immediate subject, but because this subject itself is an imitation of some part of real nature. It is not called an imitation, to express the exactness with which it copies real things; for then history would be a more perfect imitation than poetry. It is called an imitation for the very contrary reason, to intimate that it is not confined to the description only of realities, but may take the liberty to describe all such things as resemble realities, and on account of that resemblance, come within the limits of probability.[41]

This is not a pseudo-Platonic theory of general Nature; it is a theory of probability, and the conception of probability as *resemblance* to the

laws of real existence could be developed in such a way as to parallel
Aristotle's conception of probability as consisting in the inner coherence of the poetical work.

Gerard's remarks on harmony are pretty slender. He suggests an
analogy with the beauty of figure, with proportion, variety, and uniformity as principles, but makes no effort to evolve any of the immense body of *axiomata media* of music from those principles. "But
still the chief excellence of Music," he continues, "lies in its *expression*. By this quality, music is applied to a determinate subject: by this
it acquires a fitness, becomes adapted to an end, and agitates the soul
with whatever passion the artist chooses." [42]

Beyond these "simple powers of human nature"—the internal
senses being simple in feeling albeit not original—taste involves
their union with one another and their co-operation with other faculties. All the objects of the internal senses are enhanced by coexisting
with the others; although the ridiculous might be excepted from this
generalization, it is true that "taste is not one simple power; but an
aggregate of many, which, by the resemblance of their energies, and
the analogy of their subjects, and causes, readily associate and are
combined." [43] Sensibility, too, is a constituent of taste: "DELICACY of
passion must be united with vigorous internal senses, in order to give
taste its just extent." [44] This point, indeed, has been implicit throughout, that appeal to the passions enhances aesthetic effect, but that it
does not *constitute* aesthetic effect. Thus, the greatest virtue of music
is in its expressiveness, yet music is excellent not simply because it
may arouse the passions, but because the parts of the music may be
skilfully adapted to the *end* of arousing the passions; the aesthetic
virtue is this adaptation, not the passions as such. Obviously, however,
the man insensible to the passion cannot perceive the adaptation, and,
moreover, the turmoil of the passions can be converted to intensify
related aesthetic emotions (though Gerard omits to make this last
point). Sensibility, accordingly, is an integral and indispensable part
of the theory. Judgment, finally, is an ingredient of taste: "in all the
operations of taste, judgment is employed; not only in presenting the
subjects, on which the senses exercise themselves; but also in comparing and weighing their perceptions and decrees, and thence passing
ultimate sentence upon the whole." [45]

With the contributory faculties examined, Gerard can determine
the excellences of taste, commingling judgment and imagination.
These virtues of taste "may be reduced to four, *sensibility, refinement,
correctness,* and the *proportion or comparative adjustment of its sep-*

arate principles. . . . . This excellence of taste supposes not only *culture*, but culture *judiciously applied.* Want of taste unavoidably springs from *negligence;* false taste from *injudicious* cultivation." [46] It is apparent that Gerard is no relativist: there is a standard of taste superior to the preferences of individuals. The standard is proclaimed in a striking statement which concludes the first part of the *Essay:*

> There are qualities in things, determinate and stable, independent of humour or caprice, that are fit to operate on mental principles, common to all men, and, by operating on them, are naturally productive of the sentiments of taste in all its forms. If, in any particular instance, they prove ineffectual, it is to be ascribed to some weakness or disorder in the person, who remains unmoved, when these qualities are exhibited to his view. Men are, with *few* exceptions, affected by the qualities, we have investigated: but these qualities themselves are, without *any* exception, the constituents of excellence or faultiness in the several kinds. [47]

This uncompromising "absolutism" troubles modern scholars, who affect to find subjectivism the logical consequence of psychological analysis. Marjorie Grene has formulated the problem of the standard of taste in Gerard most elaborately: her intention is to state and resolve the "striking tension between a psychological theory of taste and standards apparently established on the basis of that theory, yet incompatible with it." [48] Her examination consists of rejecting one by one a series of hypotheses "implicit in [Gerard's] analysis of taste and its improvement," finding each inadequate to explain false taste. Mrs. Grene's problem is really unsolvable, for she has supposed that "an examination of the broader basis of taste in human nature . . . reveals it as a set of simple feelings which can no more be 'justified' than can the perceptions of the external senses in their character of simple givens." [49] But this is to forget that the internal senses do *not* present "simple givens" but feelings which, though simple in sensation, are derivative and complex in principle, feelings which are susceptible of reflexive analysis, in terms of which they can be adjudged proper or improper responses. It might be added that we ordinarily have no hesitation in judging the *external* senses defective upon occasion; and *a fortiori*—.

It must be noted that Mrs. Grene is not aware of the fourth part of the *Essay,* added in the third edition, a part which treats at length this very problem. [50] Even so, the kind of explanation which Gerard *must* give is apparent from the argument of the first three parts. In the first place, there is a universal element in human nature; there are faculties and mental habits which inherently tend towards, which are a potentiality for the development of, certain preferences. Custom and education, the *Zeitgeist* and individual caprice, may obstruct, warp, or overlie these natural developments; yet the acorn still tends to become the oak. What the natural tendencies *are* is not, of course, to be determined by counting noses, for that would have just the effect Mrs. Grene complains of—to erect local and temporary prejudices (in Gerard's case, those of a limited class of Edinburgh gentlemen) into universal principles. The true principles are determined by analysis of the mind; the psychological method is not incompatible with a standard—it is the method *par excellence* of determining the standard.

Such is, in fact, the fashion in which Gerard does argue in his added treatment of the standard. He is so vividly aware that diversity of tastes is real, that he rejects the test, even as established by the argument of Hume, of *quod semper, quod ubique;* even the Greek classics, he urges, enjoy only the consent of the European nations. These diversities "must be produced both by an original inequality and dissimilitude in the powers whose combination forms taste, and by the different degrees and modes of culture which have been bestowed upon these powers." [51] Taste in direct exercise, then, considered as a species of sensation, cannot admit of a standard: a man's likes depend upon his constitution and his training. But taste as a reflex act, as a species of discernment, *is* susceptible of a standard. This standard is "not something by which all tastes may be reconciled and brought to coincide: it is only something by which it may be determined, which is the best among tastes various, contending, and incapable of coinciding perfectly. It is so far from being impossible to discover a standard which may answer this purpose to the impartial, that a standard may be found, to which even they whose relish it condemns, may find themselves obliged to submit. The person who *feels* in a certain manner . . . may yet be convinced that he feels amiss, and yield readily to a *judgment* in opposition to his feeling." [52] Philosophical criticism, not universal consensus, is the only just test for new works or for the works of obscure nations. Mere sentiment is too unsteady to be accurately weighed, and precision can be secured only by studying the causes of the sentiments; sentiment is corrected and fixed by attention to the qualities producing it. General approbation, then, provides not the standard but the data from which the laws can be educed; the laws in hand, criticism can explain sentiments, however singular, and pronounce "which are most conformable to the real constitution of human nature." [53] The analytical method of Gerard and of most other eighteenth-century critics leads naturally and inevitably to this normative position, radically opposite to subjectivism. Hogarth, Burke, Hume, Kames, Alison, Knight, and other philosophical critics one and all argue for a normative position: all aim to define *true* taste by analyzing the natural effect of the qualities of objects on the faculties of the mind.[54]

Gerard was very conscious of the logic of criticism, and conceived of philosophical criticism—aesthetics—as inductive in the Baconian sense:

> In order, therefore, to form an able critic, taste must be attended with a philosophical genius, which may subject these materials to a regular induction, reduce them into classes, and determine the general rules which govern them. . . .
>
> The qualities common to the lower classes will naturally be determined first, by regular induction. But a true critic will not rest satisfied with them. By renewing the induction, and pushing it to a greater degree of subtlety, he will ascertain the less conspicuous properties, which unite several inferior species under the same genus; and will carry on his analysis, till he discovers the highest kinds, and prescribes the most extensive laws of art. . . .[55]

Only by the Baconian method of ascending induction—and Gerard quotes Bacon—"can our conceptions of all the sentiments of taste, and of the qualities by which they are excited, be rendered accurate and determinate." [56] This direct and cumulative induction is confirmed by deductive collation of the discovered laws with the principles of human nature—already established, of course, by metaphysical psychology: "To complete the criticism, and render it truly philosophical, the common qualities of the several classes, both superior and subordinate, must be compared with the principles of human nature, that we may learn by what means they please or displease, and for what reason." [57] This final deductive step saves Gerard's procedure from the danger of uncontrolled and unverified induction; indeed, the rough outline of method which Gerard urges corresponds to the Inverse Deductive Method of J. S. Mill. The inverse deductive method—empirical generalization followed by *a priori* deduction of those provisional results from fundamental principles already established, with the consilience of inductive and deductive results constituting the verification—is, as Mill shows in the well-known argument in Book VI of his *Logic*,[58] alone proper to subjects (such as aesthetics) in which a considerable variety of interacting causes participate. Plurality of causes and intermixture of effects abound in aesthetics—hence the immense variety of plausible causal analyses which aestheticians devise—and merely inductive procedures would be of slight utility. Inductions from the data supplied by taste yield empirical and provisional laws the chief use of which is to guide deduction and to verify the principles deduced from established laws of human nature.

But Gerard errs, I believe, in pushing the initial inductive procedure through successive stages, ascending to more and more general laws before deriving these same results *a priori;* the deduction from psychological principles must accompany at each stage the empirical generalizations—indeed, a rigorous aesthetics would be far more deductive than inductive in the establishment of the *axiomata media.* Gerard (somewhat inconsistently with the remarks discussed above) does in fact often operate as I have suggested, and even gives theoretic justification for so doing. Thus, when he argues that taste is but one cause of character, and liable to be counteracted by other causes, he is led to observe that, "On this account, examples of a good taste joined with gross passions or a vicious character are far from being sufficient to prove that taste has no connection with morals." This "heterogeneous composition" of good taste and bad morals causes Gerard to reflect that

> all our conclusions concerning human nature must be founded on experience: but it is not necessary that every conclusion should be *immediately* deduced from experiment. A conclusion is sufficiently established, if it be shewn that it necessarily results from general qualities of the human mind, which have been ascertained by experiment and induction. This is the natural method of establishing synthetical conclusions; especially where an effect is produced by a complication of causes. This is the case in the subject of our present enquiry.[59]

Gerard had a concern, then, with method in aesthetics, though he did not develop his views so distinctly and systematically as would have been possible, nor did he apply them with entire consistency in the *Essay on Taste,* made up as much of that work is of eclectic borrowings not entirely reduced to system. The later *Essay on Genius* is a more cogent and exhaustive work, and exhibits more vividly the strengths of Gerard's aesthetic method.[60]

CHAPTER 6

Edmund Burke

❦

T HE WORK which, after Addison's essays, was most influential on the course of British aesthetic speculation in the eighteenth century, was Edmund Burke's *A Philosophical Enquiry into the Origin of Our Ideas of the Sublime and Beautiful*. Although the *Sublime and Beautiful* was subjected to severe enough attack—Richard Payne Knight declared that he had "never met with any man of learning, by whom the philosophy of the *Inquiry into the Sublime and Beautiful* was not as much despised and ridiculed, as the brilliancy and animation of its style were applauded, and admired" [1]—it was acclaimed by Johnson ("We have an example of true criticism in Burke's 'Essay on the Sublime and Beautiful' . . ." [2]), by Reynolds ("the admirable treatise 'On the Sublime and Beautiful' " is the only modern work thus commended in the *Discourses* [3]), and by Hume (who wrote of Burke as an "Irish gentleman, who wrote lately a very pretty treatise on the Sublime" [4]); the discipleship of Uvedale Price is well enough known, and indeed, everyone after Burke either imitates him or borrows from him or feels it necessary to refute him.

Burke's book, the influence of which was felt in Germany as well as in England, owed nothing to the fame of its author, for it was the first composition to come from his hand [5]—and may have been sketched as early as Burke's undergraduate days in Trinity College, Dublin. The bibliography of the *Sublime and Beautiful* is confused; but Theodore Moore's complete and ingenious historical argument harmonizes all the apparently conflicting evidence, and establishes pretty conclusively that the first edition was published April 21, 1757, and the second January 10, 1759. [6]

Burke's program of inquiry is explicit. Observing that "the ideas of the sublime and beautiful were frequently confounded, and that both were indiscriminately applied to things greatly differing, and sometimes of natures directly opposite," he proposed to remedy this confusion of ideas "from a diligent examination of our passions in our own breasts, from a careful survey of the properties of things which we find by experience to influence those passions, and from a sober and attentive investigation of the laws of nature, by which those properties are capable of affecting the body and thus of exciting our passions." [7] These three steps of the inquiry are readily connected with the divisions of the *Sublime and Beautiful.* Part i is the examination of the emotions of sublimity and beauty—of the formal cause of the two characters. Parts ii and iii investigate the properties of things productive of the emotion of sublimity (Part ii) and that of beauty (Part iii)—they are an investigation of material causes. Part iv treats of the laws in accordance with which the assigned properties excite the emotions—it treats, that is, of the efficient cause. [8] This program is not, as some moderns have seen it, a step from the objectivism of the neoclassic to a psychological and subjective view; [9] this whole dichotomy, applied to the aestheticians here examined, is an illusion—all the aestheticians from Addison to Kant and onwards conceive of the sublime as a feeling in the mind caused by certain properties in external objects. The real differences among these men are to be sought in the methods of argument and the causal principles which they employ.

Burke has not only a clear conception of his program, but also some awareness of the techniques of argument proper to it. He lays down, in treating the influence of proportion,

> the rules which governed me in this inquiry, and which have misled me in it if I have gone astray. (*1*) If two bodies produce the same or a similar effect on the mind, and on examination they are found to agree in some of their properties and to differ in others, the common effect is to be attributed to the properties in which they agree, and not to those in which they differ. (*2*) Not to account for the effect of a natural object from the effect of an artificial object. (*3*) Not to account for the effect of any natural object from a conclusion of our reason concerning its uses, if a natural cause may be assigned. (*4*) Not to admit any determinate quantity, or any relation of quantity, as the cause of a certain effect, if the effect is produced by different or opposite measures and relations; or if these measures and relations may exist, and yet the effect may not be produced. [10]

It is not possible to accept these rules without some reservations. The first is the uncontrolled Method of Agreement, and ignores the possibility of plurality of causes. The fourth rule is really two: the first of these, that no given measure can be the cause if other measures also yield the effect, again denies plurality of causes; the second, that if the given measure is in some instances not followed by the effect it cannot be the cause, is just if corrected to read, "cannot be the whole cause." This is a fragmentary system of induction at best, scarcely rising above the Method of Agreement save for a negative application of the Joint Method of Agreement and Difference. But the inadequacy of theoretical formulation of decisive inductive methods is not crucial if they are nonetheless employed in practice; and Burke does employ them, though not with the definitive results which would have followed from a conscious awareness of their implications and conditions.

The second and third rules of Burke's listing are just consequences of an analytic philosophy, insisting upon the investigation of the parts before the whole and upon the priority of immediate to mediate causal connections. Burke's procedure is thus analytical—to separate the components of complex objects; inductive—to determine through observation the effects of the "principles" thus isolated; experiential— to compare the results computed from these simple laws with the experienced nature of the complex objects involving them. Burke is really following what J. S. Mill terms the Inverse Deductive Method: once induction has established tentatively certain empirical generalizations, Burke deduces from (what he takes to be) established laws of human nature the middle principles which account for the empirical correlations and verify them. This method is that best adapted to the nature of aesthetic phenomena, where plurality of causes and intermixture of effects often baffle attempts at steady ascending induction. It is quite wide of the mark to describe Burke's method as "a faulty rationalism imposed upon an incomplete empiricism" and to urge, presumably as a criticism, that "a priori principles are constantly applied, and, actually, the progress is made almost entirely because of such principles." [11] I urge, in contrast, that no progress can be made with a purely empirical and inductive method in a derivative science like aesthetics; that Burke's effort, though inadequate and often ill-performed, is in general rightly oriented.

To his second edition Burke prefixed an essay "On Taste," another of the many demonstrations of a standard, and appropriate enough as introduction to the *Sublime and Beautiful*, for as Burke remarks, "if taste has no fixed principles, if the imagination is not affected according to some invariable and certain laws, our labour is likely to be employed to very little purpose; as it must be judged an useless, if not an absurd undertaking, to lay down rules for caprice and to set up for a legislator of whims and fancies." [12] After a caveat against defining *a priori*, Burke hazards the *pro tempore* definition: "I mean by the word taste no more than that faculty or those faculties of the mind which are affected with, or which form a judgment of, the works of imagination and the elegant arts." [13] This statement has the unhappy effect of confining taste to art to the exclusion of nature, unless the phrase "works of imagination" is taken in a sense licentiously broad; it is not, of course, Burke's intention so to limit taste. There follows the analysis of the faculties which are conversant with such "works": the senses, the imagination, the judgment. The argument is, that the senses and imaginations of all men respond alike in principle to external objects, and that in consequence "it must necessarily be allowed that the pleasures and the pains which every object excites in one man, it must raise in all mankind, whilst it operates, naturally, simply, and by its proper powers only; for if we deny this, we must imagine that the same cause operating in the same manner, and on subjects of the same kind, will produce different effects, which would be highly absurd." [14] The obvious difference among the responses of men's senses and imaginations to objects of taste are attributable either to differences in degree of natural sensibility or to differences in attention to the object; but the chief variations in taste arise from differences in judgment. Variation of judgment, however, no more in matters of taste than in matters of "naked reason" implies absence of a standard. Taste, then,

> in its most general acceptation, is not a simple idea, but is partly made up of a perception of the primary pleasures of sense, of the secondary pleasures of the imagination, and of the conclusions of the reasoning faculty, concerning the various relations of these, and concerning the human passions, manners and actions. . . . [The] groundwork of all these is the same in the human mind; for as the senses are the great originals of all our ideas, and consequently of all our pleasures, if they are not uncertain and arbitrary, the whole groundwork of taste is common to all, and therefore there is a sufficient foundation for a conclusive reasoning on these matters.[15]

It must be noted that Burke avoids recourse to internal senses, solving the problem wholly in terms of the conventional faculties, and in this regard Burke stands apart from Hutcheson, Gerard, and Kames. There are two ways in which aestheticians may avoid the postulation of special aesthetic faculties: by explaining aesthetic responses in terms of association of ideas, and by tracing them to the action in certain modes of other faculties. Burke, it will become clear, adopts both of these devices.

Burke's theory of the sublime and beautiful led him to reject the Addisonian tradition making novelty co-ordinate with the qualities of beauty and sublimity. Accordingly, the opening section of Burke's inquiry is devoted to the pleasure of novelty, arguing that although some degree of novelty is necessary "in every instrument which works upon the mind," [16] the permanent attractions and repulsions of objects must depend on other sources of pain and pleasure. It is in the ensuing discussion of pleasure and pain that Burke's originality makes itself felt. His is a two-fluid theory: pain and pleasure are both positive qualities, and the removal of one is thus not equivalent to the addition of the other. "What I advance," Burke declares, "is no more than this: first, that there are pleasures and pains of a positive and independent nature; and secondly, that the feeling which results from the ceasing or diminution of pain does not bear a sufficient resemblance to positive pleasure to have it considered as of the same nature, or to entitle it to be known by the same name; and thirdly, that upon the same principle the removal or qualification of pleasure has no resemblance to positive pain." [17] The discrimination of relative pleasure, that arising from the remission of pain, from absolute pleasure is the foundation of Burke's distinction of the sublime from the beautiful.

"Delight" and "pleasure" are the terms which Burke hoped to affix to the two species of agreeable sensation; and the next step in the argument is to specify the causes and objects of those feelings which are pleasant or delightful. Agreeing with the sentimental system of ethics, Burke finds passions both selfish and social to be natural and original in man. The selfish passions, concerned with self-preservation, turn on pain and danger—hence on delight rather than pleasure, insofar as they are agreeable at all. And it is on these that the sublime is based: "Whatever is fitted in any sort to excite the ideas of pain and danger, that is to say, whatever is in any sort terrible, or is conversant about terrible objects, or operates in a manner analogous to terror, is a source of the *sublime;* that is, it is productive of the strongest emotion which the mind is capable of feeling." [18] Burke does not say—note well—that the sublime is always terrible; it is *either* terrible, *or* associated with something terrible, *or* acts upon us like the terrible. In fact, Burke really avoids the false issue, whether fear be sublime, or humbling and incompatible with the sublime; [19] for he insists that "when danger or pain press too nearly, they are incapable of giving any delight, and are simply terrible, but at certain distances, and with certain modifications, they may be, and they are delightful, as we every day experience." [20] Again, Burke urges that the self-glorying of the soul is "never more perceived, nor operates with more force, than when *without danger* we are conversant with terrible objects. . . ." [21] Sublimity is "tranquillity tinged with terror." [22] Gerard simultaneously with Burke was urging the agreeableness of the terrific, though he gave an explanation on different principles; before Gerard and Burke, no aesthetician had found the fearful, considered in itself, a source of aesthetic satisfaction.[23]

The social passions, which may all in one way or another afford positive pleasure, are of two sorts: those pertaining to "the society of the *sexes*," and those regarding "that more *general society* which we have with men and with other animals, and which we may in some sort be said to have even with the inanimate world." [24] Beauty—human beauty—has its special function in directing the sexual feelings towards particular individuals, though the sentiment of beauty is not itself sexual in nature. Of the passions pertaining to general society, three—sympathy, imitation, ambition—are of peculiar importance for aesthetics; and of these, two—sympathy and ambition—may produce delight as well as pleasure. Sympathy causes us to feel what others feel; imitation to do as others do, and to take pleasure in detecting imitation; ambition to excel.

The effects of sympathy lead Burke to that persistent crux, the pleasure of tragedy. He cuts the knot by arguing that we delight in the *real* distresses of others, not only in imitated distress; hence "there is no spectacle we so eagerly pursue as that of some uncommon and grievous calamity . . . [which] always touches with delight. This is not an unmixed delight, but blended with no small uneasiness. The delight we have in such things hinders us from shunning scenes of misery; and the pain we feel prompts us to relieve ourselves in relieving those who suffer; and all this antecedent to any reasoning, by an instinct that works us to its own purposes without our concurrence." [25] Compulsive and instinctual attraction to suffering is a principle noted before Burke by Hutcheson and after him by Kames, but neither of these writers developed such a paradox as Burke's delight in witnessing suffering.[26] Thus with real distress; in an imitated distress, as Burke truly says, the only difference can be in the circumstance of imitation itself. It is not that consciousness of fiction relieves us, for "the nearer [the imitation] approaches the reality, and the further it removes us from all idea of fiction, the more perfect is its power." [27] Rather, the imitation as such affords pleasure, including (I presume) that from artistry and the means of imitation. It remains the case, however, that the greater part of our response is the delight inexplicably attached to sympathy with distress, which delight is still more keen in actuality than in poetry. This explanation runs counter to the usual observation that the reality of a tragic scene is painful and only the imitation agreeable; and it is not without other problems. Not only is there the curious delight in pity itself, but the question is suggested, why should we not bring about tragic situations in order to experience this delight? To avoid this consequence, it appears to me that a second fiction must be introduced, a sense of duty which will oppose so natural a desire. Burke was not (in view of these difficulties) followed by any other writer, and Richard Payne Knight wrote a witty and destructive analysis of Burke's account.[28]

So much for sympathy. Imitation in art provides a positive pleasure often keen enough to overcome the effect of repellent originals; Burke has no notion of conversion of the passions, however, and as the effect of a displeasing original is thus simply subducted from the pleasure of the imitation, there is no encouragement to artists to deal with such subjects.

Ambition, finally, may join with the selfish passions concerned with self-preservation to produce the sublime:

> Now, whatever, either on good or upon bad grounds, tends to raise a man in his own opinion, produces a sort of swelling and triumph that is extremely grateful to the human mind; and this swelling is never more perceived, nor operates with more force, than when without danger we are conversant with terrible objects, the mind always claiming to itself some part of the dignity and importance of the things which it contemplates. Hence proceeds what Longinus has observed of that glorying and sense of inward greatness that always fills the reader of such passages in poets and orators as are sublime. . . .[29]

The sublime, then, is a twofold movement of the soul, a response to the object and a self-reflection, as Baillie and Gerard had already found it to be; it excites delight from presenting ideas of pain and danger without actually afflicting us, and it is accompanied with self-glorification of the soul for conceiving such objects with equanimity.

"The passion caused by the great and sublime in *nature*, when those causes operate most powerfully," Burke declares, "is astonishment; and astonishment is that state of the soul in which all its motions are suspended with some degree of horror." [30] The very word "astonishment"—as also "awe," "admiration," "reverence," "respect," all which designate inferior effects of the sublime—implies the connection of the sublime with the terrific.[31] Burke himself stressed the evidence of language in associating fear with astonishment and related passions.[32]

Whatever is terrible to sight, then, is *ipso facto* sublime, and obscurity is in general necessary to make anything very terrible, for "it is our ignorance of things that causes all our admiration and chiefly excites our passions." "A clear idea," Burke adds in the second edition, "is therefore another name for a little idea." [33] Power, too, is a source of the sublime, because of its association with violence, pain, and terror; those instances in which power is stripped of all danger serve to prove that its influence is indeed the consequence of its association with terror. "All *general* privations," Burke continues, "are great, because they are all terrible; *Vacuity, Darkness, Solitude*, and *Silence*." [34] Greatness of dimension, too, is sublime, and infinity fills the mind with that "delightful horror" which is the essential effect of sublimity, an effect which is approximated by the "artificial infinite" of succession and uniformity (as in a colonnade), the imagination continuing beyond the actual limits of the object. A work implying immense force and effort to execute it is sublime, and difficulty thus becomes by association a cause of sublimity. Yet other associations account for the sublimity of extreme light or of somber colors. Such epithets as "gloomy" and "melancholy" are repeatedly applied to the sublime, but the associations thus alluded to are never drawn out by Burke, obsessed as he is with the terrific.

The sublimity of all these properties is clearly traceable to association. Granted Burke's fundamental position, that original sublimity is a mode of terror (anticipated pain) vividly conceived but not actually raised into a passion, it follows that such circumstances will be sublime as, through original efficacy, experience, education, or custom, are fitted to suggest terror; by more remote associations, accompaniments of such circumstances too may become sublime. The task of the aesthetician should presumably be to trace out the various classes of associations; and Burke, though he does not in Part ii attempt to educe an explicit analysis in these terms, seems certainly to point to it. The sublime, we are told, is produced by whatever *is* terrible, or is "conversant about" terrible objects (association of ideas), or operates like terror (association of impressions); again, everything sublime either directly suggests danger, or is a modification of power (which is associated with danger), or produces a similar effect from a "mechanical cause." [35] The only thing in all this which is *not* clearly association is the "mechanical cause" which operates like terror. Even this, however, could be given a psychological interpretation in terms of the tendency of imagination to extend and extrapolate observed tendencies (as with the "artificial infinite").

It comes, then, as a surprise to discover, in Part iv, that association is not so much an explanation of the sublime as a confusing obstacle in the path of inquiry, one which is to be got out of the way. Burke pronounces that it would be "to little purpose to look for the cause of our passions in association, until we fail of it in the natural properties of things." [36] Abstractly, this is a sound methodological point: certainly find the immediate causes first, then look for the mediate and remote. But what are the immediate causes which Burke detects? Not ideal, not pathetic, not moral—but physiological. Pain and fear (we are told) consist in "an unnatural tension of the nerves" [37]—and Burke means this tension to be a literal stretching. The causal connection is reversible: if the nerves are stretched (by some "mechanical cause") a feeling like pain or terror will be produced. All that remains is, that Burke should show how this can become agreeable; and this is easy, for it is a commonplace that moderate exercise tones up the body. To have the nerves "in proper order, they must be shaken and worked to a proper degree." [38] "As common labour," Burke continues,

> which is a mode of pain, is the exercise of the grosser, a mode of terror is the exercise of the finer parts of the system; and if a certain mode of pain be of such a nature as to act upon the eye or the ear, as they are the most delicate organs, the affection approaches more nearly to that which has a mental cause. In all these cases, if the pain and terror are so modified as not to be actually noxious; if the pain is not carried to violence, and the terror is not conversant about the present destruction of the person, as these emotions clear the parts, whether fine or gross, of a dangerous and troublesome encumbrance, they are capable of producing delight; not pleasure, but a sort of delightful horror, a sort of tranquillity tinged with terror; which, as it belongs to self-preservation, is one of the strongest of all the passions. Its object is the sublime. [39]

Here is the system, complete in all its parts. Already difficulties crowd upon us. The sublime should be, by this account, simply a weaker degree of terror—enough to tone up but not to overstretch the nerves. But this is not conformable to experience, for an emotion of the sublime may be far stronger than a faint emotion of terror—somewhere a qualitative difference must come in, and this cannot be on Burke's mechanical hypothesis.

Burke undertakes to show that the various sublime properties, properties appealing to all the external senses, all cause tension of the nerves. A vast object, for instance, consists of more points which must be imaged on the retina, and consequently produces a more violent vibration of that membrane. As Payne Knight later suggested with some sarcasm, one's pen a foot away makes a greater impression on the retina than Salisbury steeple at a mile, and the sheet of paper on which one writes would be more sublime than the Peak of Teneriffe.[40] Even if we allow for the modification of the actual sense impression by habitual judgment ("improved perception")—and it is difficult to see how Burke can allow for this—there is the further difficulty that "the ideas of great and small are terms almost entirely relative to the species of the objects, which are infinite,"[41] as Burke well puts it. This is association: how is it to be reconciled with the stretching of nerves and muscles which know nothing of the species of things? The artificial infinite is fortunately susceptible of a more satisfactory explanation on Burke's hypothesis through the analogy to the percussion and vibration of stretched cords. But this fiction becomes absurd again when we read that darkness and the resulting dilatation of the pupils, by distending the muscles of the iris produce a species of pain allied to the sublime. Goldsmith pointed out that the iris really relaxed in dilating; but Burke rejoined in his second edition with the argument that the radial antagonist muscles were distended in dilatation.[42] One wonders whether fogged spectacles would produce sublimity; that Burke should give such a line of reasoning preference over his own obvious associational account (Part iv, sec. 14) illustrates pretty vividly the power of system to wrest data into conformity. This physiological theory was reckoned an absurdity even in the eighteenth century, and Uvedale Price, Burke's most vigorous champion, laid slight stress on the physiology, unobtrusively shifting most of the superstructure onto new foundations.[43]

Beauty, for Burke, is "that quality or those qualities in bodies by which they cause love, or some passion similar to it." Love, in turn, is "that satisfaction which arises to the mind upon contemplating anything beautiful."[44] This neat circle is not a flaw in the argument, however, but only indicates that the basic emotions can be designated but not described. Before entering upon his own analysis, Burke pauses to brush aside erroneous theories. He has little trouble in showing that beauty is not resolvable into proportion. The ratios of proportion must operate either mechanically, or customarily, or through fitness.[45] But since pleasing proportions are infinitely various, and since, indeed, beauty is often most perfect when proportion is least conspicuous, proportion can not be a necessary cause of beauty. Definite measures have, then, no natural power, but custom (it might be argued) may adapt us to certain proportions within each species. Burke replies with a distinction: violation of the usual measures of a species produces deformity—but not ugliness. Conformity to these measures is mediocre, indifferent to the passions, and quite distinct from beauty. Beauty, indeed, is so far from being an adjunct of custom that it strikes us by its novelty as much as does the deformed.[46] Proportion may be conceived, finally, as the suitableness of means to ends. Burke does not deny that perception of fitness is pleasurable —but to term fitness "beauty" is a usage figurative and improper. The snout of the hog is not lovely because adapted to its office; such fitness produces only acquiescence of the understanding and cool approbation—the imagination and passions are untouched. "On the whole," Burke concludes,

> if such parts in human bodies as are found proportioned, were likewise constantly found beautiful, as they certainly are not; or if they were so situated, as that a pleasure might flow from the comparison, which they seldom are; or if any assignable proportions were found, either in plants or animals, which were always attended with beauty, which never was the case; or if, where parts were well adapted to their purposes, they were constantly beautiful, and when no use appeared, there was no beauty, which is contrary to all experience; we might conclude that beauty consisted in proportion or utility. But since, in all respects, the case is quite otherwise; we may be satisfied that beauty does not depend on these, let it owe its origin to what else it will.[47]

It is unfortunate that Burke did not differentiate fitness from design and utility. Design, with the intellectual and moral traits it implies, and utility, with the human concerns and feelings it touches, both appeal more strongly to imagination and emotion than fitness in the more circumscribed sense. Burke's doctrine on fitness itself, however, was influential, and most later aestheticians who treated the relation at length considered it a negative beauty, absence of which is felt more keenly than its presence.

Burke is concerned also to discourage declamation about the beauty of virtue. "The general application of this quality to virtue," he declares, "has a strong tendency to confound our ideas of things; and it has given rise to an infinite deal of whimsical theory. . . . This loose and inaccurate manner of speaking has therefore misled us both in the theory of taste and of morals; and induced us to remove the science of our duties from their proper basis (our reason, our relations, and our necessities) to rest it upon foundations altogether visionary and unsubstantial." [48] Some virtues, nonetheless, are analogous to beauty—those softer merits "which engage our hearts, which impress us with a sense of loveliness." Those virtues "which cause admiration, and are of the sublimer kind, produce terror rather than love. . . ." [49] This division of virtues into soft and severe, amiable and venerable, reaches back at least as far as Cicero, but Burke's relating it to his dichotomy of self-preservation and society, and to the beautiful and sublime in nature, is perhaps original.

If beauty does not depend upon proportion or fitness nor yet, in general, upon virtue, Burke concludes "that beauty is, for the greater part, some quality in bodies acting mechanically upon the human mind by the intervention of the senses." [50] The properties which so act prove to be smallness, smoothness, gradual variation, delicacy, and colors of various hues, of low saturation and high brilliance. Each of these traits was already or was to become the focus of aesthetic controversy. That the beautiful must be small is the point most controverted, but usually because of systematic differences which give the term "beauty" varying significances. William Gilpin, for instance, argues that there is a species of beauty exciting admiration and respect more than love; [51] but this contention stems from the circumstance that Gilpin does not radically distinguish the sublime from the beautiful, considering all objects yielding serious aesthetic pleasure to be beautiful, and the sublime and picturesque to be subspecies with additional differentiae. Aristotle (it will be recalled) had remarked that beauty implies greatness of body, that small people may be "pretty" but not beautiful. The Aristotelian distinction between prettiness and beauty is echoed, perhaps unwittingly (though Thomas Twining had commented on classical ideas of beauty and size in his commentary on the *Poetics*), by Uvedale Price; consistently with his own system, Price argues for beauty as a golden mean between grandeur and prettiness. [52] Dugald Stewart follows Price and Twining; [53] and Payne Knight analyzes associations which may make either the large or the small beautiful in different instances. [54] None of these writers except Price, however, attempts a systematic opposition of the sublime and the beautiful; and even Price departs from Burke's principles though adhering to his dichotomy. Burke himself concedes an aesthetic pleasure from largeness conjoined with all or most of the other traits of beauty; objects exhibiting this combination he terms "fine" or "specious." [55] This distinction goes a good way towards resolving the apparent conflict, for the "beautiful," the "handsome," the "*beau*" of writers not concerned to make a sharp differentiation between sublime and beautiful are much like Burke's "fine."

Even smoothness, where Burke finds a near consensus in his support, can be denied as a predicate of beauty. Richard Payne Knight was later to urge by a subtle argument that strictly visible beauty depends on broken light and color, that it is incompatible with the harsh reflections from smooth objects, and that the beauty of smoothness depends upon association.[56]

Burke appears to have written this portion of the *Sublime and Beautiful* before Hogarth's *Analysis of Beauty* came to hand, for in his second edition he drew upon Hogarth to support his contention for the beauty of gradual variation. Burke's criticism of Hogarth is not searching, for he does not penetrate to Hogarth's principles, and his correction of Hogarth for allowing angularity to be beautiful (Hogarth does admit an inferior degree of beauty to various angularity) is another logomachy like that over the beauty of large objects. Burke himself admits another category, the "elegant," which is characterized by regularity, and regularity may well be—usually is—angular. "When any body is composed of parts smooth and polished, without pressing upon each other, and without showing any ruggedness or confusion, and at the same time affecting some *regular shape*, I call it *elegant*. It is closely allied to the beautiful, differing from it only in this *regularity;* which, however, as it makes a very material difference in the affection produced, may very well constitute another species. Under this head I rank those delicate and regular works of art, that imitate no determinate object in nature, as elegant buildings and pieces of furniture." [57] Here again Burke is led by his desire to oppose the beautiful to the sublime to limit the beautiful very narrowly, and to cast into other and inferior categories much which other writers comprehend under beauty.

Beyond the physical beauty on which Burke's emphasis principally falls, there is a beauty of expression in the face and a beauty or grace of posture and motion. And these visual beauties (like visual sublimity) have their analogies in the other senses. There is a beauty of touch consisting in smoothness, softness, gradual variation, moderate warmth; [58] a beauty of sound, clear, even, smooth, and weak, without any great variety or quick transitions to disturb "that sinking, that melting, that languor, which is the characteristical effect of the beautiful as it regards every sense"; [59] and a beauty, finally, of smell and taste—smoothness and sweetness. These beauties of the various senses serve once again as the instances to which the Method of Agreement is to be applied in ferreting out the common causes. The common effect—an inward sense of melting and languor (together with a somewhat comic collocation of outward manifestations)—suggests at once, to a mind attuned to the suggestion, "that beauty acts by relaxing the solids of the whole system." [60] As before, Burke confirms this hypothesis by showing that each constituent of beauty has separately a tendency to relax the fibers: smoothness to touch is manifestly relaxing, and heads the train; smoothness and sweetness to taste, gradual variation, smallness, and color follow in sequence.

The inferiority of fineness to beauty is accounted for through the combination in fineness of qualities which are inconsistent in their physiological effects: "The affection produced by large bodies adorned by the spoils of beauty, is a tension continually relieved; which approaches to the nature of mediocrity." [61] Presumably the regularity of the elegant, by taking off from the various and even flow of the beautiful, is similarly inferior. And although the sublime and beautiful are often commingled, each very naturally produces its best effect when pure: "If the qualities of the sublime and beautiful are sometimes found united, does this prove that they are the same; does it prove that they are any way allied; does it prove even that they are not opposite and contradictory?" [62]

A fifth part of the *Sublime and Beautiful* treats of the production of sublimity and beauty through words, and is a conventional application of the associational theory to language. Understandably, however, it is this part of the treatise which has proved most attractive to modern literary scholars. McKenzie judges this the most interesting part of the inquiry because Burke is "directly opposed to the notion of his contemporaries that the power of poetry depends upon specific imagery. . . ." [63] And William Guild Howard finds here the germs of Lessing's differentiations of poetry from painting: "Painting, then," Howard concludes, "presents ideas through clear images affecting the mind but little; poetry stirs the emotions through obscure images, or without raising images at all." [64]

Burke himself had urged simply that words produce three effects in the mind of the hearer—the sound, the picture, and the affection of soul produced by either or both of the foregoing. In terms of their meanings, words are distinguished by Burke into *aggregate* ("such as represent many simple ideas *united by nature* to form some one determinate composition"), *simple abstract* (which "stand for one simple idea of such compositions"), and *compound abstract* ("formed by an union, an *arbitrary* union of both the others, and of the various relations between them").[65] Aggregate words, that is, are names of substances, abstract words of attributes; simple abstracts are the names of single qualities or connected groups (for "square"—one of Burke's instances—is surely no simple idea!); compound abstracts are names of complexes which are not even apparently simple. Now, the compound abstracts produce only the first and third of the possible effects of words; they operate "not by presenting any image to the mind, but by having from use the same effect on being mentioned, that their original has when it is seen." [66] And though aggregate and simple abstract words *can* raise images, they commonly do not do so in the hurry of actual use, and operate just as do the compound abstract. The power of words to raise affections is little hindered by the absence of the image, however; the "picturesque connection is not demanded, because no real picture is formed, nor is the effect of the description at all the less upon this account." [67] Words, indeed, may affect us even more strongly than the things they represent, for they carry the contagion of sympathy and impassioned expression, represent things which may be seldom or never experienced in reality, and combine circumstances in a way more affecting than nature.

This whole account is associational—compare it, for instance, with Hume's study of abstract words in the *Treatise of Human Nature*.[68] When McKenzie speaks of Burke's "disregard of association," he is thinking of the association of particular ideas in the form of images, instead of association of mental habits with the sound of words; it may be granted, however, that Burke deserves credit for popularizing an important idea in criticism when the general taste was, as McKenzie says, "for images that were accurate, clear, vivid, and special." [69] Howard, however, errs in thinking that the usual absence of distinct images in poetry allocates poetry to the sublime, and that the clear ideas of painting allocate it to the beautiful; in noting that "paintings are apt to be comparatively small, and suggestive of smoothness; their figures are of undulating, or at least not angular outline; they are delicate, not glaring, but diversified in color," Howard confuses inextricably the painting as an object with the painting as an imitation.[70]

Burke never revised or expanded his theory after the second edition. When years later, in 1789, Malone proposed to him to rework the *Sublime and Beautiful,* "which the experience, reading, and observation of thirty years could not but enable him to improve considerably," Burke replied that the whole bent of his mind had been turned from such subjects so that he was less fitted for such speculations than in youth, and that in any event "the subject was then new, but several writers have since gone over the same ground, Lord Kames and others." [71] Somewhat earlier, however—in 1773—Burke had agreed to write an article on aesthetics, including an abstract of the *Sublime and Beautiful,* for a "Dictionary of the Arts and Sciences" which Goldsmith projected but which was never actually undertaken.[72] It is very probable that Burke would have had nothing to add to his treatise in later life, and it is very doubtful that he would have desired to subtract from it; the book stands an isolated monument of speculation. There is a tendency among aestheticians and scholars, unhappily, to regard the *Sublime and Beautiful* as valuable chiefly for its collection of aesthetic data but as negligible philosophically. Lessing, writing to Moses Mendelssohn, said of Burke as early as 1758, "Das heisst ohne Zweifel sehr commode philosophiren! Doch, wenn schon des Verfassers Grundsätze nicht viel taugen, so ist sein Buch doch als eine Sammlung aller Eräugnungen und Wahrnehmungen, die der Philosoph bey dergleichen Untersuchungen als unstreitig annehmen muss, ungemein brauchbar. Er hat alle Materialen zu einem guten System gesammlet. . . ." [73] And this condescending judgment has been often echoed since. I cannot share it; if the physiological theory of Part iv were replaced by a more thorough analysis of association—if it were simply deleted—the *Sublime and Beautiful* would remain a brilliant if incomplete system, of merit not historical but absolute and permanent.

CHAPTER 7

Lord Kames

※

THE *Elements of Criticism* of Henry Home, Lord Kames, remains today one of the most elaborate and systematic treatises
on aesthetics and criticism of any age or nation; and it ranks, alongside Archibald Alison's *Essays on Taste,* as the major effort of philosophical criticism in eighteenth-century Britain. The *Elements* went
through six editions within a dozen years of its first publication in
1762; and more than thirty subsequent editions in the United States
and Britain, editions both complete and abridged, testify to the
widespread and prolonged reputation of Lord Kames.[1] But with the
gradual predominance of German philosophy during the nineteenth
century, the *Elements* lost its influence among thinkers, though it
continued in use as a textbook; and Bosanquet, writing in 1892, mentions only a few scattered thoughts of "Kaimes," treating them as
stimuli to or anticipations of Lessing.[2]

Notwithstanding the obscurity in which the *Elements* is now involved, the extensive and various aesthetic and critical system it pro-
pounds remains of singular philosophical interest. Kames had some
pretensions as a metaphysician, and the examination of his aesthetics
should begin, accordingly, with an exposition of his metaphysics; that
metaphyics is developed in the first two chapters and Appendix
("Terms Defined or Explained") of the *Elements,* and in the *Essays
on the Principles of Morality and Natural Religion* (Edinburgh,
1751). The Appendix is of especial importance, for the "definitions"
are arranged not as a glossary but in a logical sequence which gives a
succinct conspectus of the system.

Like other philosophers after Descartes, Kames seeks principles in
the contents of the mind. And although he writes before publication
of any of the treatises of the Scottish school, he anticipates the Scottish answers to Hume; his philosophy has a reactionary cast, and his

effort is constantly to reassert the truths obscured by the skepticism of Berkeley and Hume—the identity of the self, the reality of the external world, the existence and attributes of the Deity. These objectives are achieved largely through appeal to a variety of "senses," faculties giving intuitive knowledge of the outer and inner worlds. The most striking characteristic of Kames's thought, a trait which he shares with the entire Scottish school, is the tendency to reduce every phenomenon directly to some sense or intuition peculiarly devoted to it by Providential design. Analysis, so prominent in Hume's thought—the reduction of a given range of phenomena to other and more basic phenomena—is minimal in the philosophy of Lord Kames; in place of Hume's analytical subtlety in reducing all phenomena to a very few principles, there is a vast proliferation of principles appropriated to the various classes of phenomena, all attested by an appeal to sense and feeling. "Fond of arguments drawn from the nature of things," cautions Kames, "we are too apt to apply such arguments without discretion; and to call that demonstration, which, at bottom, is nothing but a conviction from sense and feeling. Our perceptions, which work silently, and without effort, are apt to be overlooked; and we vainly imagine, we can demonstrate every proposition, which we perceive to be true." [3] Hume is repeatedly criticized for substituting subtle reasoning in place of the plainest feelings; and no doubt he would counter with the observation that Kames takes every association of ideas or impressions for a direct perception.

Treatises on aesthetics, like other intellectual efforts, are liable to two opposed defects. A writer may seek out in remote corners of the intellectual world the scattered and dismembered parts in order to form from these heterogeneous members the complete and perfect body of truth; or, pitching upon some few principles as indemonstrable verities, he may seek to re-create from these an image of the universe in all its variety. The world of experience can impose itself upon us in kaleidoscopic complexity, or it can be forced upon the Procrustean bed of a rigid dogmatism; and if Hume falls occasionally into the latter error, Kames rarely emerges from the former.

It is not easy to give an orderly presentation of Kames's metaphysics, for neither the *Elements* nor the *Essays* is a metaphysical work: psychology enters one as part of the groundwork of a system of morals and theology, the other as substructure to a system of aesthetics and criticism. There are no differences in doctrine between the two works, although the emphasis and order of presentation vary. In the *Essays*, the chief end is the explanation of our knowledge of

Deity, and the order of development is determined towards this conclusion. The second, and more speculative, part begins with the examination of belief, and Kames's judgment is that "there is a certain peculiar manner of perceiving objects, and conceiving propositions, which, being a simple feeling, cannot be described, but is expressed by the word belief. . . . [All belief], mediately or immediately, is founded upon the authority of our senses. We are so constituted by nature, as to put trust in our senses. Nor, in general, is it in our power to disbelieve our senses: they have authority with us irresistible." [4] This authority is not difficult to establish. There is an original feeling or consciousness of self, for instance, which accompanies all, or virtually all, other impressions, ideas, and actions, and which is the basis of personal identity. Perception of the self is direct, moreover, whereas all other subjects are known through attributes, a circumstance which makes self-consciousness the most vivid of perceptions.[5] Nor is the authority of the external senses more difficult to support, since Kames takes as unanalyzable any feeling or perception which seems strong and decisive. Sight and touch perceive not only an assemblage of qualities but a substratum in which the qualities inhere— a substratum termed "substance" in the case of sight, "body" in that of touch. "That the objects of our senses really exist in the way and manner we perceive," Kames declares, "is a branch of intuitive knowledge." [6] In a lengthy note added to the third edition of the *Elements,* Kames observes that from Aristotle onwards the fallacy has imposed itself upon mankind, that the immediate objects of perception are in the mind; and Kames's own anticipation of Reid is evident in the pronouncement that "an impression may be made upon us, by an external object, in such a manner, as to raise a direct perception of the external object itself." [7] Until Berkeley, idealism led to little harm beyond confusion in metaphysics, but that divine, giving the doctrine a sinister turn, contrived to "annihilate totally the material world. And a later writer [Hume, of course], discovering that Berkeley's arguments might with equal success be applied against immaterial beings, ventures still more boldly to reject by the lump the immaterial world as well as the material; leaving nothing in nature but images or ideas floating *in vacuo,* without affording them a single mind for shelter or support." [8] It is perhaps one of the striking ironies in the history of philosophy that two writers each of whom thought he was at length placing our belief in the external world on its true and firm foundation, should be accused of this wild skepticism.

Of importance, too, is the doctrine that it is possible to conceive of subjects divorced from any (though not from every) attribute.[9] Attributes, in contrast, cannot be conceived independently of their subjects, nor parts independently of the wholes to which they belong, although either can be represented in reasoning by abstract terms. In any case, perception is of the object as qualified, not of its qualities merely, for "as an action is not resolvable into parts, a perception, being, an act of sense, is always simple," however complex the object.[10]

It is interesting to note, before turning to Kames's aesthetics, that his deism depends for its philosophic justification on still more perceptions and intuitions. For we are assured of power (i.e., of causal force) in external objects by direct perception through the eye when we observe such objects to effect alterations. Kames rejects Hume's explanation of the feeling of necessity as mental custom, arguing that "power is perceived as a quality in the acting body, and by no means is an operation of the mind or an easy transition of thought from one object to another." [11] Here as in so many places, Kames's refutations of "skepticism" depend upon an *ignoratio elenchi,* upon stating the issue in such a way as to make refutation of his opponent's views almost superfluous. The perception of power includes the notion that the cause is proportioned to the effect, and if the effect exhibits adaptation to an end, the direct perception includes the idea of an intelligent, designing cause—if a good end, a benevolent cause as well. Another internal sense assures us that nature is uniform—that, for example, the power of a cause continues to exist after the moment of exertion. With all this "grand apparatus of instinctive faculties," [12] as Lord Kames rightly terms it, it is no wonder that *arguments* for the existence and attributes of Deity can be pretty largely dispensed with. An intricate chain of reasoning, however, is devoted to explaining away the greater part of evil in the universe and ascribing the rest "to the pre-established order and constitution of things, and to the necessary imperfection of the nature of all created beings." [13]

The starting point of Kames's aesthetics is the observation that sight and hearing differ from the other senses in that they perceive objects at a distance, with no consciousness of organic impression and no sensation accompanying the perception.[14] Impressions of unusual intensity, to be sure, must be exceptional to this generalization; and Payne Knight was later to base one part of his aesthetic system on the notion that the eye *is* conscious of organic impression, of pleasure and pain, in its perceptions generally. But granting with Kames that this is a circumstance which sets perceptions of sight and hearing apart from those of the grosser senses, and elevates them to a position less inferior to the perceptions of intellect, it follows that the impressions of pain and pleasure accompanying visual and auditory phenomena not only *are* but *seem to be* in the mind. The dignity and moderately exhilarating character of these pleasures, are devices whereby "the author of nature, by qualifying the human mind for a succession of enjoyments from the lowest to the highest, leads it by gentle steps from the most groveling corporeal pleasures, for which only it is fitted in the beginning of life, to those refined and sublime pleasures which are suited to its maturity." [15] Not only do the aesthetic pleasures of nature and art have such a moral influence, but criticism itself is attended with advantages intellectual and moral. Intellectually, criticism provides a rational enjoyment; by strengthening our reasoning faculties, it prepares us gently for the more strenuous exertions of the sciences; and by analogy it enhances our capacity for the reasonings which regulate conduct. Morally, the development of a just taste in the arts harmonizes the temper and moderates the selfish affections, invigorates sympathy and the social affections, and by cultivating "a just relish of what is beautiful, proper, elegant, and ornamental, in writing or painting, in architecture or gardening, is a fine preparation for discerning what is beautiful, just, elegant, or magnanimous, in character and behaviour." [16]

The pleasures of eye and ear, then, are the matter of aesthetics, and the *Elements* investigates them in order to regulate them; "the following work," says Kames, in a labored dedication to George III, ". . . treats of the fine arts, and attempts to form a standard of taste by unfolding those principles that ought to govern the taste of every individual." [17] By inquiring into "such attributes, relations, and circumstances, as in the fine arts are chiefly employ'd to raise agreeable emotions," [18] Kames aims to establish practical rules for the arts—not in detail, but "to exhibit their fundamental principles drawn from human nature, the true source of criticism." [19] Indeed, alongside the criticism which is his declared subject, Kames admits that "all along he had it in view, to explain the nature of man, considered as a sensitive being capable of pleasure and pain. . . ." [20]

The organization of the treatise is adjusted appropriately to the philosophic standpoint and the results aimed at. The author's plan "is, to ascend gradually to principles from facts and experiments; instead of beginning with the former, handled abstractly, and descending to the latter." [21] Helen Whitcomb Randall, in an ingenious and plausible account, shows that Kames's procedure of "ascending" from psychological experiments and facts to general principles of man's sensitive nature and then establishing the "rules" for art on those principles, is in accord with Newtonian philosophy.[22] But without wishing to depreciate Newtonian influence, I can add that the method has advantages in terms of Kames's own theory. It is not merely that the method is "empirical"; it provides a natural delight. In the opening chapter of the *Elements* ("Perceptions and Ideas in a Train"), two points of peculiar importance for aesthetics are made: there is a principle of order "implanted in the breast of every man" which governs the arrangement of perceptions, ideas, and actions, so that the whole precedes the part, the principal the accessory, the cause the effect, and so forth; but (secondly) this principle of order is counteracted in scientific reasonings and in some other cases by the natural delight in the dilatation of mind which results from precisely the opposite process of going from small to great (a modification of grandeur) or of ascending from particular to general (a modification of elevation). The method which Lord Kames adopts in the earlier parts of the *Elements*, then, by proceeding from particular observations to general principles, satisfies this natural bent of the soul, though the contrary (deductive) method would have better satisfied the sense of order. The original resemblance of feeling between the movement of the mind in illation from particular effects to general causes and mounting upwards affords a basis, subsequently, for transferring grandeur and sublimity from material to intellectual objects.

The succession of perceptions and ideas, considered merely as a succession at a certain tempo, has itself numerous consequences for the arts; but it is the theory of "Emotions and Passions" making up the lengthy second chapter of the treatise which is most fruitful in aesthetic consequences. Passions and emotions (both internal motions or agitations of the mind, but different in that passions are accompanied by desire [23]) are raised through perceptions of eye and ear, and it is the business of art to appeal through those senses to the natural and cultivated capacities for agreeable passions and emotions. Kames works out an intricate apparatus of distinctions—of passion proper from appetite; of instinctive from deliberative passions; of social, selfish, and "dissocial" passions (which last involve no motives but only instinctive impulses). Only two points concerning the efficient causes of the emotions and passions require mention, however. The "sympathetic emotion of virtue," so important subsequently in the analysis of drama, is of a curious nature; for though it is accompanied with a vague impulse to imitate the virtue exciting it when observed, this is an impulse without an object, analogous to the desires prompted by instrumental music. There appears to be no corresponding "sympathetic emotion of vice," presumably because of an original repugnance to vice; licentious comedy, Kames notes, allures only by conjoining vice with wit.[24] The second point with an especial bearing upon criticism is the raising of emotion through ideal (as opposed to actual) presence of objects. Memory, fancy, or language may evoke an ideal presence indistinguishable, without reflection, from real presence, and equally productive of emotion; such ideal presence is quite different from reflective remembrance. The theater, of course, is the art which most completely effects ideal presence; painting is less powerful; and reading much less yet. (It does not, however, follow that painting has more power over the passions than history and non-dramatic poetry, for its confinement to a single point of time limits its influence.)

Pleasure and pain can be treated only after this study of the efficient causes of emotions; and Kames is as fertile in distinctions as ever. "Agreeable and disagreeable," he notes, ". . . are qualities of the objects we perceive; pleasant and painful are qualities of the emotions we feel. . . ."[25] But emotions are sometimes taken reflexively *as* our objects, and in such case *they* are felt to be agreeable or disagreeable, as well as pleasant or painful. Now in general, what is pleasant is agreeable, and what is agreeable is pleasant. It is invariably the case that a pleasant emotion is produced by an agreeable object; and this is not a mere tautology, since the "agreeableness" is a special perception separate from the pleasure and implanted in us for wise purposes. The agreeableness of emotions themselves is governed by the rule that every "feeling that is conformable to the common nature of our species, is perceived by us to be regular and as it ought to be; and upon that account it must appear agreeable."[26] It is, then, possible for painful passions which we feel to be "specific" to be agreeable on survey, and for pleasant passions to be disagreeable.

Emotion resembles mechanical motion (Kames urges), in that it "requires the constant exertion of an operating cause, and ceases when the cause is withdrawn."[27] This denial of Newton's first law reads strangely for 1761 (and casts some doubt on the Newtonian character of Kames's method), but is of a piece with other reactionary positions in the philosophy of Lord Kames.[28] The principles governing the growth and decay of emotions are too complex to recount here; but those describing the coexistence of emotions have great significance aesthetically. Coexistent emotions produce from their combination two kinds of pleasure—an additive pleasure, greater in proportion as the mixed emotions are more similar and more closely connected by their causes (a "double relation of impressions and ideas," as Hume would have termed it), and an harmonic pleasure proportioned to the similarity of the emotions and the *disparity* of their causes. Dissimilar emotions forced into union by connection of their causes tend to weaken one another; totally opposite emotions, or dissimilar emotions arising from unconnected causes, tend to alternate until one gains the ascendant or both are obliterated. Coexistent passions are governed by an additional principle as well: fusion depends partly upon the coincidence of tendency, compatibility of the attendant desires. This system has the elaborateness, but not the neatness of Hume's analysis; Hume's study of the passions, and of their four modes of interaction (vectorial addition, alternation, chemical combination, and conversion), is more comprehensive in scope yet requires less proliferation of original principles. Kames is rich in analysis of addition and alternation, but only partly perceives the utility of conversion as an analytical device and does not treat the possibility of a *tertium quid* except in the very different sense that the emotions produced by the separate qualities of a single visible object, or by concordant sounds, become one complex emotion. His aesthetic occasionally suffers from these limitations—as, for instance, in the declaration that music should not accompany words expressing disagreeable passions because the passions and the music (which, to be music, must be agreeable) would conflict; this view belittles the power of harmony to *express* the disagreeable without *being* disagreeable, through conversion of the passions.

"That many emotions or feelings bear a certain resemblance to their cause," Kames remarks, "is a truth that can be made clear by induction; though, so far as I know, the observation has not been made by any writer." [29] Lord Kames's frequent claims to originality often exceed the real limits of his innovations, and in the present case his originality is not entire, for (among other anticipations) Hogarth had remarked upon the sympathetic uneasiness from apparent instability, and Gerard had stressed the conformance of the mind to its objects, a conformance which in some cases at least is a resemblance. But Kames illustrates the principle much more fully—sluggish motion causes a languid feeling, a low sound depresses the mind, an elevated object makes the spectator stand erect, &c.; and of course the sympathetic emotion of virtue is also an instance of this general truth. Certain modern aesthetics have pitched upon an aspect of this principle (empathy) and used it as a foundation for an entire system; but in the more complex systems of the eighteenth century, the principle remains an incidental part.

The analysis of passions and emotions terminates with an appeal to final causes, and it is not surprising to discover that these feelings are made subservient to beneficent purposes. Nothing, indeed, is more characteristic of Lord Kames than the regular detection of benevolent contrivance in every phenomenon:

> By every production that shows art and contrivance, our curiosity is excited upon two points; first, how it was made; and, next, to what end. Of the two, the latter is the more important inquiry, because the means are ever subordinate to the end; and in fact our curiosity is always more inflamed by the *final* than by the *efficient* cause. This preference is no where more visible, than in contemplating the works of nature: if in the efficient cause, wisdom and power be display'd, wisdom is not less conspicuous in the final cause; and from it only can we infer benevolence, which of all the divine attributes is to man the most important.[30]

A concern to vindicate the Architect of the Universe leads very naturally to an emphasis on finality, and, deist that he is, Kames always sees finality as deliberate purpose. One of the conspicuous features of Kamesian aesthetics is the tendency to stop short in the investigation of efficient causes—usually with the postulation of a sense which is original and unanalyzable—and to replace such investigation with specious indications of finality. I consider this to be a philosophical vice. If we have (as Lord Kames assures us we do have) an inborn tendency to complete any task under way,[31] and another such determination to rejoice in order and connection, we must in consequence desire to see effects traced back to their ultimate efficient causes, and must delight in contemplating the mechanism by which few causes give rise to many effects. It is in finding efficiency, moreover, that the real difficulties lie, and it is in overcoming these that the sublimity of genius would be displayed. For if explanations are sought in teleology, a difficulty can be ended as readily as a purpose can be invented; if the immediate consequences of some circumstance appear happy, *this* is the final cause, and if the reverse, we turn our eye to remote and indirect consequences. No philosopher, to be sure, can ignore efficiency, and Lord Kames does not. But his concern with finality (together with a reluctance to force nature into an artificial system) too often leads him to dismiss the problem of efficient causation in too offhand a manner. When a class of mental phenomena proves resistant to analysis, he too readily posits an internal sense appropriated by providence for wise, or at any rate plausible, purposes. His human nature involves almost as many distinct causes as classes of effects.

The general chapter of emotions and passions is followed by a series of chapters treating in detail of certain emotions peculiarly pertinent to aesthetics. "I propose," says Kames in one of his occasional indications of the plan he pursues,

> to confine my inquiries to such attributes, relations, and circumstances, as in the fine arts are chiefly employ'd to raise agreeable emotions. Attributes of single objects, as the most simple, shall take the lead; to be followed with particulars which depending on relations, are not found in single objects. Dispatching next some coincident matters, I proceed to my chief aim, which is to establish practical rules for the fine arts, derived from the principles above explained.[32]

The first such property is beauty, the "most noted of all the qualities that belong to single objects." The term "beauty," Kames assures us, "in its native signification, is appropriated to objects of sight."[33] Color, figure, size, motion—all the visible qualities—may be beautiful; and the object in which several of these beauties coalesce yields a complex emotion still more pleasant. A perception so various and so striking easily lends its name to express anything agreeable—not only other physical qualities but also moral and intellectual traits. Kames confines his analysis, however, to the literally beautiful qualities, common denominator of which is that they all produce emotions maintaining "one general character of sweetness and gaiety."[34] Even of this literal beauty there are two species: an *intrinsic* beauty inherent in single objects, and a *relative* beauty dependent on the relations of things. Intrinsic beauty is perceived immediately by sense; relative beauty involves an intellectual recognition of fitness or utility. Yet relative beauty is perceived as belonging to the object, not the relation, for association transfers the beauty perceived from the effects to the object which is their cause; and beauty remains in all cases an "attribute of single objects."

Intrinsic beauty results from size, color, motion, and figure, yet only the last is treated in the chapter on beauty, for size more usually pertains to grandeur than to beauty, the beauty of color is "too familiar to need explanation" (one might suppose that this familiarity is what requires explanation), and motion is treated with respect to both beauty and grandeur in another chapter. Beauty of figure, then, is resolvable into regularity and simplicity as traits of the whole, and uniformity, proportion, and order as traits of the constituent parts. Kames appears to follow Addison in detecting a specific beauty not wholly dependent on ordinary beauty: "The beauty of the human figure, by a special recommendation of nature, appears to us supreme, amid the great variety of beauteous forms bestowed upon animals." [35] But the remark is casual, and no stress is laid upon this specific beauty. Some account is given of the mechanisms by which the properties of general beauty please; simplicity, for instance, is found pleasing because it permits a single and more telling stroke upon the mind, and because the mind in elevated mood descends only with reluctance to minute ornaments. There remains, however, after all such explanations, a large irreducible surd. One would expect an inquiry how such various properties as simplicity, proportion, order, and the rest produce such similar effects. But this question is dismissed: "To enquire why an object, by means of the particulars mentioned, appears beautiful, would, I am afraid, be a vain attempt: it seems the most probable opinion, that the nature of man was originally framed with a relish for them, in order to answer good and wise purposes" [36]—purposes which are expounded forthwith. They prove to be truisms: beauty is an aid to apprehension; it adds to the delight of life; the determination of our nature to see it as objective attaches us to external objects and promotes society.

Beauty of motion is caused by the inherent agreeableness of motion itself, an agreeableness greatest when the motion is regular, correspondent in speed to the natural rate of flow of perceptions, accelerated, upwards, and undulating. Slight explanation is given of these circumstances, though it is clear from Kames's own observations (that, for instance, undulating motion is more free and natural) that the phenomena could be explained in part at least by association.

A great part of what is ordinarily termed beauty is handled by Kames under the general rubric of relations—beauty in his own terminology being a property of single facts. His judgments on resemblance and contrast are in no wise novel save in his forward-looking views on gardening; the treatment of variety and uniformity, however, is managed very skilfully in terms of the train of perceptions which was the starting point of the *Elements*, in terms of the velocity and variety of the train and the different modes of pain and pleasure which result. Kames casually demolishes the Hutchesonian law of beauty:

> It may surprise some readers, to find variety treated as only contributing to make a train of perceptions pleasant, when it is commonly held to be a necessary ingredient in beauty of whatever kind; according to the definition, "That beauty consists in uniformity amid variety." But after the subject is explained and illustrated as above, I presume it will be evident, that this definition, however applicable to one or other species, is far from being just with respect to beauty in general: variety contributes no share to the beauty of a moral action, nor of a mathematical theorem; and numberless are the beautiful objects of sight that have little or no variety in them. . . . The foregoing definition . . . is only applicable to a number of objects in a group or in succession, among which indeed a due mixture of uniformity and variety is always agreeable, provided the particular objects, separately considered, be in any degree beautiful; for uniformity amid variety among ugly objects, affords no pleasure.[37]

It is obvious, however, that Kames understands variety in a different sense from that in which Hutcheson (if it is Hutcheson here alluded to) took it. Variety to Kames involves a succession of perceptions of different kinds: he can say truly, then, that there is no variety in a mathematical theorem. Looking at the theorem as Hutcheson did, however, it does exhibit unity in variety: for it is true of multitudes of instances which, though not actually perceived, can be conceived by reflection. Again, Kames speaks of a globe as the most uniform of figures, the least various; and it is certainly true that half a globe is perceived at one *coup d'oeil*. But the surface of a globe is changing direction at every point, and in this light we can say with Hutcheson that it exhibits maximum variety conjoined with greatest uniformity, in that the incessant change takes place according to a single rule. Such differences are not, however, a consequence merely of two writers taking a term "in different senses"; for the senses in which they employ the term are consequences of their general philosophic orientations. Hutcheson's method is analogical, and his aim is to find *one* beauty which is the essence of all the various modifications of beauty. Such a method and aim require that the key terms be loosely defined; if we are to speak of the "variety" of a still life and of a law of physics, we are assuredly going to use the term "variety" in a variety of senses! If, in contrast, method is literal and analytical, and the aim is to discriminate all the different aspects of things which are in one way or another agreeable, terms will be multiplied and their meanings more narrowly ascertained. If variety is discriminated from the several species of simple beauty and from novelty, unexpectedness, congruity, propriety, sublimity, and so on, it is evident that variety is not going to be the great leading trait of all things, physical, moral, and intellectual.

Sublimity, like beauty, is a property of single facts, and like beauty has two species, though there is nothing parallel in the distinctions. "Nature," observes Lord Kames, "hath not more remarkably distinguished us from the other animals by an erect posture, than by a capacious and aspiring mind, attaching us to every thing great and elevated." [38] Great magnitude produces the feeling of *grandeur;* great elevation, that of *sublimity.* "The emotions raised by great and by elevated objects, are clearly distinguishable, not only in the internal feeling, but even in their external expressions. A great object dilates the breast, and makes the spectator endeavour to enlarge his bulk. . . . An elevated object produces a different expression: it makes the spectator stretch upward and stand a tiptoe." [39] In the first two editions of the *Elements,* Lord Kames produces experiments to show that grandeur and sublimity are distinct emotions from all others, and that they are in every case pleasant in themselves; and he argues that in proportion as an object is great, regularity is less required. The third and later editions, in which this argument is considerably revised, emphasize that mere bulk (though agreeable as such) does not constitute grandeur, but that some regularity, proportion, or other beautiful qualities are requisite to make the magnitude grand. It is conceded, however, that grandeur requires less of these qualities than beauty; indeed, in its more impressive manifestations, grandeur (or sublimity) raises an enthusiasm impatient of confinement and the strictness of regularity and order. The terms "grandeur" and "sublimity" come to be used figuratively of other objects, physical, moral, and intellectual, which raise in us emotions similar to those of literal grandeur and sublimity. No quality is more grand, Kames mentions, than great force, especially when exerted by a sentient being; but this grandeur derives from the association of impressions, and there is in Kames no tendency to interpret material sublimity as merely significant of force or other moral traits. In the figurative applications of "grandeur" and "sublimity," the distinction between them is largely lost.

It should be mentioned that Kames admits that the sublime may be attended with a humbling of the mind in some instances. He decides the controversy between Boileau and Huet over the Mosaic

"God said, Let there be light, and there was light," noting that
Boileau has rightly perceived that the primary effect of this passage
is an emotion of grandeur, but that Huet has seen more deeply that
this emotion is but a flash and that the depressing effect is more sensible and lasting. It is "scarce possible," Kames remarks, "in fewer
words, to convey so clear an image of the infinite power of the Deity:
but then it belongs to the present subject to remark, that the emotion
of sublimity raised by this image is but momentary; and that the
mind, unable to support itself in an elevation so much above nature,
immediately sinks down into humility and veneration. . . ." [40]

Kames devises, in concluding his discussion of sublimity, some
rules for achieving the sublime in art—rules of a rather disappointingly general character, as that capital circumstances should be gathered together and minute or low circumstances omitted, or that abstract and general terms should be avoided except where they comprehend multitudes of individuals, and so forth.

Kames appears to follow the list of topics marked out by Addison,
for after beauty and greatness he addresses himself to novelty: "Of
all the particulars that contribute to raise emotions, not excepting
beauty, nor even greatness, novelty hath the most powerful influence." [41] Kames argues that novelty, while agreeable in itself as gratifying curiosity, may at the same time have an opposite indirect effect: it may aggravate terror if the new object appear dangerous. Now
this is something like a theory of conversion of the passions: a pleasant emotion is transformed into a painful and more powerful feeling.
But Kames does not generalize this phenomenon, and it remains an
isolated curiosity in his system. Novelty, which gives rise to wonder,
is distinguished from unexpectedness, which creates surprise. (Surprise, unlike wonder, has no definite character of its own, but accen-
tuates, when moderate, any emotion which it accompanies—a subject
on which Kames is more than usually acute in pointing out efficient
causes.) The differentiation of novelty from unexpectedness is another instance of a tendency pervading the system to dichotomize
feelings or qualities often taken as simple. Thus grandeur was distinguished from sublimity, and thus the risible is distinguished from
the ridiculous, congruity from propriety, dignity from grace, custom
from habit. In making each differentiation, Kames appeals to an internal sense or senses, and the properties or relations treated are duly
connected with the economy of the universe. This dichotomizing
never yields dialectical distinctions of real and apparent, one and
many, changeless and changing: it has, in fact, no systematic necessity;

there is simply an extraordinary proliferation of clear-cut literal distinctions. This elaborateness of differentiation without systematic necessity gives the *Elements* an eclectic air; but Lord Kames is not eclectic in the sense of explicitly adopting and interweaving the doctrines of his predecessors. On the contrary, he often regards himself as the first to investigate many of these phenomena, and although Kames must have been familiar with the books of Addison, Hutcheson, Hume, Hogarth, Burke, and Gerard, the aesthetic doctrines of these writers are nowhere canvassed in the *Elements*. Kames writes as if he owed no debts and anticipated no objections.

The final chapter in the group treating of the aesthetic qualities of objects taken singly is devoted to the risible. Throughout the eighteenth century, most aestheticians tended to ignore the ridiculous and risible and to confine themselves to the serious traits—beauty, sublimity, picturesqueness. Only those writers who deal largely with literature, in which the comic element plays a pronounced role, are led naturally to treat of the ludicrous; writers whose concern is with painting and sculpture, and still more those whose chief interest is in gardening, architecture, or external nature itself, tend equally naturally to ignore a quality of such slight importance in their subjects.[42] The risible (I return to Lord Kames) provokes the emotion of laughter, and does so by exhibiting matters not important enough to engage serious feelings but in which there is some excess or defect not deviating so far from the norm as to become monstrous. In the ridiculous—which, since it presupposes the senses of propriety and dignity, falls under the rubric of relations—a mixture of the improper with the risible causes contempt to mingle with laughter. Kames enters upon a pretty elaborate account of ridicule and wit; but the exposition of these matters, interesting and often subtle though it is, is not pertinent to the present enterprise.

Among the relationships yielding agreeable emotions are the resemblance and contrast, the variety and uniformity, already noticed; these are "primary" relationships, having a real existence independent of the perceiving mind. But there are also "secondary" relationships dependent upon the peculiar structure of the mind and without objective existence; such is the sense of congruity and propriety.[43] There are, as usual, two related properties; but one sense suffices for both, since propriety is nothing but the congruity of sensible beings with their thoughts, words, and actions. Kames's bent for elaborating literal distinctions is nowhere more evident than in the denial that congruity is an element of beauty: "Congruity is so nearly allied to beauty, as commonly to be held a species of it; and yet they differ so essentially as never to coincide: beauty, like colour, is placed upon a single subject; congruity upon a plurality: further, a thing beautiful in itself, may, with relation to other things, produce the strongest sense of incongruity." [44] Yet another internal sense is that which perceives dignity and meanness: "Man is endued with a sense of the worth and excellence of his nature: he deems it to be more perfect than that of the other beings around him; and he perceives that the perfection of his nature consists in virtue, particularly in virtue of the highest rank. To express this sense, the term *dignity* is appropriated." [45] The "rank" of virtues, incidentally, is not determined by utility but (consistently with Kames's system) by the direct impression they make upon us; man being, in Kames's estimation, more an active than a contemplative being, the active virtues of generosity, magnanimity, heroism are the noblest. That elusive quality, grace, is treated in a few pages appended to the chapter on dignity in the third and later editions of the *Elements*; it is finally defined as "that agreeable appearance which arises from elegance of motion and from a countenance expressive of dignity." [46]

After a discussion of custom and habit, in which the various phenomena are drawn out at some length and brought under the proper causes, efficient and final, the argument begins to move gradually from these universals to the species and genres, the components and techniques, of art. The transition is made through a study first of the external signs of emotions and passions, then of sentiments, then of language dictated by passion. Thus far, the method is to move from causes (emotions and passions) to effects (gesture and expression, sentiment, language). The argument then begins constructively with a theory of language itself; upon the basis of this theory, together with the psychology of the emotions and the account of qualities and relations already canvassed, a theory of comparisons and figures is constructed; then a critique of the modes of writing (narration and description) is developed; and finally, theories of particular genres (tragedy and epic) are devised.[47] The practical bias of the *Elements*, the aim of forming taste and regulating creativity, becomes more obvious as the argument leaves the realm of universal traits and relations: positive rules and the elaborate classification of faults enforce doubly the practical bearing of the complicated analysis. Kames follows in each part of the discussion of language and literature a rather mechanical plan adapted to his practical purposes: a list of positive rules is set forth, based (usually explicitly) on aesthetic principles and elaborately illustrated both in fulfillment and defect; then faults are enumerated, proved to be such when error is obstinate, and illustrated at length. These latter portions of the system appear to me free from the faults of which I have complained hitherto. For, the apparatus of universals once established securely (however artificially) with their original senses and final causes, Kames can analyze the complex particulars of art altogether in terms of that apparatus. His criticism—as distinguished from his aesthetics—has great particularity and precision, and a very considerable degree of systematic consistency. (The reduction of critical principles to more general aesthetic principles can often be discerned even in the minutiae of criticism; the distinction of inverted and natural style, for instance, hinges on the argument that substances can be conceived independent of any one attribute, whereas attributes can not be conceived independently— accordingly, a style is inverted when the attribute precedes a circumstance intervening between it and its subject, but is still natural if the subject precedes the intervening circumstance.)

The external signs of passions and emotions are partly voluntary, partly involuntary; and the voluntary signs are either artificial (words) or natural (gestures and actions which express the passions, usually through resemblance to them). But external signs of whatever kind produce other emotions and passions in spectators. Pleasant passions have agreeable signs which in turn produce pleasant passions according to the usual rule; the feelings of the spectator, accordingly, vary with those of the patient. Painful passions which are disagreeable have external signs which repel; painful passions agreeable in survey have signs disagreeable in themselves (and which raise, therefore, painful feelings in spectators), but which nevertheless, by a skilful contrivance of providence, attract. Distress pictured on the countenance, for instance, inspires the observer with pity, which, although painful in itself, nonetheless impels him to afford relief. Kames's explanation of this phenomenon of sympathy turns, quite characteristically, on an original principle and on a conception of finality in nature, in contrast with Hume's account in terms of association of ideas and impressions; Kames, moreover, rests interpretation of the external signs of passions on intuition rather than experience. All this has clear implications for the arts, and especially for painting, which depends so heavily upon gesture and expression. And the doctrine that agreeable painful emotions produce in spectators painful but attracting emotions contains, to Kames's mind, the answer to the problem, why tragedy pleases: "The whole mystery is explained by a single observation, that sympathy, though painful, is attractive, and attaches us to an object in distress, the opposition of self-love notwithstanding, which should prompt us to fly from it. And by this curious mechanism it is, that persons of any degree of sensibility are attracted by affliction still more than by joy." [48] This view does not, however, account for any difference in the response to actual and simulated catastrophes.

Besides the natural expression of feelings in gesture and facial aspect, there is an artificial and arbitrary expression through language; chapters on "Sentiments" ("Every thought prompted by passion merely, is termed *a sentiment*" [49]) and on the "Language of Passion" accordingly conclude this division of the *Elements*. The ensuing treatment of language as such, as sound, signification, or imitation, contains what is perhaps the most subtle and extensive treatment of versification in the eighteenth century. In treating of these problems, and those of comparisons and figures, Kames is able to refer the multitudinous phenomena to the principles already established, so that his study is not only minutely detailed but also rational and ordered. The numerous "beauties" pointed out are not, of course, "beauty" in the strict sense: they are only excellencies appealing to our various senses and faculties. Beauty in the proper sense appears but rarely; a simile may involve a comparison with some object literally beautiful which the words call before the mind's eye, and such a simile, appropriately employed to embellish or clarify the context, is beautiful not only in the more narrow sense but also in the sense of being meritorious as a simile. Similes and some other figures may also be grand by representing great or sublime objects, thoughts, or actions; and occasionally the distinction of great from sublime may be noted in the subjects of a simile.

The discussion of narration and description contains, beyond the rules and analysis of blemishes which we expect, a "curious inquiry": why the depiction or description of ugly objects may please. For many critics, one answer would serve for both this problem and that of tragic pleasure; but Lord Kames characteristically divides and distinguishes. The case of tragedy is singular, involving as it does a painful emotion which is nonetheless agreeable. In imitation of the ugly, however, the pleasure of imitation itself (in painting) or of language (in poetry) overbalances the disagreeableness of the subject. In tragedy, accordingly, the attraction is greater as the distress represented is greater; but in description there is "no encouragement to deal in disagreeable subjects; for the pleasure is incomparably greater where the subject and the description are both of them agreeable." [50] Disagreeable subjects—ugly, disgusting, unmanly, horrible, or whatever—subduct, then, from the pleasure of a performance. Terrific objects, however, constitute a kind of exception, for they "have in poetry and painting a fine effect. The picture, by raising a slight emotion of terror, agitates the mind; and in that condition every beauty makes a deep impression. May not contrast heighten the pleasure, by opposing our present security to the danger we would be in by encountering the object represented?" [51] This is clearly conversion of the passions; yet Kames does not employ this principle in accounting for the effects of tragedy, presumably because of the curious interpretation he gives of tragic fear (of which below). It must be remarked, too, that Kames does not connect the terrific with the sublime; it serves rather to heighten sensibility to "beauties" or excellencies of (presumably) whatever kind.

The conventional literary kinds are at last arrived at through the constructive argument which has been described. Since these genres are not defined as objects of a certain kind (in the manner of Aristotle), but rest all alike upon a general theory of the mind, they are not sharply differentiated. "Literary compositions," says Kames, "run into each other, precisely like colours: in their strong tints they are easily distinguished; but are susceptible of so much variety, and of so many different forms, that we can never say where one species ends and another begins." [52] The fine arts generally are distinguished from the useful arts by being calculated to make agreeable impressions; and this differentia of all the arts may be supplemented in the case of particular arts, genres, or varieties, by instruction. Of course even those works which have no didactic aim affect the character, but this is rather a proprium than a differentia. The species of narrative poems are determined, accordingly, rather through the ends subserved by such compositions than through distinctions in construction as such. Aristotle's division of simple and complex plots is accordingly replaced: "A poem, whether dramatic or epic, that has no tendency beyond moving the passions and exhibiting pictures of virtue and vice, may be distinguished by the name of *pathetic*. But where a story is purposely contrived to illustrate some moral truth, by showing the natural connection betwixt disorderly passions and external misfortunes, such composition may be denominated *moral*." [53] Both varieties of plot have a moral influence, for the pathetic plot through the sympathetic emotion of virtue cultivates feelings productive of virtue, and through exercising the sympathies humanizes the mind; but the moral species "not only improves the heart . . . but instructs the head by the moral it contains." [54] Moral tragedy raises alongside pity the self-regarding passion of fear—fear not for the protagonist but for *ourselves*, lest we fall into similar errors.[55] Once the distinction of pathetic from moral is effected on these ethical grounds, so that criteria of suitable actions can be devised, action becomes the principal part of the poem, and manners are adjusted to the fable, sentiments to manners, and diction to sentiment.

It is not my aim to enter upon merely critical questions in any detail, but Kames's treatment of the three unities cannot be entirely passed over. His is the most philosophical treatment of this vexed topic in English criticism, both preceding and surpassing Johnson's analysis, which has rather undeservedly got credit for extraordinary courage and acuity. Unity of action finds support, when properly qualified, in the principles of Kamesian aesthetics; but the unities of time and place go by the board. Arguing from the conception of ideal presence, Kames urges preservation of these unities within continuous acts, and comparative freedom from these rules in intervals between acts.

But despite keen interest in critical issues in the arts and the determination to establish rules, Lord Kames's concern remains rather more with the "elements" than with the "criticism." The arts entertain by raising agreeable feelings in the mind, and critical questions therefore always illustrate, and are always resolved by, principles of psychological aesthetics. Such reference might handicap the arts if the psychology were narrow; but Kames's aesthetics, however superficial at some points, is not dogmatically constricted, and the number and variety of principles which can be brought to bear upon the particular phenomena of, say, tragedy or landscape gardening is adequate for explication of some of the most complex problems of art. Kames's aesthetics is not a mere *ad hoc* sanctification of modes of art currently fashionable. The freedom and originality of the system is striking (for instance) in the discussion of gardening (chapter xxiv), which is equally free from dogmatic attachment to the prevailing style of gardening and from insistence on some rigidly conceived set of reforms. Kames's conception of a garden is, that every part should exhibit beauty, but that each part should be characterized by some expression supervening to the beauty—grandeur, melancholy, gaiety. These parts, seen successively (for a large garden is a temporal as well as a spatial art), give maximum pleasure by variety and contrast; near the house, regularity should be studied, but at greater distances a wilder and more various style is proper. Kames admired the gardens of Kent, but his theory calls for gardens far more varied and expressive than these—it looks forward through the era of Capability Brown to the gardens of the picturesque school. The theoretical treatment is far different from that given by Price and Knight—rather more like that of Repton—but the taste which it justifies is as broad. The prescriptions for architecture are, though in precision and comprehensiveness less adequate to the subject, equally forward-looking. Uniformity, proportion, regularity, order, utility, expression, congruity, custom, and yet other principles are introduced into the discussion, a discussion which, worked out more fully, would yield a system of architectural criticism as detailed, though not so systematic, as that of Alison.[56]

Elements of Criticism culminates in a demonstration of the standard of taste. It is a curiously perverse tendency among modern scholars to argue that the philosophical critics of the eighteenth century, by tracing aesthetic responses to their roots in passions, senses, faculties, and association, subvert the neo-classical system of rules and absolutes, and thus open the way for rampant subjectivism. McKenzie, who speaks of the "nearly incurable subjectivity" of the whole "mechanist" tradition,[57] considers that Kames's escape from this welter of individualism was "simply to assume that standards exist as the result of many men's experiences and to expect the critic to acquaint himself with them," a solution evolved at "very considerable cost to the validity of the method, since it is directly contradictory to an empirical approach"—being, in fact, an insidious outgrowth of outmoded neo-classicism.[58] This interpretation appears to me to be indefensible. Setting aside the fiction of neo-classical rules, arbitrary, absolute, and objective, it is apparent that each philosophical aesthetician of the century subscribed to the idea of a standard of taste superior in authority to individual predilections; each supposed himself to be placing the admitted standard on its just foundations. All found the standard connected in one way or another with human nature, a nature universal and in some sense fixed. The derivation of the standard from human nature could, and did, take many courses. With Lord Kames, the argument involves, consistently with the rest of his thought, postulation of an internal sense which discerns conformity to our nature. Since all men speak of a right and wrong taste, there must be a foundation in nature for so universal a practice; the foundation is, that

> we have a sense or conviction of a common nature, not only in our own species, but in every species of animals. . . . This common nature is conceived to be a model or standard for each individual that belongs to the kind. . . .
>
> With respect to the common nature of man, in particular, we have a conviction that it is invariable not less than universal; that it will be the same hereafter as at present, and as it was in time past; the same among all nations and in all corners of the earth. . . .
>
> We are so constituted as to conceive this common nature, not only to be invariable, but to be also *perfect* or *right;* and consequently that individuals *ought* to be made conformable to it. Every remarkable deviation from the standard, makes accordingly an impression on us of imperfection, irregularity, or disorder: it is disagreeable, and raises in us a painful emotion. . . .[59]

Even those whose taste is perverted, still are conscious of the common nature of man and grant that it ought not to be subjected to their peculiar taste. All this by no means denies that men's tastes in art and morals is actually highly variable: how is the true taste to be ascertained? It is fixed by appealing to the most general and lasting preferences among polite nations where rationality and delicacy have been cultivated. The good judge has natural delicacy of taste, improved by education, reflection, and experience, and preserved by regular and moderate living. But the standard need not be determined by an intricate and uncertain process of selecting good judges; for Kames as for Gerard, it is to be arrived at deductively from the psychological principles governing the sensitive part of our nature. "In a word, there is no means so effectual for ascertaining the standard of taste, as a thorough acquaintance with these principles; and to lay a foundation for this valuable branch of knowledge, is the declared purpose of the present undertaking." [60] This demonstration of the standard of taste appropriately concludes the *Elements of Criticism,* for, while all the foregoing analysis serves to establish the particular principles of taste, the proof of the perfection and universality of the standard reflexively ascertains the principles already brought to light.

A few words should yet be said on the connection of aesthetics and morals in this system: judgment arises in each case from internal senses; these senses are in each case devised for beneficent purposes;

aesthetic feelings may have moral consequences, and moral feelings may be taken as the matter of art; the theoretician may pursue parallel inquiries in the two sciences. Some of the aesthetic senses, moreover, are essentially and exclusively moral in character; propriety, dignity, the agreeableness of passions all depend on our sense of our specific nature; and even those aesthetic senses which address themselves to physical properties and relations may apply also by extension and analogy to the moral world. But the "order" of the physical world is not really identical with that of the moral world; and "beauty," which in its proper signification designates a secondary property of visible objects, is extended to mental properties only through the resemblance of the effects on the percipient; the same association accounts for the figurative "grandeur" and "sublimity" of the moral and intellectual realm. Moral standards, moreover, are more definitely fixed with the progress of civilization than are aesthetic; for, the objects of moral feeling being more clearly distinguishable from one another, moral feelings are stronger and more definite. And this difference exhibits contrivance once more: were aesthetic feelings stronger, they would abstract attention from matters of greater moment; were they less vague, there would be no differences in feeling, and in consequence no rivalry and improvement in the arts.[61] And so, despite the manifold connections and analogies between ethics and aesthetics, aesthetics remains a separate science with at least partly independent principles and criteria.

CHAPTER 8

Hugh Blair

AMONG the various activities of Henry Home, Lord Kames, in behalf of the intellectual and literary life of Scotland, was the establishment in 1748 of a series of public lectures on language and literature. Adam Smith delivered the first lectures at the University of Edinburgh; in 1759 the post was vacant, and the appointment fell to Hugh Blair, littérateur and distinguished preacher and minister of the High Church of St. Giles.[1]

Blair's lectures, after 1760 given only to students of the University (where Blair became Professor of Rhetoric in 1760 and Regius Professor of Rhetoric and Belles-Lettres in 1762), remained unchanged in essentials for the quarter-century of Blair's professorship. Though Blair spoke of "adding to and improving" his lectures,[2] there is no reason to question Schmitz's judgment that "a student who sat before Blair in 1760 heard very much the same lectures as were delivered in the class of 1783, the year of Blair's retirement and publication of the lectures." [3] That Blair "kept up with" the aesthetic discussion of the age is evidenced by a footnote discussion in the printed *Lectures* of the Appendix on the Imitative Nature of Poetry added to the third edition of Gerard's *Essay on Taste* as recently as 1780.[4]

The *Lectures on Rhetoric and Belles Lettres,* together with *A Critical Dissertation on the Poems of Ossian, the Son of Fingal,* constitute Blair's contribution to aesthetic, rhetorical, and critical theory.[5] Though he was neither a comprehensive nor a profoundly original writer, Blair was of immense importance as a popularizer of aesthetic and critical speculation; there are more than sixty editions of the *Lectures* in English, almost fifty editions of abridgments, and translations into German, French, Italian, Spanish, and Russian.[6] Blair's rhetorical theory is still studied, but the almost entire absence of comment on his theory of the sublime and beautiful testifies to the disregard into which his aesthetics has fallen.

The introductory lecture of Blair's course is a recitation of truisms designed to enforce the importance of the study of writing and the advantages of the pursuits of taste. There is no striving for paradox or novelty as Blair reiterates a sentiment which echoes down the century: "PROVIDENCE seems plainly to have pointed out this useful purpose to which the pleasures of taste may be applied, by interposing them in a middle station between the pleasures of sense, and those of pure intellect. . . . The pleasures of taste refresh the mind after the toils of the intellect, and the labours of abstract study; and they gradually raise it above the attachments of sense, and prepare it for the enjoyments of virtue." [7] Yet there is often real novelty concealed beneath the platitudinous manner so characteristic of Blair. His rhetoric is a systematic return from the trope-and-figure tradition to the Ciceronian emphasis on argumentative content: "If the following Lectures have any merit, it will consist in an endeavour to substitute the application of these principles [reason and good sense] in the place of artificial and scholastic rhetoric; in an endeavour to explode false ornament, to direct attention more towards substance than show, to recommend good sense as the foundation of all good composition, and simplicity as essential to all true ornament." [8] Such generalities are, to be sure, commonplaces; but Blair's lectures carry out the program in earnest.

Rhetoric, however, falls outside the scope of this study, which is confined to the first group of the lectures as Blair outlines them: "They divide themselves into five parts. First, some introductory dissertations on the Nature of Taste, and upon the sources of its pleasures. Secondly, the consideration of Language: Thirdly, of Style: Fourthly, of Eloquence properly so called, or Public Speaking in its different kinds. Lastly, a critical examination of the most distinguished Species of Composition, both in prose and verse." [9] The four last groups are arranged in an evident synthetic pattern: language merely, then language given a character expressive of a writer's manner of thinking and peculiarity of temper, and finally the two branches of composition—rhetoric and belles-lettres—in which style is applied to subject under the influence of heart and imagination. The connection of the opening dissertations on taste is less evident, and indeed, the essays of this part constitute a subsidiary unity within the lectures, intelligible apart from what follows, and not indispensably prerequisite to it.

Since, however, taste is the faculty appealed to in disquisitions on the merit of composition, Blair may treat of it as a preliminary. He defines the faculty as "the power of receiving pleasure from the beauties of nature and of art"; [10] and finds this power to be "ultimately founded on a certain natural and instinctive sensibility to beauty," though reason "assists Taste in many of its operations, and serves to enlarge its power." [11] This formulation, so independent of any particular philosophic context—supported, indeed, by a footnote reference to Gerard, D'Alembert, Du Bos, Kames, Hume, and Burke—is a mark of Blair's eclecticism; his aesthetic doctrine is less a system than a conspectus of eighteenth-century opinion.

Determination of the constituent faculties of taste gives the material cause; and consideration of the culture and improvement of these natural powers yields the formal cause—a good taste. Here, too, the doctrine is conventional, and in distinctions and terminology appears to be based very largely on Gerard. The psychology underlying these distinctions is in Blair, however, very much abbreviated. Discussion of "correctness" leads to the problem of the standard: are we to hold, "according to the proverb, [that] there is no disputing of Tastes; but that whatever pleases is right, for that reason that it does please?" [12] Blair observes (as Hume and others had done before him) that no one really accepts the proverb in its full extent, and (further) that though Truth is one, Beauty is manifold, and there is a legitimate latitude and diversity of objects of taste. Such diversity, however, "can only have place where the objects of Taste are different"—that is, where different aspects of the object are isolated for commendation or reprehension. But direct contradiction of preference does also occur, and here a standard is requisite. Human nature, of course, provides it: "were there any one person who possessed in full perfection all the powers of human nature, whose internal senses were in every instance exquisite and just, and whose reason was unerring and sure, the determinations of such a person concerning beauty, would, beyond doubt, be a perfect standard for the Taste of all others." [13] Since such an ideal critic does not exist, the problem is to construct his judgments hypothetically. "That which men concur the most in admiring, must be held to be beautiful. His Taste must be esteemed just and true, which coincides with the general sentiments of men. In this standard we must rest. To the sense of mankind the ultimate appeal must ever lie, in all works of Taste." [14] But the eighteenth-century critics, men as various as Gerard and Kames, Hume and Johnson, were wont to demonstrate the inadequacy of the argument from alleged universal consensus, and Blair is not an exception:

> But have we then, it will be said, no other criterion of what is beautiful, than the approbation of the majority? . . . By no means; there are principles of reason and sound judgment which can be applied to matters of Taste as well as to the subjects of science and philosophy. He who admires or censures any work of genius, is always ready, if his Taste be in any degree improved, to assign some reasons of his decision. He appeals to principles, and points out the grounds on which he proceeds. Taste is a sort of compound power, in which the light of the understanding always mingles, more or less, with the feelings of sentiment.[15]

Reasonings on taste always appeal ultimately to feeling as criterion, of course—but to the feelings men have about the general properties which make up objects rather than to the superficial feelings evoked by complex objects themselves, unanalyzed by reason.

Blair is not so sensible as Gerard of the difficulties of establishing a consensus, or so aware of the existence of cultures which do not, even ultimately, coincide with Western culture in preferences; and he suggests that the rules of art can be determined inductively from works which have in fact commanded general approbation. His conception of philosophical method in aesthetics is oversimple, and depends too heavily upon ascending from particular instances to general principles. I have already argued, in treating of Gerard's method, that mere ascending induction from the empirical data is questionable when applied to problems where the contributing causes are so many and so subtle as in aesthetics. Following Mill and one of Gerard's own pronouncements, I argued for the inverse deductive method: obtaining provisional empirical laws by direct induction and afterwards connecting these with established principles of human nature by deduction—consilience constituting verification. Although Blair, like Gerard, does call for ultimate deductive verification, the *a priori* part of the process is too abbreviated.

For his principles, Blair turns back to Addison, declaring that "the advances made since his time in this curious part of philosophical Criticism, are not very considerable; though some ingenious writers have pursued the subject." [16] This inadequacy is explained by remarking that "it is difficult to make a full enumeration of the several objects that give pleasure to Taste; it is more difficult to define all those which have been discovered, and to reduce them under proper classes; and, when we would go farther, and investigate the efficient causes of the pleasure which we receive from such objects, here, above all, we find ourselves at a loss. . . . These first principles of internal sensation, nature seems to have covered with an impenetrable veil." [17] Like Addison, Blair takes refuge in final causes, which are, as he says, more readily ascertained. This is not an auspicious beginning: in aesthetics, as in biology, only the investigator who disregards finality can have the enthusiasm for efficient causes requisite to discovery.

Sublimity, as a topic traditional for rhetoricians, and as the narrowest and most precisely definable of the pleasures of imagination, is the first quality of which Blair treats. He declines to distinguish (with Kames) grandeur from sublimity, unless "sublimity" be merely "Grandeur in its highest degree." Sublimity produces "a sort of internal elevation and expansion; it raises the mind much above its ordinary state; and fills it with a degree of wonder and astonishment, which it cannot well express. The emotion is certainly delightful; but it is altogether of the serious kind: a degree of awfulness and solemnity, even approaching to severity, commonly attends it when at its height; very distinguishable from the more gay and brisk emotion raised by beautiful objects." [18] Simplest of the qualities of objects productive of this emotion is vastness, unboundedness of space or time or number. Blair makes the conventional observation that the effect of height is more intense than that of length but less so than that of depth; yet no effort is made to account for these differences. Sublimity is found also in loud sounds, the burst of thunder or the shouting of multitudes. Great power and force are the most copious source of sublime ideas; and "all ideas of the solemn and awful kind, and even bordering on the terrible, tend greatly to assist the Sublime; such as darkness, solitude, and silence." [19] Blair follows Burke in finding obscurity sublime: "In general, all objects that are greatly raised above us, or far removed from us either in space or in time, are apt to strike us as great. Our viewing them, as through the mist of distance or antiquity, is favourable to the impressions of their Sublimity." [20] The moral and sentimental sublime, finally, produces "an effect extremely similar to what is produced by the view of grand objects in nature; filling the mind with admiration, and elevating it above itself." [21] This mental sublimity "coincides in a great measure with magnanimity, heroism, and generosity of sentiment. Whatever discovers human nature in its greatest elevation; whatever bespeaks a high effort of soul; or shews a mind superior to pleasures, to dangers, and to death; forms what may be called the moral or sentimental sublime." [22]

Blair's procedure thus far has been to describe the emotion of sublimity, and to collect the chief qualities which produce it. Two steps of an adequate account remain: to find the common traits (if any) in virtue of which the various qualities produce similar effects, and to discover, preferably by deduction from established principles of human nature, the intervening steps of the mechanism. "A question next arises," as Blair puts it, "whether we are able to discover some one fundamental quality in which all these different objects [productive of sublimity] agree, and which is the cause of their producing an emotion of the same nature in our minds? Various hypotheses have been formed concerning this; but, as far as appears to me, hitherto unsatisfactory." [23] Blair's account of the theories of his predecessors is scarcely just. "Some," he tells us in patent allusion to Gerard, "have imagined that amplitude, or great extent, joined with simplicity, is either immediately, or remotely, the fundamental quality of whatever is sublime; but we have seen that amplitude is confined to one species of Sublime Objects; and cannot, without violent straining, be applied to them all." [24] This is not an adequate statement of Gerard's position, for Gerard has a pretty complicated set of devices (several species of relations and associations) through which the manifold phenomena of sublimity can be connected with the simplest and most evident of them, quantity. These devices do perhaps necessitate some subtle analysis, but might be defended against the charge of "violent straining." Burke is described as proposing the theory, "That terror is the source of the Sublime, and that no objects have this character, but such as produce impressions of pain and danger. It is indeed true, that many terrible objects are highly sublime; and that grandeur does not refuse an alliance with the idea of danger . . . yet he seems to stretch his theory too far, when he represents the Sublime as consisting wholly in modes of danger, or of pain." [25] Burke does not say quite this, however: only that sublime objects are capable of exciting terror, or are associated with terror, or act upon our "nerves" in a fashion analogous to terror. And in any event, Burke does not maintain that danger and pain constitute sublimity, but that the remission of them does. Blair's point that "the proper sensation of sublimity appears to be very distinguishable from the sensation of [danger and pain]; and, on several occasions, to be entirely separated from them," [26] is, then, an *ignoratio elenchi*, and one of which a host of critics of Burke are guilty.

Blair's own conjecture, presented without much effort at substantiation, is that

> mighty force or power, whether accompanied with terror or not, whether employed in protecting, or in alarming us, has a better title, than any thing that has yet been mentioned, to be the fundamental quality of the Sublime; as, after the review which we have taken, there does not occur to me any Sublime Object, into the idea of which, power, strength, and force, either enter not directly, or are not, at least, intimately associated with the idea, by leading our thoughts to some astonishing power, as concerned in the production of the object.[27]

This conjecture is very closely related to the doctrine later advanced by Payne Knight, that the sublime turns on energy.

Blair's principal concern in the lectures is, of course, the literary arts, and he treats of the sublime in "objects" only so far as this investigation is ancillary to a consideration of sublimity in discourse; his concern is in this respect more like that of Longinus than like that of Gerard and Burke. Ruling out at once the conception of sublimity in writing which Jonathan Richardson and a variety of others had given—"any remarkable and distinguishing excellency of composition"—Blair does not hesitate to censure Longinus himself, for "many of the passages which he produces as instances of the Sublime, are merely elegant, without having the most distant relation to proper Sublimity; witness Sappho's famous Ode, on which he descants at considerable length." [28] And Longinus' very plan is defective, for the three heads dealing with language (figures, diction, composition) "have no more relation to the Sublime, than to other kinds of good Writing; perhaps less to the Sublime than to any other species whatever; because it requires less the assistance of ornament." [29] The sublime pertains to nature, not artifice, and the true conception of "Sublime Writing" is, "such a description of objects, or exhibition of sentiments, which are in themselves of a Sublime nature, as shall give us strong impressions of them." [30] Since Blair defines the sublime of discourse in terms of the natural sublime, he can put off to a kind of appendix at the end of his chapter treatment of the two opposites to the sublime, frigidity and bombast. For Longinus, however, operating in purely literary terms, the discussion of these faults must come first, because it is through this analysis that he defines the sublime.

The foundation of sublimity in writing, then, is in the nature of the object described. "Unless it be such an object as, if presented to our eyes, if exhibited to us in reality, would raise ideas of that elevating, that awful, and magnificent kind, which we call Sublime; the description, however finely drawn, is not entitled to come under this class." [31] The description of such an object must be simple, concise, and made up of striking circumstances, rules which find their rationale in the nature of the sublime emotion: "The mind rises and swells, when a lofty description or sentiment is presented to it, in its native form. But no sooner does the poet attempt to spread out this sentiment or description, and to deck it round and round with glittering ornaments, than the mind begins to fall from its high elevation; the transport is over; the beautiful may remain, but the sublime is gone." [32] In all good writing, the sublime lies in the thoughts, which, when truly noble, clothe themselves in a native dignity of language. Its sources "are to be looked for every where in nature," and no art can isolate them. The sublime "must come unsought, if it come at all; and be the natural offspring of a strong imagination." [33]

Often in the course of the *Dissertation* on Ossian, Blair speaks of "the sublime and pathetic," a coupling which requires comment. Blair uses "pathetic" in such contexts to refer not to passion generally—though this *is* often the meaning in other contexts—but to tender and melting emotion opposite to the astonishment and elevation of the sublime, though like it serious and intense. The two great characteristics of Ossian's poetry are tenderness and sublimity; he "moves perpetually in the high region of the grand and the pathetic." [34] In this commingling of strains, indeed, Ossian is the superior of Homer, for "the sublimity of moral sentiments, if they wanted the softening of the tender, would be in hazard of giving a hard and stiff air to poetry. It is not enough to admire. Admiration is a cold feeling, in comparison of that deep interest which the heart takes in tender and pathetic scenes; where, by a mysterious attachment to the objects of compassion, we are pleased and delighted, even whilst we mourn." [35]

Blair's view accords with the fashionable primitivism of his age when he opines that "the early ages of the world, and the rude unimproved state of society, are peculiarly favorable to the strong emotions of Sublimity," [36] to glowing imagination, violent passions, bold expression. The ancient poems of nations disclose to us the history of human imagination and feeling "before those refinements of society had taken place, which enlarge indeed, and diversify the transactions, but disguise the manners of mankind." Such poetry offers some of the highest beauties of poetical writing: "Irregular and unpolished we may expect the productions of uncultivated ages to be;

but abounding, at the same time, with that enthusiasm, that vehemence and fire, which are the soul of poetry. . . . That state, in which human nature shoots wild and free, though unfit for other improvements, certainly encourages the high exertions of fancy and passion." [37] The passages of sublime and pathetic which Blair brings forward are most often drawn from such works—from Scripture, from Homer, Ossian, and Milton (whose subject and character alike withdrew him, I presume, from the insipid elegance of artificial society).

Beauty is distinguished from sublimity by its more gay and brisk emotion, an emotion felt to be calmer, more soothing, less elevating but more serene, and susceptible of longer continuance. As this list of traits already suggests, with its emotion both gay and soothing, brisk and serene, "the feelings which Beautiful objects produce, differ considerably, not in degree only, but also in kind, from one another." The term "beauty," accordingly, is equivocal, being "applied to almost every external object that pleases the eye, or the ear; to a great number of the graces of writing; to many dispositions of the mind; nay, to several objects of mere abstract science." [38] Blair infers very plausibly that there is no one common trait among beautiful objects, and that beautiful things please by means of various principles of human nature; the "agreeable emotion which they all raise, is somewhat of the same nature; and, therefore, has the common name of Beauty given to it; but it is raised by different causes." [39] Blair's hypothesis that power is the root trait of all sublimity is grounded on association of ideas; his hypothesis concerning beauty turns on association of like impressions.

The simplest beauty is that of color, and the efficient cause which Blair postulates is the structure of the eye, though he grants without emphasis that association of ideas has influence. Beauty of figure is of several sorts: regularity, Blair suggests, is beautiful chiefly "on account of its suggesting the ideas of fitness, propriety, and use." [40] Variety is a more powerful principle, and Hogarth is vouchsafed some condescending approval; "he pitches upon two lines," Blair remarks, "on which, according to him, the Beauty of figure principally depends; and he has illustrated, and supported his doctrine, by a surprising number of instances." [41] The tone is a little supercilious; Blair doubtless considers Hogarth an enthusiast who has taken a part for the whole. Hutcheson's combination of unity amid variety will not serve, however—not even for the beauty of external figured objects, for many beautiful objects have slight variety while others are intricate. The beauty of motion—gentle, undulating, and ascending—completes the roster of merely physical beauties. Each of these properties yields a distinct feeling, yet sufficiently similar "as readily to mix and blend in one general perception of Beauty, which we ascribe to the whole object as its cause: for Beauty is always conceived by us, as something residing in the object which raises the pleasant sensation; a sort of glory which dwells upon, and invests it." [42] "Perhaps the most complete assemblage of beautiful objects that can any where be found," Blair illustrates, "is presented by a rich natural landscape, where there is a sufficient variety of objects: fields in verdure, scattered trees and flowers, running water, and animals grazing. If to these be joined, some of the productions of art, which suit such a scene; as a bridge with arches over a river, smoke rising from cottages in the midst of trees, and the distant view of a fine building seen by the rising sun; we then enjoy, in the highest perfection, that gay, cheerful, and placid sensation which characterises Beauty." [43] But such an assemblage of beautiful objects really lays bare the inadequacy of the elementary principles of beauty which Blair has brought forward, and the almost total lack of middle principles connecting these with concrete phenomena.

In treating of the beauty of the countenance, Blair is led to moral and sentimental beauty, those "social virtues, and such as are of a softer and gentler kind; as compassion, mildness, friendship, and generosity." [44] There is, finally, an intellectual beauty of design and art. But Blair makes no effort to see associations with these beauties in external objects. The beauty of discourse is less a problem than the sublime, for it is less a definite and isolable quality. Beyond the unmeaning use of "beauty" to mean merely "good," is its employment to designate a certain manner, "such as raises in the reader an emotion of the gentle placid kind, similar to what is raised by the contemplation of beautiful objects in nature; which neither lifts the mind very high, nor agitates it very much, but diffuses over the imagination an agreeable and pleasing serenity," [45] a style like that of Virgil, or Fénelon, or Addison.

Imitation yields a pleasure of taste, though a pleasure distinguished by Blair from that of beauty. Although poetry and eloquence have greater capacity of affecting us by their representations than other arts, they are not (in general) strictly imitative. In a truly mimetic art, "imitation is performed by means of somewhat that has a natural likeness and resemblance to the thing imitated, and of consequence is understood by all," whereas "the raising in the mind the conception of an object by means of some arbitrary or instituted symbols" is more properly termed "description." [46] Given these definitions, it is clear that only dramatic poetry is strictly imitative; a footnote to the published lectures concedes, however, the justice of Gerard's argument for the imitative nature of poetry (in the Appendix to the third edition of the *Essay on Taste*).

Other pleasures of taste Blair does not analyze. The single paragraph accorded to novelty testifies to the demotion of that relation to the status of an incidental effect. Melody and harmony, wit, humor, and ridicule, Blair omits; for the first do not bear upon rhetoric and belles-lettres, and the last require (it appears) no explanation previous to treatment of the literary forms in which they are embodied.

CHAPTER 9

Sir Joshua Reynolds

THE *Fifteen Discourses of Art*[1] of Sir Joshua Reynolds are more a system of criticism for painting than a philosophical inquiry into the universal traits of aesthetic experience: and this is quite natural, for the discourses were delivered by an artist to an audience of artists and connoisseurs with the practical aim of directing the practice of painters and forming the taste of amateurs. Nevertheless, Reynolds repeatedly enters upon the higher and more philosophical issues, and, indeed, the very method and viewpoint he adopts tend to do away with any sharp distinction of aesthetics from criticism: his dialectic plays constantly between the most general issues of psychology and the most particular questions of technique. As is usually the case in such dialectics, it is not possible to separate for analysis one element or part of the system without prejudicing the intelligibility of the whole, and accordingly, the entire system will be reviewed here, without attempt to single out for analysis Reynolds' views on beauty or sublimity.

Reynolds alone among the philosophical critics and aestheticians of the eighteenth century is generally read today. This circumstance is attributable partly to his stature as a practicing artist, which has transferred an adventitious authority to his critical doctrines. But in part also, Reynolds' still flourishing reputation as a critic is due to the peculiar character of his thought, which, standing in some measure apart from the general current of eighteenth-century empiricism, has better escaped the dogmatic reaction of the nineteenth century.

Yet although Reynolds is widely read and respected today, the coherency of his doctrine and the purity of his method are usually disregarded; both his critics and his defenders interpret his thought in the light of modern preconceptions, philosophical, critical, or historical. It is a matter of importance to this study, as well as of considerable autonomous interest, to re-establish the aesthetics of Reynolds as a system self-consistent, systematic, and fruitful.[2]

Modern criticism of the theory of Reynolds has concerned itself chiefly with two issues, though neither has been stated in such wise as to admit of a solution. There is, in the first place, a sense of baffling contradictions in the thought of Reynolds, a feeling which has persisted since the attacks of Blake and Hazlitt. Roger Fry observes, in his admirable edition of Reynolds' *Discourses*, that it is not possible to acquit Reynolds "of confusion of thought and inconsistency in the use of words," and he instances (among other inconsistencies) the apparently incompatible senses of the central term "nature," used (*1*) to designate visible phenomena not made by artifice, (*2*) "in an Aristotelian sense as an immanent force working in the refractory medium of matter towards the highest perfection of form," and (*3*) to signify what is inherently agreeable to the mind.[3] Michael Macklem has more recently attempted to show "how the diversity of meanings attached to the idea of nature indicates the diverse principles of neoclassical art," finding that Reynolds concurrently and inconsistently thought of art as producing a general image of nature, as representing an Ideal transcending nature but from which nature is derived, and as affording a wish-fulfilling idealization of the actual.[4] Thompson, too, asserts that "inconsistencies in Reynolds's statements can easily be detected; for the first paper in the *Idler* appeared in 1759, and the last address was delivered in 1790. Moreover, the artist did not always practice what he preached."[5] The correlation of theory and practice (a matter often brought to the fore in discussions of Reynolds) is not germane to the present analysis; but I may observe that Reynolds' theory involves a hierarchy of genres and styles, and that the "rules" are analogically applicable to each, so that every genre and style has its appropriate excellence (however low in the total scheme) and artists may exercise their talents legitimately at every level. Accordingly, the criteria on which Reynolds based his choice of "fields" were more personal and social than philosophical; his talents lay in the direction of portraiture and coloring, coinciding happily with the demand of his age for portraits executed with fashionable splendor of style. In recommending to artists to follow the path which Michael Angelo had marked out, Reynolds says: "I have taken another course, one more suited to my abilities, and to the taste of the times in which I live. Yet however unequal I feel myself to that attempt, were I now to begin the world again, I would tread in the steps of that great master. . . ."[6]

Joseph Burke specifies more of the contradictions which the *Discourses* display:

> In the first Discourse Reynolds recommends an implicit obedience to the rules of art, and adds that the models provided by the great Masters should be considered as perfect and infallible guides. In the third Discourse he states that there are no precise invariable rules, nor are taste and genius to be acquired by rules; and in the fourteenth, that the moment the artist turns other artists into models he falls infinitely below them. In the sixth Discourse, he says that 'by imitation only, are variety and originality of invention' produced. On the other hand, he had already stated, in the third Discourse, that the perfection of art did not consist in 'mere imitation.' [7]

Those writers who do not emphasize outright contradictions in Reynolds' theory usually escape this conclusion only by discovering a progressive development of his thought. Clough, for instance, traces three stages in this development; the *Idler* papers constitute the first, and two of the *Discourses*, "the seventh and the thirteenth, might almost be taken to stand for the whole number, epitomizing as they do his middle and last periods"; the early discourses exhibit Reynolds' "adherence to the standard neo-classical code," but by the time of the thirteenth, "Reynolds makes a tentative advance toward the more popular aesthetic of his time, by referring art to human nature." [8] These hypotheses of self-contradiction and chronological development are obviously devised to account for the reiterated paradoxes which are so prominent a feature of the discourses. In some cases the detection of inconsistencies depends on overlooking or confounding the several stages which Reynolds prescribes for the education of artists. More often such obvious misreading is not involved; rather, the inconsistencies are found by juxtaposing passages without regard to the "level" of their argumentative contexts. The reconciliation of the paradoxes is readily accomplished if allowance is made for the methodological devices which Reynolds consistently employs.

The second persistent theme in recent discussion of Reynolds is his Platonism or Aristotelianism. Fry argues that "it was probably from a passage in Bellori . . . that Reynolds actually derived his main ideas," and that the ultimate source of such Renaissance art theories was Aristotle. [9] Bredvold urges that although "the analysis and formulation of Neo-classical principles for each specific art was generally a form of Aristotelianism," the conception of Ideal Beauty underlying all the arts "is nevertheless a conception which leads beyond Aristotle, and which Reynolds . . . definitely thought of as

Platonic rather than Aristotelian." [10] Macklem, too, finds both an Aristotelian and a Platonic strain in the *Discourses*, the first in the conception of specific forms, the second in the Ideal transcending natural experience.[11] In opposition to the consensus, however, Trowbridge argues that Reynolds "shows a tendency away from Platonism much more prominently than any attraction to it," that "the true philosophical affinity of Reynolds' classicism is not Plato but John Locke," and that Reynolds adapted the traditional Platonic theory of painting to be consistent with an empirical metaphysics and psychology.[12] Though denying the Platonism of Reynolds in regard to his philosophic principles, Trowbridge points out that in *method* Reynolds might justly be dubbed a Platonist. This problem of Reynolds' Platonism, then, like that of his doctrinal consistency, depends for adequate statement and for solution upon study of the method of the *Discourses*, and upon distinguishing problems of method from those of philosophic principle.[13]

The primary and ubiquitous principle of Reynolds' aesthetic system is the contrariety of universal and particular. Whether the discourse is of nature or of art, of invention or imitation, of subject or style, of taste or genius, the analysis proceeds in a dialectic of the one and the many, the changeless and the transient. The distinction of general and particular is the constant analytic device, and universality the invariable criterion of excellence. It is natural, therefore, to see Reynolds as the intellectual descendant of Plato; [14] yet the dialectic of the eighteenth-century critic differs sharply from that of the Grecian philosopher. Plato's system did not encourage the demarcation of an aesthetic realm which could be treated in detail apart from moral, social, and theological considerations; and Plato's reference was ultimately to a reality independent of the mind. Reynolds, *per contra*, despite his analogies between aesthetics, ethics, and science, treats the work of art, its subject, its producer, and its critic in a world of discourse largely divided off from other matters; and the unchanging, the universal, the Nature to which he appeals is contingent upon the faculties and functions of the mind—human nature rather than cosmic nature is the source of his philosophic principles: "The first idea that occurs in the consideration of what is fixed in art, or in taste, is that presiding principle . . . the general idea of nature. . . . My notion of nature comprehends not only the forms which nature produces, but also the nature and internal fabrick and organization, as I may call it, of the human mind and imagination." [15]

This shift in orientation is seen in the treatment of the end of art: "The great end of all the arts is, to make an impression on the imagination and the feeling. The imitation of nature frequently does this. Sometimes it fails, and something else succeeds. I think therefore the true test of all the arts is not solely whether the production is a true copy of nature, but whether it answers the end of art, which is to produce a pleasing effect upon the mind." [16]

The reference of these and other problems to human nature is characteristic of Reynolds' age; the confinement of the scope of the dialectic to the aesthetic world—the artist, his work (subject and style), and the audience which appreciates or judges it—is the characteristic of the system which some critics have taken for a resemblance to Aristotle; for it is this concentration on an aesthetic realm which permits the elaboration of rules fitted to particular arts. Nevertheless, the elements which enter into the discussion (artist, work, and audience) are analogous to the elements of Aristotle's theory of *rhetoric* rather than to those of his analysis of *poetic*; and attributions to Aristotle are valid only if by "Aristotle" we mean the interpretation of Aristotle by Platonizing critics and philosophers. The real Aristotle was not the author of the theory of Ideal Beauty. The passage usually cited to indicate Aristotle's supposed endorsement of this theory is his remark that "poetry is something more philosophic and of graver import than history, since its statements are of the nature of universals, whereas those of history are singulars" (*Poetics* 1451^b 6–8). But Aristotle is discussing the probability or necessity by which a poem has an inner coherence independent of accident, whereas Reynolds, like Plato, is discussing the participation of individuals in transcendent universals. Frances Blanshard argues from this passage that Aristotle (like Reynolds) was trying to answer Plato's attack on art, and that this answer consisted in showing that by imitating the general form of a species art gives knowledge of nature's unrealized ends. Reynolds (we are told) took this up, and used the empiricism of Locke and Hume to explain the generalizing process.[17] But for Aristotle, to consider art as *essentially* supplying knowledge would be a confusion of the poetic and theoretic sciences.

Reynolds does make occasional excursions outside the restricted domain of art. These may be regarded analytically as relics of the original universal dialectic, though historically it might be more accurate to see them as tentative efforts to expand a more rigidly contracted tradition. However this may be, Reynolds frequently stresses the affiliation of aesthetics and ethics, taste and virtue:

> It has been often observed, that the good and virtuous man alone can acquire this true or just relish even of works of art. . . . The same disposition, the same desire to find something steady, substantial, and durable . . . actuates us in both cases. The subject only is changed. We pursue the same method in our search after the idea of beauty and perfection in each; of virtue, by looking forwards beyond ourselves to society, and to the whole; of arts, by extending our views in the same manner to all ages and all times.[18]

And as here taste is analogized to virtue, so it may be identified with the love of truth:

> The natural appetite or taste of the human mind is for TRUTH; whether that truth results from the real agreement or equality of original ideas among themselves; from the agreement of the representation of any object with the thing represented; or from the correspondence of the several parts of any arrangement with each other. It is the very same taste which relishes a demonstration in geometry, that is pleased with the resemblance of a picture to an original, and touched with the harmony of musick.[19]

Thus, the True, the Good, and the Beautiful become, when perfected, equivalent: all are Nature.[20] The theoretic, the practical, and the productive sciences, which Aristotle carefully separated, are here, however tentatively, merged: and these easy analogies are not found among the literal writers of the century, however fond many of them are of paralleling ethics and aesthetics.

Nature and Art are related complexly and paradoxically in the aesthetics of Reynolds, for both "nature" and "art" are analogical terms and have multiple meanings in the system. Of course "art"— as opposed to "nature"—always means something learned or made: the works themselves, their subjects (for the great source of inspiration and often the model of imitation is the art of the past), the techniques of their production, the training of the artist, and the formation of taste in the audience; all are in some sense art. The interrelation of art and nature is discussed in terms of "imitation." [21] Art imitates nature; yet it is equally true that art may imitate art, and that great art transcends imitation. These paradoxes are made possible by, and are resolved by reference to, the contrariety of general and particular. Imitation in the lowest sense is mere copying of particular art works, an "imitating without selecting" in which the "powers of invention and composition . . . lie torpid." [22] It is distinguished both from "borrowing" (incorporation of a thought, action, or figure from another painting, which "is so far from having any thing in it of the servility of plagiarism, that it is a perpetual exercise of the mind, a continual invention" [23]) and from a true and proper imitation of the masters. This higher imitation is a catching of the spirit, a subjection to the same discipline; in a passage often compared to Longinus, Reynolds urges: "Instead of copying the touches of those great masters, copy only their conceptions. Instead of treading in their footsteps, endeavour only to keep the same road. . . . Possess yourself with their spirit. Consider how a Michael Angelo or a Raffaelle would have treated this subject: and work yourself into a belief that your picture is to be seen and criticized by them when completed." [24] Taken in this sense, imitation is "the true and only method by which an artist makes himself master of his profession; which I hold ought to be one continued course of imitation, that is not to cease but with his life." [25] Imitation of *one* master is discouraged, a general and eclectic imitation demanded; yet the artist can enter into a generous contention with the men whom he imitates, and by correcting what is peculiar in each, transcend all. The entire course of study which Reynolds lays out for the student is a course in imitation, first of the object set before him, then of the manner of great workers in the art, then (while imitation of artists is not discontinued) of the abundance of nature itself. This progressive broadening of the object and manner of imitation culminates in the formation of a mind adequate to all times and all occasions.

The last stage of this training directs attention to the imitation of nature rather than of art; and Reynolds can say in one discourse that art is *not* merely imitative of nature without contradicting other pronouncements that it is *essentially* imitative. When imitation is deplored, it is imitation of particular nature; when it is applauded, it is imitation of general nature, either of the ideal specific forms of external nature or of the principles of the mind. All "the arts receive their perfection from an ideal beauty, superior to what is to be found in individual nature." [26] For "a mere copier of nature can never produce any thing great; can never raise and enlarge the conceptions, or warm the heart of the spectator"; all the arts "renounce the narrow idea of nature, and the narrow theories derived from that mistaken principle, and apply to that reason only which informs us not what imitation is,—a natural representation of a given object,—but what it is natural for the imagination to be delighted with." [27]

Indeed, the chief subject of the discourses is "that grand style of painting, which improves partial representation by the general and invariable ideas of nature." [28] This general nature is, consistently with Reynolds' philosophical principles, a conception in the mind of the artist; for although the conception is formed by abstraction from external reality, the ideal itself has only a potential existence prior to its comprehension. Accordingly, the same distinction between copying (on one hand) and invention, recombination, and improvement (on the other) obtains in the imitation of nature as in the imitation of artists: "Upon the whole, it seems to me, that the object and intention of all the Arts is to supply the natural imperfection of things, and often to gratify the mind by realizing and embodying what never existed but in the imagination." [29]

It is noteworthy that in the *Discourses* Reynolds does not advance the peculiarly literal conception of general nature which he expounded in the third of his *Idler* papers.[30] Beauty was there arbitrarily confined to form alone, and was found to be the medium or center of the various forms of a species or kind (that form which is more frequent than any one deviation from it—not necessarily an average); this definition carried as corollaries, that the beauty of an individual could not be judged prior to the collection of statistics on its species, and that there could be no comparison in point of beauty between species. Refutations of Reynolds' theory from the eighteenth century to the present day have more often than not directed their battery against this paper, either directly or by reading the *Discourses* as an expansion of it and criticizing them accordingly. Thus, Sir Uvedale Price, who attempts to account for beauty by a mechanism partly nervous, partly associational, criticizes the *Idler* theory sharply, for beauty to Price does not depend on comparison within a species; Richard Payne Knight, who employs an elaborate faculty psychology in accounting for the several "beauties" of the various faculties, sees Reynolds as confining his notions to the intellectual qualities of things exclusively; and Dugald Stewart, attempting to subsume previous theories with the aid of a theory of philosophical language, finds the Reynolds view narrow and inadequate.[31] The moderns, diverting attention from the systematic interrelations of Reynolds' ideas to their sources, or the sources of the terminology in which they are couched, rarely see Reynolds' thought as more than a *pasticcio*; but Roger Fry at least has deemed the theory of the central form worthy of refutation.[32]

I shall not enter upon the question of the validity of this doctrine; rather, I should like to consider briefly the formal or constitutive question of its appropriateness to Reynolds' system as a whole. I think that, viewed in this light, it is a misstep. The peculiar virtue and merit of a Platonic system of criticism consists in the flexibility or "ambiguity" of its terms, a flexibility which permits their analogical application to a range of subjects and the consequent isolation in those subjects of the universal traits or "ideas" to which the terms refer. If it be asked, how can undefined terms isolate anything? the reply must be, that each such term receives definition in each context by comparison with and opposition to other terms of the system; in each application the meaning of the term emerges from its use in the argument, the "dialectic." If this indeterminacy of terms is a prerequisite for a Platonic system that is not to be dogmatic, it is apparent that Reynolds erred in attempting to tie down so literally the meaning of "beauty" in the *Idler* papers. Ideality is not to be defined or given statistical delimitation.[33]

In the *Discourses,* the first of which was delivered ten years after the *Idler* papers were written, the freedom of the dialectic is unimpaired by dogmatic definition. Yet Reynolds never abandoned outright his early theory. In a letter to Beattie in 1782, commenting on the manuscript of the essay on beauty which Beattie had submitted to him, he observes: "About twenty years since I thought much on this subject, and am now glad to find many of those ideas which then passed in my mind put in such good order by so excellent a metaphysician. My view of the question did not extend beyond my own profession; it regarded only the beauty of form which I attributed entirely to custom or habit. You have taken a larger compass, including, indeed, everything that gives delight, every mental and corporeal excellence. . . ." And blandly (if not plausibly) Reynolds subsumes Beattie's system under his own:

> What you have imputed to convenience and contrivance, I think may without violence be put to the account of habit, as we are more used to that form in nature (and I believe in art, too) which is the *most* convenient. . . . I am aware that this reasoning goes upon a supposition that we are more used to beauty than deformity, and that we are so, I think, I have proved in a little Essay which I wrote about twenty-five years since, and which Dr. Johnson published in his *Idler.* . . .
>
> May not all beauty proceeding from association of ideas be reduced to the principle of habit or experience? You see I am bringing everything into my old principle, but I will now have done, for fear I should throw this letter likewise in the fire [the fate of an earlier and longer reply]. . . .[34]

In the discourses, too, Reynolds speaks of "presenting to the eye the same effect as that which it has been *accustomed* to feel, which in this case, as in every other, will always produce beauty. . . ." [35] But habit is not advanced as the single cause of all beauty, and in the discourses the earlier theory is quietly modified by sloughing off all the literal limitations on the concept of beauty. By so doing, Reynolds made his system one of the permanent alternatives of aesthetic theory.

It is apparent that beauty, treated in the manner of Reynolds, has the energy and grandeur customarily associated with the sublime; and, indeed, it is difficult to see how there could be more than one ideal type of general nature—Reynolds' mode of reasoning automatically obviates the distinction between sublime and beautiful. Yet a distinction so pervasive in the literature of the century is certain to leave its mark; and Reynolds occasionally bifurcates his concept of the beautiful, setting the sublime against the "elegant." [36] These two characters are not co-ordinate; the dichotomy is between a higher beauty, the sublime, and a lower, the elegant. The elegant may be paired with taste and fancy, while the sublime is connected with genius and imagination; alternatively, the elegant may be judged sensual. But the sublime, in any event, sweeps all before it: "The sublime in Painting, as in Poetry, so overpowers, and takes such a possession of the whole mind, that no room is left for attention to minute criticism. The little elegancies of art in the presence of these great ideas thus greatly expressed, lose all their value, and are, for the instant at least, felt to be unworthy of our notice. The correct judgment, the purity of taste, which characterize Raffaelle, the exquisite grace [elegance] of Correggio and Parmegiano, all disappear before them." [37] When Reynolds is treating of art, Raffaelle stands for him "foremost of the first painters," [38] but when attention is directed towards genius and sublimity, then Michael Angelo, though he cannot match Raffaelle in balance and completeness of artistic equipment, is supreme.

There are passages in which Reynolds' sublime and elegant correspond pretty closely in application with Burke's sublime and beautiful. Reynolds draws, for instance, the inescapable contrast between the sublime landscapes of Salvator and the elegant scenes of Claude, between bold projections and gentle slopes, abruptly angular and gradually inclined branches, clouds rolling in volumes and gilded with the setting sun, and so forth. It is significant, however, that this coincidence of doctrine occurs in discussion of landscape, precisely where the difference of the two systems is minimum. In landscape, the sublime is not of higher order than the elegant; both Claude and Salvator are painters of the first rank, and the distinction between their styles is literal and descriptive. But in human subjects, the sublime springs from and appeals to higher faculties. The tastes of Burke and Reynolds, to be sure, are less different than their fashions of accounting for their tastes; but the difference in their accounts is radical. Burke's literal distinction of beauty and sublimity is often dissolved by Reynolds, and when not abandoned it is so transformed in content and established on so different a foundation that only in isolated contexts does any considerable resemblance appear. Burke's famous distinction had become a verbal commonplace for succeeding aestheticians, to no two of whom did it convey the same meaning.

Although Reynolds refers to Burke as a truly philosophical aesthetician, and although Burke is the only writer so praised, his influence on Reynolds' thought was slight.[39] Even the essay on taste prefixed to the second edition of the *Sublime and Beautiful* (to which Thompson and Bryant assign some weight in determining Reynolds' opinions) has no clear relation to the theory of Reynolds.[40] For Burke, taste is "that faculty or those faculties of the mind which are affected with, or which form a judgment of, the works of imagination and the elegant arts," whereas for Reynolds taste is "that faculty of the mind by which we like or dislike, whatever be the subject," a faculty which judges in the productive, practical, and theoretical sciences alike.[41] In the system of Burke, the aesthetic excellences rest upon very different foundations from the moral virtues, but throughout the system of Reynolds there runs a recurrent analogy between beauty and virtue, and another between beauty and truth. Burke, in short, operates within a scheme of separate sciences and is in search of closely literal definitions of the aesthetic qualities he treats (even though those qualities pervade both nature and art), while Reynolds tends always to analogize the sciences and to "define" analogically and dialectically. The occasional verbal and doctrinal resemblances, then, are only isolated points of community in systems which are radically and fundamentally distinct.[42]

The criterion of taste for Reynolds is of course generality. Not only should the audience whose taste is appealed to *be* universal (always and everywhere), but it should appeal to general principles in judging works and their producers. Nature (true art) is distinguished from fashion (false art) by the test of enduring and universal fame. Great works, therefore, "speak to the general sense of the whole species; in which common . . . tongue, every thing grand and comprehensive must be uttered." [43] Yet at the same time, the artist may envisage an elect few—his great predecessors—as his audience; and this is not a contradiction, for *these* are the few who have sloughed off fashion and rejected particularity—they are not men, but Man. Indeed, the appeal is never to the untutored taste of the multitude (which will always exhibit local and temporary particularity) but always to the taste the natural potentialities of which have been cultivated by art. For criticism both *is* an art and is developed through art, requiring for its cultivation the enthusiasm inspired by works of genius: "It must be remembered," says Reynolds, "that this great style itself is artificial in the highest degree, it presupposes in the spectator a cultivated and prepared artificial state of mind. It is an absurdity, therefore, to suppose that we are born with this taste, though we are with the seeds of it, which, by the heat and kindly influence of . . . genius, may be ripened in us." [44] There is a hierarchy of criticisms as there is a hierarchy of imitations, each stage more inclusive than the preceding: comparison of works and masters within an art (which first test "must have two capital defects; it must be narrow, and it must be uncertain" [45]); comparison of arts and their principles with one another; and comparison of all such principles "with those of human nature, from whence arts derive the materials upon which they are to produce their effects," which style is at once the highest and the soundest, "for it refers to the eternal and immutable nature of things." [46]

Taste so conceived is no different from genius, save that to genius there supervenes a power of execution. Indeed, all the elements of the system—artist, audience, style, and subject—are merged when in their perfected state: "The *gusto grande* of the Italians, the *beau ideal* of the French, and the *great style, genius,* and *taste* among the English, are but different appellations of the same thing." [47] Genius, then, is only the imaginative power of apprehending general nature; but it is related to the universal in another sense as well, since it involves a collective effort, each artist being inspired by his own predecessors. Many of the Longinian passages in the discourses center about this last theme: "Whoever has so far formed his taste, as to be able to relish and feel the beauties of the great masters, has gone a great way in his study," Reynolds declares, "for, merely from a consciousness of this relish of the right, the mind swells with an inward pride, and is almost as powerfully affected, as if it had itself produced what it admires"; [48] I need not quote the eulogy of Michael Angelo with which the discourses conclude. Even the "genius of mechanical performance," the painter's genius *qua* painter, participates in generality: it consists in "the power of expressing that which employs your pencil . . . *as a whole*," [49] contracting into one whole what nature has made multifarious by working up all parts of the picture together instead of finishing part by part.

The paradox that genius is the product of art is the chief purport of the discourses: "The purport of this discourse, and, indeed, of most of my other discourses, is, to caution you against that false opinion . . . of the imaginary powers of native genius, and its sufficiency in great works." [50] Because of the identifications already remarked upon, the purpose of the discourses can also, of course, be stated in terms of taste ("My purpose in the discourses . . . has been to lay down certain general positions, which seem to me proper for the formation of sound taste" [51]) or in terms of the art itself (it became necessary, in order to reconcile conflicting precepts, "to distinguish the greater truth . . . from the lesser truth; the larger and more liberal idea of nature from the more narrow and confined; that which addresses itself to the imagination, from that which is solely addressed to the eye. . . . [The] different rules and regulations which presided over each department of art, followed of course . . ." [52]). Keeping, however, to the aspect of the discourses which centers upon genius—it was certainly not Reynolds' view that natural powers have no efficacy, or that an Academy can make a Michael Angelo of any daubing student; a "man can bring home wares only in proportion to the capital with which he goes to market." [53] But natural powers are only a potentiality, and as a professor addressing students, or (more widely) as an aesthetician addressing artists and critics with the view of forming taste and directing practice, Reynolds deals with what is within human powers to alter, not with what is given by nature; the question is, how to realize natural endowment and how to direct its efforts. Thus the relation of genius to rules can be stated variously: the opposition of genius to the narrow rules of any rigid intellectual system is a conventional topic; nonetheless, Reynolds urges, "what we now call Genius, begins, not where rules, abstractedly taken, end; but where known vulgar and trite rules have no longer any place. It must of necessity be, that even works of Genius, like every other effect, as they must have their cause, must likewise have their rules. . . ." [54] These rules depend on the imagination and passions. The active principle of the mind demands variety, novelty, contrast; the pas-

sive, uniformity, custom, repose; and perfection lies in a mean. This
is all obvious; noticeable is the slightness of the *axiomata media*
under the guidance of which the universal qualities are found or
embodied in particular works. But it is generally true of Platonic
systems of criticism that instead of "rules" governing the relations
of parts in a whole directed towards a specific end, "touchstones"
are supplied which facilitate the recognition of the universal virtues
in their concrete manifestations. So while Reynolds occasionally
vouchsafes a rule (as that the masses of light in a picture be always
of a warm, mellow color), these rules are few and slender, and the
emphasis is on a complicated balancing of artists who embody the
various aesthetic virtues and defects.

All the problems of genius, of taste, and of art, then, are given
their peculiar form in Reynolds' aesthetics by the dialectical method
and psychological orientation of the system. Since the root is not a
supernal nature but a terrestrial, the ideal universe being a product
of imagination, the faculties of the mind play a crucial role. But
Reynolds' view of the faculties is neither original nor complex; sense
perceives, fancy combines, reason distinguishes. Appropriately, since
imagination is the combining and generalizing power, the arts depend
upon it for their higher qualities, and upon sense only by a condescension to the necessities of human nature. Such condescension is inevitable, however, and art strives to give each faculty gratification:
"Our taste has a kind of sensuality about it, as well as a love of the
sublime; both these qualities of the mind are to have their proper
consequence, as far as they do not counteract each other; for that is
the grand error which much care ought to be taken to avoid." [55] In the
same way, opinion as well as truth must be regarded by the artist,
and its authority is proportioned to the universality of the prejudice;
"whilst these opinions and prejudices . . . continue, they operate as
truth; and the art, whose office it is to please the mind, as well as in-
struct it, must direct itself according to opinion, or it will not attain
its end." [56] Such concessions, however guarded, mark the difference
of this system from that of Plato, for whom the highest art of
Reynolds would be second-best; for Plato, true art is dialectic,
whereas for Reynolds, such an identification is prevented by the laws
of the mind. Reason (as discriminating faculty) plays its role not in
dictating the subjects of art but in assisting the artist to "consider and
separate those different principles to which different modes of beauty
owe their original . . . to discriminate perfections that are incompatible with each other." [57] Reason and taste may be identified with

one another in some contexts, but when reason is "grounded on a partial view of things," in contrast with the habitual sagacity of imagination, it must give way—in art, imagination is "the residence of truth." [58]

The distinction of levels of argument is often accompanied by the bifurcation of concepts and the identification of the concepts on the higher level. This tendency is in Reynolds sometimes imperfectly realized or difficult to trace. Imagination and fancy, for instance, are not consistently or radically distinguished by him; in only one passage are they explicitly contrasted: "Raffaelle had more Taste and Fancy; Michael Angelo more Genius and Imagination. The one excelled in beauty, the other in energy. . . . Michael Angelo's works . . . seem to proceed from his own mind entirely. . . . Raffaelle's materials are generally borrowed, though the noble structure is his own." [59] The couplings here suggest a difference of degree, imagination rearranging more freely and powerfully. Fancy is sometimes "capricious" and connected with the picturesque.[60] But although the distinction made familiar by Coleridge is here sought in vain, there is an obvious differentiation of artistic powers paralleling the contrast of the arbitrary, fashionable, and ornamental with the natural, simple, and beautiful. The distinction of sublime from elegant, and the identification of taste, genius, and style on the higher level, have been enough insisted upon.

Reynolds' elaborate hierarchy of styles and species is made possible by the differentiation of mental powers and aesthetic characters which has been outlined. One set of distinctions depends upon dignity of subject: history, genre, landscape, portraiture, animal painting, still-life, and so on—many of which classes are themselves susceptible of subdivision. Cutting across this hierarchy of genres is the contrast of a higher and a lower manner. In history, for instance, the grand style of Rome and Florence is set against the ornamental style of Venice and Flanders; and in the lower genres of the art, there is "the same distinction of a higher and a lower style; and they take their rank and degree in proportion as the artist departs more, or less, from common nature, and makes it an object of his attention to strike the imagination of the spectator by ways belonging specially to art. . . ." [61] Arts employing different means from painting are handled similarly in terms of object and manner, although some media may render the lower manner intolerable: sculpture (which Reynolds instances at length) must design in simplicity proportioned to the simplicity of its materials. Even the "non-imitative" arts of architecture and music exhibit parallel distinctions, with the higher quality related to the imagination by association rather than imitation, and the lower connected with utility and sense. The argument is always flexible, however; excellence in a lower style is preferred to mediocrity in a higher (a principle which Reynolds illustrates in the critique of Gainsborough), and it is erroneous to introduce the grand manner into a lower rank to which a different mode of achieving a qualified generality is appropriate. In portraiture, for instance, universality is achieved not by idealizing beyond recognition but by catching the likeness "as a whole." Still another dimension is introduced in discussion of the "characteristical" style, peculiar to the cast of mind of an individual painter; while such peculiarity is not referable to a true archetype in nature, and is not a proper object of imitation, it has its proper excellence in consistency and unity, "as if the whole proceeded from one mind." [62]

But Reynolds' attention returns always to the grand style, the keystone of the arch. The grand style is universal in cause and in effect, in subject and in style; it is beautiful by abstracting from the particular forms of nature, simple by rejecting the influence of fashion. Although grandeur requires simplicity—which is truth—it is still contrary to truth, when truth is particular and historical.[63] The grand style concerns itself rather with "that ideal excellence which it is the lot of genius always to contemplate, and never to attain." [64]

CHAPTER 10

Thomas Reid

THOMAS REID was the dean of that group of Scots whose thought has come to be known as "the Scottish philosophy," a philosophy devised to combat what its propagators took to be the pernicious skepticism of Berkeley and (more especially) Hume. James Beattie, James Oswald, George Campbell, and Dugald Stewart were among the leading figures of the group. Gerard, Lord Kames, and Alison, moreover, were all associated with Reid; Kames, indeed, anticipated (in print) many of Reid's teachings.[1]

Reid had expounded his thought in lectures at King's College, Aberdeen, and later as Professor of Moral Philosophy at Glasgow, for thirty years before he published his major work, the *Essays on the Intellectual Powers of Man* (Edinburgh, 1785), the only work of Reid which touches upon the phenomena of aesthetics.[2] The eighth and last of the essays, "Of Taste," is Reid's only contribution to aesthetic theory. Upon this brief statement, however, a considerable (and as I think, undeserved) reputation is grounded. Monk declares that Reid's was the "first attempt to use the sublime as an integral factor of a philosophical system" (a goal at last achieved by Kant),[3] and Robbins maintains that "Reid's aesthetics is the most philosophical and least amateurish of the whole English eighteenth-century speculation. In this way, as in other ways, it may be compared favorably to contemporary German aesthetics."[4] The paucity of comment on Reid's aesthetics, however, in contrast with the numerous discussions of his metaphysics and ethics, suggests some doubt that Reid can be either profound or original. Indeed, the conclusion appears to me inescapable, that Reid cared nothing for aesthetics *per se,* and added the brief and perfunctory essay on taste to his *Intellectual Powers* only for the sake of systematically drawing all psychology under his favorite principles.

In the first chapter of the essay, "Of Taste in General," Reid pursues an extended analogy between taste the external sense and taste the internal sense; a discrimination of the differences from the resemblances of the two faculties permits a description of taste adequate for Reid's rather limited purposes. The initial "definition" of the internal sense is conventional: "That power of the mind by which we are capable of discerning and relishing the beauties of Nature, and whatever is excellent in the fine arts, is called *taste*." [5] The analysis of this faculty is conducted in the terms characteristic of the Scottish school: the sensations of taste are distinguished intuitively from the real qualities of which they are the signs. "In the external sense of taste," Reid notes, "we are led by reason and reflection to distinguish between the agreeable sensation we feel, and the quality in the object which occasions it." [6] And in precisely the same way, "when a beautiful object is before us, we may distinguish the agreeable emotion it produces in us, from the quality of the object which causes that emotion." [7] This is commonplace and unexceptionable: the only novelty is that Reid should announce such doctrine as if it *were* novelty. Reid complains of the "fashion among modern philosophers, to resolve all our perceptions into mere feelings or sensations in the person that perceives, without anything corresponding to those feelings in the external object . . . [so that] there is no beauty in any object whatsoever; it is only a sensation or feeling in the person that perceives it." [8] But this is an opinion which no one ever held—the "modern philosophers" (Descartes, Locke, Berkeley, Hume) make just the analysis which Reid performs, finding sensations or feelings in the mind and the causes of these in objects. Sir William Hamilton very justly points out that the position which Reid struggles to refute on secondary qualities is a fiction: "There is thus no difference between Reid and the Cartesians," Hamilton concludes, "except that the doctrine which he censures is in fact more precise and explicit than his own." [9]

Further analogy between external and internal taste is found in the diversity of the sensations in each of these faculties; in the influence of custom, fancy, and casual associations on both; and in the subordination of the determinations of each to a standard. Indeed, the establishment of a standard of taste is implicit in the distinction already drawn between sensation and real quality: "Every excellence has a real beauty and charm that makes it an agreeable object to those who have the faculty of discerning its beauty; and this faculty is what we call a good taste." [10] To be sure, there remains the chief question, how we are to ascertain these objective excellences? But this much is gained, that disputes in taste are put on the same footing as disputes in questions of truth; every affirmation or denial of beauty expresses judgment. Reid very evidently considers that by introducing judgment into the decisions of taste, he is overturning the "modern philosophy": "If it be said that the perception of beauty is merely a feeling in the mind that perceives, without any belief of excellence in the object," he cries, "the necessary consequences of this opinion is, that when I say Virgil's 'Georgics' is a beautiful poem, I mean not to say anything of the poem, but only something concerning myself and my feelings. Why should I use a language that expresses the contrary of what I mean?" [11] Consistently with his intuitional system, Reid perpetually argues in this fashion from the forms of language: he even asserts that "no instance will be found of a distinction made in all languages, which has not a just foundation in nature." [12] This device really results, however, not in the more ready solution of problems, but in the shifting of argument from the things themselves to the implications of the idioms of speech about them.

The internal taste differs from the external in this: that though some of the beauties it perceives are indescribable and occult, unknown causes of the effects we feel (and thus resembling the secondary qualities perceived by external taste), other beauties are explicable, and like primary qualities of matter can be isolated as causes of our aesthetic feelings. The internal sense differs, moreover, from all the external senses in that it is a reflex sense, depending on antecedent perception of the nature of the object: one may hear the ringing of a bell (Reid illustrates) with no other perception of the bell, but it is impossible to perceive beauty unless the object is already perceived by some other faculty—the ear must hear the bell before taste can appreciate the beauty of its sound.

So much for taste. The objects of it "Mr. Addison, and Dr. Akenside after him, have reduced . . . to three—to wit, *novelty, grandeur,* and *beauty.* This division is sufficient for all I intend to say upon the subject, and therefore I shall adopt it—observing only, that beauty is often taken in so extensive a sense as to comprehend all the objects of taste; yet all the authors I have met with, who have given a division of the objects of taste, make beauty one species." [13] It is curious that Reid should retain this antique and exploded classification, for he observes at once that "novelty is not properly a quality of the thing to which we attribute it, far less is it a sensation in the mind to which it is new; it is a relation which the thing has to the knowledge of the person." [14] Reid lays no claim to originality in his observations on novelty, and his treatment, including reference to final cause, is conventional.

The emotion raised by grand objects, Reid finds, is "awful, solemn, and serious"; the highest form of it is devotion, "a serious recollected temper, which inspires magnanimity, and disposes to the most heroic acts of virtue." This feeling is raised in us by perception of "such a degree of excellence, in one kind or another, as merits our admiration." [15] "Admiration," it will be recalled, was one of the inferior degrees of Burke's terrific sublime; Reid's piety and his realism alike preclude his accepting terror as the basis of the grand. Dread and admiration are alike grave and solemn, but differ in that "admiration supposes some uncommon excellence in its object, which dread does not." [16] Such excellence is found above all in Deity, then in human virtue, then in matter considered as in some wise the effect or sign or analogue of mind; but though a key concept in the system, "excellence" remains undefined and unexamined. Reid pauses to argue against the "spirit of modern philosophy," which would lead us to suppose value only in our minds and not inherent in objects; but the argument consists only in an appeal to the judgment of mankind as "expressed in the language of all nations, which uniformly ascribes excellence, grandeur, and beauty to the object, and not to the mind that perceives it," [17] together with the rhetorical question, can we conceive of a constitution of human nature which would prefer (what we now consider) inferiority to excellence? As so often, Reid is involved in an *ignoratio elenchi:* the "modern philosophers" were engaged in the inquiry, *why* do we value certain qualities? Reid answers, "Because they really *are* excellent," a reply which begs the question proposed. If asked to account for our awareness of this excellence, Reid retires behind an intuition and declines the challenge.

The most striking feature of Reid's aesthetics, however, is not this simple objectivism which bypasses the most intricate and important questions, but his denial that matter itself can have aesthetic value:

> When we consider matter as an inert, extended, divisible, and movable substance, there seems to be nothing in these qualities which we can call grand; and when we ascribe grandeur to any portion of matter, however modified, may it not borrow this quality from something intellectual, of which it is the effect, or sign, or instrument, or to which it bears some analogy? or, perhaps, because it produces in the mind an emotion that has some resemblance to that admiration which truly grand objects raise? [18]

This doctrine follows, perhaps, from the notion of excellence as the essence of grandeur, since it is difficult to see what "excellent" would mean as applied to matter as such. And it is this position which was to be adopted by Alison—but adopted into a different systematic context and justified by elaborate inductions. For Reid, too, this is a derivative, not a primary truth; matter is connected with mind through the relations of cause and effect, sign and significatum, agent and instrument. And matter may exhibit a similitude or analogy to acts and affections of mind; there is such an analogy "between greatness of dimension, which is an object of external sense, and that grandeur which is an object of taste. On account of this analogy, the last borrows its name from the first; and, the name being common, leads us to conceive that there is something common in the nature of the things." [19] Robbins objects that Reid's denial of the beauty and grandeur of matter is in contradiction with his criterion of linguistic usage, since men clearly speak of beauty and grandeur as if they pertained to matter.[20] Reid accounts adequately, however, for our habit of transferring these qualities from one relative to the other; we know mind (our own excepted) only as expressed in matter, and very naturally transfer to one what truly belongs to the other. But Reid does not explain in any detail this associative process; it is by giving detailed expositions of these phenomena, grounded on careful inductions, that Alison converts this doctrine from a dogma to a philosophical theory.

It should be noted that Reid preserves a distinction between grandeur and sublimity—not that which Lord Kames had maintained, but rather a differentiation which preserves the Longinian "sublime" as a character of discourse: "What we call sublime in description, or in speech of any kind, is a proper expression of the admiration and enthusiasm which the subject produces in the mind of the speaker." [21] Like the other aestheticians of his century, Reid subordinates art to nature and finds the true sublime to rise from grandeur in the subject and a corresponding emotion in the speaker: "A proper exhibition of these, though it should be artless, is irresistible, like fire thrown into the midst of combustible matter." [22] The sublimity of the *Iliad* is, then, the expression of the grandeur of the mind of Homer, or that of the persons of the action. "Upon the whole," Reid concludes with unction, "I humbly apprehend that true grandeur is such a degree of excellence as is fit to raise an enthusiastical admiration; that this grandeur is found, originally and properly, in qualities of mind; that it is discerned, in objects of sense, only by reflection, as the light we perceive in the moon and planets is truly the light of the sun; and that those who look for grandeur in mere mat-ter, seek the living among the dead." [23]

Reid treats of beauty in the same terms as of grandeur: feeling and judgment, subjective response and objective excellence. What is found common to the beauty of objects of sense, of speech and thought, of arts and sciences, of actions, affections, and characters, is no identity or similarity of quality, but two circumstances common to our responses to these various beauties: "*First,* When they are per-ceived, or even imagined, they produce a certain agreeable emotion or feeling in the mind; and, *secondly,* This agreeable emotion is ac-companied with an opinion or belief of their having some perfection or excellence belonging to them." [24] The term "beauty" is sometimes so extended as to comprise all objects of taste, including novelty and grandeur, sometimes so restricted as to be confined to objects of sight. To ascertain the meaning, Reid had adopted the trichotomy of nov-elty, grandeur, and beauty; novelty being excluded as a mere rela-tion and no objective quality, it becomes clear that "every quality in an object that pleases a good taste, must, in one degree or another, have either grandeur or beauty. It may still be difficult to fix the pre-cise limit betwixt grandeur and beauty; but they must together com-prehend everything fitted by its nature to please a good taste—that is, every real perfection and excellence in the objects we contemplate." [25] The emotions excited differentiate the two characters, for the object of admiration is grand, that of love and esteem beautiful. More fully, "the emotion produced by beautiful objects is gay and pleasant. It sweetens and humanises the temper, is friendly to every benevolent affection, and tends to allay sullen and angry passions. It enlivens the mind, and disposes it to other agreeable emotions, such as those of love, hope, and joy. It gives a value to the object, abstracted from its utility." [26] As the feeling is in the mind, so is the judgment a judg-ment of excellence in the object. Like all judgments, this must be true or false; when the judgments of men concur, we may conclude (Reid assures us) that there really is an objective excellence.

Our sense of beauty is partly instinctive, partly rational. In some instances (Reid mentions the colors and forms of flowers) we per-ceive an occult beauty or excellence the causes of which in the object we cannot analyze; in others (as in a well-contrived machine) we can give reasons for our judgment and point to the perfections which please. Beauty itself may be original or derived, and if "the distinc-tion between the grandeur which we ascribe to qualities of mind, and that which we ascribe to material objects, be well founded, this distinction of the beauty of objects will easily be admitted as perfectly analogous to it." [27] *Derived* beauties depend upon transference between sign and significatum, cause and effect, end and means, agent and instrument, and upon inexplicable similitude. *Original* beauty is sought in those qualities of mind which are the natural objects of love, "the whole train of the soft and gentle virtues." [28] Intellectual talents like sense, wit, cheerfulness, taste; and bodily talents like health, strength, and agility have also an original beauty, though the bodily talents (we are told) are perfections because they render the body a fit instrument for the mind. (It is a question, why the physical talents, being thus instrumental to the mind, are not derived rather than original beauties.) Reid does not stress the grandeur of talents, though he does mention cursorily that "we admire great talents and heroic virtue"; [29] intellectual power and physical strength both seem more admirable than lovely.

Reid attributes his opinion that beauty originally dwells only in the moral and intellectual perfections of mind, and in its active powers, and that these are the sources of all the beauty of the visible world, to the "ancient philosophers," and—among the moderns—to Shaftesbury and Akenside. I doubt, however, that any of these authors, classical or modern, would subscribe to the opinion as Reid has developed it; his originality is greater than he claimed in his published works. In an oft-quoted letter to Archibald Alison, however, acknowledging Alison's complimentary copies of the *Essays on the Nature and Principles of Taste,* he states that Plato, Shaftesbury, and Akenside "handle the subject of beauty rather with the enthusiasm of poets or lovers, than with the cool temper of philosophers," and that Hutcheson and Spence (to all whom Alison had attributed the doctrine) do not really seem to subscribe to a view like his own. "On these grounds," he continues, "I am proud to think that I first, in clear and explicit terms, and in the cool blood of a philosopher, maintained that all the beauty and sublimity of objects of sense is derived from the expression they exhibit of things intellectual, which alone have original beauty. But in this I may deceive myself, and cannot claim to be held an impartial judge." [30] This doctrine, though but slightly developed by Reid himself, remains his major contribution to aesthetic theory.

Minds other than our own are perceived only through their signatures impressed on visible objects, and the chief expressions of mind are in fitness and design, save where (as in the human person) there can be a direct expression of moral excellence; in every form, matter "derives its beauty from the purposes to which it is subservient, or from the signs of wisdom or of other mental qualities which it exhibits." [31] In general, Reid slights the beauties of expression of emotion and character except where such expression is patent (as in the countenance); his analysis, dwelling upon fitness and design, is more that of a natural theologian than that of an aesthetician. He thinks of the botanist as the proper critic of floral beauties—and surely the soul of an artist would wither in tracing the "thousand beautiful contrivances of Nature [in plants], which feast his understanding more than their external form delighted his eye." [32] There are, in consequence, no devices for comparing in point of beauty different specific forms, equally fit for equally noble ends. Is an ostrich as beautiful as a bird of paradise? If Reid is to deny that it is, he must have recourse to the inexplicable and occult beauty which is apprehended instinctively—and occult causes are not satisfying as explanations. What is lacking in Reid is an aesthetic of form and color, such as that which Alison was to devise without abandoning Reid's principle that matter has no inherent beauty.

What Reid does say on the derived beauty of sound, color, form, and motion, is occasionally fanciful, as in the remarkable argument that the terms "concord" and "discord" are literally applicable to conversation and only analogically to music. There is a partial truth in this view etymologically; but it is unrealistic to appeal to etymology, for in actual usage men apply "concord" and "discord" literally to music and figuratively to social interchange—the evidence of language is against Reid. Reid even appears to say, that the voices of persons engaged in amicable conversation are *acoustically* harmonious; this is truly "forcing all nature to submit." The admonition which Dugald Stewart directed to Horne Tooke is perhaps applicable to Reid as well: "to appeal to etymology in a philosophical argument (excepting, perhaps, in those cases where the word itself is of philosophical origin,) is altogether nugatory, and can serve, at the best, to throw an amusing light on the laws which regulate the operations of human fancy." [33] In the case of concord, Reid is led to ignore the mechanical pleasure of harmony in favor of a subtle analogy from which (I think) little or no pleasure proceeds.

Reid draws his rubrics for treatment of human beauty from Spence's *Crito*—color, form, expression, and grace—pointing out, of course, that all are ultimately expression. The slenderness of this system is apparent when Reid tells us that (casual associations aside) the beauty of coloring depends solely on the expression of health and liveliness, and in the fair sex softness and delicacy, or that beauty of form is expression of strength or agility in the male, delicacy and softness in the female. Even the beauty of expression proper shares this simplism—indications of meekness, gentleness, benignity are beauties, &c. And grace, the "last and noblest part of beauty," consists in those motions, either of the whole body, or of a part or feature, which express "the most perfect propriety of conduct and sentiment in an amiable character." [34]

Grandeur and beauty, though between them they exhaust the realm of taste, are nonetheless not exclusive. In some instances the very qualities which are beautiful in ordinary degree become grand in extraordinary. It is this circumstance, perhaps, which accounts for the sketchy treatment of grandeur. Inadequate as is Reid's aesthetic of beauty, it is at any rate more comprehensive and detailed than the aesthetic of grandeur, which provides no discussion of the grandeur of the material world. Reid is content to make his point that material grandeur is a reflection of mental; with this principle in hand, he is able to approach the more extensive quality, beauty, in its principal manifestations. The content of a Reidian analysis of grandeur must be arrived at by extrapolation.

Actually, Reid seems to have been little interested in aesthetics, apart from the desire methodically to fill out his system, and to have had slight aesthetic sensibility. His thought, perplexed with intuitions, unanalyzed principles, implausible reductions, and gaping lacunae, would be of minor importance had it not provided a principle which Alison was shortly to put to such effective use in a very different system.

CHAPTER 11

Archibald Alison

٭

THE REVEREND Archibald Alison's *Essays on the Nature
and Principles of Taste* appeared at Edinburgh in 1790. This
first edition of a book which was to revolutionize aesthetic speculation in Britain, and which exhibited an originality, complexity, and
logical coherence unmatched in British aesthetics, was little heeded.
A review, to be sure, appeared in the *Monthly;*[1] but when Payne
Knight mentioned Alison slightly and slightingly in his *Analytical
Inquiry* of 1804, the reference must have puzzled many a reader.
Price had written his *Essay on the Picturesque* and its sequels without
alluding to Alison; Repton and the anonymous author of *Essays on
the Sources of the Pleasures Received from Literary Compositions*
(1809) do not mention him. The philosophers Reid and Stewart
knew and esteemed Alison and his treatise. Reid's works were all in
print by 1790, but he wrote a letter of considerable interest on receiving complimentary copies of Alison's *Essays;*[2] Stewart refers with
approbation to the *Essays* in the first volume of his *Elements of the
Philosophy of the Human Mind* (1792), and in the *Philosophical
Essays* of 1810 enters upon the only serious discussion of Alison to
appear before the second edition of the *Essays.*[3] Burns wrote enthusi-
astically to Alison on reading a gift copy of the treatise.[4] But this is
all; the *Essays on Taste* had pretty well gone under when the second
and enlarged edition was published in 1811. This edition met with a
far different reception. Favored by the proselytizing efforts of Jeffrey,
who played Huxley to Alison's Darwin, the theory of associationism
came to be widely accepted as the new gospel.[5] Editions appeared
in quick succession in 1812, 1815, 1817, 1825, and 1842; this last
and those thereafter reprint Jeffrey's critique as a prolegomenon to
Alison's treatise. Brown's fifty-sixth lecture (printed in the *Lectures*
of 1820) treats of Alison's theory; and other references to it in philo-

sophic and aesthetic literature, especially among the Scottish school, become frequent. It is symptomatic of the change, that when Sir Thomas Dick Lauder edited *Sir Uvedale Price on the Picturesque* in 1842, he did so partly with the idea of supplying the proper associational underpinnings for Price's theories, his introductory "Essay on the Origin of Taste" being a version of Jeffrey's version of Alison. Bosanquet has condescended to notice the importance of Alison as an influence, though he sees the influence as pernicious (arguing that "the real problem, viz., what is accidental in association and what is not," was untouched by the associational writers).[6] The importance of Alison's work to the theory and practice of the romantic period has never been assessed, but is beyond the scope of this study, and I turn to examination of the system itself.

Alison's purpose is essentially speculative rather than practical. His concern is with aesthetics as a branch of psychology and metaphysics rather than as a science directed towards establishing rules for practice. His investigations of course do have practical implications: "They have an immediate relation to all the Arts that are directed to the production either of the Beautiful or the Sublime; and they afford the only means by which the principles of these various arts can be ascertained."[7] But only on occasion, and never at length, does Alison draw out the critical rules which depend from the aesthetic.

"Taste is, in general, considered as that Faculty of the Human Mind, by which we perceive and enjoy whatever is Beautiful or Sublime in the works of Nature or Art."[8] This, the opening sentence of the treatise, suggests the three inquiries which the total investigation would include: certain *properties of things* produce certain *states of mind* through the medium of a certain *faculty*. This is a causal analysis: the emotions of taste are the effect, and the problem is to determine through what mediating links the properties of natural and artificial objects are efficient in producing these emotions. This is, of course, the traditional method of British aesthetics; the novelty in Alison's theory is in the causes discovered. There are, then, three inquiries for Alison. First (1) comes ascertainment of the effects to be accounted for. Accepting as he does most of the traditional vocabulary, Alison naturally sees this inquiry as an analysis of the emotions of beauty and sublimity. Involved by implication is another and subordinate investigation (1A) into the origin of the beauty and sublimity of the qualities of matter. "To this subordinate Inquiry I shall devote a separate Essay," Alison writes, an essay designed to "shew that all the Phenomena are reducible to the same general Principle, and that the Qualities of Matter are not beautiful or sublime in themselves, but as they are . . . the Signs or Expressions of Qualities capable of producing Emotion." [9] The main inquiry into our emotions of taste will uncover a certain mechanism of association; this subordinate inquiry will show that certain types of ideas are always involved in the association. It must be granted that it presses rather hard upon the second inquiry, which is (II) to "investigate the NATURE of those QUALITIES that produce the Emotions of TASTE" [10]—to determine, that is, the sources of the beautiful and sublime in nature and art. This investigation will show that any simple emotion, together with the appropriate activity of the imagination, may give rise to emotions of taste, and will determine "what is that LAW of MIND, according to which, in actual life, this exercise or employment of imagination is excited; and what are the means by which, in the different Fine Arts, the artist is able to awaken this important exercise of imagination, and to exalt objects of simple and common pleasure, into objects of Beauty or Sublimity." [11] Subjoined to this inquiry are two other investigations, into (IIA) that familiar problem, how painful subjects can be beautiful, whether in nature or in art, and into (IIB) the distinction, both in the emotions and in their causes, of the sublime from the beautiful. The third principal inquiry (III) is "to investigate the NATURE of that FACULTY, by which these Emotions [of Taste] are received." [12] And subordinate to this discussion is treatment (IIIA) of another familiar crux for the empirical aestheticians—the standard of taste. Finally, Alison (who was, after all, a divine) proposed to illustrate (IIIB) the final cause of this constitution of our nature.

The *Essays* as written correspond, strictly speaking, to inquiries I and IA. The discussion of IA, however (as I have suggested above), involves much of the material which would be employed for II, and affords pretty good hints for IIB. The treatment of I, in the same fashion, affords some insight into Alison's views on III; and the coda to the final chapter of the second essay is really IIIB. This leaves us lacking only the discussion of the two cruxes—the pleasing effect of painful subjects and the standard of taste. I do not think it difficult to conjecture at the approach which Alison would have used in treating these two problems. Indeed, for Alison to have followed out his plan in full would have necessitated intolerable repetition of argument and illustration. We may regard the existing *Essays* as constituting the basis and outline of the entire system. The system is developed by specifying as closely as possible the two variables in an associationist theory—the component ideas and impressions, and the relations which connect them. It is not necessary to recapitulate in full the content of the analysis; this exposition will be accomplished incidentally in investigation of the logic by which Alison establishes his hypothesis.

The first of the two essays is intended to separate the emotions of taste from their accidental concomitants and to resolve them into their several components. Previous aestheticians, as Alison saw it, had fallen into one or other of two errors: either (as with artists and amateurs, who attend more to the causes of their emotions than to the emotions themselves) they traced the emotions of taste directly to original laws of our nature, supposing a sense or senses appropriated to the perception of beauty and sublimity; or (as with introspective philosophers) they resolved the phenomena of taste into some more general law of our mental constitution. But both approaches have been based on the delusive notion that the emotions of taste are qualitatively simple; the first stage of Alison's analysis is designed to show that they are complex.[13]

The conclusion of the first essay is that the emotions of taste are felt "WHEN THE IMAGINATION IS EMPLOYED IN THE PROSECUTION OF A REGULAR TRAIN OF IDEAS OF EMOTION."[14] I shall examine in detail the reasoning which leads to this summary proposition, for in it we find for the first time in aesthetic theory an adequate inductive argument.

The first major division of that argument (the first chapter) is designed to prove that the effect produced on the mind by objects of beauty and sublimity consists in evocation of an associating activity of the imagination. Alison's own words suggest the three evidences for this judgment: "that whenever the emotions of Sublimity or Beauty are felt, that exercise of Imagination is produced, which consists in the indulgence of a train of thought; that when this exercise is prevented, these emotions are unfelt or unperceived; and that whatever tends to increase this exercise of mind, tends in the same proportion to increase these emotions."[15] The first of these three evidences is manifestly an application of the Method of Agreement,[16] though in truth the concomitance of the emotions of taste with this associative activity of imagination is rather asserted than proved; the instances are rather illustrations than the basis for a complete induction. "Thus," Alison observes in characteristic style, when we feel either the beauty or sublimity of natural scenery,—the gay lustre of a morning in spring, or the mild radiance of a summer evening, the savage majesty of a wintry storm, or the wild magnificence of a tempestuous ocean,—we are conscious of a variety of images in our minds, very different from those which the objects themselves can present to the eye. Trains of pleasing or of solemn thought arise spontaneously within our minds; our hearts swell with emotions, of which the objects before us seem to afford no adequate cause; and we are never so much satiated with delight, as when, in recalling our attention, we are unable to trace either the progress or the connection of those thoughts, which have passed with so much rapidity through our imagination.[17]

Such instances, however, are sufficient to render Alison's theory credible as an hypothesis, and this is really all that the Method of Agreement can do, for the phenomena coincidence of which is indicated in this fashion may be joint effects, or may be casually and indifferently combined while plurality of causes obtains.

The second section of the chapter goes much further towards a conclusive proof; if it be successfully proved that without the excitation of imagination, the emotions of taste are unfelt, we have fulfilled (considering this result conjointly with that of the first section) the conditions of the Joint Method of Agreement and Difference. Indeed, in some of the instances the conditions of the Method of Difference itself are very nearly fulfilled; the subject, however, is insusceptible of conclusive application of the Method of Difference, and Alison's proof is as firm an induction as can be obtained. The particular phenomena adduced within the section are three. Alison notes, first, that if the state of mind is such as to obstruct the play of fancy, aesthetic sensibility is correspondingly dulled. The sunset or the poem which at one time is so affecting, is at another indifferent to us; on the former occasions, the mind is unembarrassed by engrossing objects of thought and free to receive all the impressions which the objects before us can produce, but "the seasons of care, of grief, or of business, have other occupations, and destroy, for the time at least, our sensibility to the beautiful or the sublime, in the same proportion that they produce a state of mind unfavourable to the indulgence of imagination." [18] Here is the disinterestedness, the detachment from practical desire, on which the German aestheticians have insisted so strongly as a characteristic of aesthetic experience; the simple practical emotions do not involve, unless accidentally, this employment of imagination.

Secondly (I return to the three evidences for the indispensability of this role of imagination), the exercise of the critical faculty diminishes or destroys the perception of beauty. "The mind, in such an employment," Alison writes, "instead of being at liberty to follow whatever trains of imagery the composition before it can excite, is either fettered to the consideration of some of its minute and solitary parts; or pauses amid the rapidity of its conceptions, to make them the objects of its attention and review. In these operations, accordingly, the emotion, whether of beauty or sublimity, is lost, and if it is wished to be recalled, it can only be done by relaxing this vigour of attention, and resigning ourselves again to the natural stream of our thoughts." [19]

And thirdly, Alison remarks that permanent differences of character produce corresponding differences in sensibility. The relation chiefly operative in the associative trains of taste is resemblance, and men differ by nature in their susceptibility to this relation; those who are attentive rather than imaginative, those whose associations are directed by habits of business or of philosophic investigation, are so far insensible to beauty. It must be noted that this third evidence is less cogent than the two previous, for it involves a comparison of different persons. The same individual, however, may be at one moment abstracted, at another at leisure, at one moment critical, at another sensitive; such cases go beyond the crude application of the Joint Method to approach the Method of Difference. Of course, no psychological phenomenon so complex as taste can be brought under the Method of Difference in the strictest sense, for it is impossible amid such intermixture of effects to be certain that only one element has been changed.

What has already been adduced amounts to a tolerable induction. But it can be strengthened; if it can be shown that aesthetic sensibility varies directly as the mobility of imagination, the Method of Concomitant Variations lends its force to the conclusion. That sensibility does so vary, Alison makes clear in the final section of this first chapter: every variety of association—personal, historical, national, professional—may swell our emotions of beauty and sublimity, and the strength and character of the emotions does vary proportionately to the kind and number of these associations which can attach themselves to the object of immediate experience. Again, this same effect of enrichment is produced by what Alison terms "Picturesque Objects." The term "picturesque" becomes here a systematic or technical term; it has a meaning derived from and peculiarly appropriate to Alison's mode of analysis. An object is picturesque if it is such as to awaken a train of associations additional to what the scene as a whole is calculated to excite. Picturesque objects are "in general, such circumstances, as coincide, but are not necessarily connected with the character of the scene or description, and which, at first affecting the mind with an emotion of surprise, produce afterwards an increased or additional train of imagery." [20] Thus, an old tower in the middle of a deep wood, an evening bell at sunset—whatever is distinct from but capable of blending with, the general character—is picturesque. Yet another confirmatory circumstance is the influence of an early acquaintance with poetry upon the appreciation of nature. One is tempted to add as a parallel (and I think a stronger) instance, the influence of the seventeenth-century landscape painters in forming the taste of the eighteenth century, or that of the great British landscape artists in forming the taste of more recent times.

This opening chapter of the two which constitute the essay has proved that trains of association are indispensable to the emotions of beauty and sublimity, that they are a part of the cause of aesthetic feeling. But a part only, for trains of association constantly pass through the mind without being attended by such emotions. The peculiar character which defines aesthetic trains of thought consists, Alison asserts, "1*st*, In respect of the Nature of the ideas of which it is composed, by their being ideas productive of Emotion: and 2*dly*, In respect of their Succession, by their being distinguished by some general principle of connection, which subsists through the whole extent of the train." [21] This is an exhaustive distinction. For in an associational psychology there are two variables only—the nature or quality of the component ideas, and the fashion in which they come into being. (It will be recalled that of Hume's seven philosophical relations of ideas, four—resemblance, contrariety, quality, and quantity—depend on the *nature* of the ideas related, while three—identity, causation, relations of space and time—depend on the *mode of existence* of the related ideas.) When Alison develops a thorough treatment of each of these variables, he has exhausted the potentialities of his system.

The three sections of the second chapter of the essay are devoted, the first to the statement of the two branches of this doctrine, the second and third to the inductive proof of these two branches. Alison's position on the *nature* of the ideas comprised in aesthetic trains of association is, "That no objects, or qualities in objects, are, in fact, felt either as beautiful or sublime, but such as are productive of some Simple Emotion. . . ." [22] Such emotive ideas Alison terms, by a sort of metonymy, "Ideas of Emotion." His contention is supported by noting that some simple affection is always excited before the more complex emotion of taste is felt. That this in turn is true, is supported by a series of observations: "if it is found, that no qualities are felt, either as beautiful or sublime, but such as accord with the habitual or temporary sensibility of our minds; that objects of the most acknowledged beauty fail to excite their usual emotions, when we regard them in the light of any of their uninteresting or unaffecting qualities; and that our common judgments of the characters of men are founded upon this experience,—it seems that there can be no doubt of the proposition itself." [23] The reasoning on this head is not, however, so subtle nor so complex as to demand minute criticism.

But the organization of the final section of the chapter is neater and more systematic. The doctrine here to be supported is, that the ideas composing a train of aesthetic association are strung on the thread of a single pervading emotion, whereas the components of an ordinary train of thought are connected each with the adjacent ideas before and after but without any one general relation informing the entire train. To establish this point, Alison examines the principles of composition in a series of arts—gardening, landscape painting, descriptive poetry, narrative and dramatic poetry. He does not, of course, assemble all the instances for a complete induction, an impossible task with artifacts which do not have a common specific nature; rather, he gives illustrations which call upon general experience in support of their implications. It is still an inductive argument, albeit an induction manqué. The conclusion is, "that, in all the Fine Arts, that Composition is most excellent, in which the different parts most fully unite in the production of one unmingled Emotion; and that Taste the most perfect, where the perception of this relation of objects, in point of expression, is most delicate and precise." [24] Notice that while the discussion of each art individually is a cursory application of the Joint Method of Agreement and Difference (since both "good" and "bad" instances are adduced), the consecutive handling of the four arts fulfills the conditions of the Method of Concomitant Variations. For painting exceeds gardening in its power of selecting and combining into wholes of greater purity and simplicity of expression; descriptive poetry, and above all narrative and dramatic poetry, enjoy yet greater power over their materials. And as the power of the art over its subjects is greater, the insistence of taste upon achievement of unity is proportionately more exacting.

The peculiar aesthetic pleasure, then, must be "composed of the pleasures which separately attend the exercise of these faculties [passion and imagination], or, in other words, as produced by the union of pleasing Emotion, with the pleasure which, by the constitution of our nature, is annexed to the exercise of Imagination." [25] I judge Alison's opinion to be, that the two pleasures coexist without producing any *tertium quid*, that we can still discern in their union the separate components. This, however, does not follow necessarily from the positions previously established; these arguments had proved that the emotions of taste were caused by (*1*) excitation of a simple emotion, and (*2*) stimulation of the imagination in a certain way. Now there are three manners of causation: the causes may continue to exist commingled, the effect being only their coexistence; they may perish in producing an effect wholly different from its causes; or they may produce an effect distinguishable from themselves, yet coexist with it. Alison's observation that beauty is always cheerful, sad, or elevated, according with the primary emotion upon which it is based, certainly rules out the second of these three alternatives. The suggestion that the term "delight" be appropriated to aesthetic "pleasure" suggests the third; yet other passages suggest the first, or blur these distinctions. It would at any rate be possible for an Alisonian to elect the third of the alternatives I have specified, to argue that in beauty caused by, say, gaiety or serenity, the serenity or gaiety might be still perceptible throughout the experience, yet that the beauty *qua* beauty might be characterized by a feeling peculiar to itself. All beauty might be thought (as Poe thought it) melancholy, this feeling existing alongside whatever emotion was the stimulus of the aesthetic feeling.

Be this as it may. We have followed the reasoning of the first, the "metaphysical," essay in the proof that the complex emotions of taste are felt "WHEN THE IMAGINATION IS EMPLOYED IN THE PROSECUTION OF A REGULAR TRAIN OF IDEAS OF EMOTION." [26] The second essay (rather more than three quarters of the treatise) is devoted to determining the source "Of the Sublimity and Beauty of the Material World." It will be recalled, that in discussing the outline of Alison's whole plan for his system, it was difficult to locate this second essay with precision, for it appears to comprehend both "1A" and "11"—both the inquiry into the origin of the beauty and sublimity of matter, and the investigation into the qualities producing the emotions of taste. The explanation of this difficulty is not far to seek. The beautiful and sublime of material qualities is a crux for Alison, since he thinks that "it must be allowed, that Matter in itself is unfitted to produce any kind of emotion. The various qualities of matter are known to us only by means of our external senses; but all that such powers of our nature convey, is Sensation and Perception; and whoever will take the trouble of attending to the effect which such qualities, when simple and unassociated, produce upon his mind, will be satisfied, that in no case do they produce Emotion, or the exercise of any of his affections." [27] This is a problem in the nature of *effects,* and may appropriately be treated in connection with "I"—ascertainment of the effects to be accounted for. Yet it involves *causes* too, once removed by association, for the qualities of matter produce emotion by association with mental traits. Alison is thus led to treat "II" together with "IA"; his plan could not be completed as originally sketched without repetition. Still remaining for his second division, of course, would be the knotty problem of explaining how *mental* properties produce emotions in percipients—but this, I suspect, is not explicable unless in terms of final causes.

McCosh considers that Alison's treatise leaves untouched two great problems: "The question arises, What starts the train [of association]? and a farther question follows, What gives the unity and harmony to the train? An answer to these questions, or rather to this question—for the questions are one,—may disclose to our view an objective beauty and sublimity very much overlooked by Alison, and the supporters of the association theory." [28] I do not conceive that these objections are fatal to Alison's theory, or that he need postulate some objective beauty to evade them; it is true, however, that much of his analysis depends from a theory of the passions which is nowhere presented to us, and that he does not discuss the interaction of association and attention in channeling the mental train.

Solution of the paradox that material qualities produce aesthetic effects although matter is inherently incapable of arousing emotion occupies the bulk of the essay; the argument is succinctly stated by Alison himself:

> The illustrations that have been offered in the course of this ESSAY upon the origin of the SUBLIMITY and BEAUTY of some of the principal qualities of MATTER, seem to afford sufficient evidence for the following conclusions:
>
> I. That each of these qualities is either from nature, from experience, or from accident, the sign of some quality capable of producing Emotion, or the exercise of some moral affection. And,
>
> II. That when these associations are dissolved, or in other words, when the material qualities cease to be significant of the associated qual-

ities, they cease also to produce the emotions, either of Sublimity or Beauty.

If these conclusions are admitted, it appears necessarily to follow, that the Beauty and Sublimity of such objects is to be ascribed not to the material qualities themselves, but to the qualities they signify; and of consequence, that the qualities of matter are not to be considered as sublime or beautiful in themselves, but as being the SIGNS or EXPRESSIONS of such qualities, as, by the constitution of our nature, are fitted to produce pleasing or interesting emotion.[29]

The method, then, in examining each class of material properties, is the Joint Method of Agreement and Difference (sometimes approximating very closely to the Method of Difference); and from these particular conclusions, the general conclusion is arrived at by the Method of Agreement. Despite Alison's disclaimer that his inquiries are "only detached observations," [30] it could be argued that he examines so many aesthetically significant properties of matter that the last generalization is not mere Agreement but approximates a "perfect induction"—what is true of each is necessarily true of all.

One gets the impression, to be sure, that Alison knows *a priori* that matter cannot produce emotion. Such a view he could have imbibed from Reid. He knew Reid; Reid had already maintained that the beauty and sublimity of matter is derived wholly from mind; [31] Alison refers to Reid on this very question in the conclusion of the second essay.[32] Such an idealist doctrine, is, at any rate, a major point of contrast between Alison and most other British aestheticians. All the picturesque school, contemporaries of Alison, argue in one fashion or another that matter is in itself aesthetically efficient (though they do not deny the role of association). Lord Kames, too, had found the properties of matter affecting independent of expression. Some part of the contradiction between Kames and Alison can be explained away by noting that for Alison perception is of qualities, whereas for Kames it is of the object as qualified. For Kames, that is, perception of the features of the countenance is perception of a face, not of mere forms, and the perception is thus immediately connected with other attributes. Yet Kames would also find a ceramic tile beautiful in itself, and in this case the object does not include a mind (apart from design and use); the difference from Alison remains real and irreducible.

It is repeatedly asserted that the associational system employed by Alison is that of Hartley; [33] but there is no decisive indication of this debt in the essays, either in an explicit acknowledgement or in the character of the psychology. There is no trace of a physiological basis for association; Alison's system is wholly ideal. Indeed, it bears a far greater resemblance to the system of Hume than to that of Hartley, and a Humeian could easily reduce Alison's instances of association to contiguity, resemblance, and cause-and-effect. Alison does not often appear to have Hume consciously in mind, however, and there are a number of points at which his language or thought contrasts with that of Hume.[34] Alison's speculation might well be regarded as in great measure his own reflection within the general tradition of British empiricism after Locke.

Curiously enough, Alison thought that his analysis of material beauties into mental coincided with the doctrine of the "PLATONIC SCHOOL," a doctrine traceable ("amid their dark and figurative language"[35]) in the philosophical systems of the East, and to be found in modern times in Shaftesbury, Hutcheson, Akenside, Spence, and Reid.[36] In his first edition, Alison appeared anxious to qualify the doctrine that "Matter is not beautiful in itself, but derives its Beauty from the Expression of MIND."[37] Granting, to be sure, that the beauty of matter "arises from the Expressions which an intelligent Mind connects with, and perceives in it," Alison nonetheless hesitates to proclaim that "MATTER is beautiful only, by being expressive of the proper Qualities of MIND, and that all the Beauty of the MATERIAL, as well as of the INTELLECTUAL World, is to be found in Mind and its QUALITIES alone. . . ."[38] For there are objects of knowledge and taste which are neither qualities of Mind nor qualities of Matter—there are "Qualities which arise from RELATION; from the relation of different bodies or parts of bodies to each other; from the relation of Body to Mind; and from the relation of different Qualities of Mind to each other. . . ."[39] Novelty, harmony, fitness, utility—all these are relational. The conclusion which Alison finally formulates is, "That the Beauty and Sublimity of the Qualities of Matter, arise from their being the Signs or Expressions of such Qualities as are fitted by the constitution of our Nature, to produce Emotion."[40] In the second edition, however, Alison reformulated his doctrine to conform to the "Platonist" position. The various "relations" are shown to be merely *indirect* expressions of mental qualities, and the ultimate conclusion is restated accordingly: "that the beauty and sublimity which is felt in the various appearances of matter, are finally to be ascribed to their expression of mind; or to their being, either directly or indirectly, the signs of those qualities of mind which are fitted, by the constitution of our nature, to affect us with pleasing or interesting emotion." [41] And Alison adds an elaborate classification, in a scheme evidently derived from Reid, of the ways in which the association of matter and mind is effected. The qualities of matter may be either

I. [ACTIVE MIND] immediate signs of *powers* of mind; thus works of art are indicative of the various capacities of the artist, and works of nature may indicate the powers of God; or material properties may be

II. [PASSIVE MIND] signs of *affections* of mind, either

A. *directly*, as voice, facial expression, and gesture are immediate expressions of mental affections, or

B. *indirectly*, by means of less universal and less permanent relations, such as

1. *experience*, through which material properties may become the means of producing affections (as with utility and fitness),

2. *analogy*, or resemblance of the qualities of matter with those of mind,

3. *association* ("in the proper sense of that term") by means of education, fortune, or historical accident, and finally,

4. *individual association* to our private affections or remembrances.[42]

In this reinterpretation of the Platonist doctrine (which, Alison concedes, "when stated in general terms, has somewhat the air of a paradox"), anything dialectical in method or mystical in purport is replaced by the empirical and literal.

Alison adopts the usual position that aesthetic experience is confined to the senses of hearing and (more especially) sight. I shall not enter into a recapitulation of the intricate details of his analysis of the aesthetics of sound. It is, however, of interest to observe that he divides his subject neatly in terms of the kinds of associations involved. He treats first, simple sounds (in order of increasing complexity, those produced by inanimate objects, by animals, and by the human voice), and then composed sounds (i.e., music). The procedure is (I deliberately oversimplify) to show that sounds similar in themselves are productive of very different effects when the vehicle of different expressions, and that sounds very different in themselves produce similar effects when conveying similar expressions; this is, of course, the Joint Method of Agreement and Difference working both ways—simultaneously establishing that the physical sound is *not* the cause of the aesthetic effect, and that the attached associations *are*. Sometimes Alison is able to arrange an experiment conforming to the Method of Difference; thus, a sound which had seemed sublime becomes indifferent when an attached association is suddenly stripped away (as when we discover that supposed thunder was only the rumble of a passing cart).

But although the effect of any sound depends upon the associations which it evokes, it remains true that general rules emerge from our experience; it is possible to assert, for instance, that (*caeteris paribus*) the most sublime sound is loud, grave, lengthened, and increasing in volume. Such principles guide us in responding to sounds with which we have no more particularized associations, and they afford the basis for an art of music. In the treatment of music, Alison is obliged to skirt a difficulty for his system—that by "a peculiar law of our nature, there are certain sounds of which the union is agreeable, and others of which the union is disagreeable." [43] The difficulty is avoided by insisting that the "mechanical pleasure" of harmony is qualitatively different from beauty; any complicated composition of harmonies, moreover, even if not expressive of any passion, is expressive of the skill of composer (and performer), and this expression may be the basis of beauty—but such beauty, too, is distinguishable from the physical pleasure which the harmonies afford. In general, Alison's remarks on music suffer from inadequacy of technical knowledge and the drastic oversimplification which he imposes on the subject; it might well be possible, however, to develop on Alison's principles a musical aesthetic which could provide a basis for practical criticism.

In treating of the beauty and sublimity of objects of sight, Alison is hampered by no technical inadequacies, and his system is most intricately complex. The sense of sight is, of course, vastly predominant in our aesthetic experience, a predominance which Alison attributes to the fact of our seeing "all that assemblage of qualities which constitute, in our imaginations, the peculiar nature of such objects," and to our discovering by sight most of the relations among objects through which associations are transferred.[44]

The beauty of colors presents a problem very like that of the beauty of harmonies, for there is a "mechanical pleasure" independent of the aesthetic pleasure. "Whether some Colours may not of themselves produce agreeable Sensations, I am not anxious to dispute," Alison declares, "but wherever Colours are felt as producing the Emotion of Beauty . . . it is by means of their Expression, and not from any original fitness in the Colours themselves to produce this effect. . . ." [45]

Form, however, is the chief source of aesthetic experience, constituting as it does the "essence" of objects. "The most obvious definition of FORM," remarks Alison, "is that of Matter, bounded or circumscribed by Lines." [46] His treatment of it, accordingly, is almost wholly in terms of lines, simple and composed—a treatment which minimizes the influence of light and shade in defining form. Although it is true that chiaroscuro is, in general, less important aesthetically than line, this omission is nonetheless a lacuna in the system. The aesthetic character of form falls under the heads of *natural* beauty and sublimity, *relative* beauty, and *accidental* beauty. The natural sublimity of form is found to turn partly on the nature of the objects distinguished by the forms (so that forms characterizing objects of danger, power, splendor, solemnity, and such are sublime), and partly on the magnitude of the forms. Alison's system does not lead him to reduce sublimity to one original, and he avoids, in consequence, the endless disputes whether sublimity is based on fear, on power, on energy, on size, yet without falling into a vapid eclecticism. Lord Kames's differentiation of sublimity from grandeur appears when Alison notes that magnitude in height expresses elevation or magnanimity; in depth, danger and terror; in length, vastness or infinity; in breadth, stability and duration. The treatment of beauty in the same way subsumes all the partial theories which Alison's predecessors had elaborated—that beauty consists in proportion, or in variety in uniformity, or utility, or specific norm, or peculiar line. The philosophical error of systematic oversimplification and the vulgar error of supposing original and objective beauty in each of the multitude of beautiful forms are alike skirted; beauty *is* reducible to one principle—association—but that principle is of such a nature that the multiplicity of experience can be reconstructed from it. Hogarth's principle, for example, is caught up when Alison notes that natural beauty of form arises from the expression of fineness, delicacy, and ease, the last of which especially is so often indicated by the waving line. But in a series of ingenious inductive experiments, Alison shows that the beauty of line depends on expression, not on serpentinity: that common language refers beauty to expression rather than to form as such; that when other lines than the serpentine acquire the same expression, they become beautiful; that when serpentine lines fail of appropriate expression they are not beautiful. Yet in Alison's judgment, Hogarth's is "perhaps of all others the justest and best founded principle which has as yet been maintained, in the investigation of the natural Beauty of forms." [47] Note, however, that what for Hogarth was *the* operative law of beauty has become for Alison an approximate empirical generalization applicable to one species of beauty.

Hutcheson's uniformity in variety also appears transformed in the Alisonian aesthetic. When a form is characterized by the composition of angular and curvilinear lines (instead of being determined by a single line of given character), Alison concedes that the union of uniformity and variety is "agreeable, or is fitted by the constitution of our nature to excite an agreeable sensation in the Sense of Sight" [48]— but this sensation assumes a place in the rank of mechanical pleasures, together with harmony and color. The beauty of such composition—so far as it is *natural* beauty—depends upon associated feeling, greater sameness being required by strong emotions and those bordering on pain, greater variety by the weaker emotions and those belonging to positive pleasure.[49] It follows that Hogarth's rule for practice—maximum variety—is false;[50] the true rules are:

1. An expressive form should be selected as the ground of the composition.
2. The variety of parts should be adapted to the nature of this expression.
3. In independent forms, the beauty is greatest when the character, whatever it is, is best preserved.
4. In dependent forms, the beauty is greatest when the character is best adapted to that of the milieu.[51]

The distinction which pervades British aesthetic theory between natural and artificial beauty is of course natural to systems the chief terms of which apply to both nature and art. Alison makes more of this distinction than does any other writer of the century, and by doing so is more adequate on the side of art than most of the eighteenth-century aestheticians; most principles of criticism can find a niche and an explanation in his aesthetic theory. The beauty of art, as far as different from that of its natural subject, is termed by Alison "relative beauty." Like natural beauty, relative beauty is expressive; it expresses not a content of affections, however, but efficient and final causes. We perceive art to be the product of *design*, and are moved by the exhibition it affords of the powers of the mind; and we perceive it to be adapted to an end, whereby both the *fitness* of the adaptation and the *utility* of the end affect us.

Alison produces experiments which indicate that the beauty of regularity is wholly attributable to the expression of design. This account of regularity explains very neatly for Alison the course of historical development of the arts, a history which in turn lends support to the theory. The development of each art, as Alison sees it, exhibits three stages: a primitive period in which the novelty of art causes stress to be laid on the design which differentiates it obviously from nature, so that uniformity is the governing principle; a stage of mature development in which variety is increasingly introduced and becomes the leading principle of art, which comes to express the passions rather than the artist's ingenuity; an era of decline in which the rivalry of artists and the unregulated desire for novelty in the audience make the display of art itself again prevalent over the expression of the subject. A just taste requires that expression of design should be subject to expression of character; for expression of character is more deeply affecting, more universally felt, and more permanent, arising from the invariable principles of human nature.

One of the omitted parts of Alison's plan, it will be recalled, is discussion of the enjoyment of painful subjects, especially as represented in art. Alison alludes only cursorily to this subject, but it is possible to conjecture at the judgment he might have made. It is apparent that artistry may yield a pleasure which can overbalance pain produced by the subject, especially since this pain is weakened by imitation. There may in addition be "mechanical pleasures" accompanying the beauty of design which might reconcile us to loss of the beauty of character. Yet Alison's principle that beauty of design is of an order inferior to beauty of character would necessarily relegate works handling painful subjects to an inferior rank. This principle is less limiting than might be supposed, however, for Alison's conception of beauty is so comprehensive that many subjects one might casually term "painful" are really beautiful in actuality as well as in art; melancholy, for instance, is eminently fitted to be the substratum of beauty, the physical signs of age are beautiful as representing or suggesting a range of moral sentiments—and so forth. The artist imitating such subjects, moreover, can point up the beautiful aspects and suppress or minimize the ugly, painful, and indifferent, just as he does in treating any other subjects. Cases would remain, doubtless, where the very facts of imitation and design alone reconcile us to subjects with displeasing expressions. The question might be raised, whether Alison could adopt Hume's notion of conversion of the passions, that the pain of the subject, weakened by removal, produces an excitement of the mind which can be turned to reinforce the emotion of beauty evoked by the artistry. There is nothing incompatible with Alison's thought in this idea. But the fact that he does not present it points to a limitation in his system. This limitation is, that he works almost wholly with ideas rather than with emotions; emotions are constantly referred to as the basis of beauty, to be sure, but there is no analytic of emotion in the *Essays*.[52] I have already noticed that Alison passes by the question whether beauty has a peculiar emotional tone of its own, apart from that of the passion on which it is based and the pleasure arising from associative activity. And I think that he would not concern himself with the problem of interaction of passions, to which the theory of conversion is a partial contribution.

Relative beauty arises not only from inferences about the efficient cause, but from apprehension of the final cause. The complicated problems of proportion are brought by Alison under the head of fitness. The great principle of Reynolds—the central form—becomes a special case of proportion: in natural forms in which the fitness of proportions is not decisively determined either *a priori* or by experience, "the common Proportion is generally conceived to be the fittest, and is therefore considered as the most beautiful."[53] The most curious problems of proportion arise with regard to architecture; Alison devotes some fifty pages to a minute survey of the external and internal proportions of architecture. His evidences are of the usual sort—a careful discrimination of sentiments, an examination of the customary uses of language, and a series of experiments which serve to determine the causal relations obtaining among the different variables. It may be useful to give a specimen of Alison's conclusions on such a topic. He considers the "internal" proportions of architecture—those of rooms—and finds that they depend upon three species of fitness: for the superimposed weight, real or apparent; for the emotional character of the apartment (elegant, magnificent, gay, somber, or whatever); and for the particular purpose for which the apartment is destined. "The two first Expressions constitute the PERMANENT Beauty, and the third the ACCIDENTAL Beauty of an apartment."[54] The first is really a negative condition, the second the source of positive beauty; these two must unite in every beautiful apartment, as the first and third must in every convenient apartment. "The most perfect Beauty that the Proportions of an apartment can exhibit," Alison concludes, "will be when all these Expressions unite; or when the same relations of dimension which are productive of the Expression of sufficiency, agree also in the preservation of Character, and in the indication of Use."[55]

Alison does not pause over the beauty of utility, merely referring the reader to Adam Smith's *Theory of the Moral Sentiments*. And he hurries through the *accidental* beauty of forms, which depends upon local, temporary, or personal associations. Since accidental beauty is thus limited, it has scant interest for a general theory of taste. It is interesting to note in this connection that associationism is often taken by its critics and by modern scholars as doing away with the possibility of standards in taste. Monk, for instance, argues that by translating beauty and sublimity into purely mental emotions, Alison's system shifted attention away from the object of aesthetic experience, that if taste is a matter of association of ideas it is a matter of environment and chance and we must fall back on the adage, *de gustibus non disputandum est,* "itself the very negation of absolute beauty and absolute sublimity, as well as of a critical code which based its judgments upon *a priori* conceptions of nature and beauty and truth." [56] But this opinion is not peculiar to Monk. Christopher Hussey tells us that Alison "denied absolutely the existence of objective qualities inherent in objects, accounting for all emotions by the association of ideas aroused in the mind of the spectator. Anything might be beautiful if it aroused pleasant and therefore beautiful ideas. . . . The truth of Alison's theory cannot be denied. Its gradual abandonment has been caused, not by any fallacy, but by its devastating effect on every standard of beauty. According to it, every man's taste is as good as another's." [57] Kallich tries to show that Alison, while a hypercritical neo-classicist, was at the same time a romantic relativist.[58] And McKenzie urges that given Alison's method, it is impossible to get beyond the reflection of individual experience.[59] But it is entirely clear that Alison saw no such implication in his theory, which is a remarkable circumstance if it be so obvious as the modern scholars would have us believe. I think it apparent that Alison would have carried out his projected analysis of the standard of taste by making the obvious distinction between universal associations and those which are local, temporary, or personal. The test of truth, Alison remarks (quite incidentally) at one point, "must finally rest upon the uniformity of our sentiments." [60] Again, he observes that only through knowledge of philosophical criticism can the artist tell whether his creations are "adapted to the accidental prejudices of his Age, or to the uniform constitution of the human Mind." [61] The scholars cited all very much exaggerate the idiosyncratic aspects of personality; the universal traits of human nature, the common core of experience, really bulk far larger. It may be true, as an historical proposition, that Alison's views, distorted and quoted out of context, have encouraged and justified antinomianism in aesthetics; that the doctrine properly understood has any such bearing is, I maintain, false.

The normative criterion, when the different beauties of form can not all be preserved together, is always universality and permanence. In ornamental forms, beauty of character takes precedence over beauty of design, and of course beauty of design over accidental beauty. In useful forms, beauty is proportional to expression of character, utility being equal; when such expression is incompatible with use, "that Form will be *most universally and most permanently* beautiful, in which the Expression of Utility is most fully preserved" [62]—even though the beauty of utility produces a sentiment in itself weaker than that evoked by beauty of character.

Since the sense of sight perceives not only color and form but also motion, Alison devotes a chapter to motion, as he had to sound, to color, to form. The associations into which he resolves motion are of two kinds—those associated to the motion as such, and those associated to the body moved. The conclusion with regard to the former is that both the sublimity and the beauty depend upon the expression of power (as opposed to external compulsion), sublimity being the effect of great power, beauty of moderate or playful power. "The most sublime Motion," Alison maintains, "is that of rapid Motion in a straight Line. The most beautiful, is that of slow Motion in a line of Curves." [63] In general, however, the expression of the body moved predominates over that of the motion itself; naturally, the aesthetic effect is most perfect when the two expressions coincide.

The second and subsequent editions of the *Essays* were embellished with an additional chapter of two hundred pages' length, devoted to analysis "Of the Beauty of the Human Countenance and Form"; the burden, as we anticipate, is that the whole beauty and sublimity of countenance, form, attitude, and gesture is attributable to expression, direct or indirect, of mental traits. The conclusion with regard to the countenance (more particularly) is that there are three beauties: that of form and color (as previously analyzed), that of direct expression of character, and that of direct expression of transient affections of the mind; each is perfect when the composition of the face preserves pure and unmingled the predominant expression; the highest beauty or sublimity is attained "when all fall upon the heart of the Spectator as one whole, in which Matter, in all its most exquisite forms, is only felt as the sign of one great or amiable Character of Mind." [64] With regard to form, the doctrine is that its beauty rises from the expression of physical fitness or propriety as a precondition, and positively from the expression of interesting or affecting characters of mind, and that the beauty of composition arises (as in all other cases) from the unity of expression. But enough: the analysis is subtle, intricate, and exhaustive; and it fairly represents the power of an associational psychology to deal with the most complex of aesthetic problems.

Certain problems within this analysis have a bearing on Alison's method generally. Instances of four of Mill's canons of induction have been cited hitherto; but there has been no occasion to adduce an instance of the Method of Residues, except in the broad sense that the whole procedure of the second essay is the Method of Residues. (The second essay, that is, proceeds by this method in arguing that since the sublimity and beauty of matter are *not* the result of material properties as such, they must be the consequence of material properties as signs of something else.) But it will be illuminating to examine the application of this method in the details of the system. By its very nature, the Method of Residues will be employed most usually in the latter parts of a system, and accordingly we find the most elaborate applications of it in this final chapter. When Alison considers the aesthetic character of the variable colors of the countenance, he lays it down that the beauty of color must here arise from either an original beauty in the colors themselves, or some law of our nature by which such colors appearing in the countenance immediately produce the emotion of beauty, or their significance to us of certain qualities capable of producing pleasing or interesting emotions. Now, the first of these alternatives has been already ruled out in the chapter on color; no color is originally beautiful (though some may yield a mechanical pleasure). The second alternative is now shown to be untenable; the consequences of the hypothesis are drawn out and found to be in contradiction with experience. The Method of Residues now points to the third alternative; and evidence drawn up inductively under several heads is marshalled in confirmation of this inference and in explication of the particular qualities signified by the variable colors of the countenance.

It is important to observe—especially as a point of contrast with Lord Kames—that Alison never begs the question whether the knowledge of the expressions of matter is implanted in us by nature or arises through experience. It is a question which, for aesthetics, need not be settled, provided that the *fact* of the expression be clear. But one feels more certain of the fact itself when its ground is known; and it is, moreover, of interest to determine the causes of this phenomenon. The chapter now under consideration affords several vivid illustrations of Alison's cautious procedure. In treating of interpretation of the permanent coloring of the countenance,[65] of the expression of the features,[66] and of the figure,[67] Alison endeavors to isolate cursorily the experiences underlying the associations. He had done the same much earlier in discussing the expressive power of tempo in music.[68] On other occasions, he leaves the issue unresolved; he does not attempt to determine why we always attribute regularity to design,[69] why motion with no visible cause suggests volition,[70] or how we come to interpret the "language" of gesture and attitude.[71] But the tendency of Alison's system to explain such phenomena, to reduce the number of inexplicable principles in human nature, is a great advance in philosophic method.

The chapter on the human face and form involves Alison in another problem, substantive rather than methodological. Throughout the century, following a tradition inherited from continental art critics, aestheticians attempted in a variety of ways to assimilate that elusive quality, grace, to a variety of systems. Alison, too, feels obliged to treat of grace, which appears in his system (as elsewhere) as a kind of finishing touch to beauty and/or sublimity. It is found in the positions and motions of the human figure, in the movements of some animals, and (by personification) even in insensitive objects; and it is the chief object of painting and sculpture. Grace is "different from Beauty, though nearly allied to it," [72] being distinguished by an emotion of respect and admiration apart from the nexus of feelings touched by simple beauty or sublimity. It appears to consist in an expression, ordinarily superimposed upon expression of emotion, of self-command, "of that self-possession which includes in our belief, both the presence of a lofty standard of character and conduct, and of the habitual government of itself by this high principle." [73]

Few eighteenth-century aestheticians—and certainly not a divine— could treat of beauty and sublimity without exhibiting the final causes served by such a constitution of our nature. Curiosity is not satisfied in scientific inquiry, Alison tells us, "until it terminates in the discovery, not only of design, but of benevolent design: and the great advantage . . . which man derives from inquiry into the laws of his own mind, is much less in the addition which it gives to his own power or wisdom, than in the evidence which it affords him of the wisdom with which his constitution is framed, and the magnificent purposes for which it is formed." [74] Despite this asseveration, however, it is apparent that this inquiry into final causes is no necessary part of the system. For Addison, for Lord Kames, final causes were a kind of particular providence, to be adduced as *deus ex machina* whenever efficient causes proved esoteric; for Alison, final causes are like the providence of a deist—things would go on quite as well without them.

These purposes of the Creator which Alison divines include the general and impartial dispersion of happiness (which would be arbitrarily and capriciously restricted if beauty were "objective") and the perpetual encouragement of the mechanic and liberal arts (which would soon become static if an "objective" beauty were once attained). But more important: since the emotions of taste are blended with moral sentiment, the pleasures of taste conduce to moral improvement. The moral influence of our appreciation of external nature is described in language as ardent as that of Wordsworth:

> While the objects of the material world are made to attract our infant eyes, there are latent ties by which they reach our hearts; and wherever they afford us delight, they are always the signs or expressions of higher qualities, by which our moral sensibilities are called forth. It may not be our fortune, perhaps, to be born amid its nobler scenes. But, wander where we will, trees wave, rivers flow, mountains ascend, clouds darken, or winds animate the face of Heaven; and over the whole scenery, the sun sheds the cheerfulness of his morning, the splendour of his noon-day, or the tenderness of his evening light. There is not one of these features of scenery which is not fitted to awaken us to moral emotion; to lead us, when once the key of our imagination is struck, to trains of fascinating and of endless imagery; and in the indulgence of them to make our bosoms either glow with conceptions of mental excellence, or melt in the dreams of moral good. Even upon the man of the most uncultivated taste, the scenes of nature have some inexplicable charm: there is not a chord perhaps of the human heart which may not be wakened by their influence; and I believe there is no man of genuine taste, who has not often felt, in the lone majesty of nature, some unseen spirit to dwell, which, in his happier hours, touched, as if with magic hand, all the springs of his moral sensibility, and rekindled in his heart those original conceptions of the moral or intellectual excellence of his nature, which it is the tendency of the vulgar pursuits of life to diminish, if not altogether to destroy.[75]

But beyond all else, "nature, in all its aspects around us, ought only to be felt as signs of . . . [the Creator's] providence, and as conducting us, by the universal language of these signs, to the throne of the DEITY." [76]

Such views as these lead to the final question of this survey of the Alisonian aesthetic: What is the precise connection between ethics and aesthetics in this system? Are they even distinguishable disciplines dealing with distinct subject matters? Alison is a remarkably systematic writer, and he seems consistently to reduce aesthetic phenomena to ethical. This is sufficiently obvious from the whole of the second essay; but particular citations may give suitable emphasis to the point. Thus, after demonstrating that beauty is found in the most opposite compositions of the countenance (and that, consequently, no physical law governs this beauty), Alison observes that "the union of every feature and colour has been experienced as beautiful, when it was felt as expressive of amiable or interesting sentiment; and . . . the only limit to the Beauty of the Human Countenance, is the limit which separates Vice from Virtue; which separates the dispositions or affections we approve, from those which we disapprove or despise." [77]

Yet the aesthetic phenomena do not become merely and purely ethical. For our sense of moral judgment pronounces directly and simply, without dependence on trains of associated imagery. Aesthetic feelings, it is true, fall within the same genus as moral sentiments; both are evaluative judgments relating—one immediately, the other mediately through the first—to the passions and faculties of the mind. But aesthetic feelings are differentiated from simple moral feelings by the peculiar mode of association which it was the function of the first essay to describe. When Alison argues that if there were an original beauty in the countenance, "the emotion of Beauty would be a simple and unassociated sentiment; and . . . language everywhere would have conveyed it with the same unity and accuracy, as it does the sentiments of right or wrong, of justice or injustice," [78] he is only stating explicitly a distinction which is implicit throughout the *Essays on Taste*.

II

Beautiful, Sublime,
and
Picturesque

CHAPTER 12

The Picturesque

❦

"T̶HE WORD *Picturesque,* as applied to the antiquities of English cities," declared the noted antiquary John Britton early in the nineteenth century, ". . . will be clearly recognised and understood by readers who are familiar with the works of Gilpin, Alison, Price, and Knight. It has become not only popular in English literature, but as definite and descriptive as the terms grand, beautiful, sublime, romantic, and other similar adjectives. . . . [In] speaking, or writing, about scenery and buildings, it is a term of essential and paramount import." [1]

This word "picturesque" had been naturalized in England for half a century before it was used as a term in theoretical aesthetic discussion. As early as 1685, William Aglionby had said of free and natural execution in painting, "This the Italians call working A la pittoresk, that is boldly" [2]—a usage strikingly like that of the picturesque school a century later. By 1705, Steele could employ the word in dramatic dialogue in the sense "after the manner of painters," though the manner in question was allegorical and academic, hardly that of which writers of the picturesque school think. Pope praised two lines of Phillips for being "what the French call very *picturesque"*; and notes to his *Iliad* pronounce two Homeric descriptions picturesque. [3] By mid-century the word was becoming a stock epithet in description and criticism. And although "picturesque" was never included in Johnson's dictionary, Johnson did employ it, in three instances at least, to define other words. [4]

Details of the etymology are mooted, and the etymologies contended for are usually employed to bolster theories of the picturesque; but there is of course no doubt of the Romance origin. Nonetheless, there is reason to suppose that the Dutch "schilderachtig" antedated development of the Italian and French synonym. Such a

Dutch art critic of the early seventeenth century as Carel van Mander
employed "schilderachtig"; [5] and the word was taken into German
half a century later by Joachim von Sandrart. Sandrart applies it,
much in the fashion of Uvedale Price, to the painting of Rembrandt:

> Er hat aber wenig antiche Poetische Gedichte, alludien oder seltsame
> Historien, sondern meistens einfältige und nicht in sonderbares Nach-
> sinnen lauffende, ihme wohlgefällige und schilderachtige (wie sie die
> Niderländer nennen) Sachen gemahlet, die doch voller aus der Natur
> herausgesuchter Artigkeiten waren.[6]

It is possible that the concept has its origin in the Netherlands; but
such speculation is at present too conjectural to pursue.

The spelling of "picturesque" is as variable as its meaning. Beside
the usual form one finds "pittoresk," "pittoresque," "pictoresque,"
"picteresque," "picturesk," and "peinturesque." "Pittoresque," like
Aglionby's "pittoresk," is early, reflects the Italian original—and is,
as we shall see, productive of much speculation. "Pictoresque" and
the exceptional "picteresque" display equally clearly in their etymology a reference to the painter. "Picturesk" is a late effort at Angli-
cizing "picturesque"; "peinturesque," also a rather late form, reflects (perhaps was invented to accord with) a different view of the
etymology—a reference to the art rather than the artist.[7]

In the early decades of the eighteenth century, "picturesque"
usually bore one of two meanings: when applied to literary style, it
meant "vivid" or "graphic," by an obvious metaphor; when applied
to scenes in nature, and sometimes when applied to imitations of
these on canvas or in words, it meant "eminently suitable for pictorial
representation," as affording a well-composed picture, with suitably
varied and harmonized form, colors, and lights. The first of these
meanings became (and in some measure still is) a commonplace in
the discussion of rhetoric and poetry; Blair (for instance) repeatedly
praises epithets, figures, and descriptions as "picturesque," as conjuring
up distinct and forcible images. But in Blair the two meanings I have
discriminated are rarely separate; he speaks of "poetical painting,"
and declares that "a good Poet ought to give us such a landscape, as
a painter could copy after." [8] Writers less concerned with literature
stress the pictorial sense of "picturesque," and it was this sense which
was destined to become predominant and fashionable.

After the publication of "Estimate" Brown's letter on Keswick
(1767) and Young's tours (1768-71), the picturesque insinuated itself more widely into popular literature, and to illustrate its use in

this period, just before Gilpin's picturesque travels set a standard for picturesque taste, I shall discuss briefly the picturesque in Smollett's *The Expedition of Humphry Clinker,* first published in 1771. The literary use of "picturesque"—"vivid"—appears as Matthew Bramble claims for Commissary Smollett's "Ode to Leven Water" the merit of being "at least picturesque and accurately descriptive." And the plastic sense—"pictorial"—appears frequently. Jerry Melford finds the scene of Clinker admonishing the felons in their chains, the grouping and expression, picturesque—fit for a Raphael. And Lismahago proves to be a highly picturesque appendage. His horror is "divertingly picturesque" when, acting Pierrot, he is chased by the skeleton. And when he escapes from the fire at Sir Thomas Bulford's in his nightshirt, Jerry Melford reports the scene as a subject for painting: "The rueful aspect of the lieutenant in his shirt, with a quilted night-cap fastened under his chin, and his long lank limbs and posteriors exposed to the wind, made a very picturesque appearance, when illuminated by the links and torches which the servants held up to light him in his descent." Sir Thomas cries out, "*O che roba!*—O, what a subject!—O, what *caricatura!*—O, for a Rosa, a Rembrandt, a Schalken!—Zooks, I'll give a hundred guineas to have it painted—what a fine descent from the cross, or ascent to the gallows! what lights and shadows!—what a group below! what expression above!—what an aspect!"[9] Sir Thomas is eccentric in his humor but not in his sense of the picturesque, for serious writers too apply the term to comic scenes: Malone remarks of an early *caricatura* of Reynolds that "it was a kind of picturesque travesty of Raffaelle's SCHOOL OF ATHENS."[10]

These examples have all referred to history or to genre painting, or to their comic equivalents; but this is not the peculiar locus of the picturesque, for although the picturesque point of view had on its first introduction into England a strong tie with history painting, landscape soon became the field for picturesque vision. And *Humphry Clinker* abounds with appreciations of (especially Scottish) scenery. Matthew Bramble often finds sublimity; Jerry is not impressed so deeply, yet he thinks that the Orkneys and Hebrides make a "picturesque and romantic" view. Here picturesque vision has less direct connection with painting; and there is one passage which prefigures satirically the later and more sophisticated sense of "picturesque": Lydia Melford thinks the meretricious and miscellaneous objects at Vauxhall "picturesque and striking." Even to an ingenue, Vauxhall would not, I think, have seemed "like a picture"—but striking it certainly was, and "striking" is a fair synonym for some of the applications of "picturesque" after that term was in some measure divorced from especial connection with painting.

But the popular uses of the word which I have illustrated were soon supplemented. Once "picturesque" became a part of technical aesthetic vocabulary, it was inevitable that, while ascertained from the vagueness of popular use, it would acquire the systematic ambiguity of other philosophical terms. As the picturesque was fitted into a variety of systems of aesthetics, the term "picturesque" acquired a corresponding variety of meanings.

It is this variety which makes a history of the picturesque—the term or the character—difficult of accomplishment. There are, as my introductory chapter has indicated, three ways in which such an account can be managed. It can be handled as a philological inquiry, with the influence of philosophical and methodological principles minimized; it can be composed dialectically, previous theories of the picturesque being examined in the light of a schematism, a superior theory, provided by the historian; finally, a closely literal survey of the arguments of conflicting theoreticians can be written, with attention directed upon philosophical issues where these are important, but without the superimposition of a more comprehensive theory of the analyst upon the theories which are his subject. The first of these modes tends to ignore the intellectual causes determining the propositions enunciated by theorists; the second implicitly impugns the integrity and adequacy of the theories; and the third (which is here attempted) has its defect too—for, since discussion of the picturesque, like that of other philosophical issues, is never brought to a close, the problems never settled, the differences never reconciled, it is difficult to give either an order or a termination to the account of the discussion. This study terminates at 1810, just at the time when picturesque attitudes had become generally adopted and when practical applications of the picturesque were being most fully developed; the theory and practice of the nineteenth century and modern times, as the picturesque gradually declined in public and critical favor, are wholly omitted, and so is the renaissance of the picturesque in very recent years.

But before entering upon my account, it may be useful to describe briefly instances of philological and dialectical histories of the picturesque. The most ambitious attempt to settle this philosophic problem by examination of language is that of Robert Bridges in one of his Society for Pure English tracts entitled "Pictorial. Picturesque. Romantic. Grotesque. Classical." Bridges does not admit intrusion of philosophic principles into the eighteenth-century usage of "picturesque"; he argues, in fact, that since the word "pictorial" did not come into general use before 1800,[11] the word "picturesque" *must* have been appropriated to the meaning which "pictorial" has for us. How this can be true of writers like Uvedale Price, who aim to divorce the term from its reference to pictorial representation, Bridges does not explain. The exclusion of all concern with ideas in the discussion of terms is made still more emphatic by the declaration that "What it was the fashion in his [Gilpin's] day to deem essentially pictorial is a minor question." [12] Now, however, with both "pictorial" and "picturesque" ready to hand, Bridges considers that we *must* differentiate their meanings (even, I suppose, if we subscribe to a theory which calls for their identification). To accomplish this differentiation, Bridges imports Hegel's classification of art as Symbolic, Classical, or Romantic, each of which genera contains three analogous species. From this classification, and from Ruskin's account of the picturesque school in England, "the right use of the words *pictorial* and *picturesque* may be deduced." All painting is Romantic; but "the term *picturesque* has lost its generic meaning, and has its proper definition in denoting an ultra-romantic school which has its own proprieties and excesses [i.e., "picturesque" = romantic-Romantic]. The word *pictorial* should therefore come to its own, to designate Hegel's mid-species, which he styles classical-Romantic, denoting such 'forms' as have been commonly recognized by all painters as suitable and effective in their art." [13]

Now despite the use of two philosophical aestheticians in arriving at these definitions, this is clearly a linguistic argument. For nothing of the philosophical principles or method of analysis of either Hegel or Ruskin is taken over, only a schematism of categories, stripped of all but the most general connotations. It is apparent that the definition of Bridges is of no use precisely in all those cases where accurate definition should be of most use—in systematic and technical discussions. Even if these pseudo-Hegelian meanings be taken over for popular conversational use, how can conversational use be set up as a norm for philosophy or science to follow? And is it true that even in everyday parlance we always use "picturesque," or should always use it, in this one sense alone?

In sharp contrast to this verbal treatment of the problem is the discussion of Christopher Hussey in *The Picturesque: Studies in a Point of View*, the very title of which implies an examination of ideas rather than of words. This book is universally acknowledged—and I acquiesce in the judgment—to be the most valuable study of the topic. It displays taste, scholarship, and wit; but Hussey has his own "point of view" which sometimes throws the picturesque theorists into a false perspective. Hussey sees the picturesque as "a long phase in the aesthetic relation of man to nature," a phase in which, through the pictorial appreciation of nature, "poetry, painting, gardening, architecture, and the art of travel may be said to have been fused into the single 'art of landscape.' The combination might be called 'the Picturesque.'" The picturesque phase was in the case of each art a transition from classicism to romanticism, and "occurred at the point when an art shifted its appeal from the reason to the imagination." Classic art addresses the reason, romantic art the imagination, and "the picturesque interregnum between classic and romantic art was necessary in order to enable the imagination to form the habit of feeling through the eyes. Pictures were in each case taken as the guide for how to see, because painting is the art of seeing . . . [but] as soon as the imagination had absorbed what painting had to teach it, it could feel for itself, and the intermediate process . . . could be dropped." Picturesque art thus "accentuated visual qualities at the expense of rational ones on the one hand, and of associated ideas on the other. . . . Picturesque art is imperfect art, but not necessarily bad art." [14] Imperfect as it is, picturesque art is the first step towards abstract aesthetic values; and it was natural that the first step should be the appreciation of visual qualities in nature through education of the eye to recognize qualities which painters had previously isolated. "Each art passed through a phase of imitating painting before developing into the romantic phase that came after, when the eye and the imagination had learnt to work for themselves. The period of imitation is the picturesque period." [15] This is history arranged in accordance with a scheme of dialectical contraries: classic—romantic, rational—imaginative, objective—subjective, and so forth. The analysis is neat, the progression smooth; but it appears to me to involve distortion of many of the data, and to prejudge the merits of the picturesque point of view, to underrate its artists and belittle its theoreticians.

Wylie Sypher has set the picturesque in a different dialectical framework. Drawing from all the arts, but basing his distinctions primarily upon painting, Sypher finds that the "suavity and gaiety" of Burkeian beauty identify it with the rococo, and that "sublimity is a tremor, felt at a distance, from the monstrous baroque agitation of

Michelangelo or Milton." Temperamentally, "the XVIII Century found it embarrassing to surrender so recklessly, and thus sought in the picturesque, a sentimentalized sublimity, the excitement of the sublime without its abandon. The picturesque was a characteristic XVIII Century appropriation of the baroque." [16] In Sypher's analysis, however, both sublime and picturesque are more shallow than the baroque from which they derive, for they do not reflect "internal or otherwise inherent tensions. In consequence, no drama is available to either picturesque or sublime (which are lyric) . . . both are akin to pathos rather than to tragedy. . . ." [17] Sypher's account is highly abstract, and finds little enough support in the concrete data, for not only do none of the theorists of the picturesque seem conscious of the motives ascribed to them, but the picturesque has, in its origins, a more evident connection with beauty than with sublimity. Sypher's analysis, even more than Hussey's, makes the entire picturesque movement trivial and inferior. One purpose of this study will be to view the picturesque, and the writers on the picturesque, without pejorative implication and without refraction through an alien theory, to restore the theories of the picturesque to some measure of philosophic respectability.

CHAPTER 13

William Gilpin

❧

"P"ICTURESQUE" was rescued from the indeterminacy of fashion
by William Gilpin, who made it the key term of the new aesthetic
attitude of which he was himself the earliest exponent. The "venerable
founder and master of the picturesque school," Gilpin exerted a profound and lasting influence upon the taste not only of England but of
Europe, though his analysis of the picturesque was soon superseded
by the more subtle and philosophical studies of Uvedale Price and
Payne Knight.[1]

In the youthful and anonymous *Dialogue at Stow* (1748),[2] Gilpin
uses the term "picturesque" conventionally: the picturesque is that
which is suited to pictorial representation. There is already apparent,
however, the tendency to consider rough and irregular scenes of nature especially picturesque, to find in landscape the peculiar locus of
the picturesque. In the later and more widely influential *Essay on
Prints*,[3] to be sure, the subject itself demanded that Gilpin avoid the
appropriation of the picturesque to wild and intricate scenes exclusively, and the term is employed, accordingly, in its more general
acceptation. The definition given in the preliminary "Explanation of
Terms" is simply this: "a term expressive of that peculiar kind of
beauty, which is agreeable in a picture."[4] The entire *Essay on Prints*
is implicitly a discussion of picturesque beauty in this traditional sense,
in its various aspects of composition, lighting, drawing, expression,
execution, and so forth. The *word* "picturesque," however, is very
sparingly employed. The landscapes of Ridinger are praised for being "picturesque and romantic," a phrase applied also to the landscapes of Sadler; and this is the use of the word which Gilpin was to
make conventional. But when Ridinger's scenes of hunting are said
to be didactic and "least picturesque of any of his works," the application is the older and broader—suitable for a picture.

It was in Gilpin's picturesque travels, which began to appear in 1782, that the picturesque of roughness and intricacy was defined and popularized; the extension of the term was pretty well fixed by Gilpin, though philosophical dispute over its intension was later to engross aestheticians, gardeners, painters, and amateurs. The most theoretical of these works of Gilpin is his *Three Essays: On Picturesque Beauty; On Picturesque Travel; and On Sketching Landscape: to Which is Added a Poem, On Landscape Painting.*[5] The general principles developed in these essays are reduced to principles of landscape in the *Remarks on Forest Scenery, and Other Woodland Views, Relative Chiefly to Picturesque Beauty Illustrated by the Scenes of New Forest in Hampshire. In Three Books.*[6] This work, then, is of an intermediate degree of abstraction, and the middle principles devised in it are applied in the six volumes of tours—all which bear titles of the form, *Observations [upon some part of Great Britain] Relative Chiefly to Picturesque Beauty.*[7] All of these volumes, illustrated by Gilpin's fine aquatints, were immensely popular and greatly affected British taste in natural and artificial scenery.

In this study, however, attention must be confined to the theoretical essays, in which, unhappily, Gilpin is least impressive. The first of the *Three Essays*, "On Picturesque Beauty," attempts to dispel the confusion (which all philosophers lament, and which each claims the honor of terminating) about the nature of beauty: "Disputes about beauty," Gilpin declares, "might perhaps be involved in less confusion, if a distinction were established, which certainly exists, between such objects as are *beautiful* [merely], and such as are *picturesque*—between those, which please the eye in their *natural state;* and those, which please from some quality, capable of being *illustrated by painting.*"[8] Gilpin is careful to emphasize that the picturesque is a species of beauty, not a distinct character, and in his dedicatory letter defends himself against the charge of "supposing, *all beauty* to consist in *picturesque beauty*—and the face of nature to be examined *only by the rules of painting.*"[9] The pleasures of imagination are various, and the picturesque is only one additional mode. The problem of Gilpin's essay is to define the causes of that mode: "*What is that quality in objects, which particularly marks them as picturesque?*"[10]

When Gilpin remarks that "in examining the *real object*, we shall find, one source of beauty arises from that species of elegance, which we call *smoothness*, or *neatness*,"[11] the phrase, "the *real object*," suggests that his theory deals not with art itself but with nature considered as a subject for art; and this is, indeed, an obvious consequence of the general sense Gilpin assigns to the "picturesque." But in picturesque representation, neatness and smoothness, "instead of being picturesque, in reality strip the object, in which they reside, of all pretensions to *picturesque beauty*." [12] In fact, Gilpin continues, "*roughness* forms the most essential point of difference between the *beautiful*, and the *picturesque*; as it seems to be that particular quality, which makes objects chiefly pleasing in painting.—I use the general term *roughness*; but properly speaking roughness relates only to the surfaces of bodies: when we speak of their delineation, we use the word *ruggedness*. Both ideas however equally enter into the picturesque; and both are observable in the smaller, as well as in the larger parts of nature. . . ." [13] A quick induction supports this principle: the painter prefers ruins to perfect architecture, an overgrown cart track to a finished garden, an aged face with dishevelled locks to the smoother beauty of youth, a human figure in action to one in repose, a cart horse or an ass to a polished Arabian. (Sydney Smith summed up the difference between beautiful and picturesque in remarking that "the Vicar's horse is *beautiful*, the Curate's *picturesque*." [14]) Price and others urge that the induction is imperfect; but Gilpin casts about anxiously to discover reasons for what he conceives to be this general preference.

The painter's love of the shaggy stems partly from the encouragement a rough subject gives to a sketchy facility of execution. It is not only that a rougher touch is easier to master than a smoother and more elegant style—Gilpin does not stress this point, which is not likely to appeal to the spectator expecting skill in the artist; rather, "a free, bold touch is in itself pleasing." [15] Gilpin gives no reason for this effect, though it is pretty clear that associations with ideas of unconstrained ease underlie it. But "it is not merely for the sake of his *execution*, that the painter prefers *rough* objects to *smooth*. The very essence of his art requires it." [16] Picturesque composition, in the first place, "consists in uniting in one whole a variety of parts; and these parts can only be obtained from rough objects." [17] Rough objects, again, alone yield what Gilpin terms "effect of light and shade"— massed and graduated lights and shades, with richness of minute variations, and "catching lights" on prominences. In coloring, too, roughness affords greater variation. In sum, roughness is more various; the taste for the picturesque is a taste for a greater measure of complexity and intricacy than either beautiful or sublime affords. Gilpin supports his reasons with an experiment. One of his aquatints exhibits "a smooth knoll coming forward on one side, intersected by a smooth knoll on the other; with a smooth plain perhaps in the middle, and a smooth mountain in the distance," [18] while a companion aquatint shows the same general scene broken into irregular and jutting forms, marked by rugged rocks, clothed with shaggy boskage, and enlivened by two figures and a ruined castle. This experiment can not, however, quite pretend to be an instance of the Method of Difference: the second print is not merely rougher; it brings with it all the interest of complicated imitation and all the charms of manifold associations. Gilpin passes over the crucial question, how much of the effect is to be attributed to these causes?

He does, however, pause to explain away apparent exceptions to the principle that roughness is the ideal subject for art. Those really smooth objects which may have a good effect in a picture, he argues, are apparently rough or highly varied: the lake seems rough from the broken light on its surface undulations, or from the reflection of rough objects; the horse's smooth coat displays the play of muscle beneath; the smoothness of plumage is only the ground for its breaking coloration; the polish of the column only displays the irregularity of the veining. Or (if the preceding does not convince) smoothness may be picturesque by contrast, adding piquancy to roughness. These explanations are specious, but it is clear that there is a difficulty, and that it has not been met so adequately as to remove all doubt; Price was subsequently to direct a part of his criticism of Gilpin to this vulnerable point.

This difficulty set aside, however, Gilpin seems to have solved his problem. But instead, he resumes the analysis: "Having thus from a variety of examples endeavoured to shew, that *roughness* either *real*, or *apparent*, forms an essential difference between the *beautiful*, and the *picturesque*; it may be expected, that we should point out the reason of this difference. It is obvious enough, why the painter prefers *rough* objects to *smooth:* but it is not so obvious, why the quality of *roughness* should make an *essential difference* between objects of *beauty*, and objects suited to *artificial representation*." [19] This is a subtle distinction. The question is, why do we come to approve *in nature* of things which would look well *in pictures?* Implicit in the very question is the recognition that our liking for the real objects is not merely from an association with painting, but has an independent basis (although, perhaps, a basis so concealed and obscured that a knowledge of painting is usually requisite to cultivate the natural aptitude). If this *is* Gilpin's point, he should be led here into the kind of inquiry in which Price later engaged; if it is *not*, his inquiry should have terminated with the determination of the reasons why the rough and rugged pleases in painting.

In any event, Gilpin fails to discover the natural basis of the "essential difference" between objects of natural beauty and those suited to artificial representation. Four hypotheses are tested and rejected: (*1*) That "the picturesque eye abhors art; and delights solely in nature: and that as art abounds with *regularity,* which is only another name for *smoothness;* and the images of nature with *irregularity,* which is only another name for *roughness,* we have here a solution of our question." [20] But art is not invariably regular; and many art objects—drapery, shipping, ruined castles, et cetera—are excellent subjects in painting. (*2*) That the picturesque is based upon the *"happy union of simplicity and variety,* to which the *rough* ideas essentially contribute." [21] But the beautiful in general equally with that species of its denominated picturesque is characterized by this happy union. (*3*) That the imitative art of painting can more readily imitate rough objects. This, however, is false in fact. (Gilpin had, to be sure, asserted something like this in treating facility of execution; the present point, however, concerns *fidelity,* not mechanical facility, of imitation.) (*4*) That painting is not strictly imitative, but *deceptive;* that the rough touches of the painter permit concealment of the deception; and that rough objects permit rough touches. But rough objects may be executed by smooth touches and these last are then picturesque.

It is interesting to observe that, the second excepted, these conjectures are drawn from considerations involving art. Now, the question to which they are addressed has meaning only if we suppose that the reason of the essential difference of picturesque and beautiful is found in nature and *not* in art; for, if the delight in the picturesque is based only on some kind of association with art, the reasons already given for the painter's preference of it are sufficient, and no problem exists. Gilpin's conjectures, then, are an *ignoratio elenchi;* the answer to the question must be found elsewhere, perhaps in the directions taken by Price, or Knight, or Alison, or Stewart. Thwarted by his methodological error, Gilpin throws up his hands in despair: "Thus foiled, should we in the true spirit of inquiry, persist; or honestly give up the cause, and own we cannot search out the source of this difference? I am afraid this is the truth, whatever airs of dogmatizing we may assume. Inquiries into *principles* rarely end in satisfaction. Could we even gain satisfaction in our present question, new doubts would arise. The very first principles of our art would be questioned. . . . We should be asked, What is beauty? What is taste?" [22] To clinch his argument, Gilpin pretends to examine the debates of the learned on taste; he hears authors contend for the cultivation of innate talents, for utility, common sense, a special sense of beauty, proportion generally, and particular canons of proportion. "Thus," he concludes, "in our inquiries into *first principles,* we go on without end, and without satisfaction. The human understanding is unequal to the search. In philosophy we inquire for them in vain—in physics—in metaphysics—in morals. Even in the polite arts, where the subject, one should imagine, is less recondite, the inquiry, we find, is equally vague. We are puzzled, and bewildered; but not informed, all is uncertainty; a strife of words. . . ." [23]

Such a disclaimer can not be expected to satisfy the pride of philosophers; Gilpin leaves an opening here for re-examination of the entire question. Before advancing to such re-examinations, however, I shall describe briefly the other essays of the present volume. Baffled in his search for causes, Gilpin turns, in the second essay, "On Picturesque Travel," to closer examination of the effects. Picturesque travel has for its object natural and artificial beauty of every kind, but especially, of course, the picturesque. [24] The distinction between beauty and sublimity might be expected to afford a corresponding division of the picturesque; but since Gilpin has defined "picturesque" to denote *"such objects, as are proper subjects for painting,"* [25] it must be granted that *"sublimity alone* cannot make an object *picturesque."* [26] Mere vastness, the merely terrific, does not lend itself to depiction; only an admixture of the beautiful can render sublimity picturesque. Granted this proviso, Gilpin is ready to admit the sublime, too, as an object of picturesque travel, and even descants on scenes of *"picturesque horror."* [27] The third member of Addison's triad, the novel, is rarely picturesque; the picturesque eye is not attracted to the curious and fantastic, but "is fond of the simplicity of nature; and sees most beauty in her *most usual* forms." [28] These usual forms are not, however, insipid; the strongly marked, the "characteristic," is most picturesque. So essential, indeed, is the characteristic to the picturesque that Gilpin even remarks of a scene beautiful as a whole but with no strongly characteristic parts, that "it exhibits such a specimen of the picturesque (if I may speak in terms seemingly contradictory) as is not well calculated to make a picture." [29]

"After the *objects* of picturesque travel," says Gilpin (with a little flourish of organizational skill), "we consider it's *sources of amusement. . . .*" [30] These consist in the pursuit itself and the attainment. In the attainment we are sometimes so happy as to come upon an agreeable whole, but are usually reduced to admiring parts. Our pleasure may be "scientifical," conjecturing amendments and forming comparisons with scenes of nature or works of art; but the great pleasure from natural scenes is enthusiastic: "We are most delighted, when some grand scene, tho perhaps of incorrect composition, rising before the eye, strikes us beyond the power of thought. . . . In this pause of intellect; this *deliquium* of the soul, an enthusiastic sensation of pleasure overspreads it, previous to any examination by the rules of art. The general idea of the scene makes an impression, before any appeal is made to the judgment." [31] But beyond contemplation of the object itself, new vistas of delight open before us: our general ideas are formed,[32] and from these we learn to sketch, first by way of remembrance, then as a free exercise of fancy, an exercise which can be indulged even without the pencil. "There may be more pleasure," Gilpin declares,

> in recollecting, and recording, from a few transient lines, the scenes we have admired, than in the present enjoyment of them. If the scenes indeed have *peculiar greatness*, this secondary pleasure cannot be attended with those enthusiastic feelings, which accompanied the real exhibition. But, in general, tho it may be a calmer species of pleasure, it is more uniform, and uninterrupted. It flatters us too with the idea of a sort of creation of our own. . . .[33]

It is noteworthy that Gilpin finds objects of art less capable of arousing enthusiasm than the works of nature. The picturesque traveler, in fact, is apt to acquire some contempt for the haunts of men, which have so often a poor effect on landscape. The unnaturalness of the garden, the limitations of painting become more obvious to the enthusiast of the picturesque. "The more refined our taste grows from the *study of nature,*" Gilpin generalizes, "the more insipid are the *works of art.* Few of it's efforts please. The idea of the great original is so strong, that the copy must be pure, if it do not disgust. But the varieties of nature's charts are such, that, study them as we can, new varieties will always arise: and let our taste be ever so refined, her works, on which it is formed (at least when we consider them as *objects,*) must always go beyond it; and furnish fresh sources both of pleasure and amusement." [34] There is a paradox here: a system which isolates a certain property of nature for admiration, a property defined by its excellence as a subject for art, comes at last to reject the art for the nature which was at first only its subject. I have observed above that Gilpin is led to the point of redefining the picturesque as a universal complex of properties pervading both nature and art, and acting upon our physical organism or our mental associations to produce an effect peculiar to itself. Here again a picturesque with a basis independent of art is needed to resolve the paradox of setting out to find the qualities of pictures in nature and returning with a preference of nature to pictures.

Gilpin's third essay deals with one of the "sources of amusement" afforded by picturesque travel: sketching landscape. His precepts have a practical bent, yet they rest upon the aesthetic ideas of the first essay. The subject is handled in a natural order: composition (both *design* in the selection of subject and its parts, and *disposition* in arrangement of them), chiaroscuro, coloring—the order of execution. Sketching is based upon general ideas picked up in picturesque travel; even more than in finished drawings and pictures, in sketches "general ideas only must be looked for; not the peculiarities of portrait." [35]

Before turning to the criticism of Gilpin's work by Uvedale Price, which leads directly into the burst of picturesque theory and practice in the last decade of the century, I should mention the observations of Reynolds on the picturesque. Using Mason as an intermediary, Gilpin submitted a draft of his three essays to Reynolds as early as 1776. The latter replied with a letter on the picturesque, addressed to Mason, a letter which Mason forwarded to Gilpin.[36] Gilpin's distinction of picturesque from ordinary beauty is neatly reduced by Reynolds, whose dialectical method and generalizing tendency hardly allow for according the picturesque either co-ordinate status with the beautiful or even that of a distinct species of the beautiful. With characteristic politeness, Reynolds seems to put Gilpin's argument on a firmer basis as he brings it into his own system:

> An object is said to be picturesque in proportion as it would have a good effect in a picture.
> If the word is applied with propriety, it is applied solely to the works of nature. Deformity has less of nature in proportion as it is deformed or out of the common course of nature. Deformity cannot [be]; beauty only is picturesque. Beauty and picturesque [Reynolds regularly omits the article] are therefore synonymous. This is my creed, which does not contradict any part of the Essay; but I think is the great leading principle which includes it.[37]

Reynolds grants that "roughness, or irregularity is certainly more picturesque than smoothness or regularity, because this carries with it the appearance of art, nature being more various and irregular than art generally is. . . . Where art has been, picturesque is destroyed,—unless we make this exception, which proves the rule, that nature itself, by accident, may be so formal or unnatural as to have the effect of art . . . you may then make nature more picturesque by art, by making her more like herself, that is, more like what she generally is." [38] In fact, Gilpin's first rejected hypothesis about the essential nature of the picturesque satisfies Reynolds well; "my opinion is perfectly expressed" by it, he declares, and he is puzzled that Gilpin thinks it unsatisfactory. Reynolds explains away the contrary instances which Gilpin had adduced—those draperies, ships, and ruined castles which appear to advantage in painting—and with them Gilpin's principle that "*a painter's nature* is whatever he *imitates,* whether the object be what is commonly called natural, or artificial." [39] The castle (for instance) is found to please from "an association of ideas by sending the mind backwards into antiquity and producing some new sentiment—or by being marked by time, and made a sort of natural object. . . ." [40]

For Reynolds, irregularity is nature, nature is beauty, and beauty is picturesque. But this picturesque is not the shaggy picturesque of Gilpin, the rough textures, fragmented outlines, and broken colors of which would be, to Reynolds, all in some measure defects. Accordingly, fifteen years later, when Gilpin was at last ready to publish his essays and sent them again for the *imprimatur* of Reynolds, Reynolds took a different tack, suggesting that "picturesque" as Gilpin describes it is "applicable to the excellences of the inferior schools, rather than to the higher. The works of Michael Angelo, Raphael, &c. appear to me to have nothing of it; whereas Reubens, and the Venetian painters may almost be said to have nothing else." [41] This comment applies not to the *definition* of picturesqueness, the statement of its denotation as comprising objects suitable for painting, for higher and lower schools alike depict objects suited for painting; it applies rather to the *description* of qualities which Gilpin's induction had indicated were peculiarly fitted for pictorial representation—to the connotation, that is, which does not (so Reynolds is arguing) correspond to the denotation.

Reynolds appears to retract, in the last paragraph of his letter of 1791, his opinion of fifteen years earlier: "Whatever objections presented themselves at first view," he confesses, "were done away on a closer inspection; and I am not quite sure, but that is the case in regard to the observation, which I have ventured to make on the word *picturesque.*" [42] But it does not seem to me that Reynolds has really changed his mind. His earlier remarks, which appear to be directed at the definition, reject this new aesthetic character as anything different from beauty; his later remarks, which appear to discuss the *description* rather than the definition, accord the picturesque an inferior status, that already granted it in the tenth discourse, which was written almost at the time of the first letter.[43] If there be any change, it might be that Reynolds is no longer so insistent on excluding art works as subjects for painting; but this is no fundamental part of his doctrine, and, stated as flatly as he puts it in 1776, seems false.

Gilpin sees the distinction of definition from description and in his brief answer reaffirms the definition while confessing his ignorance of the grand style and conceding that his roughness is probably characteristic of the lower styles. This is implicitly an admission that his analysis of the picturesque was imperfect, as being based on a partial survey of painting, and that his description does not tally with his definition—although it may describe something genuinely distinct. Picturesque theory developed by keeping the description and seeking for new definitions and for new causal analyses.

Vague as are the indications which Gilpin gives of a causal analysis of the picturesque, it is possible to conjecture that he would have been more sympathetic to an associational than a physiological account. He is decisive in proclaiming that the picturesque eye sees through the imagination—that "the picturesque eye has nothing to do with tunics, irises, and retinas." [44] At times, Gilpin's picturesque appears to depend upon association with concrete wholes, as in his repeated resentment at the intrusion of art into natural scenes. But this kind of association is not prominent in Gilpin; his picturesque depends chiefly upon associations with abstract qualities—with roughness of texture, with irregularity of outline, with contrasting lights and shades, with variegated and graduated colors. These associations he does not attempt to trace, and this omission invites further exploration of the picturesque.

CHAPTER 14

Sir Uvedale Price

❦

UVEDALE PRICE, a gentleman of landed property in the west of England, was a Whig parliamentarian—he was created Sir Uvedale, Bart., for party services; a gentleman farmer—he contributed occasionally to Arthur Young's *Annals of Agriculture;* something of a classical scholar—as a young man he translated from Pausanias, and late in life prepared a study of Greek and Latin pronunciation which is said to anticipate modern views. But it is as a man of taste, as champion and theorist of the picturesque, that Price became, and in some measure still remains, an important figure. Like his neighbor in adjoining Shropshire, Richard Payne Knight, Price was no mere theorist; he laid out Foxley, his Herefordshire estate, on picturesque principles, and combined the speculations of the philosopher with the practical taste of the artist. His works on the picturesque remain the principal monument of picturesque doctrine.[1]

Gilpin had left picturesque theory involved in paradox: though understanding the picturesque to be merely that which appears to advantage in pictorial representation, Gilpin gave an account of picturesque qualities which unrealistically delimited the real scope of the painter's art. Still more important, he sought, inconsistently with his definition of the picturesque, some essential difference in nature between the picturesque and the merely beautiful, a difference independent of the special requirements of the painter's art. Since Gilpin had pointed out an assemblage of qualities bearing *some* special relation to the art of painting, and yet had failed to discover the essential nature and efficiency of those properties, the way was open for a reformulation of the problem which would avoid these embarrassments.

Price undertakes just such a reformulation. "There are few words," he observes, "whose meaning has been less accurately determined than that of the word picturesque."[2] Noting that the popular sense

Aquatints from WILLIAM GILPIN's Three Essays (1792) mentioned on pages 194–95. The first portrays a scene without picturesque adornment; the second presents the same general scene enhanced by picturesque composition.

("depictable") is not properly distinguished from "beautiful" and "sublime," to which terms Burke had given precision, Price insists that such distinction must exist, for no one supposes the terms synonymous. Gilpin erred in adopting this common acceptation as exact and determinate; but Gilpin's definition, Price declares, is "at once too vague, and too confined": too vague, because it does not isolate the qualities which Price and Gilpin agree in deeming picturesque from other qualities which please equally in painting; too confined, because of the exclusive reference to a particular art. Price intends to show "that the picturesque has a character not less separate and distinct than either the sublime or the beautiful, nor less independent of the art of painting." [3]

But Price's aim is more comprehensive than this. His works on the picturesque are intended, theoretically, to determine the general causes and effects of the picturesque in all the works of nature and art, and (more narrowly) to point out "the use of studying pictures, for the purpose of improving real landscape"; practically, his books are to open new sources of aesthetic enjoyment and (more narrowly) to demolish the system of modern gardening introduced by Kent and aggravated by Brown. Price aims, in short, to solve the problem which Gilpin was constantly on the verge of stating, but never succeeded in isolating: What is it in the *nature* of picturesque objects which renders them different from beautiful objects independently of reference to pictures? Having determined, in his first essay, the general character of the picturesque, Price declares,

> The next step was to shew, that not only the effect of picturesque objects, but of all visible objects whatever, are to be judged of by the great leading principles of Painting; which principles, though they are really founded in nature, and totally independent of art, are, however, most easily and usefully studied in the pictures of eminent painters. On these two points . . . rests the whole force of my argument. If I have succeeded in establishing them, the system of modern Gardening, which, besides banishing all picturesque effects, has violated every principle of painting, is of course demolished. [4]

The inquiry, as Price puts it,

> is not in what sense certain words are used . . . but whether there be certain qualities, which uniformly produce the same effects in all visible objects, and, according to the same analogy, in objects of hearing and of all the other senses. . . .

If it can be shewn that a character composed of these qualities, and

distinct from all others, does universally prevail . . . it surely deserves
a distinct title; but with respect to the real ground of inquiry, it matters
little whether such a character . . . be called beautiful, sublime, or
picturesque, or by any other name, or by no name at all.[5]

The analytical apparatus which Price brought to this problem was
in part borrowed from Burke. Price professes throughout to be a disciple of that eminent man, but (as is usual) the master's doctrine
undergoes considerable transformation in the hands of the disciple.
Burke distinguishes sublime from beautiful by means of a psychology
of pleasure and pain and of the passions; he then isolates the material
properties which are fitted to arouse these feelings; and finally he
conjectures at a nervous physiology to account for the production of
such effects by such causes. Price makes a shift at following the same
method; but the physiological theory is considerably attenuated, and
even less plausible than Burke's. Burke holds (as Price indicates in
a brief but accurate précis) that the natural sublime produces astonishment by stretching the nervous fibers beyond their normal tone,
so that the motions of the soul are suspended as if in horror; the
beautiful produces love and complacency by relaxing the fibers below
their natural tone, which is accompanied by melting or languor. "In
pursuing the same train of ideas," Price continues, "I may add, that
the effect of the picturesque is curiosity; an effect, which, though less
splendid and powerful, has a more general influence. . . . [Curi-
osity] by its active agency keeps the fibres to their full [i.e., their nat-
ural] tone; and thus picturesqueness when mixed with either of the
other characters, corrects the languor of beauty, or the tension of
sublimity." [6] Now, this notion is attended with a difficulty. How does
the stimulus of the picturesque, which keeps the fibers to their natural tone, midway betwixt languor and tension—how does this differ
from no stimulus at all? It might be allowed that the assemblage of
qualities which Price treats somehow produces an effect peculiar to
itself; but the apparatus of elastic nerves does not seem elastic enough
to embrace these new phenomena. A fiber endued with a certain original tension may be tensed further or it may be relaxed; but it is
not easy to conceive of any third possibility. It may be that a physiological theory of greater elaborateness might be devised, with a
variety of kinds of fibers, so that combinations could be struck out—
a nerve organ, so to speak. But in this case, it would be a question
why only these few harmonies are possible; why not a host of similar aesthetic characters? It seems prudent to avoid such fanciful con-

jectures, and to trace the mental associations and reactions as far as possible to their origins, but to leave unbridged the chasm between mind and body.

That Price subscribed to the general method of Burke is unquestionable: "I certainly am convinced," he states, "of the general truth and accuracy of Mr. Burke's system, for it is the foundation of my own. . . ."[7] Yet he rarely appeals to this materialist physiology to account for details of the phenomena he investigates; his works are confined pretty largely to careful discrimination of the effects and painstaking analysis of the material properties which stimulate them. It is in the particular material causes rather than in the general effects, moreover, that the distinction of the character is best seen, and "it is from having pursued the opposite method of reasoning," Price suggests, "that the distinction between the beautiful and the picturesque has been denied."[8]

Price exhibits an eclectic tendency, and owes fealty not only to Burke but to Sir Joshua Reynolds; he contrives to employ both of these radically different systems to support his own, which is different from either. "An Introductory Essay on Beauty," prefixed to Price's *Dialogue on the Distinct Characters of the Picturesque and the Beautiful*, undertakes to reconcile Burke and Reynolds and to subsume both under Price. As he presents a rather full précis of Burke's views, Price begins to slip a new foundation beneath them; the foundation is this, that "if there be any one position on this subject [beauty] likely to be generally admitted, it is, *that each production of nature is most beautiful in that particular state, before which her work would have appeared incomplete and unfinished, and after which it would seem to be tending, however gradually, towards decay.* . . ."[9] No qualities are so accordant with our ideas of beauty (as Price had put it in the *Essay* of 1794) "as those which are in a high degree expressive of youth, health and vigour, whether in animal or vegetable life; the chief of which qualities are smoothness and softness in the surface; fulness and undulation in the outline; symmetry in the parts, and clearness and freshness in the colour."[10]

Burke had included Hogarth's doctrine of the line of beauty in his own theory; but the last of Reynolds' *Idler* papers, as Price very reasonably interprets it, includes a sharp criticism of Hogarth's theory, and thus by implication of Burke's.[11] Price nonetheless sees no real contradiction in the methods of Burke and of Reynolds, urging that although the method of considering beauty as the central form, and as being produced by attending only to the great general ideas inherent in universal nature, be a grander way of treating the subject; and though the discriminations of Mr. Burke may, in comparison, appear minute; yet, after all, each object . . . must be composed of qualities, the knowledge of which is necessary to a knowledge of it's distinct characters. Such a method is more easily apprehended, than the more general and abstract one which Sir Joshua proposes; and when allied with it, is more likely to produce a just estimate of the character altogether, than any other method singly.[12]

But Price can not ignore the obvious contradiction in doctrine, and sets himself to undermining that part of Sir Joshua's position which denies the possibility of comparing species in point of beauty; he even questions the notion that *custom* determines us to prefer the "central form." Price concedes that the beauty of form does consist in a central type, a type isolated for the human figure by the Greek sculptors—an "invariable general form," but not that which nature most frequently produces; rather, that which she may be supposed to intend in her productions. Since both Burke and Reynolds appeal to the same model of beauty—antique statues of young and graceful persons—Price concludes that their notions coincide, "and the only difference between them is, that the one treats of the great general abstract principles of beauty; the other of its distinct visible qualities." [13] Finally, Price concludes with triumph, "if it appear, that those qualities which are supposed to constitute the beautiful, are in all objects chiefly found to exist at that period, when nature has attained, but not passed, a state of perfect completion, we surely have as clear, and as certain principles on this, as on many other subjects, where little doubt is entertained." [14]

To establish beauty in this fashion—to make it a response to signs of freshness and youth—is to establish it on the association of ideas. Commentators on Price have not recognized the importance of association in his aesthetics; Hussey, indeed, denies that Price admitted any role to association. Yet despite Price's effort to champion the theory of Burke, association assumes a place of very great though undefined importance in his own analysis. "All external objects," he declares, "affect us in two different ways; by the impression they make on the senses, and by the reflections they suggest to the mind. These two modes, though very distinct in their operations, often unite in producing one effect; the reflections of the mind, either strengthening, weakening, or giving a new direction to the impression received by the eye." [15] In this passage from "On Architecture and Buildings," Price attributes to the "eye" the pleasures arising from form, light and shadow, and color; and to the "mind" the pleasures stemming from utility, historical connections, and so forth. Elsewhere, however, much even of the effect of the physical properties is traced to association. Throughout, in fact, Price appeals both to inherent efficiency and to association, and rarely troubles to make clear what aspect and proportion of the total effect is to be attributed to each severally. The weakness of his theory is not that he denies "subjective" factors,[16] but that he constantly employs association as an analytic device without anywhere presenting a theory of association or an outline of its implications for aesthetics.

This problem of association can be clarified by employing the matrix of distinctions developed in my introduction. Associations among the perceptions of the different senses, so that, e.g., tangible properties come to be "seen," are of crucial importance; for it is thus that smoothness becomes beautiful to the eye. Still more pervasive in Price are associations of the sensible qualities of things with human traits and feelings. It might be argued, indeed, that these associations are the essential feature of the picturesque as Price understands it; for the picturesque depends less on the nature of the concrete whole than on the visual and tactile properties comprised therein. Of this kind is that crucial connection between the beautiful and ideas of freshness and youth, and the association of the picturesque with age and decay. Price notes, for instance, that ruins, though vegetation overgrowing them may have produced an air of softness and insensible transition, are still not "beautiful"; for the mind, "from the powerful and extensive influence of that principle, called *association of ideas,* is unwilling to give them a title, which, as I conceive, implies the freshness of youth; or, at least, a state of high and perfect preservation." [17] The connection of the picturesque with curiosity, again, may be dependent upon association of ideas as well as upon association of impressions through resemblance of the sense impressions with the passion.

There are, moreover, associations of objects, of concrete wholes, with human traits and feelings. Concretes as such may exhibit utility, design, fitness, naturalness, congruity, propriety, and so forth— all which relations enter into the aesthetic response, and all which are repeatedly stressed by Price. Or the concrete wholes may, as signs, suggest historical, social, poetical, or other affecting circumstances. Blenheim, its brilliant ornaments gilded by the setting sun, seems an enchanted palace, and the viewer perhaps thinks of Alcina and Armida; or the village washing scene becomes an image of peace and security, and suggests the appropriate passage from Homer.[18] Gothic architecture, rich with associations to the romance, the violence, the faith of the middle ages, suggests further to the cultivated mind paintings in which it has figured, and to which it had itself originally lent a charm.

When Price speaks of the "poetry" of painting, he refers to associations with the subjects of the art; and when he speaks of "the art itself," he refers, not to technique, but to the aesthetic characters and the principles of their admixture. The associations constituting the poetry of painting may suggest to us modes of life, historical epochs, remote or fascinating places. The aesthetic characters which constitute the "art" itself are also, at least in part, associational, but the associations are of a different order—they are associations of the abstracted qualities of line and shadow and color with one another and with the basic feelings of human nature. It is perhaps the predominance in Price of such abstract association over poetical association that has misled scholars into considering him an "objectivist." It is true that Price often posits a direct nervous action of formal properties on the mind; but still more frequently he supposes an associational mechanism. It is because the use of associational psychology is not accompanied with metaphysical fanfares that it has been minimized or overlooked.

Price, in short, despite reiterated allegiance to the principles of Burke, is in fact eclectic both in the method and the substance of his theory. It is only his modification of Burke's principles which enables him to introduce the picturesque as a middle character coordinate with the beautiful and the sublime.[19]

It is now possible to turn from discussion of Price's method to the content of his doctrine. The gist of it is set forth in the *Essay on the Picturesque* of 1794. The organization of this book is rhetorical; it is designed to lead the reader by gradual induction to "believe in" the picturesque, the abstract theory of which is presented only at the end of the first part of the treatise. The opening chapter treats the study of pictures for the purpose of improving grounds, concluding, with embittered irony, in a description of an improver at work adjusting a Claude to his notions. The second chapter moves from art to nature, and shows how the attractively picturesque qualities of a hollow lane would be destroyed by "improvement." These instances suggest the reality of the picturesque character, and the third chapter, accordingly, takes up the question at large, comparing this new quality with the beautiful in various works of art and nature; the fourth chapter performs the same function for picturesque and sublime. The fifth treats of the mixture of beautiful and picturesque, with an eye to improvement. Price turns then to detailed examination of picturesque material qualities, dwelling especially on the nervous effects of smoothness and roughness; he treats of form and light and shadow (in the sixth chapter), with especial attention to breadth of light and shadow (in the seventh), and finally of color (in the eighth). The final chapter of this first part introduces the negative characters of ugliness and deformity, and works out the analogies and contrasts among all five characters. The second part of the *Essay* turns to examination of the system of gardening with which Kent and Brown had altered the face of England; the first chapter treats the general characteristics and defects of this system; the second discusses trees; the third, water; and a final chapter is a peroration, divided between denunciation of the current mode of gardening and appeal for the principles of painting to prevail.

This organization is appropriate both to Price's aims and to his method. The general purpose of establishing the picturesque is accomplished in the first part; the narrow aim of investigating the utility of painting as a guide for gardening is handled chiefly in the second part, the prolegomena of the first having prepared the ground. Put differently, it might be said that the first division develops an aesthetic science, the second an art dependent on that science, and that both science and art have consequences in practice, one in aesthetic appreciation generally, the other in gardening especially.

Price's effort to establish picturesqueness parallel with beauty and sublimity is temporarily arrested by the circumstance of the obvious etymology of the name, tying the picturesque to painting. But this circumstance Price ingeniously and plausibly turns to his advantage. "*Pittoresco*"—and the Italian word is the original of the French and English—"is derived, not like picturesque, from the thing painted, but from the painter; and this difference is not wholly immaterial." [20] For painters are struck with numberless circumstances to which an unpracticed eye pays little attention: "Quam multa vident pictores in umbris et in eminentia, quae nos non videmus!" is the motto from Cicero which Price prefixes to his book. The qualities of picturesqueness are of this nature—not immediately appealing, and hence unnoticed and unnamed by the run of mankind, yet nevertheless seen, admired, and isolated by the genius of painters; and hence the name.

Again, in the preface to his second volume, Price suggests another and more ingenious origin of the term: the word "picturesque," he writes, "may possibly have been invented by painters to express a quality not merely essential to their art, but in a manner peculiar to it: the treasures of the sublime and the beautiful, it shares in common with Sculpture; but the Picturesque is almost exclusively its own. . . ." By "picturesque" is "meant, not all that can be expressed with effect in painting, but that which painting can, and sculpture cannot express . . . and the etymology of the word . . . sanctions the use I have made of it, and the distinction I have given to its character." [21]

But the phrase, "picturesque beauty," is a misnomer, Price holds, for "in reality, the picturesque not only differs from the beautiful in those qualities which Mr. Burke has so justly ascribed to it, but arises from qualities the most diametrically opposite." [22] Beauty is characterized by smoothness and gradual variation, qualities which necessarily limit the variety and intricacy essential to the picturesque. [23] Roughness and sudden variation, joined to irregularity, are the most efficient causes of the picturesque. This proposition is illustrated by a rich and various catalog of picturesque objects—Gothic cathedrals and old mills, gnarled oaks and shaggy goats, decayed cart horses and wandering gypsies, the paintings of Mola and Salvator. [24] Beautiful and picturesque are further differentiated in that symmetry, which accords with beauty well enough, is adverse to the picturesque. And the distinction of the two characters is brought under the aesthetic principles peculiar to Price, finally, by the observation that "one [depends] on ideas of youth and freshness, the other on those of age, and even of decay." [25] Striking descriptions are given of the gradual alteration of beauty into picturesqueness as time operates upon a temple, a tree, or a man. [26]

It may seem remarkable that symmetry should be pitched upon as a principal point of distinction, since Burke had explicitly ruled out symmetry as a trait of beauty. He admitted symmetry, to be sure, so far as was necessary to avoid deformity, but even in such instances it contributed to beauty only as a precondition. [27] Price's remarks on symmetry show that he had it in mind as a character chiefly of the forms of animals, or sometimes of plants and their parts, and of the non-imitative arts of architecture, furniture, and the like. The difference between Burke and Price on this point is partly one of nomenclature: Price includes the symmetrical "elegant" within the beautiful, since the difference in the sentiments excited is comparatively slight.

The picturesque is equally distinct from the sublime, both in its characteristics and its causes. The sublime is great, often infinite or apparently so, often uniform, and is founded on awe and terror. The picturesque may be great or small, but, since it so depends on the character of boundaries, can never be infinite; it is various and intricate rather than uniform, and is indifferently gay or grave.

Although the sublime and beautiful are incompatible—admixture of grandeur taking off from loveliness—picturesqueness renders beauty the more captivating. Price's doctrine is, that exclusive attention to beauty, to the total exclusion of the picturesque, produces an insipid monotony; even in painting this may be the case, and Guido's works show "how unavoidably an attention to mere beauty and flow of outline, will lead towards sameness and insipidity." [28] In nature, picturesqueness and beauty are blended; the rose, with its thorny bush and jagged leaves, is emblematic of this mixture. The happy effect of such a union has its basis in psychology: smoothness, literal or metaphorical, conveys the idea of repose; roughness that of irritation, of animation, spirit, and variety. Roughness serves as the ornament of beauty, that which gives it life and spirit, and preserves it from flatness and insipidity. Nothing "but the poverty of language makes us call two sensations so distinct from each other [as the relaxation of beauty and the lively irritation of the picturesque] by the common name of pleasure." [29] Great part of the irritation produced by roughness of whatever kind is attributable to association with the sensations of touch; it is in touch, indeed, that the difference between beautiful and picturesque is most sensibly felt. Such automatic and necessary association plays a considerable role in the theory of Price; and like Burke, Price is fond of tracing the aesthetic characters through the analogies of the various senses. He has an interest in music, and finds a picturesque of sound; there is even picturesque conversation; but in the strict sense, however, Price's picturesque is a character of visible objects.

Discussion of smoothness and roughness and the qualities associated with them is illustrated by lengthy and sometimes subtle disquisitions on the schools of painting. Form, light and shadow, that breadth of treatment which unites a scene into one whole, and color are the topics. Price dwells most at length upon breadth of lighting, for even the intricacy and variety of the picturesque require a ground to set them off, to make of them a harmony rather than a discord; this breadth produces a delight even from objects otherwise indifferent or ugly. Color, too, is brought within Price's frame of reference;

the freshness and delicacy of the colors of spring are beautiful, the warmth, various richness, and harmony of autumnal hues are more suited to painting, and are justly termed picturesque, according in variety and intricacy with the other traits of that character. Price concedes that the beauty of color is positive and independent; but the picturesque and sublime of color are relative, dependent upon accompanying circumstances and associations. What Price has to say about the picturesque in color, and in form, is consistent with the observations of Reynolds on that character. It is the Venetians who exhibit picturesque coloring; Guido and Claude pursue the beautiful; [30] the Roman school and the Mannerists employ the unbroken and distinct colors appropriate to the sublime (to the sublime of history, at least; it appears to me that the sublime of landscape requires a greater admixture of picturesque breaking of color and shadow). What strikes one as different in Reynolds and Price is that Reynolds, because of his insistent reference to generality as criterion, arranges these schools in a hierarchy of excellence: the sublime takes precedence of what Price calls the beautiful, and this in turn is higher than the picturesque. Price, instead, lays out these qualities "horizontally" rather than hierarchically. The influence of Reynolds, and the taste of his age, occasionally lead him to make evaluative judgments similar to those of Reynolds, but these are in Price expressions of personal taste rather than consequences of a philosophic system—and Price's taste is much more favorably inclined to the picturesque than that of Reynolds.

The system of the picturesque is completed by consideration of ugliness and deformity. Having used up Burke's ugly to make the picturesque, Price is obliged to find a new ugliness; this "does not arise from any sudden variation [as Burke had urged [31]]; but rather from that *want* of form, that unshapen lumpish appearance, which, perhaps, no one word exactly expresses; a quality (if what is negative may be so called) which never can be mistaken for beauty, never can adorn it, and which is equally unconnected with the sublime, and the picturesque." [32] Deformity, in contrast, consists in an unnaturally exaggerated rather than a featureless character; it depends not upon the physiological effect of the shape as ugliness does, but upon association, or lack of association, with the norm of the species or with regularity. "Deformity is to ugliness, what picturesqueness is to beauty; though distinct from it, and in many cases arising from opposite causes, it is often mistaken for it, often accompanies it, and greatly heightens its effect. Ugliness alone, is merely disagreeable; by the addition of deformity, it becomes hideous; by that of terror it may become sublime." [33] The interrelations among the five aesthetic characters are difficult to reduce to diagram. Ugliness appears to be the undistinguished potentiality from which the others may all be formed; yet at the same time it is peculiarly the negation of beauty, as deformity is of the picturesque. This, however, is consistent with Price's view of beauty, for the monotony of that quality when unenlivened by any admixture of the picturesque has more than once been emphasized, and this monotony allies it to ugliness, whereas the piquancy of the picturesque, a little exaggerated, leads towards deformity. It is nonetheless curious that ugliness is both the excess and the defect of beauty, but the defect only of the other characters.

Picturesqueness enjoys greatest facility of union with the other aesthetic characters. It holds a middle station between beautiful and sublime. It mixes with ugliness, and picturesque ugliness is agreeable in painting, thence, by association at first, in nature: "Those who have been used to admire such picturesque ugliness in painting, will look with pleasure . . . at the original in nature. . . ." [34] Beauty, sublimity, and deformity, too, all tend to become picturesque with time. This ability of the picturesque to combine agreeably with the ugly, and in some measure with the deformed, tells against any theory which reduces the picturesque to a mode of beauty.[35] There is, of course, a broad sense of the term "beauty" which signifies any kind of pleasing aesthetic effect, and in this sense both sublime and picturesque are comprised within beauty; but in the same sense, Price remarks, envy and revenge are both modes of ill will—though distinct from one another. The aesthetic characters generally exhibit obvious analogies with ethical characters, just as this mode of aesthetic thought appears to be established by analogy with ethical philosophy. It may be asked, why are the analogous ethical distinctions so much more firmly established and widely recognized? Their superior influence in practical life has made all men involuntarily moralists, whereas the aesthetic distinctions have been little attended to in the earlier stages of civilization. Price looks forward, in fact, to the development of new aesthetic distinctions, and the development of new terms for the union of the picturesque with beauty, with sublimity, or with ugliness.

Such is the general theory of the picturesque. Its application to improvement, although subordinate logically, occupies the greater part of Price's writings, and was the provocation for most of the attacks leveled against his system by gardeners and aestheticans. Yet Price's application of the principles of painting to improvement is attended with such qualifications as should have safeguarded him from some at least of these assaults. For it was not his desire to reproduce in real scenes the compositions found in paintings; gardening is not to imitate particular pictures, or even to reproduce the same kinds of scenes as are found in pictures; rather, the original compositions formed by improvers from the elements of scenery are to be guided by the general *principles* of painting.[36] "But, however highly I may think of the art of painting, compared with that of improving [protests Price], nothing can be farther from my intention . . . than to recommend the study of pictures in preference to that of nature, much less to the exclusion of it. Whoever studies art alone, will have a narrow pedantic manner of considering all objects, and of referring them solely to the minute and practical purposes of that art . . . to which his attention has been particularly directed. . . ."[37] Looking at nature merely with a view to forming pictures contracts the taste; looking at pictures with a view to improvement of our ideas of nature enlarges it. It remains true, however, that the capacity to judge of forms, colors, and combinations of visible objects "can never be perfectly acquired, unless to the study of natural scenery, and of the various styles of gardening at different periods, the improver adds the theory at least of that art, the very essence of which is connection. . . ."[38] The principles of painting—composition, grouping, harmony, unity, breadth and effect of light and shadow—are so called "because that art has pointed them out more clearly . . . but they are in reality the general principles on which the effect of all visible objects must depend, and to which it must be referred."[39] These principles are so little affected by the peculiar limitations of painting as a medium, that they may properly be taken, as Price does take them, as principles for all the co-temporary or spatial arts. Since in the spatial arts the combinations are taken in at one view, union and harmony, insensible transition of parts, is the most essential requirement. The "circumstance of insensible transition," Price declares, "is the most comprehensive principle of visible beauty in its strictest acceptation: as not being confined to lines or curves of any kind, and as extending, not only to form, but to colour, to light and shadow, and to every combination of them; that is, to all visible nature."[40]

If it be objected, why should one art dictate to another? Price is ready with his reply: the art of improving is new, it has not been distinguished by artists of transcendent genius, nor have any of its works so withstood the test of time as to become classics—indeed, the inevitable processes of growth and decay may always prevent the products of this art from attaining the venerable authority of the statues of Greece and the paintings of Italy.

Just as the picturesque improver should not seek to imitate the particular effects of paintings, so he should not attempt to imitate the particular details of uncultivated nature; here, as in the imitation of paintings, he observes the principles by which uncultivated scenes please, and endeavors by original selection and arrangement of materials to achieve analogous effects on the same principles: "I am convinced," says Price, "that many of the circumstances which give variety and spirit to a wild spot, might be successfully imitated in a dressed place; but it must be done by attending to the principles, not by copying the particulars. It is not necessary to model a gravel walk, or drive, after a sheep track or cart rut, though very useful hints may be taken from them both; and without having water-docks or thistles before one's door, their effect in a painter's foreground may be produced by plants that are considered as ornamental." [41] Price's demands for shagginess apply chiefly to the grounds, or park; the garden in the narrow sense, immediately adjacent to the house, he desires to be formal—but the ornate formality of the ancient style rather than the insipid and monotonous formality of level greens and serpentining walks. This moderate position goes pretty far, I think, in abating the force of Reynolds' objections to picturesque gardening. Reynolds, anticipating a part of the argument of Repton, Marshall, and other "practical" opponents of the picturesque school, had expressed to Gilpin his disapproval "of reforming the art of gardening by the picturesque of landscape painting." The picturesque, according to Reynolds, has nature alone for its object; a picturesque garden must therefore be totally devoid of art, and therefore not a garden. The picturesque attitude towards improvement, Reynolds writes, "appears to me undervaluing the art of gardening, which I hold to be an art that stands on its own bottom, and is governed by different principles. It ought to have apparently, if not ostentatiously, the marks of art upon it: as it is a work of art upon nature, it is a part of its beauty and perfection that it should appear at first sight a cultivated spot—that it is inhabited, that every thing is in order, convenient, and comfortable; which a state of nature will not produce." [42] These arguments, valid or not, are addressed to a position which Price at least does not hold.

Price describes the change from the Italian and Dutch styles of gardening to that of Kent and Brown by a succinct half-line from

Horace: *Mutat quadrata rotundis*. The new improvers, though they meant to banish formality and restore nature, had in fact only installed a new formality of regular curves in place of the more grand and simple straight-lined formality of the old gardens, creating a style both monotonous and affected.[43] The great defect of the new system, a defect to which it was more subject than the old had been, and in which it was most opposite to the principles of painting, was "want of connection—a passion for making every thing distinct and separate. All the particular defects which I shall have occasion to notice, in some degree arise from, and tend towards this original sin." [44] The most characteristic features of "modern gardening"—its serpentine drives and walks and canals, its clumps and belts—are dispatched in the opening chapter of the *Essay*'s second part; trees and water, the chief materials of the improver, are treated in the succeeding chapters, and the practical suggestions which Price advances are carefully adapted to his general aesthetics. The objections raised against these suggestions by Repton, George Mason, Marshall, and others, objections that they are theorizing dreams which cannot be reduced to practice, seem to me to rest partly on misapprehension of Price's plans, partly on mere habitual attachment to established modes of practice. These practical objections melted away in following years, and Price may almost be said to have formed the taste of the early nineteenth century in gardening and architecture.

In 1798, the *Essay on the Picturesque* was supplemented on the practical side by a new volume of three essays, designed to meet Humphry Repton's challenge to set forth a method of practical improvement which could be acted upon. The "Essay on Artificial Water, and on the Method in Which Picturesque Banks May be Practically Formed" really handles the whole problem of natural foregrounds, a problem of especial importance to improvers, who have less control than painters over the distant parts of their scenes; the "Essay on the Decorations near the House"—the garden in the narrow sense—treats avowedly artificial foregrounds, which only are in character with architecture. The final essay completes the progression from the extremities of the estate towards its center; it is "An Essay on Architecture and Buildings, as Connected with Scenery," as, that is, subject to the landscapist rather than the builder.

An aspect of Price's system of "natural" gardening which was much ridiculed, an aspect of peculiar importance in these practical essays, was the reliance upon time and accident—gardening by neglect.[45] But Price does not suggest leaving natural processes uncontrolled. Nature must give the finishing roughness to the gardener's work, but the art of the gardener directs nature's operations; nature must crumble the banks of the lagoon, but the improver can undermine and support them in such wise as to determine where and to what extent nature can operate. "As art is unable by an immediate operation to create those effects, she must have recourse to nature, that is, to accident; whose operation, though she cannot imitate, she can, in a great measure, direct." [46]

Improvers have been self-defeated in their attempts at beauty, so Price says, by their insistent repetition of smoothness and flowing lines. For the most essential trait of beauty is insensible transition, and in landscape these transitions are effected best by a certain degree of irregularity and roughness. Only this much is granted to the serpentine—that the same bareness and formality cut into angles would be less beautiful yet. It could be argued that this conception of natural beauty dissolves the distinction between picturesque and beautiful; Price grants that

> the two characters are rarely unmixed in nature, and should not be unmixed in art. In the wooded river, I have supposed roughness and abruptness to be so blended with the ingredients of beauty . . . as to produce altogether those insensible transitions, in which . . . consists the justest, and most comprehensive principle of the beautiful in landscape. The whole, then, assumes the soft and mild character of beauty. But should any of these rough, abrupt parts be more strongly marked . . . then the picturesque would begin to prevail: and in proportion as that distinct and marked roughness and abruptness increased, so far the character of the beautiful would decrease. . . . [But] it would be no less absurd to make picturesque scenes without any mixture of the beautiful, (and the caution at some future period may not be unnecessary,) than to attempt what has so long, and so idly been attempted—to make beautiful scenes, without any mixture of the picturesque. [47]

The characters remain analytically distinct, but when manifested in concrete objects do not produce a good effect unless in some degree mingled. I might urge an analogy with external taste: sweet and sour are not the less distinct for their being more pleasing when mingled. The analogy is the closer in that tartness (like picturesqueness) is usually not pleasing until we are made accustomed to it by artificial productions, and in that sweetness, which is alone pleasing at first, subsequently becomes insipid unless varied with some sharper flavor.

The excellence of Italian gardens, even in their perfect state, rests upon the combination of beautiful and picturesque elements:

> All persons . . . are universally pleased with smoothness and flowing lines; and thence the great and general popularity of the present style of gardening; but on the other hand those who have paid any attention to scenery, are more *struck* with sudden projections and abruptnesses . . . for in all such rugged abrupt forms, though they may be only picturesque, there is still a tendency towards the sublime; that is, towards the most powerful emotion of the human mind. The great point, not merely in improvements, but in all things that are designed to affect the imagination, is to mix according to circumstances, what is striking, with what is simply pleasing. . . . The same principle seems to have been studied in many of the old Italian gardens.[48]

The beauty of such a garden, of course, consists in symmetry and regularity rather than in serpentinity; even the less grand and beautiful Dutch style, with its hedges, labyrinths, and straight canals might be indulged, although Price condemns the extravagancies of topiary work.

Yet there is a use for the system of modern gardening, too, though in the hands of most practitioners it banishes equally all present decoration and all future picturesqueness. With some of its absurdities corrected, it serves as a transition from the formal architectural garden near the house to the wilder park. The ideal estate, then, would have a grand Italianate garden near the mansion, with parterres, hanging and balustraded terraces, statues and fountains; beyond the last terrace there would be a smooth pleasure-ground, with gravel walks sweeping easily among its ornamental shrubberies and trees; and at a distance the wooded park, in which the gravel walk gives place to the grassy lane, the smooth lawn to the forest glade, and the plantations of ornamentals to the intricate variety of wild nature.

The final essay of Price's second volume treats of "Architecture and Buildings as Connected with Scenery." The country house is necessarily connected with scenery primarily rather than with other buildings, and there is a consequent necessity of giving it a picturesque appearance from a large number of viewpoints. Ruins, especially the ruins of once-beautiful structures, are the most picturesque of buildings. Structures designed for use and habitation can hardly be made ruinous, however; what does give such structures picturesqueness is the turning of their windows to views suitably framed by trees, which, *pari passu*, gives the building an intricate irregularity as viewed from without.[49] Connection with the scenery is effected also by disposing the offices subordinate to the central mass (instead of burying them underground or concealing them in evergreen plantations), and by planting trees close to the house to break and vary its regularity (instead of setting the house down in a meadow). Building is thus brought under the principles of painting, and the *architetto-pittore* is the prophet of the new revelation. Only the artist well acquainted with the beautiful, grand, and picturesque will know when to keep these characters separate, when and in what degree to mix them, according to the effect intended.

It is significant and characteristic that Price should remark, in treating of the sublime in buildings, that "the effects of art are never so well illustrated, as by similar effects in nature: and, therefore, the best illustration of buildings, is by what has most analogy to them—the forms and characters of rocks. . . ."[50] For Price is always ultimately concerned with the isolation of qualities which pervade both art and nature, a concern which minimizes the distinctive artificiality of art. The difference of art from nature is more marked, however, in architecture than in painting; for architecture is not in the same sense an imitative art. Since architecture is functional and creative rather than representative, the waving line, which is a principal cause of beauty in natural objects, appears only to the limited extent that associations with function permit. The beautiful in building, then, involves straight lines, angles, and symmetry. Symmetry had of course been excluded from the beautiful by Burke, on the grounds that it reduced variety and freedom; only in non-imitative arts is this argument overbalanced by other considerations. But Price is not yet free of difficulty; for it might be argued, on the basis of insensible transition, that the ruin is often more beautiful (as well as more picturesque) than the entire building, the lines of which are more distinct and hard. This paradox is avoided partly by observing that the beauty of ruins is attributable rather to the vegetation than to the fragmentary architecture, partly by noting that "the mind, from the powerful and extensive influence of that principle, called *association of ideas*, is unwilling to give them a title, which, as I conceive, implies the freshness of youth; or, at least, a state of high and perfect preservation."[51] Price's substitution of a new substructure under Burke's aesthetics has permitted him to modify Burke's conclusions without outright rejection of the master's authority.

Price reinforces his analysis by considering "the use, which both in history and landscape, some of the principal painters of different schools and countries have made of buildings, from the highest style of architecture, to the simplest cottage—from those which are in their freshest and most perfect state, to those which time has most defaced and mutilated." [52] The judgments on history paintings are so clear, once one has the knack of using Price's distinctions, that they need not be dwelt upon. The comparisons and contrasts of styles become rather subtle, and the entire passage, some fifty pages, bears a clear relation to Reynolds' classification of styles and manners. When we discover that of two pictures by Poussin and Veronese, "one is addressed to the understanding through the sight; the other to the sight only: and who can doubt which has attained the noblest end?" [53] we can conceive ourselves to be reading the academic discourses. The discussion of architecture in history painting serves rather to clarify the definitions of the aesthetic characters in architecture than to provide practical precepts; but the employment of architecture in landscape painting drives close to Price's own concern with the combination of buildings and landscape gardens. The practice of the great landscape painters, therefore, provides directly applicable principles, and even hints for practice. Especially useful are the ideas of village scenery to be gleaned from the Dutch and Flemish masters. Though Price's discussion of such village scenes turns chiefly on his enthusiasm for the picturesqueness of village life, his humanitarian sympathies concur with his aesthetic inclinations in the improvement of villages, and he dilates upon the expansion of benevolence which must accompany extension of pleasure in picturesque objects. Unhappily, moral and aesthetic criteria do not *invariably* coincide, and the socially conscious gentleman must forego half-ruining the houses of his villagers to make them more picturesque. Where there is conflict, the moral principle must prevail; and eventually it assumes an aesthetic guise, since associations of utility enter into the aesthetic as well as into the moral judgment. [54]

Before advancing into the tangled controversies among Price and Knight and Repton, it is necessary for me to return briefly to the first theorist of the picturesque, William Gilpin. The 1794 volume of Price's *Essay on the Picturesque* included, at appropriate points in the discussion, a number of lengthy footnotes in which Price set forth his differences with Gilpin. In the 1810 edition of Price's works on the picturesque, these notes were collected into an Appendix to the first volume of the *Essay;* the Appendix contains no new material, and its somewhat disjointed effect is an obvious consequence of its mode of formation. Price declares that Gilpin's *Three Essays* did not come to his hand until he had written a great part of his own work. This assertion, which I see no reason to doubt, in no way derogates from Gilpin's historical importance, for Price acknowledges having been influenced by Gilpin's earlier writings. When he first read into the "Essay on Picturesque Beauty," Price says, he thought that his own work had been anticipated. "But as I advanced," he continues, "that distinction between the two characters, that line of separation which I thought would have been accurately marked out, became less and less visible; till at length the beautiful and the picturesque were more than ever mixed and incorporated together, the whole subject involved in doubt and obscurity, and a sort of anathema denounced against any one who should try to clear it up." [55]

Gilpin, as Price sees it, has followed a will o' the wisp in trying to find a definition of the picturesque which refers to the art of painting only, a concern which has made him lose sight of the universal distinction between picturesque and beautiful. Seeing that roughness is the essential point of difference between the two characters, Gilpin was thus led to exclude smoothness from painting—except where he could show by a kind of sophistry that what is really smooth is in appearance rough, "so that," Price observes ironically, "when we fancy ourselves admiring the smoothness which we think we perceive, as in a calm lake, we are in fact admiring the roughness which we have not observed." [56] Price himself, in fact, distinguishes between Gilpin's definition of the picturesque as "adapted to painting" and "his more strict and pointed method of defining it by making roughness the most essential point of difference between it and the beautiful." [57]

Price does not, however, remark the other methodological errors into which Gilpin is led by this initial misstep. Instead, he descends to details (naturally enough, since his critique originated as footnotes to particular points in his own *Essay*). He has little difficulty in overturning Gilpin's notion that only rough, or apparently rough, objects please in painting. Gilpin (as we have seen above) concedes this point in his letter to Reynolds, but without recognizing that the concession requires a restatement of his theory. Price insists that the painter may represent objects exhibiting any of the aesthetic characters; and for him, difficulties like those into which Gilpin is led by his exclusive fondness for painting "must always be the consequence, when instead of endeavouring to shew the agreement between art and nature, even when they appear most at variance, a mysterious barrier is placed between them, to surprize and keep at a distance the uninitiated." [58] No comment could display more clearly the bent of Price's aesthetics—which is in this particular typical of the British systems—towards isolation of characters which pervade both nature and art, rather than towards the discrimination of the problems and traits of art from those of nature. Aestheticians of the Hegelian tradition also isolate universals found both in nature and in art; but they analogize nature to art instead of (like the British) subsuming art under nature. Bosanquet, for instance, declares roundly: "I have assumed . . . that Fine Art may be accepted, for theoretical purposes, as the chief, if not the sole representative of the world of beauty." [59] The British writers, in contrast, begin with nature, and by allowing for the effects of imitation and design adapt their doctrines to art. Ultimately, I suppose, this difference is a remote consequence of metaphysical differences: the British empiricists begin with a history of the perceptions of the mind, the Germans with an analysis of forms or categories inherent in the mind; in one case, then, it is simpler to treat aesthetics in terms of the more primitive phenomena (nature), in the other in terms of the more intellectual (art).

Templeman, swept away, perhaps, by the enthusiasm of the specialist, is unable to discover anything in the three volumes of Price which is not in Gilpin's little essay; he doubts that Price "has much to offer in addition to Gilpin, or in defensible disagreement with Gilpin." Despite his pompous verbosity, Price "does *not* give a definition of the picturesque" in his *Essay;* the definition he finally ventures in his letter to Repton, "what is rough and abrupt, with sudden deviations," is inadequate; and Price can no longer insist that the words "picturesque" and "beauty" never be combined.[60] To ignore, as Templeman does, the differences in analytical method between Gilpin and Price; to avow that because Price foregoes a one-sentence definition for a history of the term and a complex discrimination of the picturesque from related characters he does not define it; to imply that Price ever denied the practical combination of picturesque and beautiful or ever abandoned the analytical distinction between them—this is totally to fail to grasp Price's argument. But Templeman is at any rate refreshingly literal in his reading of the texts; most commentators on these subjects have a Theory, and in every point to make it fit, will force all writers to submit. Mayoux sees the picturesque as a stage on the road to romanticism; Price's "création du Pittoresque, à côté et audessus du beau avili, marque un progrès certain de l'esthétique romantique qui a commencé avec Burke." Mayoux notes especially that Gilpin observes picturesque scenes from fixed points of view, whereas in Price, "le pittoresque est l'objet de sensations successives. C'est une différence primordiale au point de vue esthétique, une des grandes séparations du beau classique et du romantique. On remarquera que Price au lieu de s'attacher au point de vue fixé . . . se plait à s'y mouvoir; ainsi le besoin romantique de changement, de sensations renouvelées, fait sentir son progrès." [61] I do not think that Price, or indeed any writer on the picturesque, ranks picturesqueness *above* beauty. Nor do I see in Price a "besoin romantique de changement"; with Miss Manwaring, I believe that the new knowledge of painting in eighteenth-century England, knowledge especially of the great landscape painters of the previous century, led to a habit of looking at landscape as if it were a series of paintings, a habit not at all absurd if not pursued to the exclusion of other ways of viewing landscape, and from the stimulus of which other and more natural ways of regarding scenery were sure to follow. Price, in fact, taking up the rather confused hints thrown out by Gilpin towards a general theory of picturesque aesthetics, shows their inadequacy, and develops a theory of the picturesque as a mode of beauty (in the extended sense) co-ordinate with the special beauty of Burke and with the sublime. It retains little of the connection with painting from which it sprang, and Mayoux does not allow this fact its due weight when he remarks that "c'est par là que la théorie de Price est curieuse; par tout ça romantisme visuel, dissimulé sous le détachement artistique. . . ." [62] What is true in this observation is that which I have remarked before, that poetic sensibility is less prominent in Price than the feelings excited by the more abstract qualities and their composition. In reading Price, however, this emphasis seems a consistent and integral part of his system; it should not be made the mark of a conflict, of one system of thought insinuating itself under the guise of another.

CHAPTER 15

Humphry Repton

❦

URGED, perhaps, by the fond ambition of converting to his views the leading landscape gardener of the age, Uvedale Price dispatched a presentation copy of his *Essay on the Picturesque* to Humphry Repton.[1] The personality of Humphry Repton was something of a paradox, pleasing enough in most ways, but rather like Jane Austen's Mr. Collins in its mixture of pompous solemnity with servile humility in all that related to his profession. Deferential almost in the extreme in his "humble endeavours to gratify the royal commands" or those of his noble patrons, he yet assumes a magisterial attitude when instructing his detractors and the world generally in the dignity of his profession, and confides that he feels it "a kind of duty to watch, with a jealous eye, every innovation on the principles of taste in Landscape Gardening; since I have been honoured with the care of so many of the finest places in the kingdom."[2]

Repton was not much pleased by Price's attention. He felt that the memory of "that great self-taught master,"[3] his predecessor the immortal Lancelot Brown, had been traduced; that "a direct and undisguised attack on the art [of landscape gardening]"[4] itself had virtually denied the right of the profession, and of its professors, to exist; and, which perhaps piqued him more personally, he felt that some of his own ideas had been stolen and brought out in print while his own work was still at the printer's. If he had had the most distant idea that Price was writing such a book, he complains, he "should certainly have been more guarded in my conversations with its author, who has frequently adopted my ideas; and has, in some instances, robbed me of originality. . . ."[5] While his resentment was still keen, Repton dashed off *A Letter to Uvedale Price, Esq.*, of which he caused some copies to be struck off for private distribution— Price, of course, being one of the recipients. Price, doubtless surprised by the quickness and tartness as well as by the public character of the retort, as hastily wrote off *A Letter to H. Repton, Esq. on the Application of the Practice As Well As the Principles of Landscape-Painting to Landscape-Gardening* . . . ; this was a major publication, about eight times the length of Repton's brief letter.

But the great landscape gardener had been already affronted some months before the unexpected blow from Price. For Payne Knight's *The Landscape* had excoriated the improvers, and had provoked Repton especially by, as Repton puts it, "the attempt to make me an object of ridicule, by misquoting my unpublished MSS. [the Red Book of Tatton Park, partly incorporated in *Sketches and Hints*]." [6] While these attacks on modern improvement were issuing from the presses, Repton's own *Sketches and Hints on Landscape Gardening* was languishing at the printer's, waiting for dilatory artists to complete the colored aquatints which make that book today a collector's item of great rarity. The delay permitted him, however, to append replies and apologia: a seventh chapter was added to repel Knight's attack, and an Appendix to treat Price's opinions in the *Essay on the Picturesque*. Price's *Letter to Repton*, too, came out early in 1795, with *Sketches and Hints* still hanging fire; but Repton decided against further enlargement of what he puffs as "my great work," so that it finally appeared without allusion to Price's *Letter*. There has always been an uncertainty about the date of publication of *Sketches and Hints*. The title-page bears no date, and standard reference works give, some 1794, some 1795. The 1794 date has the sanction of Repton himself, for in two passages of later works he refers to *Sketches and Hints* as published in 1794.[7] This testimony, inexpugnable as it seems, is nonetheless erroneous. The Newberry Library of Chicago possesses, bound together, copies of Price's *Essay* and *Letter to Repton* each of which was presented to Repton by the author; bound in with these two works are four manuscript letters among Price, Repton, and the publisher Robson, and these letters make clear that *Sketches and Hints* was still awaiting publication on February 5, 1795.[8]

So much for the chronology of the early phase of the controversy. My intention is to discuss the publications of Repton in such fashion as to give a proper view of his conduct of the controversy and of the later development of his practice and thought. But to throw this discussion into a proper perspective, I must first give a view of Repton's system as a whole. Repton was a professor of landscaping and architecture rather than a theoretical aesthetician. This judgment is unaffected by Repton's reiterated statements that he wished posterity to judge him by his published works rather than by the actual estates he created or altered ("It is rather upon my opinions in writing, than on the partial and imperfect manner in which my plans have sometimes been executed, that I wish my fame to be established," he declares in the preface to *Theory and Practice*[9]). For these published writings are an applied rather than a theoretical aesthetics. They contain, to be sure, frequent enunciations of general principles (no two lists quite the same), but these principles constitute rather *axiomata media* of a high order than first principles. Repton assumes almost all of his psychology; he never investigates metaphysics, but takes propositions implying metaphysical analyses for his starting points. These psychological principles serve only as the basis for deductions of particular precepts which determine the manner in which the architect or gardener manipulates his materials to fulfil the requirements of his profession. One of the most frequent phenomena in Repton's books, consequently, is the list of "rules" for managing this or that part of the art of landscapist or architect—rules for arranging the parts of an estate, rules for arched gateways, &c.; and equally frequent is the list of "principles" of some style of art, propositions which are implicitly guides for practice in that style—principles of ancient or of modern gardening, of the town house or the country house, of the Gothic, and so forth.

Now all this forms a decided contrast between Repton and Price or Knight. The two amateurs—Knight most notably—really worked out aesthetic systems; Knight carried analysis as deep as aesthetics requires, and Price, though less analytical, still gives much more of a psychology and a theoretical aesthetics than does Repton. Neither Knight nor Price, moreover, was given to making out lists of rules; they preferred to bridge the gap from theory to actual making by a cultivated taste, a taste formed (so far as things visual are concerned) on the higher painters. But Repton, without any propensity for philosophizing, and with a great concern for directing the creative work of others, can not leave so much to the variability of taste—especially since he wished to weaken the influence of painting on landscape gardening, and thus removed one of the important controls on idiosyncrasy. He therefore prescribes taste in directions more concrete than those to which Price and Knight care to bind themselves.

Since Repton is essentially an unsystematic writer, it is difficult to reduce to order the many principles which he enunciates. In general, he is concerned with discovering or providing sources of pleasure, without tracing out the causes of these pleasures in more than a common-sense way and without much effort to isolate those which are peculiarly aesthetic in quality. In the Appendix against Price added to *Sketches and Hints*, Repton gives a list of the "Sources of Pleasure in Landscape Gardening." These sources are: (*1*) *congruity*, of parts with the whole, and of the whole with the circumstances of the place and its possessor; (*2*) *utility*, by which Repton means not profitableness, but convenience, comfort, and "everything that conduces to the purposes of habitation with elegance"; (*3*) *order*, as in a walk parallel with a straight wall; (*4*) *symmetry*; (*5*) *picturesque effect*, "which has been so fully and ably considered by Mr. Price"; (*6*) *intricacy*; (*7*) *simplicity*; (*8*) *variety*; (*9*) *novelty*, which Repton deems a perilous goal to aim at; (*10*) *contrast*, a safer substitute; (*11*) *continuity*, as in an avenue; (*12*) *association*, historical or personal; (*13*) *grandeur*; (*14*) *appropriation*, the appearance and display of extent of property; (*15*) *animation*, whether of water, vegetation, or animals; (*16*) *seasons* and *times of day*.[10] The first four of these sources are "generally adverse to picturesque beauty," Repton tells us, "yet they are not, therefore, to be discarded." So far from discarding them is Repton, that he erects congruity and utility into the primary principles of his analyses: "The leading feature in the good taste of modern times, is the just sense of GENERAL UTILITY."[11] This observation pertains to taste in general; with reference to landscape gardening in particular, Repton suggests that "if any general principles could be established in this art, I think that they might be deduced from the joint consideration of *relative fitness* or UTILITY, and *comparative proportion* or SCALE; the former may be referred to the mind, the latter to the eye, yet these two must be inseparable."[12] And the observations in *Theory and Practice* are often referred to this dual head. Yet Repton can not mean that all the principles of gardening can be derived from congruity and utility, for he constantly introduces judgments based on other principles—as in the sources of pleasure enumerated above. Nor is it strictly true that scale is referable to the "eye"—only that scale is ordinarily perceived without reflection, whereas the recognition of fitness often involves some degree of conscious ratiocination. A more proper distinction would distinguish pleasures referable to some physiological or nervous mechanism (the "eye," if you will) from those attributable to the operation of ideas in association or judgment. Even this more accurate distinction, however, would not of itself carry us, or Repton, very far.

Repton's "utility" has no connection with profitableness; indeed, Repton regularly opposes ornament to profit, and regarded with disfavor the *ferme ornée* of Shenstone: "I have never walked through these grounds [Shenstone's Leasowes]," he writes, "without lamenting, not only the misapplication of good taste, but that constant disappointment which the benevolent Shenstone must have experienced in attempting to unite two objects so incompatible as ornament and profit." [13] Farm and park, in short, are incongruous. The utility Repton has in mind is, instead, a matter of convenience and comfort—gravel walks to keep our shoes dry, a southeast aspect for favorable weather, &c. Insofar as this utility is an aesthetic excellence, it must be because association has connected such circumstances with our more disinterested and apparently spontaneous responses to the general appearance of things. An exposed situation for the house, that is, might "hurt the eye" by calling up half-conscious notions of rain and cold, yet without exciting conscious reflection. Perhaps a set of Repton's rules will serve to make this point more definite. The site for a house, says Repton, is to be decided by four considerations (in order of decreasing importance): (1) the aspect; (2) the levels of the surrounding ground; (3) objects of convenience, such as water supply, space for the offices, accessibility to roads and towns; and (4) the view from the house.[14] Now only the last of these is altogether an aesthetic consideration; the first and second may perhaps come by association to be tinged with aesthetic feeling; but the third requires so conscious an exertion of the understanding that it can hardly, I think, be reckoned aesthetic at all. The first three topics together, of course, are branches of Repton's utility.

Often the semblance alone of utility is sufficient to justify ornaments: a pilaster deceptively seems to provide support. Deception is, in fact, a central concept in Repton's view of art; "the highest perfection of landscape gardening," he declares, "is, to imitate nature so judiciously, that the interference of art shall never be detected," [15] whereas formal gardening is an open display of art. More at length,

The perfection of *Landscape Gardening* consists in the four following requisites: First, it must display the natural beauties, and hide the natural defects of every situation. Secondly, it should give the appearance of extent and freedom, by carefully disguising or hiding the boundary. Thirdly, it must studiously conceal every interference of art . . . making the whole appear the production of nature only; and, fourthly, all objects of mere convenience or comfort, if incapable of being made ornamental, or of becoming proper parts of the general scenery, must be removed or concealed. . . .

Each of the four objects here enumerated, are directly opposite to the principles of ancient gardening, which may thus be stated. First, the natural beauties or defects of a situation had no influence, when it was the fashion to exclude, by lofty walls, every surrounding object. Secondly, these walls were never considered as defects; but, on the contrary, were ornamented with vases, expensive iron gates, and palisades, to render them more conspicuous. Thirdly, so far from making gardens appear natural, every expedient was used to display the expensive efforts of art, by which nature had been subdued. . . . And, lastly, with respect to objects of convenience, they were placed as near the house as possible. . . .[16]

Modern gardening, it is clear, involves a constant and pervasive deception; Nikolaus Pevsner has spoken of "the landscape garden that tries seriously to look like Nature Unadorned, the landscape garden that has deceived us all at some stage into believing it to be England's natural scenery." [17] It is amusing to see Repton occasionally entrapped by deceptive associations of his own creating. Brown and he had built so many artificial rivers with terminations deceptively concealed by "bridges," that at last Repton could not throw a bridge across a *real* river for fear of making it seem artificial! [18] Repton himself objects to art deceptively imitating art: "Deception may be allowable in imitating the works of NATURE; thus artificial rivers, lakes, and rock scenery, can only be great by deception, and the mind acquiesces in the fraud, after it is detected; but in works of ART every trick ought to be avoided. Sham churches, sham ruins, sham bridges, and everything which appears what it is not, disgusts when the trick is discovered." [19]

But "art" is not a pejorative term in Repton's writings. Repton thinks of himself as an eclectic, inheriting the best of the modern style from Brown, and leading a renaissance of the best in the old style: "I do not profess to follow either Le Nôtre or Brown, but, selecting beauties from the style of each, to adopt so much of the grandeur of the former as may accord with a palace, and so much of the grace of the latter as may call forth the charms of natural landscape." [20] Repton's formalism has occasioned a good bit of discussion, and I shall dwell upon it briefly. The Red Books of Hasells and Cobham were written, Repton states, "in the year 1790, before Mr. Price published his *Essays*"; and on both estates Repton recommended the retention or extension of formal terraces.[21] If Repton's memory is accurate, he did without question participate in the formal revival; but it is not necessary to give him credit for leading it. Price and Knight had developed their views before going into print; they are independent of Repton; they are more systematic and thoroughgoing in their formalism; and they rest their preferences on different theoretic bases. Even their taste in formal gardens does not accord with Repton's; the taste of Knight and especially that of Price is for a definitely Italianate style near the house, with ivied stone balustrades, open stairways, statuary enriched in hedges, all on a magnificent scale and style. Repton, however, leaned more and more towards the creation of a multiplicity of small and largely disconnected gardens—curiously enough, the very sort of thing which Lord Kames had recommended. This tendency became more pronounced in Repton's late work, until in such a report as that on Ashridge he designed "no less than fifteen kinds of gardens." [22] Five of these were in the modern pleasure-ground manner, a couple in a consciously antique style, and several in Repton's own manner—an arboretum, an American garden, a winter garden,[23] and two with raised beds of flowers. Repton became, in fact, the originator of what John Claudius Loudon dubbed the "gardenesque" style, with its separate compartments and its attention to the peculiarities of type-plants of various, especially exotic, species.[24]

Repton suggested numerous innovations in the landscape garden of his day: to reduce the size of the pleasure ground "within such limits that it may be kept with the utmost artificial neatness," to mark the separation of artificial from natural scene, to let the dressed grounds "rather appear to be the rich frame of the landscape than a part of the picture" from the windows, to connect the garden with the house by a sheltered way, and to provide a winter garden.[25] The tendency of the first three of these suggestions is to separate garden and park, and this is a distinction often emphasized by Repton, and connected by him with the distinctions between nature and art and between utility and the picturesque. "And while I have acceded to the combination of two words, landscape and gardening," Repton cautions, "yet they are as distinct objects as the picture and its frame. The scenery of nature, called landscape, and that of a garden, are as different as their uses; one is to please the eye, the other is for the comfort and occupation of man: one is wild . . . while the other is appropriated to man in the highest state of civilization and refinement." [26] (When Repton speaks of "acceding" to the term "landscape garden," he forgets that twenty years earlier, in the Introduction to *Sketches and Hints*, he had claimed the term as his own.) The garden proper is defined to be "every part of the grounds in which art, rather than nature, is to please the eye, the smell, and the taste," or again as *"a work of* ART, *making proper use of the materials of* NATURE." [27] All this implies a preference for the garden rather than the park. Price remarks that whereas he had spoken largely of the park, Repton answered by speaking of the garden; and this bias increased pronouncedly in later years. In 1811 Repton suffered an injury to his spine in a carriage accident, and this fortuitous circumstance had a curious influence on the development of the art, for it turned Repton's attention more exclusively to the improvement of houses and gardens rather than of parks or forests; he speaks of the design for Ashridge as "the child of my age and declining powers: when no longer able to undertake the more extensive plans of *landscape,* I was glad to contract my views within the narrow circle of the *garden,* independent of its accompaniment of distant scenery." [28] The influence of years and of infirmity is manifested in numerous details of Repton's theory and practice: after being a life-long advocate of the gravel path (as opposed to the picturesque grass walk), he suddenly advocates grass glades—for the accommodation of wheel chairs; and, unable to stoop to pick a flower from the ground, he creates the raised flower bed, which went far to modify the character of the English garden in the nineteenth century.

When Repton presented his ideas more fully, he usually distinguished three "distances": the garden, the park, and the forest or open country. Now in outline this is also Price's view of a large estate; it seems still more like Price when Repton tells us that "in forest scenery we trace the sketches of SALVATOR and of RIDINGER; in park scenery, we may realize the landscapes of CLAUDE and POUSSIN: but, in garden scenery, we delight in the rich embellishments, the blended graces of WATTEAU, where nature is dressed, but not disfigured, by art; and where the artificial decorations of architecture and sculpture are softened down by natural accompaniments of vegetation." [29] Price had used Salvator, Claude, and Watteau in the same analogy in his *Letter to Repton.* [30]

Repton rarely shows any independent knowledge of painting, and he is vigorously opposed to Price's notion of bringing gardening under the principles of painting. Sometimes, granted, he speaks in the conventionalized language of picturesque vision—often repeating that the landscape and garden are as the picture and its frame. But despite these locutions, Repton consistently argues against the predominance of painting. "The art I profess," he cries, "is of a higher nature than that of painting, and is thus very aptly described by a French author. '—*il est, à la poèsie et à la peinture, ce que la realité est à la description, et l'original à la copie.*' " [31] Led by conversations with Price and Knight into inquiring the differences of the two arts, Repton enumerates these:

1. The point of view of the painter is fixed, whereas the gardener surveys his scenery while in motion, and from many sites.
2. The field of vision is greater in nature than in a picture.
3. The view down a hill is not representable in painting.
4. The light on a real scene shifts, and (unlike painting, where composition and keeping can be secured only by setting off light with shade) all parts of a scene may bear illumination.
5. The foreground, so essential to the picture, is usually lacking in the real landscape. [32]

And although conceding that the delight of the imagination in intricacy makes desirable distinct breaks between the reaches of a landscape, Repton denies that the three distances of a landscape painting can be created in real landscape (except in the figurative sense mentioned above), for of the three distances of the improver, "the first includes that part of the scene which it is in his power to improve; the second, that which it is not in his power to prevent being injured; and the third, that which it is not in the power of himself, or any other, either to injure or improve. . . ." [33] The idea that painting should supply models for landscaping affords opportunity for the satirical excursions in which this controversy abounds: "This idea of deriving all our instruction from the works of great painters, is so ingenious and useful, that it ought not to be confined to gardening and building. In our markets, for instance, instead of that formal trim custom of displaying poultry, fish, and fruit, for sale on different stalls, why should we not rather copy the picturesque jumble of Schnyders and Rubens? Our kitchens may be furnished after the designs of Teniers and Ostade, our stables after Woovermans, and we may learn to dance from Watteau or Zuccarelli. . . ." [34] All this despite the derivation of the term "landscape-gardening," which Repton chooses because the art can only be perfected "by the united powers of the *landscape painter* and the *practical gardener*. The former must conceive a plan, which the latter may be able to execute. . . ." The mere gardener, "without some skill in painting, will seldom be able to *form a just idea of effects before they are carried into execution.*" [35] Subsequently, however, Repton seems disposed to transfer from painter to gardener this faculty of foreseeing effects; the painter, he remarks, "sees things as *they are*," the landscape gardener "as *they will be.*" [36]

Discussion of the relation of painting to gardening leads to Repton's view of the picturesque, for Repton usually uses the term "picturesque" to mean "pictorial." "In the park and forest," he cries, "let the painter be indulged with the most picturesque objects for his pencil to imitate . . . let the active mind be soothed with all the beauty of landscape, and the contemplative roused by all the sublimity of prospect that nature can produce; but we must also provide artificial scenes, less wild, though not less interesting . . ." for the pleasure grounds of the leisured.[37] This remark suggests that Repton thought pictorial chiefly what is wild, rugged, and shaggy; this is Gilpinism, and with this clew we can follow Repton's conception of the picturesque throughout his writings.

The admiration which Repton expressed for the aesthetic theory of Burke was no doubt fostered by the reflection that Burke's theory left no room for a character alongside the beautiful and the sublime, though this polemical interest in no way obstructed Repton's theoretical grasp of Burke's theory and his skill in employing it in the analysis and construction of actual scenes. In the *Letter to Price*, it is true, Repton does seem to accept Price's conception of the co-ordinance of the picturesque with beautiful and sublime (although denying that it is a prime object of gardening); yet there is nothing in the other writings, or in the principles underlying the *Letter*, to indicate such a conviction. Repton speaks as often as not of "picturesque beauty," which is a solecism in Price's system, though consistent enough with Gilpin's usage. Gilpin and Price agree in this, that the picturesque is in some sense rough; Repton is in accord, but he sees roughness only in what is wild and unkempt. For Price, in contrast, highly dressed scenes, if intricate, various, and full of abrupt modifications of form and light, are perfectly picturesque. Repton appears to take both definition and description from Gilpin.

In architecture, Repton's taste is more like that of Price, and in his discussions of buildings "picturesque" is a term of praise rather than opprobrium. The reason is, I think, that the picturesque appears in (non-ruinous) architecture in the form of irregularity of plan and elevation and of intricacy of ornamentation. Irregularity is eminently pictorial, and at the same time is often the handiest manner of building, as accommodating a variety of sizes, shapes, and exposures for rooms and as permitting additions with greatest grace. Utility and picturesqueness thus in great measure coincide in architecture, whereas in gardening (as Repton saw it) they were largely opposed. Gothic is clearly the picturesque style in architecture, and from his first work to his last Repton preferred Gothic to Grecian. His interest in irregular architecture was, in fact, a powerful force operating on the taste of the following generation in which the Gothic Revival swept over all England. The "great principle on which the picturesque effect of all Gothic edifices must depend," says Repton, is ". . . irregularity of outline; first, at the top by towers and pinnacles, or chimneys; secondly, in the outline of the faces, or elevations, by projections and recesses; thirdly, in the outline of the apertures, by breaking the horizontal lines with windows of different forms and heights; and, lastly, in the outline of the base, by the building being placed on ground of different levels." [38] It was "Queen Elizabeth's Gothic" that Repton recommended most often rather than castle or abbey Gothic, and he laments the "mutilation of the old *halls* and *manor houses,* where the large bay windows, the lofty open chimneys, and picturesque gables of Queen Elizabeth's time, give place to the modern sashes and flat roofs, with all the garish frippery of trellis, and canvas, and sharp-pointed pea-green Gothic porches, or porticos of Grecian columns reduced to the size of bedposts." [39]

Although Repton's notion of the picturesque in architecture came in application very close to Price's (however different the underlying theories), in scenery Repton thought of the picturesque as wild and uncouth, fitter for gypsies than for English gentlemen, unless the gentlemen amused themselves with rifles or canvases. This image of picturesqueness is probably derived not only from Gilpin's nature-appreciation but from the style of landscape painting of the contemporary English school, which specialized in subjects that were wild without being great, and that of their Dutch and Italian models. In the report on Endsleigh (which I think was written early though published late), Repton discourses on the picturesque:

> This word has, of late, excited considerable interest and controversy; but the word, like many others in common use, is more easy to be understood than defined; if it means all subjects capable of being represented in a picture, it will include the pig-sties of Moreland, as well as the filthy hostels of Teniers and Ostade. . . [but it is absurd to represent all that is visible without selecting what is most beautiful]. The

subjects represented by Salvator Rosa, and our English Mortimer, are deemed picturesque; but, are they fit objects to copy for the residence of man, in a polished and civilized state? Certainly not.[40]

The picturesque is consistently connected in this way with painting; and sometimes the connection becomes very particular, as in the observation that Grecian buildings have a beautiful effect amidst pointed or conical trees not only from contrast but because Italian painting has so often blended Grecian architecture with firs and cypresses. Such association by resemblance with the subjects or modes of representation of paintings is of peculiar importance in Knight's account of the picturesque, though this is a superficial instance, since the association involves the concrete wholes represented rather than the abstract qualities themselves.

It is important to notice the importance of association in Repton's thought. Like those of Price and Knight, Repton's aesthetic rules and judgments depend heavily upon association—there is almost no trace of Burke's physiology—but the classes of association stressed are not the same. What Repton calls by the name "association" is not of the first order of importance in construction of his theory, though in actual appreciation it "is one of the most impressive sources of delight; whether excited by local accident, as the spot on which some public character performed his part; by the remains of antiquity, as the ruin of a cloister or a castle; but more particularly by that personal attachment to long known objects . . . as the favourite seat, the tree, the walk, or the spot endeared by the remembrance of past events: . . . such partialities should be respected and indulged, since true taste, which is generally attended by great sensibility, ought to be the guardian of it in others." [41] Such personal or historical circumstances involve associations with concretes rather than with abstract qualities, and they are adventitious rather than inherent; this kind of association only is so termed by Repton.

But Repton appeals also to associations with qualities taken abstractly. He claims as his discovery the observation that Grecian architecture consists essentially of horizontal lines and Gothic of vertical,[42] and the problem of purity or mixture of styles depends partly on the composition of these lines. But it depends partly also upon our habits of vision as determined by historical accident; Repton denounces the incongruous mixture of Gothic and Grecian on antiquarian grounds, though he is inclined to permit some mixture of the three Gothic styles, for "whilst every casual observer may be struck with the incongruity of mixing the Grecian with the Gothic styles,

yet the nice antiquarian alone discovers, by the contour of a mould-
ing, or the shape of a battlement, that mixture of the castle and abbey
Gothic, which is equally incorrect with respect to their different dates
and purposes." [43] It is interesting to note that Knight and Price,
whose habits of vision were formed proportionately more on paintings, were inclined to justify the mixture of Grecian and Gothic which
is so frequent in the Italian landscapes of the sixteenth and seventeenth centuries. Repton at one time became so particular that he
began to complain of the "mixed style" of Queen Elizabeth's Gothic,
for "a mixed style is generally imperfect: the mind is not easily reconciled to the combination of forms which it has been used to consider distinct . . . it feels an incongruity of character . . . it is like
uniting, in one object, infancy with old age, life with death, or things
present with things past." [44] But this archaeological sensitivity is
found only in the book explaining Repton's design for the pavilion
at Brighton—which was to be in the Hindu style. He desired to
introduce a new and safe source of novelty into British architecture
which would not be susceptible of corrupting mixture with the two
accepted systems; and it was his interest to show that the accepted
systems were not themselves wholly adequate in utility and style.
The *Fragments* subsequently betray no dissatisfaction with the "mixed
Gothic."

Habitual association resulting from historical circumstances does
not account wholly for our reactions to the materials of building, for
this depends also on the properties of the materials, their costliness
and durability. Such considerations lead us to that branch of associations with concretes which involves properties essential to the objects.
Utility, fitness, and design all include such associations as these, and
it is only insofar as they are associational that utility and fitness are
aesthetic. So long as we approve the utility of an object with a practical aim in view, our feeling is perhaps pleasurable, but does not
have the detachment and freedom of aesthetic pleasure; it is only
when perceived sympathetically, without direct practical concern-
ment or conscious reflection, that utility assumes an aesthetic guise.
The practical view of a farm gives non-aesthetic satisfaction; the distant view of an active farm scene may give a truly aesthetic pleasure
from the ideas of animation, prosperity, and happiness which it suggests. The utility of which Repton most often speaks lends itself especially well to aesthetic feeling; it is not that of a farm but of a
retirement for leisure, and the detachment and freedom of leisure
are associated to its conveniences. The merits Repton saw in formality

were of this kind, though he was not insensible to its picturesque qualities. But on occasion Repton becomes too practical for his judgments to be considered aesthetic; his analysis of the differences of town house and country house, and his rules for the layout of an estate, are so largely in terms of immediate function that they must be considered non-aesthetic;[45] Price discusses these same points, but in terms of creating visual effects.

Repton's utility has a range of moral overtones which determine his taste in beauties. Throughout his long career, Repton preferred neat and open scenes with light and animation; "cheerful" and "gloomy" are among his favorite epithets of praise and reproach, and he never tires of altering "the melancholy appendages of solitary grandeur observable in the pleasure-grounds of the last century." [46] His "favorite propensity for humanizing, as well as animating, beautiful scenery" [47] is a matter of taste and character, but is at the same time a facet of his preference of utility to picturesque beauty when the two conflict. His own tiny garden in the village of Romford was a frame to the landscape he preferred, a frame "composed of flowering shrubs and evergreens; beyond which are seen, the cheerful village, the high road, and that constant moving scene, which I would not exchange for any of the lonely parks that I have improved for others." [48]

CHAPTER 16

The Price-Repton *Controversy*

❧

REPTON'S *Letter to Price* betrays, in its lack of system and order, the haste with which it was composed; and this is the more unfortunate since Price unimaginatively organized his much longer *Letter to Repton* to answer point by point. Neither of these works of controversy impresses as a powerful or profound piece of aesthetic speculation. Repton introduces his assault with the conciliatory judgment that "in the general principles and theory of the art, which you have considered with so much attention, I flatter myself that we agree; and that our difference of opinion relates only to the propriety, or, perhaps, possibility, of reducing them to practice." [1] Repton's principles are really, however, very different from those of Price; and since Repton proceeds to show that Price's (as he understands them) are not practicable, it is a question how they could be accepted even in theory if inherently insusceptible of reduction to practice? Price perceives this paradox and is quick to point out the "very singular contrast" between Repton's opening professions of agreement upon principles and the ensuing attack upon those very principles. [2]

The principles which undergo Repton's examination are, that the painter's landscape is the model for the gardener, and that the picturesque consists in the wild and uncouth. Neither of these propositions, of course, was asserted by Price. He proposed not to copy pictures in gardens, but to apply in landscape the principles of composition governing all visual phenomena, principles isolated most readily, to be sure, in the works of the great painters. "The question, therefore, is not," Price declares, "whether the Caracci, Francesco Bolognese, or S. Rosa, would study landscapes in a flower-garden, but which of two scenes of the same character (whatever it were, from the Alps to a parterre,) had most of those qualities that accord with the general principles of their art." [3] And secondly, the picturesque is nowise incompatible with high ornamentation and the conveniences of civilized life; Price avows that he might even prefer the nation to be wholly finished by Brown rather than become one "huge picturesque forest"—the fate Repton foresaw if the "new system of improving 'by neglect and accident' " should prevail.[4] These two principles are in Repton's thought really only one; "it seems to me," Price observes in noting this coincidence, "that your principal aim through the whole of this Letter, is to shew, that by an attention to pictures, and to the method of study pursued by painters, only wild and unpolished ideas are acquired." [5] Not so, of course; the elegance of Claude, the formal grandeur of Poussin (to look no farther) refute this notion. Nor, moreover, did Price propose that the improver should abandon design to chance, but only that he should gain hints for design from observing the effects produced by neglect and accident. This use of accident is a consequence of the nature of the art, for, unlike architecture, gardening deals with the materials of nature.[6]

Repton's letter falls, after introductory compliment and blow, into three sections: the first, an examination of the relation of painting and gardening; the second, an apology for Brown's clump and belt; the third, a return to the offensive with a renewed attack on painting and the picturesque. However amateurs might be misled into supposing a great affinity amongst the several arts they cultivate, Repton remarks in taking up the first of these heads, mature consideration and practical experience have led him to realize that "*in whatever relates to man, propriety and convenience are not less objects of good taste, than picturesque effect. . . .*" [7] Price's reply to the argument from utility is revealing. After describing how a landscape painter might improve a scene, he observes that "in all this, *convenience* and *propriety* are not the objects of consideration: not that either of them is to be neglected, but that they are objects of another kind; objects of good sense, and good judgment, rather than of that more refined and delicate sense and judgment, called taste. Any glaring offense against either of them is disgusting, but the strictest observance of them will give a man but little reputation for taste, unless the general effect of the *picture* be good." [8] The argument is, that circumstances of utility are not truly aesthetic in quality—a point which I have hitherto considered at sufficient length. Price is chiefly interested in associations with abstract visual qualities, or in the direct nervous action of such qualities, and it is doubtful that he would judge aesthetic any assemblage of concretes not enriched by associations with line, color, and shade. The question to be decided is in a sense one of terminology; but the terminology hinges upon a discrimination of subtle sensations. Disinterested appreciation of utility is assuredly pleasurable, though assuredly different in feeling from pictorial values; ought the two feelings to be ranked together? Here the habits of feeling and the philosophic inheritances of the two disputants come into play. Price is by temperament highly sensitive to compositional and to romantic values, and (though a Whig humanitarian) loves seclusion and reverie. Repton is by native temperament and by the conscious habits of his professional duties concerned more with society than with contemplation, and (his visual sensitivity notwithstanding) concerned more with use than with composition or poetic feeling. Price is temperamentally disinclined from accepting convenience as an aesthetic consideration, while Repton is prompted to consider it a part, and the chief part, of taste. Add to this, that Repton had really no philosophical inheritance except those eulogies of Brownian gardening which were couched often in terms of utility, whereas Price built upon the system of Burke, the whole influence of which was against admission of the useful as a cause of beauty.[9]

In examining picturesqueness (I revert to Repton's *Letter*), Repton takes advantage of Price's distinction between beautiful and picturesque: "There is no exercise so pleasing to the inquisitive mind," he avers, "as that of deducing theories and systems from favourite opinions: I was therefore peculiarly interested and gratified by your ingenious distinction betwixt the beautiful and the picturesque; but I cannot admit the propriety of its application to landscape gardening; because beauty, and not 'picturesqueness,' is the chief object of modern improvement. . . ."[10] In reply, Price makes three observations which restate the issue cleared of the obfuscations which Repton's misreading or rhetoric had thrown over it. The picturesque, firstly, is not a reference to painting but a separate aesthetic character; it is in many cases not applicable to gardening, but the general principles of painting are always so. The landscape gardener, secondly, does more than make a garden near the house, where the picturesque must often be sacrificed; he makes a park. And thirdly, in nature the picturesque is usually mixed with the beautiful, whereas improvers have exhibited "the dangerous tendency of recommending a narrow exclusive attention to beauty as a separate quality . . . instead of a liberal and enlarged attention to beauty in its more general sense [which would include the picturesque], to character, and to the *genius loci*."[11] Price suggests, and I think plausibly, that Repton is influenced by a *jalousie de métier,* which leads him to misstate the issue on one side by taking gardening in the narrower sense rather than landscape gardening, and on the other side by taking painters' studies of *wild* nature exclusively. Those insensible transitions in which Burkeian beauty consists are, after all, best effected in gardening by a natural style of loose arrangements; Brown's effort at this beauty consisted in making the separate parts smooth or undulating, but in leaving each part—clump, belt, walk, river—perfectly distinct and sharply separated. Brown and his followers, says Price, "have been universally and professedly, smoothers, shavers, clearers, levellers, and dealers in distinct serpentine lines and edges. . . ." [12]

Repton introduces one argument on this general head which requires especial attention, the political analogy which is appealed to in one form or another both by the disputants of the eighteenth century and the scholars of the twentieth. Repton

> cannot help seeing great affinity betwixt deducing gardening from the painter's studies of wild nature, and deducing government from the uncontrouled opinions of man in a savage state. The neatness, simplicity, and elegance of English gardening, have acquired the approbation of the present century, as the happy medium betwixt the wildness of nature and the stiffness of art; in the same manner as the English constitution is the happy medium betwixt the liberty of savages, and the restraint of despotic government; and so long as we enjoy the benefit of these middle degrees betwixt extremes of each [he concludes], let experiments of untried theoretical improvement be made in some other country. [13]

Price rejoins in like vein that his pride and exultation in the British constitution "would sink into shame and despondency, should the parallel you have made, ever become just: should the freedom, energy, and variety of our minds, give place to tameness and monotony; should our opinions be prescribed to us, and, like our places, be moulded into one form," and so forth; modern improvement is "a species of thraldom unfit for a free country," he had declared in his first book. [14] This kind of political analogy had been even from the beginning of the century a feature of discussion of gardening—so much so that Nikolaus Pevsner declares that "Whig is the first source of the landscape garden," and tells us that the landscape garden was "conceived in England, because it is the garden of liberalism." [15] I. de Wolfe goes further, and makes an effort to relate picturesque theory to the political background in such a way as to be able to use the terminology of politics for discussion of landscape. [16] But really, the appeal to the British constitution is a mere rhetorical trick, whether it appears in Knight, in Price, or in Repton. All of these men are literal-minded; none makes dialectical assimilations of politics to aesthetics or vice versa. Such arguments have no real conviction for them and are mere polemical brickbats; they are rationalizations, not intellectual causes, and they are never the principal arguments relied upon, but are makeweights thrown in to overwhelm already staggering opponents. To stress them is to equivocate with terms and to distort picturesque theory.

The second of the principal divisions of Repton's *Letter* defends clump and belt, the most conspicuous features of Brown's style. The question of the clump is merely one of means, as Repton states it: the clump is the simplest way of producing a group in future. Price, however, denies that Brown ever "made a clump like a natural group, though he did make many natural groups like clumps"; [17] the inference is that he preferred distinctness to connection, and "it is by means of this *system* of making every thing distinct and separate, that Mr. Brown has been enabled to do such rapid and extensive mischief; and thence it is that he is so much more an object of the painter's indignation than his strait-lined predecessors." [18] Repton's defense of the belt, too, rests upon expediency. Man loves seclusion and safety: the park must be enclosed. He loves liberty: the pale must not show. The belt gives the reality of enclosure with the deceptive appearance of freedom. Price, instead, is inclined to suppose the belt adopted from vanity in the owners (to conceal the size of a small estate, or display that of a large) and laziness in the improvers (since it is a formula applied without regard to particular circumstances of composition). It is of interest that on clumps and belts at least, Price and Repton drew together as Repton's interest in the garden and his appreciation of picturesque effect increased. Repton even comes to sneer at the "trim imitators of Brown's defects," and to refer contemptuously to "the spruce modern seat of sudden affluence, *be-belted* and *be-clumped* in the newest style of the modern taste of landscape gardening. . . ." [19] This coincidence of opinion is not an identity, however, for Repton was contracting the pleasure grounds into a garden while Price (though formalizing them near the house) was transforming them into a forest park.

Having written this much, Repton determined on having his letter printed, and accordingly returned to the attack on the painter-gardener. He warns against amateurs "quacking" themselves; he contradistinguishes the prospect, in which everybody delights, from

the landscape, or painter's subject, and proclaims the love of prospect
to be "an inherent passion of the human mind"; [20] he decides that
painting and gardening are not sister arts but congenial natures
brought together like man and wife (the controversy reaches its most
banal); he suggests that (as a man may from habit prefer tobacco
to sugar) Knight and Price "are in the habits of admiring fine pictures, and both live amidst bold and picturesque scenery," which
may, he tells them, "have rendered you insensible to the beauty
of those milder scenes that have charms for common observers . . .
your palate certainly requires a degree of 'irritation' rarely to be
expected in garden scenery; and, I trust, the good sense and good
taste of this country will never be led to despise the comfort of a
gravel walk, the delicious fragrance of a shrubbery, the soul expand-
ing delight of a wide extended prospect, or a view down a steep
hill, because they are all subjects incapable of being painted." [21]
Price humorlessly takes up each of Repton's points, in which it will
not be necessary to follow him. His discussion of prospects, however,
is ingenious. A prospect is distinguished from a landscape, from a
composition suitable for a picture, in that the foreground and second
distance are absent or minimal. The question arises, why prospects
are enchanting in nature, though unsuited for painting? The reason
Price alleges is that painted prospects "are not *real*, and therefore
do not excite the curiosity which reality does, both as to the particular
spots, and the circumstances attending them . . ."; [22] Price might
well have granted also the sublimity of prospect. One of the circumstances the curious eye remarks in a prospect is, of course, the composition of those parts which make separate pictures. Gilpin, too,
found this fascination in the prospect; after describing a various and
extensive scene, spoiled by transfer to canvas, Gilpin sings,

> *Yet why (methinks I hear*
> *Some Critic say) do ample scenes, like this,*
> *In picture fail to please; when every eye*
> *Confesses they transport on Nature's chart?*
> *Why, but because, where She displays the scene,*
> *The roving sight can pause, and swift select,*
> *From all she offers, parts, whereon to fix,*
> *And form distinct perceptions; each of which*
> *Presents a separate picture. Thus as bees*
> *Condense within their hives the varying sweets;*
> *So does the eye a lovely whole collect*
> *From parts disjointed; nay, perhaps, deformed.*[23]

Since the painted panorama is seen at one *coup d'oeil*, the picturesque eye can not from it select such separate compositions.

To the refutation of Repton's objections Price appends a review of the whole question of the difference and mixture of the picturesque and the beautiful. For he feels about Repton's criticisms as most philosophical writers feel about the arguments of their opponents, that confusion has enveloped the subject from the uncertain and licentious use of words. The central term, "beauty," may signify comprehensively "all that allures, attracts, or pleases the eye in every style," [24] through the grand principle of union, harmony, connection, breadth, congruity; or it may have the narrower Burkeian sense as opposed to sublimity and the picturesque. The analogy of aesthetical and ethical language is again stressed; like "beauty," "virtue" has both a broad, inclusive sense, and a narrow sense referring to the most valued qualities in men (courage) and women (chastity). The analytical separation and practical blending of beautiful and picturesque are illustrated by some of Price's most luscious description. Even the topic of gravel walks and mown lawns is given a luminosity and order when drawn under Price's apparatus of terms and distinctions.

In a letter to the publisher Robson, granting permission for his *Letter to Price* to be reprinted in Price's answer, Repton speaks of adding an Appendix to "the first volume of my great work" in which "I shall more fully enter into the question between Mr. Knight, Mr. Price, Mr. Brown & myself. . . ." [25] As late as December 24, 1794, then (Repton misdates his copy of the letter 1795), Repton had not added the seventh chapter (against Knight) or the Appendix (against Price). But these additions, once made, add little to this exposition, for they have been canvassed in the treatment of Repton's scheme as a whole. He complains of Price's alleged idea-thieving; mentions the controversy over painting; proclaims his agreement with Price on artificial water (though eight years later he was to declare that "Mr. Price has written an Essay to describe the *practical* manner of finishing the banks of artificial water: but I confess, after reading it with much attention, I despair of making any practitioner comprehend his meaning . . ." [26]); defends Brown against misrepresentation; enters into the sources of pleasure in landscape gardening, neglect of some of which had misled Price and Knight; and, finally, prints a letter on gardening by William Windham. This piece of Windham's says in little almost all that Repton had said at length; the key proposition is that "places are not to be laid out with a view to their appearance in a picture, but to their uses, and the enjoyment of them in real life; and their conformity to those purposes is that which constitutes their beauty. . . ." [27] So far as the controversy stems from principle rather than personality, this is that principle which lies at its root.

The *Observations on Theory and Practice* contain a few sections devoted to the controversy; Repton has softened little, and still tilts at windmills in reading "picturesque" as "pictorial." Behind the scenes of this logomachy, however, the combatants speak well of one another, and the differences over which they cut and slash in print they gloss over in correspondence. Repton declares to Robson that he "received so much pleasure in perusing Mr. Price's work & am so charmed with the animation of his Stile and manner, that I shall not be sorry to have provoked this kind of *sparring,* so long as we both keep our muffles on our hand & our buttons on the points of our foils." [28] When Price concludes his published *Letter* in a spirit of accommodation, excusing "occasional asperity" on the grounds that "he who writes a formal challenge, must not expect a billet-doux in return," and avouching that "whatever sharpness there may be in my style, there is no rancour in my heart," [29] Repton replied with generosity, candidly acknowledging that "the difference in our opinions is by no means so great, as we either of us pretend in our publick controversy. . . ." [30]

There was little personal animosity between Price and Repton, notwithstanding the harsh sarcasms they leveled at one another in print, but towards Knight, I think, Repton did at first feel real resentment for the affront offered in *The Landscape* (of which more hereafter). When it became clear, after publication of the *Analytical Inquiry* in 1805, that there was an intellectual rift between neighbors Price and Knight, Repton naturally sided with Price. From the first he had felt that there was "a shade of difference betwixt the opinions of Mr. *Price* and Mr. *Knight,* which seems to have arisen from the different characters of their respective places; *Foxley* is less romantic than *Downton,* and therefore Mr. Price is less extravagant in his ideas, and more willing to allow some little sacrifice of picturesque beauty to neatness, near the house. . . ." [31] But the *Analytical Inquiry*'s critique of Price allows Repton to regard him as a fellow victim to the severity of Knight's criticism. In the *Fragments on the Theory and Practice of Landscape Gardening,* Repton's last book, the references to Price are mostly favorable; Repton makes incidental appeal to Price as to an authority whose concurrence lends weight to his own opinion,[32] and even quotes Price's Ciceronian motto, "Quàm multa vident pictores in umbris et in eminentiis, quae nos non videmus." [33] Most curiously, in writing on Stanage Park, Repton remarks that "the opposite opinions of two gentlemen in its vicinity [a footnote identifies Price and Knight] have produced that controversy in which I have endeavoured to become a moderator." [34] This is not quite the role in which we recall him!

Richard Payne Knight

✿

T HE LANDSCAPE, *a Didactic Poem in Three Books. Addressed to Uvedale Price, Esq.*, appeared early in 1794, the first manifesto of the picturesque controversy. Richard Payne Knight, its author, was a scholar and connoisseur with an enthusiasm for the picturesque and a knack for didactic poetry in the manner of Pope.[1] Knight was prominent in the Society of Dilettanti and one of the principals in the Elgin marbles controversy; his collection of antique coins and bronzes is today the basis of the British Museum's holdings; and he had the most valuable collection of Claudes in Europe. Downton Castle, which he himself designed, and his park along the picturesque Teme in Shropshire are among the showplaces of England. And Knight has as well some claim to the title of philosopher, partly for his system-building,[2] but surely for the keenness of his insight into human motives. The tangential dissertations on happiness, love, morals, government—dissertations scattered through both *The Landscape* and the *Analytical Inquiry into the Principles of Taste*—interrupt continuity and shatter organization, but the works would be less rich without them. Knight conjoins the urbane cynicism of Gibbon with a sympathy genuine though not mawkish; and his thoughts on political society, religion, marriage—skeptical, tolerant, just—exhibit a mind distinguished in its balance of polished intellect with unforced feeling.

The Landscape was a highly entertaining work and enjoyed a favorable reception—a reception which roused a host of defenders of the old order. *The Landscape* is, of course, primarily concerned with inculcation of a certain taste in gardening rather than with exposition of a system of aesthetics; but that taste involves implications and assumptions of immense importance. Empirical aesthetics are perhaps always best grasped in their application to visible objects, and especially to natural objects which involve few complicating factors. The theory of landscape gardening, an art which heightens and simplifies the effects of natural scenery without introducing artistic materials of its own, is thus an excellent introduction to the problems of aesthetics.

But I need not justify further the inclusion of *The Landscape* in this study. The opening argument and invocation have the faintly ironical flavor which pervades much of the poem:

> *How best to bid the verdant Landscape rise,*
> *To please the fancy, and delight the eyes;*
> *Its various parts in harmony to join*
> *With art clandestine, and conceal'd design;*
> *T'adorn, arrange;—to sep'rate, and select*   5
> *With secret skill, and counterfeit neglect;*
> *I sing.—Do thou, O Price, the song attend;*
> *Instruct the poet, and assist the friend:*
> *Teach him plain truth in numbers to express,*
> *And shew its charms through fiction's flow'ry dress.*   10

The opposition of fancy and sensation (in the second verse) is of fundamental importance for Knight, whose aesthetics connects a theory of the direct nervous action of color and light with an elaborate associational psychology. It reappears in the statement of the first principle of taste:

> *'Tis still one principle through all extends,*   35
> *And leads through diff'rent ways to diff'rent ends*
>
> .   .   .   .
>
> *'Tis just congruity of parts combin'd*
> *To please the sense, and satisfy the mind.*   40

This congruity is not to be delimited by arbitrary rules, whether in painting or in landscape gardening:

> *Nature in all rejects the pedant's chain;*   140
> *Which binding beauty in its waving line,*
> *Destroys the charm it vainly would define;*
> *For nature still irregular and free,*
> *Acts not by lines, but gen'ral sympathy.*

The true rules for gardening are illustrated by a pronouncement on approaches:

> *First fix the points to which you wish to go;*
> *Then let your easy path spontaneous flow;*

> *With no affected turn or artful bend,*   155
> *To lead you round still farther from the end:*
> *For, as the principle of taste is sense,*
> *Whate'er is void of meaning gives offence.*

It was to this passage that Knight appended a note on Repton's Red Book for Tatton; having read Repton as urging that the family arms might be placed on neighboring milestones, Knight subjects this gratification of "purse-proud vanity" to excoriating satire. Repton, naturally enough, was embittered, and added a chapter of defense and rebuttal, "Concerning Approaches; with Some Remarks on the Affinity Betwixt Painting and Gardening," to his *Sketches and Hints*. Quoting at length from the Red Book of Tatton, and from others of his reports, he defends himself pretty successfully against the charge of catering to the pride of conspicuous magnificence. It was perhaps a little pompous to suggest erecting distance markers with the family arms (not, as Knight read it, using the turnpike milestones for the purpose); but Repton is free of the desire to establish vast estates for solitary splendor. More and more, as we have seen, he urged limiting the size of parks, and advised that the public be admitted to enliven them. He is, it is true, desirous of perpetuating a hierarchy of ranks and classes; but Knight and Price, Whigs though they be, share this preference.

True taste, as Knight declares, reveals its stores cautiously:

> *Its greatest art is aptly to conceal;*
> *To lead, with secret guile, the prying sight*
> *To where component parts may best unite,*
> *And form one beauteous, nicely blended whole,*   195
> *To charm the eye and captivate the soul.*

Two plates illustrate application of this principle to landscaping; one exhibits a severely Palladian house set in a shaven lawn with an affected Chinese bridge carrying a serpentining approach—every part hard and distinct; the other shows an intricate Tudor Gothic house half-buried in a wilderness, with shaggy foreground and roughhewn rustic bridge—the "beauteous whole" of harmonious and picturesque connection. Repton (with some justice) thinks the two scenes "serve rather to exemplify bad taste in the two extremes of artificial neatness and wild neglect," and the rustic bridge (copied, in fact, from one on Knight's estate) "looks like the miserable expedient of poverty, or a ridiculous affectation of rural simplicity." [3]

Knight (we return to *The Landscape*) thinks to develop principles for gardening by analyzing the three distances of painting. Hence, he cries,

> *Hence let us learn, in real scenes, to trace*
> *The true ingredients of the painter's grace;*   258
>
> .   .   .   .
>
> *But ah! in vain:—see yon fantastic band,*
> *With charts, pedometers, and rules in hand,*
> *Advance triumphant, and alike lay waste*
> *The forms of nature, and the works of taste!*
> *T'improve, adorn, and polish, they profess;*   265
> *But shave the goddess, whom they come to dress;*
>
> .   .   .   .
>
> *Hence, hence! thou haggard fiend, however call'd,*
> *Thin, meagre genius of the bare and bald;*
> *Thy spade and mattock here at length lay down,*   285
> *And follow to the tomb thy fav'rite Brown. . . .*

This attack on Brown called forth Repton in defense; "the whole," he says, "of that false and mistaken theory, which Mr. Knight endeavours to introduce, by confounding the two ideas [of park and forest], proceeds from not duly considering the degree of affinity betwixt painting and gardening. . . ." [4] We need not examine again the opinions of Repton on this vexed question; but Repton did not spring alone to the defense of the art of Capability Brown. William Marshall and George Mason, practical gardeners both, wrote elaborate replies to *The Landscape* and to Price's *Essay on the Picturesque.* And John Matthews struck off a parody, *A Sketch from the Landscape,* matching verse for verse. Knight's adjuration to improvers to follow their master Brown to the tomb suggested Matthews' title-page vignette, which exhibits a fashionably dressed gentleman discharging the contents of a chamber pot at a tomb inscribed CAPABILITY. Around the tomb a half-dozen improvers, equipped with spade, scythe, and roller, are spattered with the discharge and fall away holding their noses, &c. Matthews' ironical comment:

> *Death has mown thee [Brown]—his heavy paw*
> *Has swept thee down his deep ha-ha,*
>   *Thou great defacer of the nation!*
> *Well did he use his scythe and broom!*
> *And now, with glee, upon thy tomb*
>   *I'll pour a suitable libation.* [5]

Another vignette at end illustrates the closing apostrophe:

> *Triumphant* KNIGHT! *to give thy name*
> *A passport to immortal fame,*
> *What shall the grateful world agree on?*
>
> . . . .
>
> *Thy statue of Colossal size,*
> *In ductile yew, shall nobly rise—*
> (*Think not thy modesty shall 'scape us*)
> *The* God of Gardens *thou shalt stand,*
> *To fright improvers from the land,*
> *A huge and terrible* Priapus.[6]

The vignette is a caricature of a formal garden, with knotted parterre, topiary work, and a cypress avenue; facing the avenue and back to us is the yew statue of Knight; two ladies are turning away in confusion (a statue of Priapus, recall). This allusion is a clever but rather cruel stroke; it refers, of course, to Knight's *Account of the Remains of the Worship of Priapus,* a book generations ahead of its age in understanding of sexual symbolism, which brought on Knight's head a storm of abuse for alleged obscenity and infidelity.

Knight's mockery of improvers for "shaving Nature" is in its turn mocked:

> *How cropt and shorn poor Nature looks!*
>
> . . . .
>
> *How could these blockheads at her toilet*
> *Shave such a charming head, and spoil it!*
>
> . . . .
>
> *Shave, then, no more, good friends, but friz*
> *The lovely locks round Nature's phiz. . . .*[7]

Again, with the misunderstanding which Hearne's engraving was likely to suggest and entrenched interest to adopt, Matthews cries,

> *That man should walk, can Nature mean,*
> *On prim-roll'd gravel fring'd with green?*
> *No—if I rightly understand her!*
> *'Midst brambles thick I'd rather chuse*
> *To trudge in dirt above my shoes,*
> *Than in such serpentines meander!* [8]

Book II of *The Landscape* is introduced by celebration of the ancient system of formal gardening—

> *Oft when I've seen some lonely mansion stand,*
> *Fresh from th' improver's desolating hand,*
> *'Midst shaven lawns, that far around it creep*
> *In one eternal undulating sweep;*
> *And scatter'd clumps, that nod at one another,*   5
> *Each stiffly waving to its formal brother;*
> *Tir'd with th' extensive scene, so dull and bare,*
> *To Heav'n devoutly I've address'd my pray'r,—*
> *Again the moss-grown terraces to raise,*
> *And spread the labyrinth's perplexing maze;*   10
> *Replace in even lines the ductile yew,*
> *And plant again the ancient avenue.*
> *Some feature then, at least, we should obtain,*
> *To mark this flat, insipid, waving plain;*
> *Some vary'd tints and forms would intervene,*   15
> *To break this uniform, eternal green.*[9]

This exordium is followed by development of principles of composition for the new picturesque park and by oft-quoted lines on picturesque buildings—

> *Bless'd is the man, in whose sequester'd glade,*
> *Some ancient abbey's walls diffuse their shade;*   255
> *With mould'ring windows pierc'd, and turrets crown'd,*
> *And pinnacles with clinging ivy bound.*
> *Bless'd too is he, who, 'midst his tufted trees,*
> *Some ruin'd castle's lofty towers sees;*
> *Imbosom'd high upon the mountains brow,*   260
> *Or nodding o'er the stream that glides below.*
> *Nor yet unenvy'd, to whose humbler lot*
> *Falls the retir'd and antiquated cot;—*
> *Its roof with weeds and mosses cover'd o'er,*
>
> .   .   .   .
>
> *Still happier he (if conscious of his prize)*
> *Who sees some temple's broken columns rise,*
> *'Midst sculptur'd fragments, shiver'd by their fall,*   270
> *And tott'ring remnants of its marble wall;—*
> *Where ev'ry beauty of correct design,*
> *And vary'd elegance of art, combine*
> *With nature's softest tints, matur'd by time,*
> *And the warm influence of a genial clime.*   275

This second book concludes with an account of the purity of taste among the Greeks,[10] its destruction by Roman tyranny and Christian bigotry, and the revival in the Renaissance:

Reviv'd again, in Charles' and Leo's days,
Art dawn'd unsteady, with reflected rays;
Lost all the gen'ral principle of grace,　　　　　410
And wav'ring fancy left to take its place;
But yet, in these degen'rate days, it shone
With one perfection, e'en to Greece unknown:
Nature's aerial tints and fleeting dyes,
Old Titian first imbody'd to the eyes;　　　　　415
And taught the tree to spread its light array
In mimic colours, and on canvas play.
Next Rubens came, and catch'd in colours bright
The flick'ring flashes of celestial light;

.　　.　　.　　.　　.　　.　　.　　.　　.

But both their merits, polish'd and refin'd
By toil and care, in patient Claude were join'd:
Nature's own pupil, fav'rite child of taste!
Whose pencil, like Lysippus' chisel, trac'd　　　　425
Vision's nice errors, and, with feign'd neglect,
Sunk partial form in general effect.

This peculiar merit of modern painting is the picturesque, the harmonious blending of tints and lights which constitutes the direct pleasure of the sense of sight. *The Landscape,* while not a treatise on aesthetics, was yet deliberately calculated to cultivate the tastes which Knight's theory, already formed, justified and demanded. Even in the Sicilian diary of 1777 are passages containing the germ of Knight's theory. On April 13 of that year, Knight writes of the ruins at Paestum, "The colour is a whitish yellow, which merges here and there into shades of greyish blue. The weather has attacked the stone, which is overgrown with moss and weeds, and neither blackened by smoke, nor rendered hideous by recent additions, as is the wont of ruins at Rome. Thus it is that the tints affect the eye in a fashion at once harmonious, pleasing, and picturesque." [11] "Affect the eye," "harmonious," and "picturesque" are all susceptible here of the technical analysis given in the *Analytical Inquiry.*

The final book of *The Landscape,* on trees, is logically only a pendant to the second and need not detain us. Gilpin, who had given an analysis of trees and shrubs, their groupings and accompaniments, in his *Remarks on Forest Scenery,* dwelt chiefly on line and form; Knight, consistently with his theory of the picturesque, operates more in terms of light and color. His prescriptions, like those of Price, are free of academic mannerism; he celebrates the beauties of native scenery—

> *Nor [he warns], plac'd beneath our cool and wat'ry sky,*
> *Attempt the glowing tints of Italy:*   310
> *For thus compell'd in mem'ry to confide,*
> *Or blindly follow some preceding guide,*
> *One common track it [art] still pursues,*
> *And crudely copies what it never views. . . .*

It is not imitation of Italian landscape, real or painted, that is required, but independent composition on picturesque principles.

When a second edition of *The Landscape* was called for in 1795, Knight added a note which, after dealing an incidental blow to Repton for his *Letter to Price*, undertook the subversion of Price's radical distinction of beautiful and picturesque. Repton, "taking advantage of a supposed distinction between the picturesque and the beautiful," maintains that "his art was never intended to produce landscapes, but some kind of *neat, simple, and elegant effects,* or non-descript beauties, which have not yet been named or classed. . . . I cannot, however [Knight declares], but think that the distinction of which this ingenious professor has thus taken advantage, is an imaginary one, and that the picturesque is merely that kind of beauty which belongs exclusively to the sense of vision; or to the imagination, guided by that sense." [12] This is the thesis of the note to *The Landscape,* and this is the thesis of the *Analytical Inquiry into the Principles of Taste* a decade later, so far as that work relates to the picturesque.

In the Introduction to the *Analytical Inquiry,* "Containing a Sceptical View of the Subject," Knight develops with some subtlety the uncertainty and instability of every standard. Since taste is a question of feeling rather than of reason, the only standard is the generality of feeling; yet no values are really general, and every age rejects the values of the preceding. "The word Beauty," Knight observes, "is a general term of approbation, of the most vague and extensive meaning, applied indiscriminately to almost every thing that is pleasing, either to the sense, the imagination, or the understanding; whatever the nature of it be, whether a material substance, a moral excellence, or an intellectual theorem." [13] All these applications of the term, moreover, are literal, notwithstanding that "all epithets, employed to distinguish qualities perceivable only by intellect, were originally applied to objects of sense . . . and are therefore applied *transitively,* though not always *figuratively,* to objects of intellect or imagination." [14] Whether applied to virtue or the human form, "beauty" signifies the result of balance and proportion. But these "proportions" are not truly the same; "I admit," Knight continues, ". . . that the word Beauty entirely changes its meaning . . . accordingly as it is applied to objects of the senses, the imagination, or the understanding; for, though these faculties are so mixed and compounded in their operations, in the complicated mind of civilized man, that it is extremely difficult to discriminate them accurately; yet the pleasures of each, though mixed in their effects, are utterly distinct in their causes." [15]

It is this analysis of the faculties which permits Knight to get beyond the expression of personal preferences. The three parts of the *Analytical Inquiry* are devoted to sensation, the association of ideas (comprehending "Knowledge or Improved Perception," "Imagination," and "Judgment"), and the passions. The appropriateness of this particular psychology will be examined later; what is to be noted here is the advance such an approach represents over that of Price. One of the difficulties in Price's analysis, and one which has left Price exposed to much misunderstanding, is the confusion in which the psychological mechanisms underlying the aesthetic characters are left. In Knight, the analysis is conducted entirely in terms of the faculties involved in aesthetic experience, so that (whatever errors may be made in the conduct of the analysis) the argument always differentiates clearly the various causes involved.

Analysis naturally proceeds from the simple to the complex, and Knight begins, accordingly, with the senses, and with those least compounded with the higher faculties—taste, then smell and touch. Having ascertained the principles of sensation generally, Knight can then move to the senses of sight and hearing, "whose objects are the proper objects of taste in the more general sense of the word, as used to signify a general discriminative faculty arising from just feeling and correct judgment implanted in the mind of man by his Creator, and improved by exercise, study, and meditation." [16]

Knight was pretty well read in British philosophy as far as Reid. He follows Berkeley and Hume in rejecting the special status of primary qualities, but not in what he supposed to be Berkeley's denial of the material world and Hume's denial of the intellectual universe as well. To escape these supposed conclusions of skepticism, Knight emphasizes a set of distinctions familiar enough to readers in the Scottish philosophy. "All its [skepticism's] wandering clouds of confusion and perplexity," he says, "seem to have arisen from employing the Greek word *idea*, sometimes in its proper sense to signify a mental image or vision, and sometimes in others the most adverse and remote, to signify *perception, remembrance, notion, knowledge,* and almost every other operation, or result of operation, of which the mind is capable." [17] Thus, we have a *perception* of an object moving when we see or feel it (and even this is more than the sensation), and a *remembrance* afterwards; of the motion of the earth we have a *notion* "acquired by comparative deductions from other perceptions"; of motion in general we have only *general knowledge* abstracted from all the above. Objects and their qualities exist really, and by experience we learn that they are the causes of sensations—though the sensations do not resemble them. But mere sensation—a modification of the sense-organ—is different from the perception in the mind, and this difference is crucial for aesthetics.

Much of the later doctrine is a consequence of the remarks on taste and smell, remarks which are carefully selected, however scattered in appearance. The doctrine is, that the sense-organs, like other animal parts, are irritable, a certain degree of irritation being always kept up by ordinary vital processes. This normal irritation may be increased or decreased by external impressions, or its modes may be changed; "but how these changes take place . . . is beyond the reach of human faculties to discover. All that we know is, that certain modes of irritation produce sensations, which are pleasant, and others, sensations which are unpleasant; that there must be a certain degree of it to produce either; and that, beyond a certain degree, all are painful." [18] The influence of custom and that of novelty are readily allowed for; with an acuteness and a cynicism altogether characteristic, Knight remarks that "the case is, that all those tastes, which are natural, lose, and all those which are unnatural, acquire strength by indulgence: for no strained or unnatural action of the nerves can ever be so assimilated to their constitutional modes of existence, as not to produce, on every re-application of its cause, a change sufficient to excite a pleasing irritation. . . ." [19] In this theory, essentially the same pleasure results from an increase in deficient irritation and from a diminution of excessive irritation, whereas in Burke's nervous physiology there are two distinct modes of agreeable sensation, according as the nerves are relaxed below their normal tension ("pleasure") or allowed to approach normality from painful distention ("delight"). Knight's theory does not readily accommodate two modes of pleasure in this way, and the result is dissolution of Burke's dichotomy of sublime and beautiful. "Among the pleasures of sense, more particularly among those belonging to touch," Knight postulates, "there is a certain class, which, though arising from negative causes, are nevertheless real and positive pleasures: as when we gradually sink from any violent or excessive degree of action or irritation into a state of tranquillity and repose . . . but why the sensation caused by the ascent of the scale [of intensity] should be called pleasure, and that caused by its descent, delight, as distinguished by an eminent writer, I cannot discover." [20]

Burke's beauty, of which the leading trait is smoothness, is also rejected by Knight, and found to depend upon "mistake of a particular sexual sympathy for a general principle," through association of ideas. Abstracted from such sympathies, the pleasures of touch arise from gentle irritation. One of Knight's crotchets is the tracing out of the influence of sexual associations on art—and rejecting what comes from this origin as aesthetic only in inferior degree.

It is in the treatment of sight that Knight is most strikingly original. The sensual pleasure of the organs of sight depends, Knight finds, on the same principle which governs the pleasure of the other senses—"that is, upon a moderate and varied irritation of the organic nerves." [21] Knight insists that this irritation of the eye is a function of light and color only. The connection of color and light with distance and magnitude is of course learned by experience with touch; and by the same token, smoothness is no source of pleasure to the eye as such:

> Smoothness being properly a quality perceivable only by the touch, and applied metaphorically to the objects of the other senses, we often apply it very improperly to those of vision; assigning smoothness, as a cause of visible beauty, to things, which, though smooth to the touch, cast the most sharp, harsh, and angular reflections of light upon the eye; and these reflections are all that the eye feels or naturally perceives. . . . Such are all objects of cut glass or polished metal; as may be seen by the manner in which painters imitate them; for, as the imitations of painting extend only to the visible qualities of bodies, they show those visible qualities fairly and impartially—distinct from all others, which the habitual concurrence of other senses has joined with them in the mind, in our perceptions of them in nature.[22]

Visible beauty, that which gives organic pleasure to the eye, consists in "harmonious, but yet brilliant and contrasted combinations of light, shade, and colour; blended, but not confused; and broken, but not cut, into masses: and it is not peculiarly in straight or curve, taper or spiral, long or short, little or great objects, that we are to seek for these; but in such as display to the eye intricacy of parts and variety of tint and surface." [23] Such are shaggy animals, irregular trees, moldering ruins—in short, all that Price had described as picturesque. Picturesque because "painting, as it imitates only the visible qualities of bodies, separates those qualities from all others; which the habitual concurrence and co-operation of the other senses have mixt and blended with them, in our ordinary perceptions. . . . The imitative deceptions of this art unmask the habitual deceptions of sight . . . by showing that mere modifications upon one flat surface can exhibit to the eye the semblance of various projecting bodies at different degrees of distance from each other. . . ." [24]

This, then, is Knight's conception of the simple picturesque (there is also a picturesque dependent on association of ideas, of which hereafter): (*1*) the pleasure of the eye is wholly in broken and gradated light and color, and (*2*) the art of painting separates this aspect of visible things from all others associated with it in practical experience. Painting can effect such dissociation because it is devoted to pleasure only, so that utility, propriety, splendor, and such do not influence us to accept those harsh oppositions of color which may please in actuality or in practical arts. Intellect and imagination are immensely predominant even in painting; "in the higher class of landscapes, whether in nature or in art, the mere sensual gratification of the eye is comparatively so small, as scarcely to be attended to: but yet, if there occur a single spot . . . offensively harsh and glaring . . . all the magic instantly vanishes, and the imagination avenges the injury offered to the sense." [25]

This conception of the picturesque affords a neat solution to the perennial problem, why pictured imitations of the ugly or offensive may please, and are therefore (in Knight's language) beautiful. Painting separates qualities pleasing to the eye, dissociating from those qualities displeasing to the other senses, or perhaps the understanding or imagination as well. It is clear also how Burke's erroneous notion of making beauty consist in the smooth and undulating should lead a man of taste like Price to discover such beauty to be insipid. Price proposed to remedy this insipidity by mixing "picturesqueness" with the "beauty." But though the taste thus displayed is correct, there is a confusion of terms from "attaching to the word beauty those ideas, which the rest of mankind attach to the word insipidity; and those, which the rest of mankind attach to the word beauty, to this nameless amalgamation, which he conceives to be an improvement of it. The difference is merely a difference of words. . . ." [26] Not quite; there is a difference in the psychology supposed by the words.

Thus far, Knight has been operating in the mode of Burke, however different his doctrine is from that of Burke; he has developed a theory essentially physical rather than mental, a theory of impressions unassociated rather than a theory of ideas associated. In this view, Knight's work is reactionary, for writing after Alison, he attempts to restore the senses as avenues of direct aesthetic feeling. But this is only a part, and not the principal part, of Knight's aesthetics. Part II of the *Analytical Inquiry* is devoted to the association of ideas. The most elementary mode of association is "improved perception"—that, for instance, by which modifications of light and color inform us of distances. But improved perception extends beyond such universally acquired and automatic habits; the ability to separate the elements of a complex impression and compare them with ideas already fixed in the mind produces the skill of a winetaster, and also enjoyment of the arts as imitation, as expression, as virtuosity. In all these instances the perception is in appearance the mere result of the sensations, but in reality is the consequence of knowledge applied automatically to the sensations as signs of non-sensory qualities, or as signs of qualities belonging properly to the other senses.

The arts can be classified according as they afford immediate sensory pleasure or please only through improved perception. "Sculpture and poetry require order and regularity: painting and music delight in wild and irregular variety; sculpture and poetry, too, are addressed entirely to the imagination and the passions; while painting and music are, in a degree, addressed to the organs of sight and hearing, and calculated to produce pleasures merely sensual." [27] The point is clear as regards sculpture, for sculpture is imitation of form, and visual pleasure results from color and light; the lights and shadows of sculpture are regular, and either too much or too little broken to suit painting or to please the eye. The case of prosody is rather different, for poetry is expressive rather than imitative. "Poetry," Knight declares, "is the language of inspiration, and consequently of enthusiasm; and it appears to me that a methodical arrangement of the sound into certain equal or corresponding portions, called verses . . . is absolutely necessary to sustain that steady rapidity of utterance and exaltation above the ordinary tone of common speech;

which alone can give a continued character of enthusiastic expression to any extensive composition." [28] This view of prosody leads Knight to criticize sharply the English blank verse, which often requires so much inversion to distinguish it from prose that rapidity of flow is lost, and especially the use of that verse by Milton.[29] Knight's observations on the musical quality of poetry are keen, and he shows by a neat application of the Method of Agreement that the melody of verse does not depend upon the sound, for modern Europeans, each mispronouncing Latin according to the fashion of his own nation, agree fully on the correctness or incorrectness of Latin verses; these points must be recognized not by the ear, then, since that hears a different pattern in each language, but by accurate memory and ready discernment, which operate so automatically that they "dupe the ear through the medium of the imagination." [30] This is improved perception, not a determination of the sense itself but an effect of knowledge unconsciously employing the sensations as signs.

Thus far Knight has dealt with those associations which so fuse with the sensations exciting them that only by philosophy can we learn to dissociate the elements of the resulting perceptions. The next step is examination of associations which do not so fuse with the organic sensations; accordingly, "Of Imagination" is the second chapter of this part on association, a chapter forming perhaps a quarter of the entire treatise. This kind of association may attach to either natural or artificial objects, or to the former through the medium of the latter. To a mind enriched with trains of ideas drawn from the productions of the arts, not only art works but all the objects of nature and society may afford gratifications through association with such ideas and imagery. "Of this description are the objects and circumstances called *picturesque*: for, except in the instances, before explained, of pleasing effects of colour, light, and shadow, they afford no pleasure, but to persons conversant with the art of painting, and sufficiently skilled in it to distinguish, and be really delighted with its real excellences." [31]

Like Price, Knight labors the etymology of "picturesque" and draws this etymology into conformity with *his* system, as Price had with his. The progress of painting, according to Knight, was from exact and distinct imitation of details (which was soon found to be rather "copying what the mind knew to be, from the concurrent testimony of another sense, than what the eye saw" [32]), to a more truly visual imitation, with massed lights and shadows blended and broken together. Still later, the Venetians and the painters of the Low Countries

carried this principle of *massing* to a degree beyond what appears in ordinary nature; and departed from the system of strict imitation in a contrary extreme to that of their predecessors. Instead of making their lines more distinct, and keeping their tints more separate, than the visible appearance of the objects of imitation warranted, they blended and melted them together with a playful and airy kind of lightness, and a sort of loose and sketchy indistinctness not observable in the reality, unless under peculiar circumstances and modifications of the atmosphere; and then only in those objects and combinations of objects, which exhibit blended and broken tints, or irregular masses of light and shadow harmoniously melted into each other.

Such are the objects, and compositions of objects, which we properly call *picturesque;* and we find that the style of painting which distinguished them as such, was invented by Georgione about the beginning, and perfected by Titian about the middle of the sixteenth century; soon after which the word made its first appearance in the Italian, and, I believe, in any language.[33]

In this remarkable passage Knight distinguishes linear and painterly, clear and unclear, in the very manner of Wölfflin. And see the consequences: Knight's treatment of sensation had shown clearly that beauty in the strictest sense, as applied to that which is pleasing to the sense of sight, consists in broken and blended tints and irregular masses of light and shadow harmoniously melted together; *the picturesque is therefore beautiful* in the strictest sense so far as it affects the sense, and this beauty is independent of connection with painting, although that art drew our attention to it and cultivated our sensibility. (In that more comprehensive sense of "beauty" which includes all that affects intellect and imagination, many picturesque objects are, of course, decidedly not beautiful.) But this very relation to painting, expressed by the word "picturesque," affords that special pleasure from association; picturesque objects "recall to mind the imitations, which skill, taste, and genius have produced; and these again recall to the mind the objects themselves, and show them through an improved medium—that of the feeling and discernment of a great artist." [34] In this comparison of nature and art, both eye and intellect acquire a higher relish for the productions of each. This picturesque of association with painting always involves sensual beauty, though it may reside in objects distasteful to imagination or intellect—a flayed carcass, a decaying hovel, &c. Since everything capable of representation to advantage in painting is to that extent picturesque, no catalog of picturesque objects is possible; very opposite styles are, in Knight's sense, picturesque—Salvator, Poussin, Claude, Rubens, Rembrandt, sometimes even Raphael, are picturesque. Claude, though, is indeed the "fav'rite child of taste"; combining sensual beauty—picturesqueness—with powerful imaginative appeal, he is for Knight the ideal painter. Knight's theory, it has been observed, is a landmark on the road to impressionism, and its remote consequence might be the "Interior at Petworth." But Turner's last phase would not, I think, be approved by Knight, for while the sensual beauty is complete, objects have so dissolved that there is less appeal to imagination and intellect; Turner's imitations of Claude would be, in this system, superior works of art.

The moldering ruin in a Claude landscape is picturesque, and so (albeit in less degree) is the magnificent architecture of a Claude seaport. The seaport less so, because its tints are more uniform and its angles sharper, so that it affords less sensual pleasure; and its regularity, neatness, and congruity are qualities which we associate with the term "beauty"—not in the strict acceptation (which refers to the sense of sight), but in that looser meaning that includes pleasures of the imagination and understanding. This tendency to think of the "beautiful" as regular and fresh very naturally appropriates the term "picturesque" to objects which, while strictly speaking more beautiful to the sense, do not have these qualities. Knight is, we see, very close to Price on the beauty of architecture, for to Price, too, the beauty of architecture consisted in regularity and neatness. But Price was actually defining the beauty of the regular arts in this way; Knight, however, does not define beauty unqualifiedly, but distinguishes the beauties of the different faculties—here he speaks of an associational beauty quite different from sensual beauty.

Led into a general discussion of gardening and architecture, as far as these arts involve association, Knight lays it down that "the mind requires propriety in every thing; that is, it requires that those properties, the ideas of which it has been invariably habituated to associate, should be associated in reality; otherwise the combinations will appear to be unnatural, incoherent, or absurd." [35] In gardening, therefore, we require all to be dressed and cultivated immediately adjoining the dwellings of opulence and luxury, "although, if the same buildings were abandoned, and in ruins, we should, on the same principle of consistency and propriety, require neglected paths,

rugged lanes, and wild uncultivated thickets; which are, in themselves, more pleasing, both to the eye and the imagination, but, unfit
accompaniments for objects, not only originally produced by art, but,
in which, art is constantly employed and exhibited." [36] Such neatness
must be confined to the environs of the house, where it appears best
in the form of Italianate gardening; park and forest are not to be
shaved and trimmed. Repton had taken umbrage at *The Landscape,*
and in the added chapter to his *Sketches and Hints* he protested
Knight's "bitterness of prejudice against all that is neat and
cleanly"—which he traced to a fanatical insistence on pictorial effect.
But it is apparent in the *Analytical Inquiry* that Knight did not desire wild forest to the very portals of the house, but (like Price)
thought of a formal garden near the house, picturesque in its varied
and intricate textures, of a wilder forest-park at some remove, and of
an open park between; even in *The Landscape* the preference for
formality near the house was evident. Repton never directly met
Knight's actual position. From the first, however, Repton was partly
in accord with Knight, thought *The Landscape* good poetry (though
this made it the more insidious), and genuinely admired Knight's
castle and picturesque estate of Downton.[37] He returns frequently to
these themes in later books, and the area of agreement appears ultimately to increase; Repton takes to "enriching" his Red Books with
quotations from *The Landscape,* even on the topic of approaches! [38]

This happy accord was prevented for a time, however, by publication of the *Analytical Inquiry.* "The elegant and gentlemanlike manner in which Mr. Price has examined my opinions, and explained his
own," wrote Repton, "left no room for further controversy"; but
Knight's book again called upon Repton to defend the art of landscape gardening, though (as he complains) his own books were given
no notice by Knight. "In perusing these works," Repton continues
with some irony, "the candid reader will perhaps discover that there
is no real difference between us; but, in contending with an adversary
of such nice discernment, such deep investigation, and such ingenious powers of expression, it is difficult to say how far we are actually
of the same opinion." [39] Repton's perplexity is increased by the controversy now developed between the two amateurs, whom he had
considered pretty nearly of a piece in their opinions, if not in their
manners. But he consoles himself with the reflection that many of
his opinions have been confirmed by being "disguised in other
words"—stolen, that is—in the *Analytical Inquiry.* He cites three
ideas in evidence, reprinting the parallel passages from his own writ-

ings and from Knight; the similarity is unquestionable, but Knight's comment (in the third edition of the *Inquiry*) seems just: that when the observations are obvious, an author ought not "to pronounce every such coincidence a plagiarism, nor triumph in the concession of what was never disputed." [40]

The truth is, that Repton did not wholly grasp the subtle and complicated theory of his amateur opponent, so that the controversy hinged, personalities aside, on points of practice, and even on these the controversialists understood one another imperfectly. The issues, then, are either the same as, or less well defined than, those in Repton's quarrel with Price; and it is unnecessary to enter into a more methodical analysis of them.

In architecture, Knight justifies that mixture of Greek and Gothic which Repton had condemned. Knight argues for the superior picturesqueness of a heterogeneous style, and this (I judge) Repton would have granted; but he makes light of that antiquarian demand for purity of style which for Repton forbade the mixture. Knight examines the history of castle and ecclesiastical Gothic, and discourses on the civil and military architecture of the ancients—all with the view of dissolving the notion of stereotyped styles, pure and unvarying. The only truly general rule is, congruity with the situation and the purpose of buildings. The moderns, however, have inflexibly copied the sacred (rather than the domestic) architecture of the Greeks, and in its least varied forms; hence the regularity of Palladian buildings, and hence the Grecian temple in the English park. Such a temple is in one sense, to be sure, as beautiful in the lawns and woods of England as on the barren hills of Agrigentum; but all the local, temporary, and accidental circumstances upon which its congruity depended are changed; in such an imitation, either of a Grecian temple or a Gothic abbey, "the scale of its exactitude becomes that of its incongruity." [41] The fundamental error of imitators, Knight protests, "is, that they servilely copy the effects, which they see produced, instead of studying and adopting the principles, which guided the original artist in producing them; wherefore they disregard all those local, temporary, or accidental circumstances, upon which their propriety or impropriety—their congruity or incongruity wholly depend: for principles in art are no other than the trains of ideas, which arise in the mind of the artist out of a just and adequate consideration of all such circumstances. . . ." [42] The real authority of style in building is the trained vision of the great landscape painters, and the best style for picturesque houses is, accordingly, "that mixed style, which characterizes the buildings of Claude and the Poussins," since it has no one manner of execution or class of ornaments, but can admit of contrast "to heighten the relish of beauty" without appearance of deceit or imposture.[43]

Another variety of association in painting is that between handling and subject. Brilliant, free, and sketchy execution is peculiarly adapted to forms which are loose and flowing; the lightness of such work is peculiarly picturesque, and Rubens is in this particular the most picturesque of painters. Such picturesque form consists precisely in "those flowing and undulating lines, which have been called the lines of grace and beauty; how truly, the compositions of Rubens, in which they always predominate, and those of Raphael, in which they are never employed, but incidentally, may decide." [44] Hogarth's famous line is, then, really the line of picturesqueness rather than of beauty unqualified. This apparent contradiction is more than a difference of taste. Hogarth's psychology dwelt on the notion of the eye tracing outlines, so that form was fundamental in his conception of beauty, and the beauty of color was treated secondarily and by analogy with that of form. Knight's theory, in contrast, rests on the idea that the eye is affected immediately only by light and color, the beauty of form entering his system only by associations of various kinds—here by an indirect association, through the handling, with facility of coloring and composing chiaroscuro.

The subtlety of Knight's system is shown nicely in the parallel discussion of form in sculpture, an art more fairly representing beauty of form than painting since it has neither tricks of light and shade nor can it leave anything to the imagination by sketchy brilliance of execution. "The forms, therefore, both of the human figure and countenance, which are peculiarly appropriate to sculpture, are directly the reverse of the picturesque forms above mentioned; this art requiring exact symmetry in limb and body, muscles and joints strongly indicated, regular and distinct features. . . ." [45] This is an associational beauty, for symmetry (in which Knight comprehends proportion) depends wholly on association, not at all on abstract reason or organic sensation; nor is it far different from that ideal beauty which Reynolds deemed requisite not in sculpture only but in the higher styles of painting as well. And since this style of beauty is especially appealing to those conversant with the masterpieces of classic sculpture, it really constitutes a *sculpturesque* analogous to the picturesque. But Price need not add this new character to his scale of taste, as Knight ironically suggests. Knight may think of the picturesque as sensual beauty together with complex associations to the art of painting, but this is not Price's conception; for Price, the picturesque is a certain composition of line, color, and light the peculiar effect of which is attributable not to association with painting nor to the pleasure of the eye in broken tints, but to association with a variety of passions and to a reaction of the nerves. Knight pursues his point with a whole train of new aesthetic characters. The grottesque, he writes, must "bear somewhat of the same relation to the *picturesque,* as he [Price] supposes the *picturesque* to bear to the *beautiful:* for the *grottesque* is certainly, a degree or two at least, further removed from the insipid smoothness and regularity of beauty, than he supposes the picturesque to be." [46] And in this same strain of unfeeling sarcasm, Price is advised "to season the insipidity of beauty" with the classical, the romantic, the pastoral, the mercantile, &c. "All these extra pleasures are from the minds of the spectators; whose pre-existing trains of ideas are revived, refreshed, and reassociated by new, but correspondent impressions on the organs of sense; and the great fundamental error, which prevails throughout the otherwise able and elegant *Essays on the Picturesque,* is seeking for distinctions in external objects, which only exist in the modes and habits of viewing and considering them." [47] And Knight pretends to find the key to Price's philosophy in a remark made by the character Seymour in Price's *Dialogue:* " 'All these ideas,' says an interlocutor, who, on this occasion, sustains his own part in his dialogue, 'are originally acquired by the touch; but from use they are become as much objects of sight as colours.' When there is so little discrimination between the operations of mind and the objects of sense, that ideas become objects of sight, all the rest follows of course; and the distinct classes of beauty may be divided into as many distinct characters, as there are distinct ideas. . . ." [48] Seymour was really intended by Price to stand for naïveté and common sense; and the remark Knight ridicules was, Price apologizes, only a careless expression—but Price's defense will be taken up later.

According to Knight's exposition of the influence of association, dignity, elevation, grace, and elegance depend wholly upon mental sympathies and association of ideas, differing only in "that while our ideas of dignity of attitude and gesture have always continued nearly the same, those of grace and elegance have been in a perpetual state of change and fluctuation: for our notions of what is *mean,* and what is *elevated,* depend upon the natural and permanent sentiments of the soul; but those of what is refined or polished; and pleasant, or

the contrary, depend much on artificial manners, which are incessantly varying." [49] Dignity and grace alike express the character of the soul mediately, through association in experience; and in this they alike differ from expression in the features and the voice, both which are immediately cognized by internal senses. It is curious that Knight, who makes so much of associational psychology, retains these additional faculties in his system, vestiges of an aesthetic method already antiquated.

Knight returns repeatedly to the denunciation of rigid system and general rules in the arts; "indeed," he says, "in all matters of taste and criticism, general rules appear to me to be, like general theories in government and politics, never safe but where they are useless; that is, in cases previously proved by experience." [50] Critics, like casuists, attempt to direct by rules matters depending on sentiment and which elude all the subtleties of logic. This is not total skepticism, however, for although there remains no test of aesthetic excellence but feeling, the discrimination of modes and causes of feeling which Knight is conducting permits a general judgment to emerge from the welter of conflicting tastes, even though such principles will rarely be universal and permanent, depending as they do on the state of the human mind in the different stages of its culture and upon variations induced by custom. Disparagement of rules carries with it a vigorous hostility towards academies. The great objection to institutionalized art is that the members quite naturally come to imitate one another, to adopt a common style which deprives them of their individual sentiments. This objection applies equally to modern European academies of painting and Roman schools of rhetoric, from the institution of which the decline of Latin eloquence may be dated. In truth, Knight declares, "the whole history of literature obliges us to acknowledge that, in proportion as criticism has become systematic, and critics numerous, the powers of composition and purity of taste have, in all ages and countries gradually decayed." [51]

Association of ideas accounts not only for improved perception and imaginative connection, but for judgment as well; and this second part of the *Analytical Inquiry* concludes with a chapter on judgment. "Judgment," Knight states, "is more properly the result of a faculty than a faculty itself; it being the decision, which reason draws from comparison: whence the word is commonly used to signify the talent of deciding justly and accurately in matters, that do not admit of mathematical demonstration; in which sense, judgment may be properly considered as a mode of action of reason." [52] This is the familiar distinction of demonstrative reasoning on relations of number and quantity from that reasoning on questions of cause and effect and resemblance which depends on association. It is of course true that Knight's analysis of this associative reason is much too simple to serve as a logic; he does not distinguish proof from probability, or develop any canons for checking less certain against more certain inferences. But for his immediate purposes, the differentiation of demonstrative from habitual reason is enough; unimportant in most matters of practical life, "it is of the utmost importance in fixing the just bounds of poetical fiction; and that is the subject, to which the nature of my present inquiry leads me to apply it." [53] Artistic probability or "truth" is the central concern throughout the discussion of judgment.

Knight illustrates the problem by the implausible Homeric account of Ulysses' three-day swim: this circumstance, however improbable, does not destroy the interest of the story; but it would be demonstratively impossible for Ulysses to appear in two places at once, "for difference and identity of substance, space and time, are matters of demonstration by number and quantity," [54] and such an invention would have destroyed our interest in the subsequent events. When demonstratively false circumstances do not obstruct the train of our ideas and feelings, we do not quarrel with fictions, for poetical probability

> does not arise so much from the resemblance of the fictions to real events, as from the consistence of the language with the sentiments, of the sentiments and actions with the characters, and of the different parts of the fable, with each other: for, if the mind be deeply interested, as it always will be by glowing sentiments and fervid passions happily expressed, and naturally arising out of the circumstances and incidents of a consistent fable, it will never turn aside to any extraneous matter for rules of comparison; but judge of the probability of the events merely by their connection with, and dependence upon each other. [55]

This principle has important application to dramatic poetry, where *real* actors are present to our senses as a part of the poem; poetic license is restricted within narrower bounds of probability, and incident and sentiment confined to what we can really believe possible to such men as we see. Unities of time and place find no justification on Knight's principles and go by the board. [56] And unity of action becomes only unity of subject, "for, where the events described or represented, spring, in their natural order of succession, from one source, the sentiments of sympathy, which they excite, will all verge to one centre, and be connected by one chain." [57]

It is interesting to contrast the argument of Knight on this whole subject of poetical belief and probabililty with that of Aristotle. Aristotle's chief concern is formal and artistic, a concern with the conditions which render the work of art a unity, a pseudo-substance with a principle of organization analogous to those of natural substances; and the reactions of the audience enter subordinately to this formal interest, only broad and casual assumptions being made about audience psychology. Knight's concern, in contrast, is pre-eminently psychological, with the principles of the mind which determine audience reaction being fundamental; the formal properties of the work are deduced as appropriate causes for such responses. Thus for Aristotle, the primary element in a poem is the plot, with character, thought, and diction following in descending sequence, each being, relative to the preceding, as matter is to form. For Knight the sentiments are primary, for the sentiments, clothed in appropriate diction, carry that enthusiasm which is the essence of poetry. But with all this opposition, it is remarkable how close the resulting analyses of particular works can be; when Knight describes the "subject" of *Macbeth* as the ambition of Lady Macbeth, which, "instigated by the prophecies of the witches . . . rouses the aspiring temper of her husband, and urges him to the commission of a crime, the consciousness of which embitters the remainder of his life, and makes him suspicious, ferocious, and cruel; whence new crimes excite new enemies, and his destruction naturally follows," [58] his statement would serve for Aristotle as statement of the "plot." The two critics, operating with very different ideas, work from contrary directions towards a common goal: statements about works which will be at once definitions of their forms and descriptions of their effects.

Knight's remarks on the realism of petty details, on the use of allegorical agents and of symbolical figures, on refined conventionalization and idealization in the different arts—all are pointed and some ingenious, but they need not be spelled out. Unusual is his distaste for Michael Angelo, who departed from nature not in the direction of a superior and ideal perfection but in that of extravagant violence: "the evil which he did, in making extravagance and distortion pass for grandeur and vigour of character and expression, still spreads with increasing virulence of contagion. . . ." [59] This dislike is really consistent with (though I would hesitate to assert that it is a strict deductive consequence of) Knight's system. Michael Angelo's art rests on form rather than on color and light; all the effect of form results from expression, and since "expression, that is not true, ceases to be expression," truth is the foundation of the power of forms; Michael Angelo's forms are assuredly not, to a severely classical taste, true.

Knight's account of association in aesthetics has now been surveyed in its entirety, and it is apparent how great, how predominating a role association plays in this system. Yet Knight is not quite a disciple of Alison; association does not for him, as for Alison, exclude other causes of aesthetic feeling. Knight complains, in fact, that by endeavoring to reduce everything to the one principle of association, Alison "seems to forget, though he abundantly exemplifies, the influence, which the association of a favorite system may acquire in every thing." [60] Knight's thought is very closely related to that of Hume, though he can not be quoted to this effect, for he mentions Hume only to oppose what he takes to be Hume's skepticism. But the outlines of the systems bear an unmistakable resemblance: Hume distinguishes ideas from impressions, and these last into sensations (which precede corresponding ideas) and passions (which usually follow them); and this is the organization of Knight's treatise— sensations, ideas, passions. The refusal to construct a system as ideal as Alison's or as sensational and pathetic as Hogarth's or Burke's is the consequence of filling out a matrix derived from Locke and Hume.

First step in the study of the passions (Part III of the *Analytical Inquiry*) is to distinguish the aesthetic from the practical role of the passions. "The passions, considered either physically as belonging to the constitution of the individual, or morally, as operating upon that of society, do not come within the scope of my present inquiry; it being only by sympathy, that they are connected with subjects of taste; or that they produce, in the mind, any of those tender feelings, which are called pathetic, or those exalted or enthusiastic sentiments, which are called sublime." [61] Knight plunges directly into the problem of delight in represented suffering—or even in real suffering, as in a gladiatorial contest—which delight he traces to sympathy, sympathy not with the suffering but "with the exhibitions of courage, dexterity, vigour, and address, which shone forth, in these combats of life and death, more conspicuously and energetically than they would have done, had the object of contention been less important." [62] Men "are not so perversely constituted by nature, as ever to feel delight in beholding the sufferings of those who never injured them," [63] but all delight in exhibitions either of the passive virtues of fortitude and patience or of the more interesting active merits of courage and dexterity. In the case of drama, the suffering is known to be fiction, but the sentiments are really expressed; "the sympathies, therefore, which they excite, are real and complete; and much more strong and effective, than if they were produced by scenes of real distress: for in that case, the sufferings, which we behold, would excite such a painful degree of sympathy, as would overpower and suppress the pleasant feelings, excited by the noble, tender, or generous sentiments, which we heard uttered." [64]

Knight's conception of poetic belief does away with the pity-and-fear formula for tragedy, for the danger is known to be unreal, the distress fictitious. Longinus had declared—and Knight harks back to the theory of Longinus after discussion of the sublime had long taken another direction—that grief, sorrow, and fear are incapable of any sublime expression. The reason alleged by Knight for this truth is, that these passions display only a selfish weakness, whereas the essence of the sublime is *energy:* "All sympathies, excited by just and appropriate expression of energetic passion; whether they be of the tender or violent kind, are alike sublime; as they all tend to expand and elevate the mind; and fill it with those enthusiastic raptures, which Longinus justly states to be the true feelings of sublimity." [65] Passions like pity, fear, sensuality are neither sublime in themselves nor capable of inspiring sublime expressions; others, while not as passions sublime, can excite "sentiments and expressions of great and enthusiastic force and vigour; with which we sympathize, and not with the passion itself" [66]—such are hatred and malignity; others yet are sublime both in themselves and in their appropriate expression, whether exhibiting active or passive energy.

It follows also from Knight's doctrine of sympathy, that "no character can be interesting or impressive in poetry, that acts strictly according to reason: for reason excites no sympathies, nor awakens any affections; and its effect is always rather to chill than to inflame." [67] On the same principle, tragedy can not exhibit examples of pure morality without becoming dull—and consequently as useless as insipid. There is nonetheless no moral danger in tragedy, for spectators do not attend the theater for examples on which to model their minds, but "to hear a certain series of dialogues, arising out of a certain series of supposed events, recited with appropriate modulations of voice, countenance, and gesture." [68] Knight achieves an appreciation of tragedy which does not require superimposition of a moral lesson, nor even postulation of an indirect moral effect; it is a view as disinterested as the mimetic analysis of Aristotle.

Tragedy entered Knight's discussion chiefly because good tragedy is sublime; the sublime and pathetic are his subject rather than the analysis of literary forms, though they are best approached through literature because it is here that the nature of sympathy appears most distinctly.[69] It is worth remarking that in real life the sublime and pathetic may be separated and opposed (as the tender to the exalted), whereas "in all the fictions, either of poetry or imitative art, there can be nothing truly pathetic, unless it be, at the same time, in some degree, sublime: for, though, in scenes of real distress, pity may so far overcome scorn, that we may weep for sufferings, that are feebly or pusillanimously borne; yet, in fiction, scorn will always predominate, unless there be a display of vigour, as well as tenderness and sensibility of mind."[70] Even in actuality sublime and pathetic are usually conjoined, and both find their ultimate vent in tears.

All sublime feelings are feelings of exultation and expansion of the mind, whether excited by sympathy with external objects or arising from internal operations of the mind. Knight is willing to accept the catalog of sublime external objects established by earlier writers; in grasping at infinity the mind expands and exalts itself, whence its feelings become sublime; so with vast natural objects, or with those works of man which represent great labor or expense; and similarly with the general privations, darkness, silence, vacuity, and with the convulsions of nature. Some permit direct expansion of the mind, others are signs of power or energy, contemplation of which permits this same expansion. Burke had argued that all of these phenomena are fearful in themselves, or are suggestive of something fearful, or operate on the nervous system in the manner of fearful things.[71] He does not argue—as Knight supposes—that the emotion of fear itself is sublime, but rather that the sublime is a feeling resulting from the remission of fear, from fear felt at a distance or by analogy or sympathy; the sublime is not pleasant but "delightful," in Burke's technical vocabulary. Knight's declaration that "fear is the most humiliating and depressing of passions,"[72] and therefore wholly incompatible with the sublime, does not really contradict Burke, who had said that "when danger or pain press too nearly, they are incapable of giving any delight, and are simply terrible; but at certain distances, and with certain modifications, they may be, and they are delightful. . . ."[73] Knight ridicules this statement for its use of "distance" to mean "degree" ("a stout instance of confusion even with every allowance that can be made for the ardour of youth in an Hibernian philosopher of five and twenty" [74]); but by "distance" I presume that Burke meant not a lesser degree of the same passion, but such a degree of probability or interest as permits us to see and be awed by the evil without engaging our direct practical concern for our safety, a meaning to which Knight could not strenuously object. Knight, of course, traces the sublime of apparently fearful objects to perception of power: "As far as feeling or sentiment is concerned . . . *that* alone is terrible, which impresses some degree of fear. I may *know* an object to be terrible; that is, I may know it to possess the *power* of hurting or destroying: but this is *knowledge,* and not *feeling* or *sentiment;* and the *object* of that knowledge is *power,* and not *terror;* so that, if any sympathy results from it, it must be a sympathy with power only." [75]

When Knight moves on to ridicule of Burke's physiological hypothesis, he drops argument for pure satire. But quite seriously he charges Burke with fathering Gothic novels, grandiose and horrific painting, preposterous attempts to create the terrific in gardening, the poems of Ossian, and other extravagances; and of the pernicious influence of Michael Angelo, Knight urges that "while it is supported by such brilliant theories as those of the Inquiry into the Sublime and Beautiful, there can be but faint hopes of its ceasing or subsiding." [76] The influence of Burke, indeed, "has principally appeared among artists, and other persons not much conversant with philosophical inquiries: for, except . . . [Price], I have never met with any man of learning, by whom the philosophy of the *Inquiry into the Sublime and Beautiful* was not as much despised and ridiculed, as the brilliancy and animation of its style were applauded, and admired." [77]

The art in which the sublime finds its fullest expression is poetry, for here sympathy with mind is most direct, and the poet's power of selection and emphasis is confined by no such laws of strict imitation as in the plastic arts. Suppression of irrelevant or disturbing circumstances in poetic description does not, however, justify the *obscurity* which Burke had found a potent cause of the sublime, for the more distinctly the energies expressed are brought before the imagination, the more effect; description "should be *distinct* without being *determinate.*" [78] Quantitative measurements are best omitted, since the imagination, raised to enthusiasm by the style of the poetry, will expand its conceptions to the bounds of probability. Knight's attention, it is clear, is directed to the precision, perspicuity, and energy of the language of description, whereas Burke's was centered upon the image created. After all, the indeterminateness which Knight finds requisite to sublime imagery is very like Burke's obscurity; what Knight is saying appears to be, that sublime imagery consists in distinct statement of the essential traits but with accidents of magnitude and relative situation left to the imagination.

This whole critique of Burke seems to me to rest partly on a difference of system, partly on a divergence of taste. Knight is unable to treat sublimity under the head of sensation, since he supposes the eye to be directly affected only by light and color, and he is thus at once in inescapable contradiction with Burke's physiology. The sublime cannot fall, moreover, under "association," for it comprises passions rather than mere associations of ideas; Knight must, therefore, treat sublimity among the passions. Burke, too, had connected the sublime with the passions, with those passions concerned with self-preservation. We have seen the extent of Knight's misinterpretations of Burke's thought on this topic, and the extent to which Burke's "terror" can be translated into Knight's system; but the difference between the two accounts is not dissolved away by such translation. When Knight tells us that the fidelity of Ulysses' hound is sublime, we can not avoid recognizing a real difference in taste. Knight speaks, here and everywhere, of a peculiar heightening which may supervene when any but a weak or selfish passion is apprehended intensely; the expression of passions moral and malignant, vigorous and tender, may all be sublime. Burke, in contrast, speaks of a more special feeling which always involves a kind of awe, usually tinged with terror or horror "at a certain distance." If these observations are just, Knight is conducting a genuine argument in the chapter on the sublime and pathetic. The sublime receives the kind of treatment proper to it in this system.[79]

Diametrically opposite to the sublime and pathetic "is the ridiculous: for laughter is an expression of joy and exultation; which arises not from sympathy but triumph; and which seems therefore to have its principle in malignity. Those vices, which are not sufficiently baneful and destructive to excite detestation; and those frailties and errors, which are not sufficiently serious and calamitous to excite pity, are generally such as excite laughter. . . ."[80] Those passions incompatible with the sublime, those belonging to self-preservation or self-gratification (fear, avarice, vanity, gluttony, &c.), are the usual subject of the ridiculous, "for, as they show vice without energy; and make human nature appear base without being atrocious, and vile without being destructive, they excite the laugh of scorn instead of the frown of indignation. . . ." [81] So much for the proper object of wit and ridicule; the technique of the ridiculous involves always some incongruous juxtaposition. Wit requires novel junctions of contrasting ideas, through which the principal subject is distorted or debased; humor consists in junction of dissimilar manners rather than images and ideas; parody involves degradation of serious compositions by analogous means; mimicry the peculiarities of individuals; and so forth. Knight virtually limits the ridiculous to what Freud has termed "tendency-wit," and indeed to one mode of tendency-wit, that which serves the purposes of aggression; "harmless wit" and the other modes of tendency-wit—the sexual, the skeptical, &c.—are not acknowledged. And despite recognition that the "proper" function of ridicule can be perverted, so that virtuous moderation rather than foolish or vicious excess becomes its object, Knight has no glimpse of any inherently antimoral tendency in ridicule.

Comedy, the literary form of the ridiculous, departs equally with tragedy from common life, one exaggerating the general energies of human nature, the other its particular weaknesses and defects as modified and distorted by artificial society. Since the characters and incidents of comedy are drawn from the ordinary ranks of society, its examples of folly—often, Knight grants, of folly triumphant—are open to all to imitate; but comedy is not therefore pernicious, for it is "a fictitious imitation of the examples of real life, and not an example from which real life is ever copied. No one ever goes to the theatre to learn how he is to act on a particular emergency; or to hear the solution of any general question of casuistical morality," [82] but only to sympathize with the energies or weaknesses of humanity free of the painful sentiments which such contemplation would occasion in real life. Literature is for Knight an object of aesthetic appreciation, not an instrument of moral reform.

The final chapter, "Of Novelty," brings us full circle; we return to the sense of flux which dominated the Introduction of the *Inquiry*. The sensations and sentiments which have been reviewed, like all others, are reduced by habit to insipidity. "Change and variety are, therefore," Knight declares, "necessary to the enjoyment of all pleasure; whether sensual or intellectual: and so powerful is this principle, that all change, not so violent as to produce a degree of irritation in the organs absolutely painful, is pleasing; and preferable to any uniform and unvaried gratification." [83] Perfection of taste and style is no sooner reached, accordingly, than the restless pruriency of innovation leads to its abandonment; the pure and perfect continues to be applauded, perhaps, but is not imitated. The desire for novelty is also, of course, a cause of progressive improvement of taste, so long as it is restrained to imitation of genuine nature; "but, when it calls upon invention to usurp the place of imitation; or substitute to genuine, or merely embellished nature, nature sophisticated and corrupted by artificial habits, it immediately produces vice and extravagance of manner."[84] The usual effect of custom is to reduce embellishment and refinement to vulgarity, so that refinement must be twice refined; hence the progress of all highly polished languages, and hence the changes of taste in landscape gardening.

But even here, in the restless principle of change itself, a standard of taste is found. There is the novelty of mere fashion, caprice, and innovation; and there is a permanent novelty. Intricacy and variety are modes of gratifying curiosity, a passion satisfaction of which produces an unmixed pleasure universally felt; a system of gardening, then, which introduces variety and intricacy as its principles—the picturesque gardening which Price and Knight invented and popularized—is novel not only in the sense of being different from the previous fashion, but also as containing a permanent novelty of composition. This self-contained newness is an achievement in which art may for a time at least escape from flux.

Inordinate gratification of the taste for mere novelty is a moral, and not merely an aesthetic, evil, resulting in atrophy of real powers of sensibility and understanding. Debilitation of the mind and the pampering of morbid sensibility are the moral dangers which Knight perceives in the fiction of his age; but in general, the moral influence of belles-lettres is slight.

> The end of morality is to restrain and subdue all the irregularities of passion and affection; and to subject the conduct of life to the dominion of abstract reason, and the uniformity of established rule: but the business of poetry . . . is to display, and even exaggerate those irregularities; and to exhibit the events of life diversified by all the wild varieties of ungoverned affections, or chequered by all the fantastic modes of anomalous and vitiated habits. It is, therefore, utterly impossible for the latter to afford models for the former; and, the instant that it attempts it, it necessarily becomes tame and vapid; and, in short, ceases to be poetry. . . .[85]

The moral good of the arts is only in their civilizing and softening mankind by substituting mental to sensual pleasures and turning the mind to mild and peaceful pursuits—the good which critics and philosophers have agreed upon since Plato called for music to soften the temper of his warriors.

The *Analytical Inquiry* concludes, as *The Landscape* had concluded, with an exposition of the general conditions of happiness. Our felicity, Knight insists, depends on novelty; man's happiness

> consists in the *means* and not in the *end:*—in *acquisition,* and not in *possession.* The source and principle of it is, therefore, *novelty:* the attainment of new ideas; the formation of new trains of thought; the renewal and extension of affections and attachments . . . and above all, the unlimited power of fancy in multiplying and varying the objects, the results, and the gratifications of our pursuits beyond the bounds of reality, or the probable duration of existence. A state of abstract perfection would, according to our present weak and inadequate notions of things, be a state of perfect misery. . . .[86]

But custom steadily reduces the possibility of novelty; imagination, which prior to possession enhances the value of every object, "immediately afterwards becomes equally busy and active in exposing its defects and heightening its faults; which, of course, acquire influence as their opposites lose it. Thus it happens that in moral as well as physical—in intellectual as well as sensual gratifications, the circles of pleasure are expanded only in a simple ratio, and to a limited degree; while those of pain spread in a compound rate of progression; and are only limited in their degree by the limits of our existence." [87] Though the objects with which we are familiar cease to give pleasure, habitual attachment to them makes the prospect of loss more painful than before, and we are protected from the effects of this irreversible tendency only by dissolution. Elaboration of this theme evokes all of Knight's acuity and his considerable powers of melancholy eloquence; Payne Knight is not only an aesthetician but a moralist of stature.

CHAPTER 18

The Price-Knight *Controversy*

❧

THE ESSENCE of Knight's position on the picturesque had been presented succinctly in the note appended to the second edition of *The Landscape:* the distinction of sensation and perception, the separation of the modes of beauty proper to the various senses and faculties, the definition of picturesque beauty as that kind of moderate and grateful visual irritation which painting serves to isolate. The "picturesque," Knight declares, "is merely that kind of beauty which belongs exclusively to the sense of vision; or to the imagination, guided by that sense." [1] The second of these alternatives, however—analysis of the associations with painting, the styles of painters, and particular pictures—is omitted from the discussion; the note to *The Landscape* is intended rather to clear the ground than to erect the finished edifice of a complete theory. Price countered this note with *A Dialogue on the Distinct Characters of the Picturesque and the Beautiful, in Answer to the Objections of Mr. Knight* (1801), and the argument of this dialogue is applicable to the more complete form as well of Knight's theory. Knight returned to the charge with comment in the *Analytical Inquiry,* comment expanded by more enthusiastic attack upon Burke's theory in the second edition; and Price, finally, added a brief Appendix to his *Dialogue* for the 1810 edition of his works.

So much for bibliography. The *Dialogue* itself is not a true philosophical dialogue, for the truth does not emerge from the debate; rather, one of the interlocutors is in possession of it from the first and needs only to triumph over the counterarguments and objections of the other speakers. The dialogue form is merely a rhetorical device to convince the simple and intrigue the bored. Airing the views of Price himself is a Mr. Hamilton; Mr. Howard, Knight's partisan, recites in fragments the note to *The Landscape;* and the two connoisseurs both seek the allegiance of Mr. Seymour, the naïve arbiter.[2]

The three friends, meeting by accident, determine on viewing a collection of paintings at a manor house nearby; they are delayed, however, some thirty pages by the charms of the real scenes they encounter by the way, a device which permits that double comparison of art and nature which is somehow involved, essentially or accidentally, in every conception of the picturesque. Price devises the incidents so that such comparisons arise quite naturally: the friends pass a real butcher shop in the village, and once in the picture gallery they find a Rembrandt of a flayed ox; they admire a prospect *en route* which is matched in the gallery by a Claude; and so forth. Soon our amateurs stumble on a group of gypsies encamped in a decayed hovel on a gloomy heath, a scene picturesque in every detail and radically removed from what is ordinarily deemed beautiful; the rhapsodies on the picturesque which this view evokes from the connoisseurs piques the curiosity of Mr. Seymour; and Mr. Howard, in the language of Knight, explains that the picturesque is the beauty peculiar to vision or to the imagination guided by vision, adding hastily an explanation of the difference between sensation and perception. Mr. Seymour perceives this difference well enough, but thinks that "perception . . . in the mind, and sensation in the organ, although distinct operations in themselves, are practically inseparable." Sight, continues Mr. Seymour (and if Howard *parle comme un livre,* as Knight protests, Seymour *parle comme un métaphysicien*), distinguishes "not only form in general, but, likewise, its different qualities; such as hardness, softness, roughness, smoothness, &c. and to judge of the distance and gradation of objects: all these ideas, it is true, are originally acquired by the touch; but from use, they are become as invariably connected with objects of sight, as the very perceptions of the colours themselves." [3] Mr. Howard explains patiently that the imitations of painting separate the visual qualities, and that by the study of pictures the eye learns to respond to these qualities in nature abstracted from all others. Seymour is not satisfied. He can not separate the visual from the tactile properties; he can not neglect the beauty of the parts separately for the sake of their harmoniously blended composition ("am I obliged to call a number of colours beautiful, because they match well, though each of them, separately considered, is ugly?" [4] he asks incredulously); he can not see why beautiful objects should not blend and compose as well as the picturesque or ugly Howard has dwelt on.

Mr. Hamilton (Price, that is) is much gratified by the objections

of Seymour, which represent for him the candor of naïveté as against
the subtlety of system; and he hastens to say that there is really but
one point of difference between Howard and himself, "and that rather
on a matter of curious inquiry, than of real moment; our general
principles are the same, and I flatter myself we should pass nearly
the same judgment on the merits and defects of any work of art, or
on any piece of natural, or improved scenery; but our friend there
[Howard] has taken a strong antipathy to any distinction or subdivision on this subject." [5] Picturesqueness is for Hamilton the concept which solves all difficulties—by its means, the pleasure which
lovers of painting derive from real scenes is accounted for without
confounding our natural ideas of beauty as soft, graceful, elegant,
and lovely.

Already we have the fundamental answer of Price to Knight's
theory of pure visual beauty: Price denies that dissociation ever proceeds so far that the parts of our complex perceptions originally
attributable to different senses are discriminated and appreciated
separately. It is true that a picture of a flayed ox, if executed by a
Rembrandt, may please, though the carcass would in reality be offensive; but then the odor and animal disgust are not present in the
imitation, and even so those parts of the picture representing the
unattractive subject are pleasing only by virtue of imitation as such
and because of the harmonious light and color. All this fits with
Howard's—Knight's—explanations too; but here the friends differ,
for Hamilton argues that these merits make the picture only a well-
done piece—an *excellent*, not strictly speaking a *beautiful* picture.
A truly beautiful work is one which, having these properly artistic
excellences, is beautiful also in its parts—which has, that is, a beautiful subject. Hamilton elicits from Seymour some further reasons
why scenes displeasing in reality may be acceptable in painting: even
"without having recourse to the operation of the other senses," Hamilton sums up, "we may account for the difference between the effect
of disgusting objects in reality, and in pictures; in which last, not
only the size of objects, and their detail, are in general very much
lessened, but also the scale both of light and colour, is equally low-
ered." [6] The diminution of resemblance effected by change in scale,
in lighting, in detail, cuts the associative ties with the real scenes
far enough to remove the unpleasant associations with the real objects, but not so far as to destroy the pleasure of imitation: here is
a theory of dissociation as efficacious as Knight's, yet which does not
require abandonment of the distinction between beauty and picturesqueness. For a Teniers scene of a woman cleaning guts in a back

kitchen is excellent but not beautiful; a Magdalen of Guido is both beautiful, and excellent as a picture. And, adds Hamilton, "where great excellence in the art is employed on pleasing objects, the superior interest will be felt by every observer; but especially by those who are less conversant in the mechanical part." [7]

The discussion wanders back and forth between beauty and picturesqueness, with Seymour's native good sense leading him gradually towards Price's point of view. The final conversion is effected by a Pannini view of St. Peter's. When Hamilton assures him that Howard would have to regard this splendid edifice as still more beautiful in ruins, common sense revolts, and Seymour rejects the theory of Knight. Price thinks it fair to allege this consequence of Knight's theory, for we all know that ruins are more picturesque than entire edifices, and Knight (we are told) denies any difference between the picturesque and the beautiful in visible objects. "It seems to me," Seymour is made to object to Howard, ". . . that, according to your system whatever is not absolute monotony, or absolute discord, is positive beauty, or, if you please, *picturesque* beauty: for that epithet, taken in your sense, only confines the term to visible objects, but makes no other discrimination." [8] This, however, is a misrepresentation; Knight does *not* say that picturesqueness is merely the beauty of visible objects; he says that it is the beauty of such objects as *merely* visible—without compounding by perceptions derived from touch, without association of imaginative or poetic ideas, without suffusion by the passions. But the beauty of St. Peter's is not primarily this pure visual beauty. In architecture the transitive meanings of "beauty" outweigh the sense which for Knight is strict; the perfect building is more beautiful than the ruin in the everyday sense of "beauty," though less beautiful in the purely visual sense —less suited, therefore, for painting—less suggestive of our ideas of painting and paintings—less picturesque.

Is there, then, no difference on this point between Price and Knight, once confusions are cleared away? [9] I repeat what I have urged before, that the psychological systems of the two men are quite different, and that this difference permeates all their disputes, underlying the verbal confusions. Knight finds, necessarily, that the picturesque has an essential relation to painting, and that other arts or activities giving us special points of view yield analogous qualities—none of them in the nature of things, all of them produced by special conditions in the mind of the observer, all of them modes of beauty. Price, *per contra*, consistently with his system finds the picturesque related only accidentally to painting, founded in the nature of things (though itself a feeling in the mind), and analytically distinct from beauty. On the particular point which led the participants of the *Dialogue* into this wrangle—that picture by Pannini—Knight would say that such a painting of splendid and perfect architecture is (however meritorious) not doing the special work of painting, is not the highest rank of picture; Price would say, *per contra*, that the best paintings are those which combine pictorial excellences with beautiful subjects, and that as far as Pannini did this he is secure from criticism. If Knight should object that pictorial excellence is not wholly compatible with such a subject as Pannini's, a subject confessedly beautiful in some sense, then at last we come to a difference in practical taste.

The three friends, sated with pictures, walk out of doors again and directly into a Brownian garden. Hamilton and Howard together make short work of it. Hamilton punctures the sophistical defense of the Reptonians—that beauty-not-picturesqueness is the object of their calling—by showing the limitations this formula really implies, and the insipidity which follows from it in practice. But he and Howard fall by the ears when Howard remarks that the Brownian garden shows just how little smoothness has to do with beauty, and reiterates his theory of beauty as mild visual irritation. It of course follows from Knight's theory, that smooth objects are harsh to the eye, rough objects soft and harmonious—that, in short, the effect of roughness on the touch is like that of smoothness on the eye, that of smoothness to the touch like that of roughness to the eye.[10] Hamilton replies at some length, pointing out (among other objections) that while roughness is always unpleasing to the touch, light is painful to the eye only in excess, and that the point at which it becomes excessive depends on the extent to which the imagination has been interested. Can it still be maintained that Price is an "objectivist" and Knight an associationist?

Seymour lends his weight, too, against the theory of abstract vision, declaring that "some of our earliest ideas are, that smoothness is pleasing, and roughness unpleasing to the eye, as well as to the touch; and these first ideas always prevail, though we afterwards learn to discriminate, and to modify them." And, he goes on, "the whole tenor of your argument [addressing Howard] goes to prove, that, with respect to colours, the mere absence of discord, is the great principle of visible beauty; whereas, if there be a positive beauty in any thing, it must be in colours: the *general* effect, I allow, will not be beautiful without harmony; but neither can the most perfect accord change the nature of dull or ugly colours, and make them beautiful." [11] Seymour has hardly time to say so much before Hamilton interposes to pronounce once more his creed, bolstered as it is by observation of Seymour's reactions during the excursion:

> had I [says Hamilton] not observed so many instances at various times, of the indifference of persons little conversant with pictures to picturesque objects—I must have given up one principal ground of my distinction. Its strongest foundation, however, rests upon the direct and striking opposition that exists between the qualities which prevail in objects which all allow to be beautiful, and those which prevail in others, almost as generally admitted to be picturesque: and till youth and age, freshness and decay, smoothness and ruggedness, symmetry and irregularity, are looked upon in the same light, and the objects in which they are prevalent give the same kind of pleasure to all persons . . . the character of the objects themselves, must, in truth, be as distinct, as the qualities of which they are composed.[12]

In the *Analytical Inquiry*, Knight picked up the quarrel again; but the issue of principle was already joined, and that discussion in the *Inquiry* which is directed explicitly upon Price's *Dialogue* adds little save on some concrete details of the dispute. Complaint is made (and with justice) that Price had distorted Knight's doctrine into the proposition that the picturesque is simply the beautiful of visible objects, so that with respect to objects of sight "beauty" and "picturesqueness" are synonyms.[13] Price returns to this issue in his 1810 Appendix, and exhibits a lamentable inability to grasp Knight's point—even though he had the answer ready to hand in the objections which "Seymour" had raised in the *Dialogue*. Price even detects that in the *Inquiry* his friend "appears *somewhat inclined* to make the same sort of distinction between the beautiful and the picturesque which I have made, and which in his note he had treated as imaginary." [14] This triumph is imaginary, but not so Price's own cause for complaint— Knight's attack on his alleged "objectivism," an assault founded on misrepresentation. One feels, in reading these last words of the controversy, that the issue had worn itself out. There was from the first, and there still remained, a real difference between the disputants, but the resolution of this difference—even clear and distinct recognition of it—was prevented by misreading and misunderstanding. Neither of the controversialists, so limited, had more to say on the issue of principle, and further discussion would have been mere combative rhetoric.

CHAPTER 19

Dugald Stewart

❦

SAMUEL MONK asserts, as the summary proposition of his survey, *The Sublime: A Study of Critical Theories in XVIII-Century England,* that the aesthetic speculations in the Britain of that age were an unconscious prolegomenon to Kant: ". . . it may be said that eighteenth-century aesthetic has as its unconscious goal the *Critique of Judgment,* the book in which it was to be refined and reinterpreted." [1] Yet it seems to me doubtful that the intellectual history of any age can be viewed, without distortion, as a progression towards some one culmination. If adequate allowance is made for backslidings, excursions into wastelands on either side of the beaten track, and new beginnings from fresh starting points, perhaps in contrary directions, no generalization can hope to subsume these multifarious particulars. Assuredly, no British aesthetician of the eighteenth century evolved a system resembling Kant's, unless in such occasional concurrence on particular points of doctrine as may be found in writers the most diverse. Monk partly recognizes the difficulty of supporting his hypothesis by a literal study of the texts, and is inclined to detect a blind *Anders-streben* at work in the mind of the century, a vague groping for a truth beyond what the men of the age could formulate, but which became more and more luminous and distinct as the century wore on.

Maintaining (as I do) that there is no tendency for multiplicity to reduce to unity in the British speculations of the eighteenth century, and in consequence no simple historical progression from inadequacy to completeness, from error to truth, I can not erect any writer as goal and terminus for the inquiry. In another sense, however, a terminus can be found in a writer who aimed to subsume and reinterpret the speculation of the century: Dugald Stewart. Stewart considered himself the first worker at the superstructure of the "Philosophy of the Human Mind," Reid having performed the pre-requisite destructive labor of clearing away the metaphysical rubbish of previous systems.[2] Yet, though considering himself partly a disciple of Reid, and partly an innovator in applying an improved inductive method in mental philosophy, Stewart was in great measure an eclectic writer; in all his works he looks reflectively over the history of thought since the revolution of Descartes, culling from conflicting schools and systems data and principles which might be welded into a comprehensive theory of human nature, a whole for which he supplies the unifying basis and method.

After publication of the first volume of the *Elements of the Philosophy of the Human Mind* in 1792, there was a period of twenty-two years during which Stewart was prevented by ill-health and by the pressure of his duties from continuing that treatise. The principal work published in that interval was the *Philosophical Essays* of 1810.[3] There are two sets of essays in this work, the first comprising "Essays of a Metaphysical Purport," the second "Essays Relative to Matters of Taste" (as Hamilton terms them); these last, which will be treated of here, have been almost wholly ignored by philosophers and scholars alike. It may be a useful preliminary to state succinctly the place of the aesthetic essays in the corpus of Stewart's works. Stewart envisioned his entire philosophy of mind as consisting of three parts: the three volumes of the *Elements* deal with the intellectual powers; the two volumes of *The Philosophy of the Active and Moral Powers of Man* comprise the second part of the system; the third portion of Stewart's plan he never published, but Hamilton includes in the *Works* two volumes of *Lectures on Political Economy* compiled from MSS and student notes.[4] The *Philosophical Essays* are an interlude in this larger program.

The first part of the *Essays* "may be regarded," Stewart explains, "as a comment on some elementary and fundamental questions which have divided the opinions of philosophers in the eighteenth century."[5] Stewart is concerned to enforce that view of the origin of our ideas which is the leading point of his philosophy and of Reid's. The view is, that though all our knowledge arises on the occasion of sensations supplied through our external senses, these sensations do not constitute this knowledge. Accompanying sensation is perception, the apprehension of some external object which is the cause of the sensation; we have, moreover, through consciousness, knowledge of the operation of the mental faculties; and beyond ideas both of perception and of consciousness, a third class of ideas arises in the mind by a suggestion of the understanding consequent on sensation and operation of the faculties—ideas of our own existence, of personal identity, of time, motion, space and its dimensions, truth, causation, the uniformity of nature, God, and so forth. All those ideas, in short, which Hume attempted to analyze are here taken to be supplied on appropriate occasions by an occult mechanism or original law of our nature. And the distinction of sensation from perception disposes of what Stewart conceives to be the fundamental error of Locke and his followers, an error prevailing since the Greeks, that ideas are the immediate objects of knowledge.

But it is not my present purpose to enter upon a discussion of Stewart's metaphysics. It suffices to say that Stewart attempts in the first four essays of his first part to show how the erroneous speculations of Locke, Berkeley, Hume, the followers of Locke in France, and the English physiological metaphysicians (Hartley, Priestley, and Darwin) arise from misconceptions of the nature and origin of ideas. The last of the essays of the first part, "On the Tendency of Some Late Philological Speculations," treats of the theories expounded by Horne Tooke in *The Diversions of Purley,* and serves as a kind of link between the metaphysical and the aesthetic essays. Stewart refutes at length and with skill Tooke's principles that all the meanings of a given word have a common element, and that this element, the essence of the meaning, is fixed by the etymology of the word. Tooke's theory is connected with the foregoing essays by the circumstance that it implies a theory about the origin of ideas: since the words designating the various phenomena of mind were originally borrowed from the sensible circumstances of matter, Tooke's etymological explanations constitute an implicit induction to the effect that "the only real knowledge we possess relates to the objects of our external senses; and that we can annex no idea to the word *mind* itself, but that of *matter* in the most subtle and attenuated form which imagination can lend it." [6] This theory Stewart had examined in the earlier essays, and he needs here only to refute the alleged evidence of language in its favor. Here as elsewhere, Stewart carefully avoids confusing genetic problems with constitutive. He reprobates strongly the pretensions of philologists to direct us in the study of the mind: ". . . to appeal to etymology in a philosophical argument, (excepting, perhaps, in those cases where the word itself is of philosophical origin,) is altogether nugatory, and can serve, at the best, to throw an amusing light on the laws which regulate the operations of human fancy." [7] Yet though philologists "are more likely to bewilder than to direct us in the study of the Mind, they may yet (as I shall attempt to exemplify in the Second Part of this volume) supply many useful materials towards a history of its natural progress;—more particularly towards a history of Imagination, considered in its relation to the principles of Criticism." [8]

This slender bond is the transition to the second series of essays: Stewart's aim in the essays on beauty and sublimity is to trace the progress of the mind in its apprehension of those characters, and the fashion in which a common appellation comes to be applied to diverse qualities. The scope of the series is conventional: "On the Beautiful," "On the Sublime," "On Taste," and "On the Culture of Certain Intellectual Habits Connected with the First Elements of Taste." The treatment which Stewart gives these topics, with its careful reference to previous writers and its constant effort to bring together the best that had been written into one systematic conspectus, justifies the role which I have assigned to him in the speculation of the period. Stewart refers to Shaftesbury, Addison, Hutcheson, Hume, Akenside, Hogarth, Gerard, Burke, Beattie, Blair, Reynolds, Lord Kames, Gilpin, Price, Knight, Repton, Alison, Twining, Reid, and Adam Smith, and among the French to Boileau, Huet, Père André, Du Bos, Buffier, Diderot, D'Alembert, Voltaire, La Harpe, Montesquieu, the Abbé Girard, and the Abbé De Lille; few names are missing from the roster.[9]

It is natural for a writer of eclectic temper, coming after a long succession of diverse theories, to be concerned with the ambiguity of terms, for it is in part this ambiguity which allows such multiplicity of theories. Stewart considers that all previous writers on beauty had made an important methodological error: all had supposed that there was ultimately one common essence of beauty pervading all the various qualities called beautiful.

We speak [Stewart urges] of beautiful colours, beautiful forms, beautiful pieces of music: We speak also of the beauty of virtue; of the beauty of poetical composition; of the beauty of style in prose; of the beauty of a mathematical theorem; of the beauty of a philosophical discovery. On the other hand, we do *not* speak of beautiful tastes, or of beautiful smells; nor do we apply this epithet to the agreeable softness, or smoothness, or warmth of tangible objects, considered solely in their relation to our sense of feeling. . . .

It has long been a favourite problem with philosophers, to ascertain the common quality or qualities which entitles a thing to the denomination of *beautiful;* but the success of their speculations has been so inconsiderable, that little can be inferred from them but the impossibility of the problem to which they have been directed.[10]

Speculations endeavoring to find properties in things corresponding to these usages of language originate, Stewart conjectures, "in a prejudice which has descended to modern times from the scholastic ages; that when a word admits of a variety of significations, these different significations must all be *species* of the same *genus*, and must consequently include some essential idea common to every individual to which the generic term can be applied." [11] But a genetic view of language dispels this illusion:

> I shall begin [he writes] with supposing that the letters A, B, C, D, E, denote a series of objects; that A possesses some one quality in common with B; B a quality in common with C . . . [et cetera];—while, at the same time, no quality can be found which belongs in common to any *three* objects in the series. Is it not conceivable, that the affinity between A and B may produce a transference of the name of the first to the second; and that, in consequence of the other affinities which connect the remaining objects together, the same name may pass in succession from B to C; from C to D; and from D to E? In this manner, a common appellation will arise between A and E, although the two objects may, in their nature and properties, be so widely distant from each other, that no stretch of imagination can conceive how the thoughts were led from the former to the latter.[12]

This theory of transitive meanings is adopted from a remark in Payne Knight's *Analytical Inquiry* and converted by Stewart into the special analytical device of his aesthetic system. The utility of his method, as Stewart sees it, lies in diverting philosophers from vain attempts to discover a common essence in things possessing a common name through habitual association, and in finding, through tracing out the associations underlying the transitive meanings, a basis for discussion of the qualities to be studied. Indeed, Stewart repeatedly insists with undue modesty that he does not aim at a theory of the beautiful or the sublime, but only at the prolegomenon to such a theory; concluding his essay on sublimity, he reminds his readers that his aim is "not to investigate the principles on which the various elements of Sublimity give pleasure to the Mind; but to trace the associations, in consequence of which the common name of Sublimity has been applied to all of them; and to illustrate the influence of this common name in re-acting on the Imagination and the Taste. . . ." [13] This apparent limitation led Jeffrey to remark that the essay on beauty is "in reality, a sort of *philological* dissertation." [14] But explanation of the transitive meanings of terms requires much prior explication of the real phenomena to which the terms refer, and Stewart's work is "philological" only in the sense in which Plato's *Republic* is an effort at definition.

Applying the device Stewart has adopted, the first problem is to find the "A"—the original application of the term Beauty. It refers primitively, Stewart concludes, to objects of sight; more narrowly, "The first ideas of *beauty* formed by the mind are, in all probability, derived from *colours*. Long before infants receive any pleasures from the beauties of form or of motion, (both of which require, for their perception, a certain effort of attention and of thought,) their eye may be caught and delighted with brilliant colouring, or with splendid illumination." [15] Stewart's approach makes it almost inevitable that color will be the original beauty, for, tracing the meaning of "beauty" genetically, we begin with qualities which affect *sight alone*—and color and light are the only such qualities. This beauty of color is for Stewart in large part a mechanical or organic pleasure, like that of harmony to the ear; and these organic pleasures are "the *parent stock* on which all our more complicated feelings of Beauty are afterwards grafted, as well as *the means* by which the various exciting causes of these feelings are united and consolidated under the same common appellation. . . ." [16]

Form is conjoined in our experience with color, and the pleasures attached to the perception of certain forms blend with those arising from color—so that the term "beautiful" is transitively applied to form, and then through form to motion. It is not, Stewart reiterates,

in consequence of the discovery of any quality belonging in common to colours, to forms, and to motion, considered abstractly, that the same word is now applied to them indiscriminately. They all, indeed, agree in this, that they give pleasure to the spectator; but there cannot, I think, be a doubt, that they please on principles essentially different; and that the transference of the word Beauty, from the first to the last, arises solely from their undistinguishable co-operation in producing the same agreeable effect, in consequence of their being all perceived by the same organ, and at the same instant. [17]

Concerned chiefly with the bond uniting the various qualities under a common term, Stewart does not always pause to account for the origin of the pleasures they afford. For the most part, he is content to refer to Alison's *Essays on the Nature and Principles of Taste* for

explanations of the separate beauties, though allowing more to organic impression in the case of color. (Stewart's reliance upon Alison,
his friend and whilom student, is one of the few notices which the
first edition of Alison's work received; it was the second edition,
championed by Jeffrey, which swept the day for associationism in
aesthetics.) That Stewart makes no effort to account for this pleasing
organic effect of colors is, I think, a serious lacuna in the system;
the pleasing effect of harmony is very well accounted for by the
physiology of the ear, but no such account is forthcoming for the al-
legedly analogous case of color.

Stewart is emphatic in insisting upon the complexity of beauty,
and he censures the theories of his predecessors as extending too far
critical inferences proper only to some part of the phenomena. The
opinions of Burke especially, recommended by so illustrious a name,
are "calculated to bias and mislead the taste." [18] The physiological
hypothesis of Burke Stewart scarcely pauses to overthrow; it is, of
course, directly contrary to his own principle that inductive mental
philosophy may legitimately concern itself with ascertaining the laws
which regulate the connection of matter and mind, but not with
efforts to explain in what manner they are united—so that theories
of subtle fluids, vibrations, or (as with Burke) tensions and relaxa-
tions, are the merest conjectures, to be eschewed by sober inquirers.[19]
But the chief weight of Stewart's criticism falls on the limitation of
Burkeian beauty consequent on Burke's supposition that there is some
common quality in the pleasing objects of the different external
senses. It is this principle which leads Burke to find smoothness so
essential to beauty. Stewart's genetic approach, in contrast, limits
beauty to such qualities as affect through the sight; there is, of course,
association among the senses, so that smoothness may *become* beautiful by association with perceptions of sight. But this effect is limited
to objects destined to be handled, and the principle is inapplicable
to objects which we do not think of touching because of their magnitude or situation. The beauty of smoothness is traced equally, moreover, to other kinds of associations than tactile—to the reflecting
properties of smooth surfaces, to sexual associations, to associations of
utility or design, and to custom.[20]

But since all of these associations may be in some circumstances in-
effectual, or counteracted, or even reversed, the rough and angular
may also be beautiful—and Stewart begins to enumerate the various
qualities and objects which Uvedale Price, from a similar awareness
of the limitations of Burkeian beauty, had termed *picturesque:*

According to Mr. Price [writes Stewart], the circumstances which please, both in natural scenes and in the compositions of the painter, are of two kinds—the Beautiful and the Picturesque. These, he thinks, are radically and essentially distinct. . . .

To this conclusion Mr. Price was naturally, or rather necessarily led, by his admission, at his first outset, of Mr. Burke's peculiar tenets as so many incontrovertible axioms. In the progress of his subsequent researches, finding numberless ingredients in agreeable compositions, that could not be brought under Burke's enumeration of the qualities which "go to the composition of the beautiful," he was forced to arrange them under some new name; whereas, he ought rather to have concluded, that the enumeration was partial and defective, and extended the application of the word Beauty, to whatever qualities in natural objects affect the mind with agreeable emotions, through the *medium* of sight.[21]

Now, both Burke and Price had objected to so general an extension of the term "beauty," on the grounds that it lumped together indiscriminately characters really dissimilar. Stewart thinks to avoid such confusion by drawing a distinction: some elements of beauty, he urges, are intrinsically pleasing, while others please only in a state of combination. Stewart makes little of this latter, "relative" beauty, though it includes much of what Price terms "picturesque." But Price's sense of "picturesque" does not escape censure: "The meaning he [Price] has annexed to the word *picturesque* is equally exceptionable with the limited and arbitrary notion concerning the *beautiful*, which he has adopted from Mr. Burke. In both cases, he has departed widely from established use; and, in consequence of this, when he comes to compare . . . the *picturesque* and *beautiful* together, he has given to many observations, equally just and refined, an air of paradox. . . ."[22] Stewart prefers Gilpin's sense of "picturesque"—that which is suited to the purposes of painters—in which event "picturesque" becomes not the name of an aesthetic character, but a qualifying epithet "to limit the meaning of the generic name Beauty in particular instances," as "romantic," "classical," "pathetic," and other such terms may also do. The picturesque is not quite a species of beauty, however, for things may be picturesque which are not beautiful: this is the old problem of pleasing imitations of unpleasant originals. Stewart notes a variety of causes for our seeing beauty in representations of what is offensive: the pleasure of imitation itself; the annihilation in a picture of what is offensive to other senses than sight; the influence of selection and emphasis (which are signs of the fancy and taste of the artist); the skill of execution and design.

The second of these points is evidently drawn from Knight; but I do not see how Stewart can consistently admit it with respect to touch —and his examples (pictures of dead fish, &c.) refer rather to smell, the objects of which are less closely associated with visual properties and are never *seen* as the objects of touch are. The fourth point parallels Hume's argument in "On Tragedy"; Stewart criticizes Hume, however, for carrying the point too far. Neither Stewart nor Hume has noted an important distinction necessary to be drawn: pictorial representations of terrific or pathetic objects (crucifixions, &c.) may yield an actual conversion of the passions, and be *more* agreeable than gayer scenes; where, however, the original is merely disgusting, the mind is not stirred and no conversion can take place, the unpleasantness of the original being simply subducted from the beauty of artistry and representation—except, perhaps, for the connoisseur, who is really delighting in the boldness of the artist in addressing his powers to such untoward subjects. Stewart overlooks, finally, the important influence of change of scale which Price had pointed out.

These criticisms have not implied any condemnation of Price's taste: "I not only agree with him in almost all the critical observations which he has introduced in the course of the discussion," Stewart declares, "but I esteem his work, as eminently calculated, in its practical tendency, to reform and to improve the public taste." [23] But with Price's causal explanations, Stewart is disposed to cavil. A distinguishing feature of all the writers of the picturesque school—Gilpin, Price, and Knight—was their insistence upon the aesthetic significance of lines, colors, textures taken abstractly from the concretes in which they occur, and this whether the effect of such qualities was attributed to immediate agency or to association. Stewart, in contrast, is inclined to lay more stress on associations involving the concrete objects as wholes, less on those associations which the separate properties carry. He complains that the "ingenious" Gilpin and Price had been led to ascribe more effect to the mere visible appearance than really belongs to it. His own emphasis on associations with concrete wholes is illustrated by analysis of the picturesqueness of the ass: Stewart points to its appearance in the Bible, in Aesop, and other writings— its use by the vagrant poor—its own manners—its appearance in Renaissance painting; Price and Gilpin emphasize instead its peculiarities of form, coloring, and roughness of coat. Stewart suggests ingeniously that these peculiarities may possess for the painter "important and obvious advantages over those which are more decidedly beautiful; inasmuch as these last, by the immediate pleasure they communicate to the organ, have a tendency to arrest the progress of our thoughts, and to engage the whole of our attention to themselves." [24] The picturesque of physical properties thus becomes ancillary to the poetical picturesque by facilitating association. Only in the poetical sense, as referring to the significance and expression of concrete objects, can "picturesque" be opposed to "beautiful"—opposed, however, only to immediate visible beauty, for the poetical picturesque pleases as a sign of understood beauties in the case of originals which are displeasing immediately.

Having in this way vindicated his conception of beauty by an argument treating partly of terminology, partly of causes, against objections which the picturesque school or disciples of Burke might raise, Stewart turns to further generalizations of beauty and the corresponding transitions of the term. In all these transitions and generalizations, "the *visible object*, if it is not the *physical cause*, furnishes, at least, the *occasion* of the pleasure we feel; and it is on the *eye alone* that any organic impression is supposed to be made." [25] Objects of touch, as we have found, come to be seen as beautiful; in some measure even objects of smell or taste enhance beauty, through association of conceptions of their pleasing sensations with the perceptions of the visible beauty.[26] But a difficulty remains: for the epithet "beautiful" appears to be directly and immediately applicable to objects of hearing, though sounds are not judged of by the eye. Certain peculiarities of sounds, however, connect their beauties with those immediately perceived by the eye. There is, first, a *picturesque* effect of sounds—by association they may call up particular scenes, as "the clack of a mill, heard at a distance, conjures up at once to the mind's eye the simple and cheerful scene which it announces." [27] More important is the *expressive* power of sounds naturally pathetic; thus "the word Beauty, which is at first transferred from the face to the mind, comes to be re-transferred from the mind to the voice; more especially, when its tones express such passions as we have been led . . . to consider as beautiful." [28] There is, further, the *significant* power of sounds through conventional speech, whereby they present pictures to the imagination. Eye and ear, finally, are associated

as the great inlets of our acquired knowledge; as the only *media* by which different Minds can communicate together; and as the organs by which we receive from the material world the two classes of pleasure, which, while they surpass all the rest in variety and duration,—are the most completely removed from the grossness of animal indulgence, and the most nearly allied to the enjoyments of the intellect. The unconsciousness we have, in both these senses, of any local impression on our bodily frame, may, perhaps, help to explain the peculiar facility with which their perceptions blend themselves with other pleasures of a rank still nobler and more refined.—It is these two classes, accordingly, of organical pleasures, which fall exclusively under the cognizance of . . . intellectual Taste. . . .[29]

Stewart of course acknowledges the original and mechanical pleasure of harmony; he has detailed all these connections between sight and hearing with the view of accounting for the extension of the term "beauty" from the objects of one to those of the other.

The intellectual and moral associations in which beauty chiefly (though not originally) consists, are treated very briefly by Stewart, since he can refer to Alison's work for illustrations, and needs only to point out the "transitions" involved. Yet there is a curious contrast between the accounts of Stewart and of Alison. Stewart declares that the term "beauty" is transferred to moral qualities through association, through those associations which are grounded on that "intimate and inseparable union, which, in the human face, connects soul and body with each other. . . . To the peculiar intimacy of this connexion . . . it seems to be owing, that the word Beauty comes . . . to be applied to certain moral qualities considered abstractly. The qualities which are thus characterized in ordinary discourse are, in truth, exactly those which it gives us the greatest delight to see expressed in the countenance; or such as have a tendency . . . to improve the *visible* beauty which the features exhibit."[30] Stewart is in accord with Alison in urging that beauty is chiefly moral and intellectual, and that it is communicated to material properties by association; but the arguments they follow to reach this position are radically opposite. Alison's technique is to apply induction directly to each trait of the beautiful and reduce each equally to its mental root; Stewart's is to trace the history of the mind as the concept is enlarged. And Stewart's history begins with the material beauty of color, in contradiction to Alison's great generalization that there is *no* material beauty. The methodological difference itself may in turn be accounted for in part by recalling that Stewart undertook his aesthetic inquiry as a part of a more general program of ascertaining the origin of our ideas: the historical method follows in consequence; "our attention," as Stewart says, "is directed to the natural history of the Human Mind, and to its natural progress in the employment of speech."[31]

A conspicuous instance of the tendency of the doctrine of general ideas to mislead theorists is afforded by the system of Reynolds. Like most writers of his age (and of our own), Stewart takes the *Idler* papers as a definitive statement of Reynolds' principles; and it must be owned that these papers (and the somewhat simpler theory of Buffier which Stewart considers conjointly) are obnoxious to serious criticism. Stewart grants (much too readily, I think) the "fact" that in every species, the central or most common form is the most beautiful, but the inference from this supposed fact, that beauty depends upon custom, he combats. His approach throughout has been to trace the transitive application of terms following lines of association from initial intrinsic effects, rather than to refer to habits formed by frequency distributions; and he of course points out, not only that Reynolds' theory affords no way of comparing species in point of beauty, but that even applied to things of the same kind it entails the corollary that no individual object can give pleasure previous to comparison with others of the kind. "The only point in dispute," Stewart concludes, "is, whether the individual objects please in consequence of their approximation to the usual forms and colours of Nature; or whether Nature herself is not pronounced to be Beautiful, in consequence of the regular profusion in which she exhibits forms and colours intrinsically pleasing?" [32]

The second portion of the essay, "On the Beautiful, When Presented to the Power of Imagination," is abruptly truncated, and we are left to conjecture by analogy Stewart's thought on the beauty of virtue, of philosophical theories, of geometrical propositions. All that Stewart performs is, to point out the leading causes of the differences between the beauties of imagination and those of perception—between the beauties of presentation and those of representation. It must be noted that imagination, in Stewart's system, is a compound faculty. Comprised in it are *fancy*, "a power of summoning up, at pleasure, a particular class of ideas,—and of ideas related to each other in a particular manner"; [33] *conception*, "that power of the mind which enables it to form a notion of an absent object of perception, or of a sensation which it has formerly felt"; [34] *abstraction*, the "power of considering certain qualities or attributes of an object apart from the rest . . . the power which the understanding has, of separating the combinations which are presented to it"; [35] and *judgment* or *taste*, "which selects the materials and directs their combination." [36] The function of this compound faculty is "to make a selection of qualities and of circumstances from a variety of different objects, and by combining and disposing these, to form a new creation of its own." [37] Stewart's pleasures of the imagination do not, then, correspond to Addison's, nor yet do they correspond precisely to Addison's secondary pleasures singly, despite Stewart's declaration that "philosophical precision indispensably requires an exclusive limitation of that title to what Mr. Addison calls *secondary* pleasures; because, although ultimately founded on pleasures derived from our perceptive powers, they are yet . . . characterized by some very remarkable circumstances peculiar to themselves." [38] For Addison's secondary pleasures are often pleasures, in Stewart's language, of mere conception and memory; Stewart's imagination is a poetical faculty creating a new world from the materials of the world of perception.

In imaginative conception the predominance of visual images is still greater than that of sight in perception; it is the *picture* which fixes attention, and "its agreeable concomitants add to the effect rather by the association of fugitive impressions or feelings, than by that of Conceptions, on which we are able steadily to dwell." [39] It is, indeed, through the *image* that poetical composition comes to be judged *beautiful:*

> In the same manner in which the *Eye* (while we actually look abroad upon nature) attaches to its appropriate objects so great a variety of pleasures, both physical and moral; so to the poet, *Language* serves as a common channel or organ for uniting all the agreeable impressions of which the senses, the understanding, and the heart, are susceptible: And as the word Beauty is naturally transferred from colours and forms to the other pleasing qualities which may be associated with these, and to the various moral qualities of which they may be expressive; so the same word is insensibly extended from those *images* which form at once the characteristical feature, and the most fascinating charm of poetry, to the numberless other sources of delight which it opens. [40]

No pronouncement could make clearer the contrast between this genetic mode of aesthetic analysis and the Aristotelian, wherein beauty resides in the magnitude and order of an organized whole, and that of a poem in its architectonics rather than in its diction.

The essay, "On the Sublime," Stewart tells us, was stimulated by the controversy between Price and Knight over the doctrine of Burke; and Stewart resolves the issue by a line of reasoning perfectly analogous to that of the essay on beauty. Previous writers had taken for granted that there must be some common quality in all objects characterized as sublime. "In their researches, however, concerning the essential constituent of Sublimity, the conclusions to which they have been led are so widely different from each other, that one would scarcely suppose, on a superficial view, they could possibly relate to the same class of phenomena;—a circumstance the more remarkable, that, in the statement of these phenomena, philosophical critics are, with a few trifling exceptions, unanimously agreed." [41] Stewart sees in the conjectures and partial truths of Burke and Helvetius, Blair and Knight, Kames and Longinus, "a great deal of false refinement . . . in bending facts to preconceived systems"— and opens his explication with the declaration that "none of these theorists have paid sufficient attention to the word *Sublime* in its literal and primitive sense; or to the various natural associations founded on the physical and moral concomitants of *great Altitude*." [42] The clew of etymology leads us from the maze: sublimity is connected with altitude originally, and the problem becomes the discovery of "the *grounds* of that natural transition which the mind is disposed to make from Sublimity, literally so called, to the numerous metaphorical uses of the term." [43] A note added after the essay was completed acknowledges Hume's prior discovery of the opposition of sublimity to gravitation, though Stewart objects to Hume's explanation of the superior effect of the sublimity of time to that of space, and that of past to future time (denying the fact itself in this latter case). [44] In Hume, the argument is given rigorously in terms of an opposition between the influences of passion and association on the imagination; opposition, if not overwhelming, stimulates the soul, and hence moving against the natural order of association causes such an expansion or exaltation. Removal in time "opposes" the natural flow of ideas more than removal in space because time seems made up of discontinuous events, and recession into the past more than removal into the future because it opposes the sequence of cause and effect. Stewart may be said to be systematically blind to Hume's argument, for by it the sublime of time would be co-original with the sublime of space, and the sublime of horizontal extent co-original with that of vertical. The only real difference between Hume and Stewart is, that Stewart insists (consistently with his program and method) in finding some *one* root sublimity, and connecting all other sublimities with this by historical analysis. In any event, the feeling caused by altitude is further qualified, in Stewart's view, by association with the upward growth of plants, the erect form of man, and the upward development of the human body coinciding with the advancement of the mind—all which circumstances tend to give an

allegorical character to literal sublimity, as does also the rising, cul-
minating, and setting of the heavenly bodies, with all the analogies
their progress suggests.

It is pretty obvious how Stewart can explain the connection of
power with sublimity, while maintaining that taking power as itself
the root of the sublime does not give so natural and easy a history of
the development of the concept as does Stewart's own notion of an
automatic psychological process stimulated by perception of physical
height. But it is curious that *terror* makes no part of literal sublimity
for Stewart—not even in analysis of the sublimity of depth. The sublime of power is closely associated for Stewart with the religious
sublime, with what he conceives to be a universal tendency for religious sentiments to carry the thoughts upward; and, indeed, Stewart
sees much of the sublime of the material world as a reflection of creative power, though this in turn is ultimately dependent upon physical
altitude for its sublimity. Stewart is led to rest upon comparatively
insecure bases sublimities which—in his own system—could be given
a more certain ground. Eternity and immensity, for instance, are made
a part of the religious sublime, although their sublimity might be
very readily explained in other ways—by extension, for instance, of
the notion of opposing gravity. And when Stewart tells us that "instead of considering, with Mr. Burke, Terror as the ruling principle
of the *religious sublime*, it would be nearer the truth to say, that the
Terrible derives whatever character of Sublimity belongs to it from
religious associations," [45] he has evidently been misled by his enthusiasm for following out a slender thread of association. Heights, and
more especially depths, are dangerous and terrible from infancy;
their sublimity is original: why slight this early and obvious connection between sublimity and terror? Happily, Stewart's taste triumphs
over his piety, and he in effect retracts this position by acknowledging in the succeeding chapter other connections of elevation with terror and power (especially, Stewart notes with formal magniloquence,
that of "masses of water, in the form of a mountain torrent, or of a
cataract," which "present to us one of the most impressive images of
irresistible impetuosity which terrestrial phenomena afford . . ." [46]).
To the admiration and awe excited by such force is superadded an
emotion of wonder when the actual fall is prevented by some extraordinary means; in a Gothic cathedral, for instance, "it is this natural
apprehension of impending danger, checked and corrected every moment by a rational conviction of our security, which seems to produce
that silent and pleasing awe which we experience on entering within

their walls. . . ." [47] Knight's sublime of *energy* is easily brought within Stewart's system, for it is merely relative, "a reflection from the sublimity of the Power to which it is opposed." [48]

Stewart is able to find additional support for his notion of the original and literal import of "sublimity" in the empathic signs of sublime emotion. That "the Mind is naturally *elevated* by the true Sublime, and, assuming a certain proud and erect attitude, exults and glories, as if it had itself produced what it has only heard," was noticed by Longinus himself.[49] The analogy of greatness of mind with greatness of stature is, Stewart declares, "the ground-work of the account of Sublimity in writing, given by Longinus; who, although he speaks only of the effect of sublimity on the Mind, plainly identifies that effect with its Bodily expression . . . [which] may be regarded as a demonstrative proof, that, in the complicated effect which sublimity produces, the primary idea which has given name to the whole, always retains a decided predominance over the other ingredients." [50]

The analysis of taste in Stewart's work is less a fresh insight into that outworn topic than a restatement of familiar truths within the special framework of his aesthetic system. Like all the more philosophical writers of his age, Stewart regards taste as a compound and derivative faculty; his originality consists in employing, characteristically, a genetic approach. Gerard and Alison had analyzed taste as it exists in a cultivated mind, says Stewart, "but it did not fall under the design of any of these writers to trace the growth of Taste from its first seeds in the constitution of our nature; or to illustrate the analogy which it exhibits, in some of the intellectual processes connected with it, to what takes place in various other acquired endowments of the understanding. It is in this point of view that I propose to consider it. . . ." [51] These other "acquired endowments of the understanding" include not only the acquired perceptions of sight but the phenomena of reading and writing, of mathematical calculation and inference in those accustomed to it, and so forth: all are apparently simple and instantaneous acts of the mind, all are really habits the acquisition of which is forgotten or unattended to.[52] In the case of taste, the apparent originality of the faculty is an illusion the more readily supported as the pleasures and pains which its perceptions excite attract attention to the effects rather than the causes.

Consistently with the plan of Stewart's entire mental philosophy, the elements of taste and the mode of their acquisition are determined inductively; in analyzing the effects of the ingredients of beauty, "we must proceed," Stewart declares, "on the same general principles by which we are guided in investigating the physical and chemical properties of material substances; that is, we must have recourse to a series of observations and experiments on beautiful objects of various kinds; attending diligently to the agreeable or disagreeable effects we experience, in the case of these diversified combinations." [53] These observations and comparisons can not be made precise and quantitative by measuring devices: the appeal is to pleasant and unpleasant emotion. But this disadvantage is compensated for by the ease with which experiments in taste can be made ideally.

The faculty consists in the discriminating perception of the circumstances which enhance or detract from aesthetic effect; and its objects fall into certain general classes: "First, those which derive their effect from the organical adaptation of the human frame to the external universe; and, Secondly, those which please in consequence of associations gradually formed by experience." This latter and more extensive class may be subdivided into "such beauties as owe their existence to associations resulting necessarily from the common circumstances of the human race," and "beauties which have no merit but what depends on custom and fashion; or on certain peculiarities in the situation and history of the individual." [54] If human nature is conceived to include the natural condition, as well as the natural constitution of man, those beauties resulting from universal associations together with the organical beauties "fall under the consideration of that sort of criticism which forms a branch of the Philosophy of the Human Mind"; and to these Universal Beauties corresponds Philosophical Taste, which "enables a writer or an artist to rise superior to the times in which he lives, and emboldens him to trust his reputation to the suffrages of the human race, and of the ages which are yet to come." [55] To the Arbitrary Beauties dependent upon accidental association corresponds a lower taste, "that humbler, though more profitable sagacity, which teaches the possessor how to suit his manufactures to the market. . . ." [56] Stewart betrays, in the terms in which he couches this distinction, the romantic bias of his era; for the popular taste is grounded in a certain facility of association acquired through intercourse with society, a habit of mind which, Stewart writes, renders both the beautiful and the right a function of fashion; whereas the philosophical taste "implies a sensibility, deep and permanent, to those objects of affection, admiration, and reverence, which interested the youthful heart, while yet a stranger to the opinions and ways of the world," and is characterized by "strong domestic and local attachments, accompanied with that enthusiastic love of Nature, Simplicity, and Truth, which, in every department, both of art and of science, is the best and surest presage of Genius." [57]

In taste which exists perfected, we find

> an understanding, discriminating, comprehensive, and unprejudiced; united with a love of truth and of nature, and with a temper superior to the irritation of little passions. While it implies a spirit of accurate observation and of patient induction, applied to the most fugitive and evanescent class of our mental phenomena, it evinces that power of separating universal associations from such as are local or personal, which, more than any other quality of the mind, is the foundation of *good sense,* both in scientific pursuits, and in the conduct of life. [58]

Beyond the primary pleasures which beauty affords, there is a secondary pleasure of taste derived from remarking the skill of the artist in his performance, which technical taste, unlike the primary, is susceptible of pain as well as pleasure, for it is offended with blemishes in artistry. Higher than this technical taste is the taste of the connoisseur, a taste based more on the study of models than of rules, "secretly, and often unconsciously, guided by an idolatrous comparison of what it sees, with the works of its favourite masters." [59] But the indigenous taste formed by cultivating and disciplining native capacity for the primary pleasures is alone entitled to be considered true and just. The pleasures of artful design are, for Stewart as for all the writers of his tradition, inferior to those of expression and of nature.

In the final essay of his series, Stewart examines the culture and training of the imagination, and his observations are penetrating and sometimes original. Instead of merely repeating the saw that the pleasures of imagination are interposed betwixt those of sense and of intellect, and fitted to allure the mind to virtue, he develops with some subtlety the suggestion that in cases where a speculative bias has caused the neglect of imagination and of taste, philosophical criticism could serve as a link connecting habits of abstract thought with the more ornamental accomplishments, whereas when the powers of imagination have gained an undue predominance over the other mental powers, this same philosophical criticism could serve as transition to the general philosophy of mind. Early culture of imagination, Stewart insists, will subject it to the supremacy of the rational powers in the more serious concerns of life; the "*momentary belief* with which the visions of imagination are always accompanied, and upon which many of its pleasures depend, will continue unshaken; while that *permanent or habitual belief*, which they are apt to produce, where it gains the ascendant over our nobler principles, will vanish for ever." [60] Nor is Stewart the dupe of the fashionable primitivism of the period; "when I speak," he warns,

> of a *cultivated imagination,* I mean an imagination which has acquired such a degree of activity as to delight in its own exertions; to delight in conjuring up those ideal combinations which withdraw the mind from the present objects of sense, and transport it into a new world. Now of this activity and versatility of imagination, I find no trace among rude tribes. Their diction is, indeed, highly metaphorical; but the metaphors they employ are either the unavoidable consequences of an imperfect language, or are inspired by the mechanical impulse of passion. In both instances, imagination operates to a certain degree; but in neither is imagination the *primary* cause of the effect, inasmuch as in the one, it is excited by passion, and in the other, called forth by the pressure of necessity. [61]

Stewart's work (review of which is now complete) did not have the influence which he anticipated: he did not lay that true foundation on which followers were to build, for these followers did not come. British aesthetics lost in the nineteenth century what unity of approach there was in the eighteenth: while some writers elaborated facets of the work done before Stewart's efforts at synthesis, others made fresh beginnings, and others yet followed in the tracks of Kant and Hegel. What Stewart really did was to review the work of the eighteenth century, and to draw from the various systems of that age insights which could, without prejudice to the truth they contained, be included in a fresh system by arrangement in a genetic account, part of the general History of the Human Mind.

Retrospect

※

THIS RETROSPECT is neither summary nor conclusion: not a summary, for the object of this study has been to display the logic of the particular systems in the details of their unfolding; not a conclusion, for the systems have been treated as entities, not as data for the induction of generalizations. Rather, in this chapter I review the aesthetic speculation of eighteenth-century Britain in a different mode of analysis. The method I have employed to examine the structure of individual systems has necessarily subordinated the continuum of concepts, distinctions, and methods of argument which persist through the period and which constitute a distinctive tradition in aesthetic thought. In this final chapter, it is my purpose to indicate briefly some at least of these general characteristics of the age, and to point out such shifts and tendencies as can be observed within that continuum. In no sense, then, is the chapter a distillation of this book: it has a different purpose, isolates a different aspect of the subject, and employs a different method. The reader who opens the book at this point to discover its nature is remanded to the Introduction.

This book is not a history: the selection of data, the organization of materials, and the purpose are not determined by historical principles. If a history, a literal history, of the aesthetic thought of the eighteenth century were attempted, its purpose must be to educe from the facts a summary proposition, or set of summary propositions, which would distill the essence of a narrative, a narrative of changes in subject, in principle, in method, and in purpose within the discussion of aesthetics. The materials would be organized to display the parts of those changes—their stages or their aspects—and the data selected would be those most indicative of the progression studied, or which were causes of that progression. Yet a system of thought, if considered as a logical entity, is an indissoluble crystal, fixed, out of time and change. It is only the minds of the authors and students of those systems—their tastes, associational patterns, predominant passions, habits of inquiry, convictions and conjectures—which can change. A literal intellectual history, then, is really a history of the choices—choices of subject, of principle, of method—made by the authors of systems, and of the causes of those choices; it is an examination of systems taken not as logical entities but as psychological products. My concern, however, has been not with the history either of speculation or of taste in eighteenth-century Britain, but with those sets and systems of ideas which were then crystallized, to examine their facets, to compare their lusters, and to note the various refractions of the same light as it is transmitted through them.

For though reality may be one, the reflections of it in thought are many; we see only the image of reality through the prism of our own thought, an image which depends more directly on the nature of that prism of concepts and distinctions and patterns of inference through which we look than upon the object of our view. It is not more in our power after examining twenty systems of aesthetics than before to answer the naïve and natural question, "What, then, *is* beauty after all?" What beauty is in itself, outside *all* system of thought, is indeterminable; we see only the image of it through the terms in which we describe it, the categories to which we refer it, the inferences by which we interpret it. The purpose which leads us to the objects of our contemplation, the presuppositions which have equipped us with a vocabulary and prepared us to distinguish some aspects of the object and to pass over others, our habits of reasoning—these circumstances make up that prism or lens through which we view reality; what our lens brings into focus, we see. Different lenses are of use for different purposes, to be sure, and we can grind our lens to fit the application; but dispense with it, we can not.

The problem in giving an account of a variety of systems of thought is to establish a set of terms and distinctions sufficiently comprehensive that the concepts and arguments of the systems discussed can be compared without prejudice in the terms of the analyst. Where the systems compared have many and major features in common— as with these British systems of the eighteenth century—this task is of course simpler. R. S. Crane has observed that the neo-classical tradition in literary criticism was not a body of doctrine; it was "a large but historically distinguishable aggregate of commonplace distinctions, of a highly flexible and ambiguous kind, out of which many variant critical systems and doctrines could be constructed" [1]—distinctions such as general and particular nature, instruction and pleasure, uniformity and variety, sublime and pathetic, and the like. A critic within this tradition might employ such of these distinctions as were useful for solution of the problems to which he addressed himself, giving the various concepts the interpretation and emphasis appropriate to the structure of his thought. The tradition which we are here examining is confined to a more narrowly defined subject— the beautiful, sublime, and picturesque—than the miscellaneous critical tradition which Crane describes, and the discussions form a more closely integrated tradition; yet here too there is great variance of doctrine within a common manner.

The common features of that manner, then. The aestheticians of this period all found their subject to be psychological: the central problem for them was not some aspect of the cosmos or of particular substances, nor was it found among the characteristics of human activity or of the modes of symbolic representation; one and all, they found their problem to be the specification and discrimination of certain kinds of feelings, the determination of the mental powers and susceptibilities which yielded those feelings, and of the impressions and ideas which excited them. For this reason, "taste" is their fundamental concern. Numerous inquiries were devoted to the faculty itself; and when this faculty was found to be derivative, consequent on special modes of action and interaction of other faculties, such inquiry could be complex enough. Even when the faculty of taste was not itself the major subject, it was still fundamental to every inquiry. Addison had declared that the arts were "to deduce their Laws and Rules from the general Sense and Taste of Mankind, and not from the Principles of those Arts themselves"; [2] and though his "Pleasures of the Imagination" papers were not devoted to analyzing the operation of taste and imagination (for he considered the efficient causes inexplicable), his attention was merely shifted to those qualities, the beautiful, great, and uncommon, which were sensed and judged by those faculties. Hutcheson's "internal sense," likewise, is a kind of taste; and his overarching purpose in the "Inquiry concerning Beauty" was to establish the existence of such a discriminating sense as propadeutic to his examination of morals in terms of similar senses. Gerard's *Essay on Taste* is only the most elaborate and analytical of a class of works common enough in this period, works having as their chief subject analysis of the faculty itself. Hume contributes his neat essay, "On the Standard of Taste." The treatises of Burke, Lord Kames, and Blair, those of Reid, Alison, and Knight open with accounts, some of them elaborate, of taste and associated faculties as a natural preliminary to examination of its objects. Stewart and Reynolds are exempted, one by his dialectical, the other by his philological, method from beginning with taste; yet one devotes a discourse, the other an essay to it subsequently. Price and Repton, too, disclose their views, though the fragmentary nature of Repton's works prevents a connected account, and Price takes the views of Burke for granted, merely introducing additions and alterations at need.

Granted, then, that though Gerard alone of the writers here studied devotes the greater part of his treatise to this as his central theme, all the writers of the century begin with presuppositions about, and most with explicit discourses on, taste. The psychology of taste which all these writers employed was genetic rather than *a priori:* their analysis of mental phenomena was essentially historical, depending always upon determination of original impressions and the reduction of more complex ideas and feelings to combinations of these primary materials. *An Inquiry into the Original of Our Ideas of Beauty and Virtue, A Philosophical Inquiry into the Origin of Our Ideas of the Sublime and Beautiful:* such titles are testimony. And when Payne Knight entitled his work *An Analytical Inquiry into the Principles of Taste,* the implication was the same: this *analysis* is the breaking down of the complicated phenomena to simpler elements and principles of combination. It is this trait of the eighteenth-century British systems, I take it, which is so often called "empirical." Continental rationalisms, and those British systems of the next century which were modeled on the German, also find their principles in psychology. But they are not genetic or historical; they appeal instead to *a priori* principles and categories of thought. It is the habit of the eighteenth-century British philosophers to analyze those principles and categories, to find explicable what the rationalists take as primary givens; and this analysis, these experiential explanations, are a major feature of what is called empiricism. Such empiricism is, to be sure, a very different thing in the writings of a Hume or Alison from what it is in a Reid or Kames; but even those Scots who took issue with the systematic reductions of Hume, who asserted a host of primary and original sensibilities and powers, still used their greater number of principles as Hume used his more simple and elegant postulates—used them, that is, as simple elements into which the parts of more complex phenomena could be resolved, and from the effects of which the effects of those more complex phenomena could be calculated.

The notion of an unanalyzable *gestalt* would be a fiction to these writers: the whole is resolvable into and explicable by its elementary parts and the relations connecting them. Alison's theory is the type of this mode of philosophizing in aesthetics, both in the simplicity of its principles and in the intricacy of its analyses. Reynolds—and Shaftesbury, too—is exceptional to this generalization, for his dialectical way of thinking requires neither such a set of elementary notions nor such analysis of complexes; the analogical principle of generality and particularity applies in one fashion or another to every branch of his subject. Yet most of Reynolds' dicta lend themselves readily to statement in the more conventional mode; Reynolds, too, is psychologically oriented, and only gives the faculty psychology of his age an unusual dialectical twist.

That taste should be the fundamental concept in the aesthetics of the eighteenth century is a consequence of the philosophizing of criticism. One of the tendencies Crane has noted in the evolution of neoclassical literary criticism is "an important shift of emphasis in the critical writing of the mid-eighteenth century—a shift that exalted the philosopher (in the current sense of an inquirer into the operations of the mind) over the artist or the mere critic as the expert best qualified to determine the rules of art and that served, hence, to bring about, within criticism, a sharper separation between criticism itself, considered as a codification of past artistic experience, and the 'demands of nature,' on which its precepts and judgments, if they are to be valid, must ultimately rest." [3] The subject of the present book has automatically selected for comment those writers of whom this new method was most characteristic: for to extract and refine the sublime and beautiful wherever they are imbedded in nature or in art requires some "tincture of philosophy" in those who would mine such ore. The rules and conventions of literary criticism might enable many a criticaster to pronounce on particular works with no more painful consequence than triteness, and even that might be redeemed by novelty of subject; but in the more abstract and philosophical examination of the beautiful, to be trite is to be worthless—only the logic of system is of value here. In aesthetics, accordingly, some degree of philosophic system was present from the first; the new character noted by Crane in the literary criticism of mid-century began in the "philosophical criticism" with Hutcheson. After Hutcheson's *In-*

quiry, no writer could pretend to importance as an aesthetician without credentials as a philosopher, or at any rate without a native bent for analysis and systematization.

Not only, then, was this mode of aesthetics founded on psychology, but upon an empirical, genetic, and usually associationist psychology: philosophic principles were sought in human nature, philosophic method was found in a mental atomism of elements and laws of combination. Such an orientation directs attention away from the technical aspects of artistic construction and towards the universal properties of natural or artificial objects which affect the perceiving mind. It is the perceiving mind, moreover, not the mind as creative, from which principles are drawn. Any psychology accounts of course for both perception and creation, taste and genius; but there may still be a difference of priority and emphasis. It would be plausible to argue that one difference between neo-classical literary criticism and that of the Romantic period is that in neo-classical criticism the principles of examination and evaluation are drawn ultimately from the nature of the audience, in Romantic criticism from the powers of the artist. It is true equally of the aesthetics of the eighteenth century as of its criticism that principles are derived from the mind beholding beauty or sublimity, the mind in which these characters subsisted as feelings. The artist's powers, as represented in his works, are considered as among the sources of aesthetic pleasure, and, like the technical problems of artistic construction, are treated subordinately to the emotions of taste. Gerard, to be sure, authored a lengthy and closely reasoned *Essay on Genius,* a work which, like Alison's *Essays on Taste,* works out in detail a mental atomism; but this essay has little to the purpose on the beautiful or the sublime. And so with the other studies of genius in the period; except for generalizations on the connection of original genius, the sublime, and primitive society where human nature shoots wild and free, or on the correlation of powers of imagination with a vague Longinian sublimity, there is little attempt to bring such studies into relation with the beautiful, sublime, picturesque.

Indeed, the chief discussion of the artist's work in this tradition (setting aside Reynolds' *Discourses,* and even these tend to resolve genius into taste) is in the controversy on the picturesque. But although Gilpin might write essays on sketching landscape, his central concern is the cultivation of the perceiving taste through the knowledge, and practice, of art; and his picturesque traveler, though he sets out on his rambles to find scenes of art from the hand of nature, returns preferring nature unimproved to the tinsel efforts of art. Repton, as a practicing artist concerned to justify his art and himself as a professor of it, uses his status only to authorize his analyses of taste. Price and Knight, again, have to do with genius or art only to the extent that they wish, partly by study of the works of art, to form a taste which will both guide artists and gratify amateurs.

The beautiful, sublime, and picturesque being feelings raised up in the mind from impressions and associated ideas, it was natural that the mind as perceiving rather than creating should have been the focus of discussion. At the same time, another circumstance in the nature of the subject militated against extensive consideration of art itself. Beauty, sublimity, and picturesqueness are found in nature as well as in art. A transcendental aesthetician, acknowledging this fact, might see in it only an excellent reason for beginning with, and largely confining himself to, art: for the whole includes the part, and to determine the beauty of art necessarily determines also that simpler and less complete beauty of nature. But this reasoning is plausible only if method is not analytic and genetic: for if we are to resolve the beauty of the complex into the beauties of its components and their relations, we will not be tempted to start with the whole. We will begin instead with the elementary and original—the elements being original not only in a logical but also in a chronological sense. What is it in colors which fascinates the child? What is the taste of men uncorrupted by artifical society—the primitives of an heroic age, the untutored but feeling rustic, the country gentleman remote from the fashions of London, or the sophisticated connoisseur whose very sophistication enables him to allow for the effects of custom, education, and vogue? What is the etymology of "picturesque"? To what objects was the epithet "beautiful" first applied? Questions such as these come naturally to the mind which habitually thinks in this vein. Since nature is prior to art both in the history of our experience and in the order of creation, and since nature is the simpler, we begin with nature—or, when we do employ art works as data, we are likely to ignore or minimize in them those characteristics distinctively artificial. In nature, then, and increasingly in natural scenery— in the gilded colors of sunsets, the tangled intricacies of wooded glens, the formless might of stormy oceans—we find our problems and data. When these data have yielded to our analyses, when we have in hand our principles of unity in variety, of the association of moral traits with line and color, or whatever they may be—then, and only then, may we approach the complicated and derivative products of art. From them we derive additional principles: we discern the influence of design and of fitness (or, if we have seen design and fitness in the works of nature, we see them here in a new relationship); we uncover the effects of imitation; and we one by one account for the differentiae of art from nature.

It remains a constant characteristic of these aestheticians—Reynolds excepted—that their analyses apply to natural objects first, or to artificial objects not distinguished from natural, and only by secondary elaboration to art works as differentiated from natural things. There is yet another common characteristic consequent on their taking as fundament human nature: that nature, being common to all men, or at any rate having common potentialities, implies that there is a normal taste. To exhibit the standard of taste is an object at which all these writers aim. Crane has noted that in neo-classical literary criticism there was a shift in emphasis between the age of Dryden and that of Johnson, that the standard was at first rested chiefly on rules induced from the works sanctioned by universal consensus, that as criticism became more philosophical the standard came to be grounded more on theories of human nature.[4] The aestheticians we are here studying put the standard from the first on the basis of human nature; though some still laid stress on the argument from consensus as well (Blair, for instance, or Reynolds, whose principle of generality naturally accords with that argument), others skeptically eschew it. Gerard and Knight are as aware as any modern relativist made skeptical by excess of knowledge, that there is no consensus except within a cultural tradition, that even taken over many ages the judgment of Peking and Tokyo does not coincide with that of Athens and London. Indeed, so long as taste is considered merely as a species of sensation it does not admit of a standard; not only do cultures vary, but each man's constitution and experience determine his peculiar likings and aversions, and these are for him preferable to any other's.

Yet each of our writers owed allegiance to the standard, or to a standard; and many—Burke, Gerard, Hume, Lord Kames, Reynolds, Knight, Stewart—devised explicit arguments to demonstrate a rightness in taste. Each might justify the standard by his own peculiar principles—Hume by shifting the argument from the impressions of sensibility to the idea of critical competence, Kames by appealing to original senses which testify to the universality and perfection of human nature, Reynolds by using his contrary of the one and the many, Burke by examining the common basis of human faculties in the external senses. But their works were all (in the language of Hogarth's subtitle) "Written with a View of Fixing the Fluctuating Ideas of Taste." For it is possible to examine the causes of our preferences and aversions, to determine which are unavoidable, which accidental; which universal to all men, which common to our culture, our era, or our class, which peculiar to ourselves. The effect on us of a complex whole can be analyzed, reduced to the operation of simple causes. Our response to these simple elements may be a matter of feeling, and the common feelings of mankind may for these be a standard; but the proper response to the complex whole becomes a matter of computation after such analysis. Taste as judgment is referred to principles and is conscious of grounds; it is (as Blair put it) "a sort of compound power, in which the light of the understanding always mingles, more or less, with the feelings of sentiment." [5] All the treatises of the century are implicitly determinations of the standard: if (for instance) the sublime be what Burke or Kames or Alison avers, and produced by the causes assigned, and we feel it not—then we feel amiss. The analytic method of this tradition is the method *par excellence* not merely of showing that there is a standard, but of determining what that standard is. The dialectic method of Shaftesbury and Reynolds pronounces with equal force that there is a true Taste, a true Beauty, but the showing forth of that taste and that beauty depends less on cold precision of analysis, more on the cultivation and eloquence of the dialectician.

So far, I have been concerned with traits common to all, or almost all, systems of the century. Was there, then, no change, no progress? Certainly there is no simple and straightforward development, no progress from shadowy intuition to the blaze of full illumination. Neither the characteristic subject matter, the philosophic principles, the prevailing method, nor even the doctrines changed in any way lending itself to ready generalization. Intellectual history, like biological, is a record of haphazard mutation and opportunistic development. In just this random way the century had opened with a triad of aesthetic characters: Addison's uncommon, great, and beautiful. Novelty, which is not co-ordinate with the great and the beautiful, remained in the discussion for a time: Hutcheson mentions it, Akenside adopts it in the first edition of his *Pleasures of Imagination*, Gerard allows it to stand as one of the internal senses. But Hume and Hogarth ignored it, and Burke struck it out, one would think for once and all, as a co-ordinate character; but there is no system in the history of systems, and Reid—in 1785!—again introduces novelty as an organizing topic, though very properly rejecting its claims to independent status.

The division of this book into two parts implies a more important shift in subject matter: beautiful and sublime become beautiful, sublime, and picturesque. Yet note: Alison, even in 1811, devotes scarcely a paragraph to the picturesque, nor is picturesqueness a major topic for Stewart. We can say truly, only that the picturesque is a topic introduced by Gilpin, and which was with some later writers a major focus of interest. Whether a writer after Gilpin finds the picturesque a topic of engrossing importance and co-ordinate with beauty and sublimity (like Price), or though important not co-ordinate (like Knight), or not important (like Alison)—these variations are functions of the systems, and the systems do not fall into a chronological pattern. The analyst can note that it was the predominance of Burke's special view of beauty which led to the distinction of the picturesque by Gilpin, and that the inadequacies of Gilpin's analysis opened the way to fresh explorations by Price and Knight: but these are the vagaries of historical accident, or at any rate the effects of extra-philosophical causes, not the inevitable rush of intellectual orthogenesis.

Another shift accompanies the evolution of the picturesque, perhaps partly causes it. Discussion of scenery and gardening runs through the century—Addison is eloquent on these topics. But as the picturesque came into favor as a taste and as a topic, the discussion of landscape and of landscape gardening came to occupy a far larger, often an overwhelmingly predominant, place in the discussion. The works of the end of the century abound alike with detached analysis of the forms, colors, and textures of scenery, with practical rules for arranging Nature to suit man's convenience or for disarranging her to suit his wilder fancy, and with poetical rhapsodies on the delights, aesthetic, moral, or religious, which Nature affords.

The philosophic method employed throughout this tradition of discussion of the beautiful, sublime, and picturesque was, as I have suggested, analytic and genetic;[6] yet some writers within the tradition performed but superficial analyses, others pursued more searching inquiries; and various authors resolved the gross phenomena into different elemental principles. A sketch of the varieties of causal explanation adduced has been included in my Introduction; but a recapitulation in different terms may not be useless here. Shaftesbury and Reynolds, it should be noted, stand pretty much outside the tradition methodologically, for though they, like the more literal and differential writers, grounded their systems on psychological principles, their method of inquiry was dialectical and organic, and their Beauty one, not a set of related beauties. Considering, however, the other writers—

Addison distinguished the three characters, great, uncommon, and beautiful, and noted some of the leading components of these characters—that, for instance, there is beauty of color, of proportion, of arrangement. Yet there is little further analysis of these components; other obvious physical varieties both of sublimity and beauty are omitted; and the complicated interconnections between the physical and mental worlds are quite ignored, even though Addison had available a rudimentary associational theory.

Hutcheson's far more philosophical theory pursued the analytic approach much further. His purpose, the demonstration of an internal sense of beauty, led him to adopt a single analytical device—the notion of uniformity in variety—with which to reduce all forms of beauty, including that beauty of mind which Addison had left out of account, to a single formula. But though physical, moral, and intellectual beauties are all treated by Hutcheson, his system (in which association plays a limited role, and often one of interference with the perception of beauty) does not lend itself to penetrating investigation of their commingling and reciprocal influence; nor does it encourage exploration of the sublime alongside that of beauty.

In the philosophy of Hume, an associationism is employed to analyze most of the phenomena of human nature to their ultimate constituents; but Hume's aesthetic is sketchy. Rather disappointingly, he does not find much connection between physical and moral beauty, has little to say on those beauties immediately pleasing, makes no effort to separate design and fitness from utility; these and other negligences are, of course, the consequence of Hume's always mentioning beauty incidentally to some other object of analysis—beauty itself was never the focus of his attention. Disappointing, too, is the fragment of a theory of sublimity which Hume invented, suggestive, like the essays on taste and tragedy, of the subtle analysis which his powerful psychology could have yielded had it been turned upon such subjects.

The method of Hume was developed by Gerard, and more rigorously and elaborately by Alison; but before Gerard published, Hogarth's theory was brought forward, employing a method very different from Hume's but equally characteristic of this tradition.

Hogarth resolves beauty into a half-dozen elements—fitness, variety, &c.—all which, however, are reduced to traits of lines: line becomes the element into which all manner of beauty is analyzed. Like Hutcheson, Hogarth does not develop a distinct aesthetic of the sublime, for this his linear analysis would not readily allow; rather, he reckons greatness only an excellence supervening to beauty. And for Hogarth, as for all analytic writers, moral and intellectual beauty is different from physical; though some dispositions of lines can signify moral traits, they are not beautiful by reason of this signification.

In the theory of Gerard, eclectic though it is, Hume's method is that largely pursued; the analysis is carried out in terms of ideas, impressions, and operations of imagination. Though Gerard (like most eighteenth-century writers) uses the term "association" to designate the less close, even the capricious or disruptive, linkages among ideas and impressions, his system is, in a wider sense of the term, associational; and its breadth of scope, flexibility of analysis, and subtlety of argument are partly attributable to Gerard's use of this powerful analytical tool. As in Hume, the connection of physical and moral beauty consists in the dependence of both taste and virtue on operations of imagination, in the similarity of the pleasures from these two kinds of excellence, and in the reciprocal influence of character and taste. Such connections of resemblance and of cause and effect are the marks of a system which essentially differentiates ethics from aesthetics. All of the analytic systems make such differentiation, for even in Hutcheson, in Reid, and in Alison the beauty of virtue is distinct from the virtue.

The system of Burke, more radically than most of the theories of this school, treats beauty and sublimity in terms of constituent elemental qualities, each producing its own part of the total effect without interaction: the beauty of an object has so many quanta of the beauty of smoothness, and so forth. Burke's logic, designed to separate the components of complex objects, and with a strong bias towards the discovery of simple natural causes operating directly upon our sensibility, is well adapted to such a system. And although Burke makes use of association, his more distinctive analysis is into physiological stimuli; since the separate elements of beauty act individually upon the nervous system without being blended, as it were, in the mind, Burke's atomism comes to lay a good deal more stress on the atoms than on the relations among them, which are largely reduced to a matter of addition and subtraction. This trait of the system produces a certain dogmatic inflexibility and a negligence of context in assessing the aesthetic effects of the simple properties. All of those theories, in fact, which suppose distinct responses by external or internal senses to separate aesthetic elements necessarily share this inflexibility, for the sense is always prepared to respond to the appropriate stimulus. The physiological apparatus of Burke's system, and of Hogarth's too, makes it especially liable to this defect. The defect can be minimized by choice of a single principle capable of many kinds of applications—as in Hutcheson—or by development of a large number of senses—as in Kames. Nonetheless, the more purely associational analyses have an inherent capacity for modulations and contextual adjustments which the systems reposing on a sense or senses lack.

Burke's postulated physiological mechanism enables him to draw the sharpest of separations between beauty and sublimity, and precludes him from admitting novelty, the picturesque, or any third character into his system. So definite was Burke's division of beauty and sublimity that even those later writers who wished to deny any absolute contrariety of the two characters—Knight, or Stewart, or (outside the analytic group) Reynolds—still often used the terms as if they constituted an exclusive and exhaustive distinction, or employed the concepts as organizing principles for their discussions.

The distinguishing feature of the system of Lord Kames, and one which he derived from, or as a member of, that sect of Scottish philosophy which arose to combat the reductive analyses of Hume, is the assertion of a multitude of original perceptions through separate senses provided by Providence for their reception. The consequence of this bent is, of course, that aesthetic phenomena are readily broken down into a variety of atomic elements, each class perceived through a special sense. The components are so varied that analyses of very considerable complexity can be worked out, and the results are sufficiently precise that Kames can build from them a synthetic system of criticism, elaborate for the literary arts, less so for gardening and architecture.

Blair's purpose is very like that of Lord Kames: to work out an analysis the results of which can be put to use in synthesis of a theory of the literary arts. But Blair's interest is more literary and less philosophical than that of Kames; his principles are fewer, his results more general, his synthetic theory more detached from the preceding analysis. Clearly inferior to Kames in connecting his aesthetic with his criticism, and kept by his eagerness to get on with the criticism from penetrating very far in the aesthetic, Blair nonetheless has one advantage: he is free of Kames's penchant for finding special senses and final causes, and he not only keeps open the investigation of efficient causes but even makes some effort to resolve the various modes of sublimity into one by association of ideas (though allowing beauty to be one only through association of like feelings from the different modes of it). His deficiency in middle principles of analysis, however, his tendency to leap from first principle to particular instance, leaves Blair's system poorly verified and somewhat meager.

With Reid, the sublime and beautiful were brought within the framework of a philosophic system, and both the merits and defects of Reid's aesthetic follow from that system. Because of Reid's theory of direct perception of the outer world, he finds that beauty and sublimity subsist as real and objective excellences in things; and since matter itself can not be "excellent" except as connected with mind by some relation, beauty and sublimity must ultimately derive from mind. But Reid brings forward little evidence to support this position; it rests on deduction from the principles of his metaphysics, which is in turn established intuitionally. Neither Reid's purpose in treating beauty nor his characteristic method of thought lead him to undertake detailed or subtle analysis, and his aesthetic system, saving only the principle that all beauty is from mind, contains little novelty either in doctrine or in demonstration.

The analytic and genetic method is given its most systematic, its most exhaustive, development by Alison. Employing an associational psychology, operating wholly in terms of ideas and habits of imagination, Alison develops an aesthetic both comprehensive and subtle, equally adapted to formulating broad principles and to making delicate adjustment to particular contexts. Not only does Alison work out all the permutations of the elements of his system—the component ideas and the modes of their combination—but he employs the most rigorous inductive method, consciously organizing data and contriving experiments to meet the requirements of inductive logic. Hume, Gerard, and Alison had, of these writers, the most complete grasp of the kind of logic appropriate to an analytic system, recognizing that neither deduction from principles of human nature (whether these be indemonstrable or established inductively) nor induction from the raw data of taste is alone adequate for proof in aesthetics, wherein plurality of causes and intermixture of effects abound. Both deductive and inductive inference must be used, and their consilience alone constitutes proof. But since the powers and sensibilities of human nature which enter into aesthetic response are several, and their operations more than ordinarily subtle, the deductive process can not be pursued safely without some view of the law towards which demonstration is to be directed; and such view is afforded by empirical generalization from the data of taste. Here is the use of consensus: to suggest empirical laws which can serve as hypotheses towards which the ratiocinative part of the process can be oriented. The ratiocination is the principal part of the proof, and that part from which the bulk of the doctrine will be evolved. Gerard lays perhaps too much emphasis on successively ascending inductions rising to more and more general laws, and tends to see the deduction as only verificative of results already arrived at inductively; and yet he does not select his data (in the *Essay on Taste* at any rate) to meet express conditions for such induction. Alison's concern is to establish the most general laws of taste, those from which the more particular rules of judgment and criticism can be deduced; and such first principles must be proved, if they are proved at all, inductively. It is in the perfection of inductive techniques for establishing these most general laws that Alison is distinguished beyond any other writer of this tradition, beyond even Hume, from whom much of the technique may have been borrowed.

It might be argued that one line of development within this tradition is in this very matter: the perfecting of inductive technique and the co-ordination of inductive and deductive procedures in the process of proof. But there is no consistent evolution. Hume, well before mid-century, had in hand such a logic; Gerard and Alison advance beyond him in applying it to aesthetic subjects; but contemporary with these men are Gilpin, Repton, and Price, with little conception of it—or, if it be judged unfair to cite men without pretensions to philosophy, Blair and Reid will serve as well. Even Payne Knight, though he is a systematic writer, has less grasp of inductive procedure than Alison. All that can be urged, I think, is that three major writers at the end of the century—Alison, Knight, and Stewart—had a more philosophic command of logic as applied to aesthetics than did any earlier cluster of writers. This is negligible as a generalization, especially if we reflect that Alison, in 1790, had advanced beyond the later writers.

Addison had set in progress the inquiry concerning the sublime and beautiful by discriminating the characters without explaining the mode of their operation; his very abandonment of the quest for efficient causes opened the question to other writers. In much the same way, Gilpin initiated a new phase of the discussion by introducing the character of the picturesque without finding any plausible explanation of its influence upon us. Addison had few predecessors and no adequate tools of analysis; Gilpin, though numerous systems lay ready to his hand, yet failed so signally to define his problem with accuracy, and performed his inductions with so little care, that his effort served chiefly as an incitement to later inquirers infected with his taste but disappointed in his analysis of its objects.

The theory of Price, brought forward shortly after, displays an interesting shift in the technique of analysis; for though Price stands forth as the champion of Burke, he defends Burke's theory mostly in foreign terms. For Burke the essential device used to explain the sublime and beautiful was a physiological hypothesis; but though Price does affirm allegiance even to this, it is not easy to justify the picturesque by the theory of Burke. The real, though but half-acknowledged, basis of Price's theory is associational. Burke, too, of course, had employed associational psychology; but in Price, what was subordinate in Burke has become predominant. The shift is real; but it is an imperfect indication of a general transformation of aesthetic theory into purely associational terms. Hume had been an associationist before Burke; Knight, writing after Gerard and Alison, after Price had attenuated the physiological part of Burke's theory, still re-introduces into the discussion a new physiological hypothesis to account for the picturesque.

The special merit of Price's method is his skilful comparison and opposition of the aesthetic characters, of beauty, sublimity, picturesqueness, and their opposites, through detailed analyses of the elements of line, texture, light, and color, and of the composition of these elements into distinct characters. But his theory was left exposed to much misunderstanding because of the confusion in which, after all, the psychological mechanisms were left, the wavering between a notion of direct action upon the nervous system and an associational theory the reaches of which were not fully explored. Knight's major work, the *Analytical Inquiry*, left nothing to conjecture, for it is organized faculty by faculty, the analysis moving by stages from simple sensation to refined judgment and complicated passion. It is in the clarity with which the beautiful, sublime, and picturesque are related to these faculties that Knight's acuteness and originality is displayed. The ambiguities of the terms "beautiful" and "picturesque" are resolved with unusual elegance through Knight's theory of transitive meanings, which permits him to assign the different meanings to the objects and operations of the different faculties.

Repton's aesthetic is more applied than theoretic; his general principles, repeatedly though not always consistently enumerated, are never systematically evolved either from empirical induction or from a theory of human nature. Taken as topics of argument, however, they allow Repton to draw up rules for the practice of his art, though the rules do not follow so inevitably from the principles as to prevent Repton's taste from undergoing considerable change in the course of his career. But Repton's aesthetic is too much an *ad hoc* justification of his style in gardening and architecture to dwell upon his method.

Stewart, however, introduces a novelty in method. Still more than the analyses of other writers of this tradition, his is historical and genetic. Alison had been content to trace each of the various modes and forms of beauty separately to its mental root; Knight to rest each upon an appropriate faculty and to treat the faculties in a sequence corresponding to the order of their development; and so with other writers—each traced the kinds of beauty individually to their origins. Stewart, however, and Stewart alone, takes the progress of the mind to be in principle like a chain, and he follows it link by link. The analytic device by which he traces the chain is the theory of transitive meanings which he adopted from Knight; the progress he studies is a progress in the wider and more various applications of terms. Stewart's view that inductive method in mental philosophy may concern itself with the laws describing the connections of matter and mind, but not with the manner of that union, allows him freedom from the rigidities imposed by physiological hypotheses or the postulation of internal senses; but his own conception of linear and stepwise development along a thread of transitive meanings imposes its own restrictions.

My partial review of the writers of this school does not disclose strongly marked tendencies or striking improvements; rather, it presents, within the limits of a broad common method, a scattered variety of particular systems. The different purposes of the authors partly account for this variety—whether the purpose is to complete a philosophical system (as with Stewart) or to prepare a prolegomenon to some other branch of philosophy (as with Hutcheson), whether to treat the nature and conditions of an art (as with Reynolds) or to justify a particular style in an art (as in Repton), whether to find the roots of the principles of taste (as with Alison) or to form a new taste (as with Gilpin). The philosophic allegiance of the authors is a factor too—whether they are dialecticians (like Shaftesbury and Reynolds), thorough analysts (like Hume and Alison), or intuitionists (like Kames and Reid). Each system, again, reflects the state and momentum of current discussion: a writer may introduce a new problem—this Addison did; or may add a new dimension to discussion already in progress—which Gilpin did; may incorporate previous efforts into a more comprehensive theory— as Burke did Hogarth's, or Price Burke's; or may demolish false views which had gained currency—as did Knight. And doubtless each system reflects the tastes of its author and of its age; Hogarth's theory might be used to justify one set of preferences, Price's another. But after all these causes, philosophical and extra-philosophical, are allowed for, there is still, as it appears to me, an element of surprise and originality; the different habits of thought arise from causes too subtle to be categorized. There is perhaps an analogy with mutations in the biological world: causes presumably exist, but all except the grossest escape us. There is little pattern, even in retrospect; and no prediction.

NOTES

BIBLIOGRAPHY

INDEX

NOTES

Introduction

1. See Ronald S. Crane, "Interpretation of Texts and the History of Ideas," *College English*, II (May, 1941), 755–65. See also Crane's "History Versus Criticism in the University Study of Literature," *English Journal* (College Edition), XXIV (October, 1935), 645–67, for a statement of the nature of a *literal* history of literature.

2. [Joseph Addison], *The Spectator*, No. 29 (April 3, 1711), ed. G. Gregory Smith (London: Dent, 1897), I, 109.

3. Archibald Alison, *Essays on the Nature and Principles of Taste* (4th ed.; Edinburgh, 1815), I, xxvii–xxviii; the quotation was added in the second edition (1811), just a century from the time Addison wrote.

4. In every writer treated there is the concession of an organic pleasure in harmony and in light or color; Alison alone denies that these organic pleasures are a part of the aesthetic response.

5. I take Greenfield to be the author of the anonymous *Essays on the Sources of the Pleasures Received from Literary Compositions* (London, 1809), which is more commonly ascribed to Edward Mangin.

Chapter 1

1. [Joseph Addison], *The Spectator*, No. 409 (June 19, 1712), ed. cit., VI, 52.

2. *Ibid.*, p. 49.

3. *Ibid.*

4. *Ibid.*, p. 51.

5. *Ibid.*, No. 411 (June 21, 1712), ed. cit., VI, 56.

6. *Ibid.*, No. 417 (June 28, 1712), ed. cit., VI, 78.

7. *Ibid.*, No. 411 (June 21, 1712), ed. cit., VI, 56.

8. *Ibid.*, p. 57. There are two possibilities altogether, not three (as Addison's grammar might suggest): ideas of memory include those of things absent; ideas of things fictitious involve powers of abstraction and combination.

9. See Clarence D. Thorpe, "Addison's Theory of the Imagination as 'Perceptive Response,'" *Papers of the Michigan Academy of Science, Arts, and Letters*, XXI (1935; Ann Arbor: University of Michigan Press, 1936), 512; and

Martin Kallich, "The Association of Ideas and Critical Theory: Hobbes, Locke, and Addison," *ELH*, XII (December, 1945), 309.

10. [Addison], *Spectator*, No. 416 (June 27, 1712), ed. cit., VI, 73. The italics are mine.

11. *Ibid.*, No. 411 (June 21, 1712), ed. cit., VI, 58. Thorpe concludes, after finding various components of Addison's psychology in Hobbes, Locke, and Descartes, that it was Descartes who "furnished most clearly the conception of the imagination as an intermediary between sense and understanding" ("Addison's Theory of the Imagination as 'Perceptive Response,'" *Papers of the Michigan Academy of Science, Arts, and Letters*, XXI [1935], 529.) But this is a commonplace in philosophy since the Greeks; we need locate no single source.

12. [Mark Akenside], *The Pleasures of Imagination* (London, 1744), Book I, ll. 139–46. In the second edition (1772), written after Burke's *A Philosophical Enquiry into the Origin of our Ideas of the Sublime and Beautiful* (1757), Akenside adopts (Book I, ll. 180–89) Burke's more logical twofold division.

13. Joseph Warton, *The Adventurer*, No. 80 (August 11, 1753).

14. Daniel Webb, *An Inquiry into the Beauties of Painting; and into the Merits of the Most Celebrated Painters, Ancient and Modern* (Dublin, 1764), pp. 35–36. (The first edition of Webb's book appeared in 1760.)

15. Thomas Reid, *Essays on the Intellectual Powers of Man*, in *The Works of Thomas Reid . . .* , ed. Sir William Hamilton (8th ed.; Edinburgh: Maclachlan and Stewart, 1880), I, 493. See *infra*, pp. 151–52, for discussion of Reid's view on the triad in question.

16. Samuel H. Monk, *The Sublime: A Study in Critical Theories in XVIII–Century England* (New York: Modern Language Association, 1935), pp.10–56 (on Longinian sublimity) and 56–59 (on Addison).

17. The eighteen papers on *Paradise Lost* are in the *Spectator*, every sixth paper beginning with No. 267.

18. [Addison], *Spectator*, No. 315 (March 1, 1712), ed. cit., IV, 257.

19. *Ibid.*, p. 255.

20. *Ibid.*, No. 412 (June 23, 1712), ed. cit., VI, 59.

21. Theodore McGinnes Moore, "The Background of Edmund Burke's Theory of the Sublime (1660–1759)," (Unpublished Ph.D. dissertation, Cornell University, 1933), p. 136.

22. [Addison], *Spectator*, No. 412 (June 23, 1712), ed. cit., VI, 59.

23. *De Sublimitate* 35.

24. See Ernest Tuveson, "Space, Deity, and the 'Natural Sublime,'" *MLQ*, XII (March, 1951), 20–38.

25. [Addison], *Spectator*, No. 412 (June 23, 1712), ed. cit., VI, 60.

26. Thus our delight in rivers, fountains, and the like is explained by referring it to the perpetual shifting of the scene (*ibid.*, pp. 60–61).

27. *Ibid.*, p. 61.

28. *Ibid.*, No. 369 (May 3, 1712), ed. cit., V, 198.

29. See Edmund Burke, *A Philosophical Enquiry into the Origin of Our Ideas of the Sublime and Beautiful*, i. 10, in *The Works of the Right Honourable Edmund Burke* (London: Oxford, 1906), I, 94–95. Compare Richard Payne Knight, *An Analytical Inquiry into the Principles of Taste* (3d ed.; London, 1806), i. 5. 27, and ii. 2. 57, pp. 86–88, and 185–86.

30. [Addison], *Spectator*, No. 412 (June 23, 1712), ed. cit., VI, 62.

31. *Ibid.*, No. 413 (June 24, 1712), ed. cit., VI, 63.

32. *Ibid.*

33. Victor Hamm is confused by this overlapping, arguing that Addison illogically treats artifacts under secondary pleasures, though they are present objects, and that in general, Nature and the plastic arts should be handled under primary pleasures, recollections and poetry under secondary, or that (from another point of view) Nature ought to be primary and all art secondary; see his "Addison and the Pleasures of the Imagination," *MLN*, LII (November, 1937), 498–500.

34. [Addison], *Spectator*, No. 414 (June 25, 1712), ed. cit., VI, 66.

35. *Ibid.*, No. 477 (September 6, 1712), ed. cit., VII, 14.

36. *Ibid.*, p. 17.

37. *Ibid.*, No. 415 (June 26, 1712), ed. cit., VI, 71.

38. F. Gregory Smith points out that Addison's passage is an almost verbatim transcript from John Evelyn's translation of *A Parallel of the Antient Architecture with the Modern; Written in French by Roland Fréart, Sieur de Chambray* . . . (London, 1664), pp. 10–11. See *Spectator*, No. 415 (June 26, 1712), ed. cit., VI, 71–72 for the passage (wherein Addison concedes a debt to Fréart), and VI, 291 for the note.

39. *Ibid.*, p. 71.

40. Burke, *Sublime and Beautiful*, ii. 9, in *Works*, I, 125, and (for the physiological explanation) iv. 11–13, in *Works*, I, 184–88.

41. [Addison], *Spectator*, No. 416 (June 27, 1712), ed. cit., VI, 75.

42. *Ibid.*, No. 418 (June 30, 1712), ed. cit., VI, 84.

43. *Ibid.*, p. 81.

44. *Ibid.* Addison remarks that "it would not be very difficult to cast under their proper Heads those contrary Objects [to the great, the beautiful, the novel], which are apt to fill it [the fancy] with Distaste and Terrour; for the Imagination is as liable to Pain as Pleasure" (*ibid.*, No. 421 [July 3, 1712], ed. cit., VI, 92), but he leaves this problem almost untouched. Are these contrary objects disagreeable apart from expectation, sympathy, and association? Addison's instances all disturb the passions via the imagination rather than pain the imagination as such.

45. *Ibid.*, No. 418 (June 30, 1712), ed. cit., VI, 81.

46. That this account is not complete is clear from the point made by Hume that we are the more affected and delighted in proportion as we are absorbed by the play and forget that it is an imitation.

47. [Addison], *Spectator*, No. 412 (June 23, 1712), ed. cit., VI, 62.

48. *Ibid.*, No. 416 (June 27, 1712), ed. cit., VI, 77.

49. Addison does not put forward the Cartesian account as one to which he necessarily subscribes; the passage presents hypothetically what "a Cartesian" *would* say. Addison's reiterated denials that the nature of the soul can be known seem, on the other hand, conclusive.

50. Clarence D. Thorpe, who has written more at length on Addison's aesthetics than any other modern scholar, sums up Addison's achievements in similar terms; see "Addison's Contribution to Criticism," *The Seventeenth Century: Studies in the History of English Thought and Literature from Bacon to Pope, by Richard Foster Jones and Others Writing in His Honor* (Stanford,

Cal.: Stanford University Press, 1951), p. 324. Thorpe's concern with evolutionary development rather than logical structure leads him to view Addison's essay as "one of the great critical documents of all time," an estimate few will share.

51. Hugh Blair, *Lectures on Rhetoric and Belles Lettres*, iii (4th ed.; London, 1790), I, 55–56.

Chapter 2

1. Full title: *An Inquiry into the Original of Our Ideas of Beauty and Virtue; in Two Treatises. In Which the Principles of the Late Earl of Shaftsbury Are Explain'd and Defended, against the Author of the "Fable of the Bees" and the Ideas of Moral Good and Evil Are Establish'd, According to the Sentiments of the Antient Moralists. With an Attempt to Introduce a Mathematical Calculation in Subjects of Morality* (London, 1725). Editions followed in 1726, 1729, 1738 (the last in Hutcheson's lifetime), 1753, 1772.

2. London, 1728; another edition appeared at Dublin in 1728, later editions coming in 1730, 1742, 1751, 1756, 1769, 1772. Hutcheson's later works, including the posthumous *A System of Moral Philosophy* . . . (Glasgow and London, 1755), I shall not consider in the present account.

3. William Robert Scott, *Francis Hutcheson* (Cambridge: Cambridge University Press, 1900), p. 287.

4. Among the more useful recent studies is William Curtis Swabey's "Benevolence and Virtue," *Philosophical Review*, LII (September, 1943), 452–67. Swabey works in some qualifications apparently modifying Hutcheson's views, but these modifications are really present in Hutcheson in other forms.

5. Hutcheson, *Inquiry*, ii. 1. 1, p. 109. My references will be to the first edition, but I shall indicate treatise numbers (according to the system given in the text) and section numbers to facilitate reference to other editions.

6. *Ibid.*, Preface, p. vi.

7. *Ibid.*, p. viii.

8. *Ibid.*, i. 1, ed. cit., pp. 6–7.

9. *Ibid.*, i. 4, ed. cit., p. 35. R. L. Brett ("The Aesthetic Sense and Taste in the Literary Criticism of the Early Eighteenth Century," *RES*, XX [July, 1944], 199–2〉〉) works with a contrary of judgment and fancy, reason and taste, and finds accordingly that eighteenth-century critics tended to divide beauty into two species—one reasonable, one sensible. He sees the general and specific beauties of *Spectator* No. 412 in this light (thereby identifying reason with sex), and finds Hutcheson's relative beauty rational, since resemblance involves reason. But not so; resemblance must always in the final analysis be perceived immediately.

10. Hutcheson, *Inquiry*, i. 2, ed. cit., pp. 15–16.

11. *Ibid.*, i. 6, ed. cit., p. 75.

12. Scott, *Francis Hutcheson*, pp. 188 and 217 (in which last passage Scott tries to identify variety with novelty).

13. See Birkhoff, *Aesthetic Measure* (Cambridge, Mass.: Harvard University Press, 1933).

14. Hutcheson, *Inquiry*, i. 4, ed. cit., p. 39.

15. Alfred Owen Aldridge ("A French Critic of Hutcheson's Aesthetics," *MP*, XLV [February, 1948], 184) declares that this whole section "has no real

place in a treatise on aesthetics"; Scott, on the other hand, argues that "beauty, understood as regularity or uniformity, has always with Hutcheson a precise reference to an end, conceived by some intelligent 'designer' " (*Francis Hutcheson*, p. 191).

16. Hutcheson, *Inquiry*, i. 6, ed. cit., p. 76.

17. *Ibid.*, i. 8, ed. cit., pp. 93–97. There is a circularity in this argument: the sense is implanted to fit man for the world, and the world created to match the sense. All that is shown is self-consistency; the question eluded is, why *this* self-consistent system instead of some other?

18. See Hutcheson's statement in almost these words at the conclusion of the Introduction to the "Inquiry concerning Virtue."

19. Hutcheson, *Essay*, iii. 1. 1, ed. cit., pp. 5–6. In the *Inquiry*, ii. 5. 2, 3, ed. cit., pp. 197–201, honor and gratitude appear to involve distinct senses, but in any event both are reflections of our own goodness in the feelings of others, one involving personal obligation, the other detached.

20. See *Inquiry*, ii. 5. 7, ed. cit., pp. 209–15 for the clue which might serve to reduce the sense of dignity under the moral sense: the nobler faculties, abilities, and pleasures are less selfish or are presumably applied for public weal.

21. The nomenclature of the senses is that of the "Essay on the Nature and Conduct of the Passions" (1728), but the doctrine is all contained in the "Inquiry concerning the Original of our Ideas of Virtue or Moral Good" (1725), even though the earlier work is largely devoted to the moral sense. It is unnecessary and false to read these two works as successive stages in a march towards, or away from, Truth.

22. Hutcheson, *Essay*, Preface, ed. cit., pp. xvi–xvii.

23. *Ibid.*, iii. 3. 10, ed. cit., p. 165.

24. The formula is developed in *Inquiry*, ii. 3. 11, ed. cit., pp. 168–72. In the first edition there was some ambiguity about "I"—whether it stood for self-love or personal gain; the second edition clarified the matter by defining $I = S \times A$, wherein "I" is the moment of personal good, "S" is self-love, and "A" abilities.

25. For the analysis of sympathy, see David Hume, *A Treatise of Human Nature*, eds. T. H. Green and T. H. Grose, ii. 1. 11 (new ed.; London: Longmans, 1882), II, 111–14. Parts ii and iii of Book III of the *Treatise* are concerned with reduction of the moral sense to more original principles; for reduction of the public sense, see *Treatise*, iii. 2. 1, ed. cit., II, 255–56, where Hume flatly denies any love of mankind merely as such; and for the sense of honor see *Treatise*, iii. 1. 11, ed. cit., II, 110–17, a discussion which introduces the most elaborate account of sympathy in the *Treatise*. See also on this question the letters of 17 September 1739 and 10 January 1743, both to Hutcheson, in *The Letters of David Hume*, ed. J. Y. T. Greig (Oxford: Clarendon Press, 1932), I, 33–34 and 47–48.

26. Hutcheson, *Inquiry*, ii. 6. 3, ed. cit., p. 229.

27. *Ibid.*, ii. 6. 7, ed. cit., pp. 240–41. Number and measure exhibit absolute beauty (i. 4), metaphor and similitude relative beauty (*ibid.*). Prosopopeia is the figure eminent for moral beauty (*ibid.*, ii. 6. 7, ed. cit., p. 242).

28. Hutcheson, *Essay*, iii. 3. 3, ed. cit., p. 69. This sympathetic notion of virtue enters Hutcheson's thought more systematically than it does Lord Kames's; in section 3 of the "Essay on the Passions," Hutcheson is drawing out the sources

of our passions, and finds six passions arising from each of a number of senses. The sympathetic emotion of virtue gives rise to a *desire* of that virtue; if the imitation desired is successful, *self-approving joy* results; if not, *remorse*. Three corresponding feelings result from the reaction to vice.

29. Hutcheson, *Inquiry*, ii. 5. 8, ed. cit., pp. 217–18. On tragedy, see also *Essay*, iii. 3. 5 for discussion of the moral state and change of fortune of the protagonist. Hutcheson rather mars his analysis by adducing admiration of providence as one of the emotions of tragedy; pity is felt only if suffering is disproportionate to transgression—and if disproportionate, why admire providence?

30. Hutcheson, *Inquiry*, ii. 2. 8.

31. *Ibid.*, i. 6, ed. cit., p. 78.

32. Clarence DeWitt Thorpe, "Addison and Hutcheson on the Imagination," *ELH*, II (November, 1935), 233.

33. The essay is included in De Villette's *Oeuvres mêlées* (Dublin, 1750); I draw my information about it from Alfred Owen Aldridge's article, "A French Critic of Hutcheson's Aesthetics," *MP*, XLV (February, 1948), 169–84.

34. De Villette, *Oeuvres mêlées*, p. 158, as quoted by Aldridge, "A French Critic of Hutcheson's Aesthetics," *MP*, XLV, 178.

35. Aldridge states that "in considering merely the general outlines of Hutcheson's and De Villette's systems, we do not find fundamental differences. . . . De Villette does less to show us that Hutcheson's theory is wrong than that his essay is superficial and incomplete" ("A French Critic of Hutcheson's Aesthetics," *MP*, XLV, 183–84). It appears to me, however, that the difference is more fundamental, that similar doctrines are set upon different foundations.

Chapter 3

1. See Monk, *The Sublime, passim*; Gordon McKenzie, *Critical Responsiveness: A Study of the Psychological Current in Later Eighteenth-Century Criticism* ("University of California Publications in English," XX [1949]; Berkeley: University of California Press, 1949), *passim*; Teddy Brunius, *David Hume on Criticism* ("*Figura*, Studies Edited by the Institute of Art History, University of Uppsala," No. 2 [Stockholm: Almqvist and Wiksell, 1952]), p. 127; *et al.*

2. "Of the Standard of Taste" and "Of Tragedy" appeared, together with "The Natural History of Religion" and "Of the Passions," in *Four Dissertations* (London, 1757). My references are to the version in *Essays Moral, Political, and Literary*, eds. T. H. Green and T. H. Grose (London: Longmans, 1875).

Vols. I and II of the *Treatise* were published at London, 1739; Vol. III, London, 1740. My page references are to the edition of T. H. Green and T. H. Grose (new ed.; London: Longmans, 1882).

3. I shall not attempt in this brief chapter to comment on the immense body of secondary materials on Hume. Brunius discusses much scholarship on Hume's critical and aesthetic position in *David Hume on Criticism*, and himself enters into a lengthy account—from which, however, the present analysis often differs rather widely.

4. Hume, *Treatise*, Introduction, ed. cit., I, 307. Logic deals with ideas; morals, politics, and criticism with impressions—passions, habits, moral feelings, and aesthetic emotions.

5. *Ibid.*, i. 1. 1, ed. cit., I, 314. On the following pages Hume admits one trifling exception to this principle—the possibility of making interpolations in a series without specific experience.

6. *Ibid.*, i. 1. 3, ed. cit., I, 318.

7. *Ibid.*, ii. 1. 1, ed. cit., II, 76. This "vulgar and specious division" is employed by Hume only to divide his subject; it must be noted, however, that the principle of the distinction is similar to that of the distinction between impressions and ideas.

8. *Ibid.*, ii. 1. 8, ed. cit., II, 96.

9. *Ibid.*, ii. 1. 5, ed. cit., II, 85.

10. *Ibid.*, ii. 1. 8, ed. cit., II, 96.

11. *Ibid.*, pp. 95–96.

12. *Ibid.*, iii. 3. 1, ed. cit., II, 347.

13. *Ibid.*, p. 336.

14. *Ibid.*, ii. 2. 5, ed. cit., II, 151.

15. Hume, *An Enquiry Concerning the Principles of Morals*, i (LaSalle, Ill.: Open Court, 1946), p. 5.

16. Monk, *The Sublime*, p. 64.

17. James McCosh, *The Scottish Philosophy* . . . (New York: Scribner, 1890), p. 149.

18. Hume, *Enquiry Concerning Morals*, v, ed. cit., p. 59.

19. Monk, *The Sublime*, p. 98.

20. *Ibid.*, p. 74.

21. Hume, *Treatise*, ii. 3. 7, 8.

22. *Ibid.*, ii. 3. 7, ed. cit., II, 207.

23. *Ibid.*, ii. 3. 8, ed. cit., II, 209–10.

24. *Ibid.*, pp. 210–11.

25. Hume notes elsewhere that weak ideas are painful to the mind; hence we seek to have our notions buttressed by the consensus of others, &c.

26. Hume of course refers tacitly to the etymology of "sublime" as well as to its literal English signification of elevation. In contexts not involving literal or figurative elevation, Hume speaks of "grandeur" rather than of "sublimity."

27. See Dugald Stewart, *Philosophical Essays*, Part II, Essay II, chap. ii, in *The Collected Works of Dugald Stewart, Esq. . . . .*, ed. Sir William Hamilton (2d ed.; Edinburgh: T. & T. Clark, 1877), V, 445–47, note EE.

28. Hume, "Of the Standard of Taste," *Essays*, I, 266.

29. *Ibid.*

30. *Ibid.*

31. *Ibid.*, p. 268.

32. *Ibid.*, pp. 268–69.

33. For Hume there are seven philosophical relations which may obtain between ideas. Four depend only on the nature of the ideas, and can be determined by comparison: resemblance (same quality), degree of quality (partly the same), contrariety (different quality), degree of quantity; three depend on the mode of existence of the ideas, and can be determined only by experience: identity (same idea recurring), time and space (ideas occurring contiguously), causation (ideas with an apparent necessary connection). See *Treatise*, i. 1. 5, ed. cit., I, 322–23.

34. Hume, "Of the Standard of Taste," *Essays*, I, 269.
35. *Ibid.*, p. 270.
36. *Ibid.*
37. *Ibid.*, pp. 271–72.
38. *Ibid.*, p. 272.
39. *Ibid.*, p. 273.
40. *Ibid.*, pp. 273–74.
41. *Ibid.*, p. 275.
42. *Ibid.*, p. 276.
43. *Ibid.*, p. 277.
44. *Ibid.*
45. *Ibid.*, p. 279.
46. *Ibid.*, p. 280.
47. *Ibid.*, p. 281.
48. *Francis Hutcheson*, p. 124.
49. "Reason and Genius," *PQ*, XXIII (January, 1944), 53. Stuart Gerry Brown ("Observations on Hume's Theory of Taste," *ES*, XX [October, 1938], 193–98), attempts to make out an internal contradiction between subjective and objective, romantic and classic, and completely fails to grasp Hume's argument. Brunius (*David Hume on Criticism*, pp. 74–87) gives a clear account of the essay but does not remark its logical relation to Hume's basic distinctions.
50. Hume, "Of Tragedy," *Essays*, I, 258.
51. For detailed analysis of the argument of "Of Tragedy" in terms of Hume's system of logic developed in the *Treatise*, see my article, "The Logic of Hume's Essay 'Of Tragedy,' " *The Philosophical Quarterly*, VI (January, 1956), 43–52.
52. Abbé Jean Baptiste Du Bos, in *Réflexions critiques sur la poésie et sur la peinture* (Paris, 1719).
53. Hume, "Of Tragedy," *Essays*, I, 259.
54. Bernard le Bovier de Fontenelle, in *Réflexions sur la poétique* (Paris, 1742).
55. Hume, *Treatise*, i. 3. 9, ed. cit., I, 414.
56. See Baxter Hathaway, "The Lucretian 'Return upon Ourselves' in Eighteenth-Century Theories of Tragedy," *PMLA*, LXII (September, 1947), 672–89.
57. See Hume, *Treatise*, iii. 3. 2 for the opposition of sympathy and comparison, and *Treatise*, ii. 2. 7, 8 for discussion of sympathy and comparison in compassion, malice, and envy.
58. *The Letters of David Hume*, ed. J. Y. T. Greig (Oxford: Clarendon Press, 1932), I, 313. Smith replied in later editions of *The Theory of Moral Sentiments* (i. 3. 1) by distinguishing between the emotion communicated sympathetically and the emotion arising from perception of the coincidence of original and communicated passion, the latter only being in every case agreeable. This subtlety does not resolve the issue.
59. Hume, "Of Tragedy," *Essays*, I, 261.
60. Hume, *Treatise*, ii. 2. 8, ed. cit., II, 162.
61. *Ibid.*, ii. 3. 4, ed. cit., II, 198.
62. *Ibid.*, ii. 3. 9. There is also a passing reference to conversion in *Treatise*, ii. 3. 6, ed. cit., II, 203.
63. Hume, "Of Tragedy," *Essays*, I, 262.

64. See Earl R. Wasserman, "The Pleasures of Tragedy," *ELH*, XIV (December, 1947), 283–307, for some account of objections to Hume's theory from the school of sympathy; Wasserman appears to agree that Hume's theory postulates an intellectual taste.

65. Hume, *Treatise*, i. 1. 7, ed. cit., I, 330.

66. A number of eighteenth-century aestheticians touch upon this problem, but none of them connect it with the conversion theory. See especially Lessing, *Laocoön*, 24–25, and Stewart, *Philosophical Essays*, note X, in *Works*, V, 440–41 (cited *infra*, pp. 291–92).

67. Hume, "Of Tragedy," *Essays*, I, 265.

Chapter 4

1. See Joseph Burke, *Hogarth and Reynolds: A Contrast in English Art Theory* (The William Henry Charlton Memorial Lecture, November, 1941; London: Oxford, 1943), pp. 4 ff., and Stanley F. Read, "Some Observations on William Hogarth's *Analysis of Beauty*: A Bibliographical Study," *HLQ*, V (April, 1942), 360–73. See also Joseph Burke's definitive edition of *William Hogarth: The Analysis of Beauty, with the Rejected Passages from the Manuscript Drafts and Autobiographical Notes* (Oxford: Clarendon Press, 1955), pp. xiii ff., and Peter Quennell, *Hogarth's Progress* (New York: Viking Press, Inc., 1955).

2. Sandby's prints are described in F. G. Stephens and E. Hawkins, *Catalogue of Prints and Drawings in the British Museum*, Division I, Vol. III, Pt. 2, 1877 (years 1753 and 1754). Several are reproduced in Burke's edition of the *Analysis*.

3. See Stanley E. Read, *A Bibliography of Hogarth Books and Studies, 1900–1940; with an Introductory Essay on Trends in Hogarth Criticism, 1764–1940* (Chicago: De Paul University, 1941), for references. A few of the general histories of aesthetics comment on the *Analysis; Bosanquet (History of Aesthetic*, pp. 206–9) criticizes Hogarth without having read him (cf. *ibid.*, p. 496).

4. Marjorie Bowen (pseudonym of G. M. V. Long), *William Hogarth, the Cockney's Mirror* (2d ed.; New York: D. Appleton Century Co., 1937), p. 315. Even those moderns who admire the *Analysis* seem to do so because it can be construed to support some modern crotchet; thus, R. H. Wilenski finds Hogarth important because his three-dimensional line of grace "brings him at once in touch with the aesthetic attitude of our own time, the attitude behind Cezanne's landscapes and the Cubist movement . . ." (*English Painting* [London: Faber, 1933], p. 275).

5. William Hogarth, *The Analysis of Beauty, Written with a View of Fixing the Fluctuating Ideas of Taste* (London, 1753), Preface, p. xii. (To facilitate reference to the editions of 1772 and after, I give chapter as well as page references.)

6. *Ibid.*, Introduction, p. [1].

7. *Ibid.*, p. 6

8. *Ibid.*, p. 4.

9. *Ibid.*, pp. 7–8.

10. *Ibid.*, p. 8.

11. *Ibid.*, p. 9. In Joseph Burke's rather different interpretation of the technical memory (*Analysis* [1955 ed.], pp. xxxvii–xli), the shell-view made no

part of the system, which comprised only linear abstractions, essentially two-dimensional.

12. *Ibid.* (1753 ed.), pp. 11–12.

13. J. Burke, *Hogarth and Reynolds*, p. 8, and "A Classical Aspect of Hogarth's Theory of Art," *Journal of the Warburg and Courtauld Institutes*, VI (1943), 151–53.

14. In *Memorabilia* iii, Xenophon explains how Socrates "helped those who were eager to win distinction by making them qualify themselves for the honours they coveted" (iii. 1. 1); my quotation is from the debate with Aristippus (iii. 8. 7); the visit with Cleiton is in iii. 10. 8. See also the discussion with Pistias the armorer, wherein Socrates argues that good proportion is relative to use (iii. 10. 9–15), and the identification of useful and beautiful in iv. 6. 9.

15. Hogarth, *Analysis*, ii, ed. cit., pp. 16–17.

16. *Ibid.*, iii, ed. cit., pp. 18–19.

17. *Ibid.*, x, ed. cit., p. 63.

18. *Ibid.*, iv, ed. cit., p. 21. The pyramid exhibits most variety in fewest parts among straight-lined figures; the title-page ornament of the *Analysis* shows the serpentine line enclosed within a pyramid erected on a rectangular base. On the same principle, the oval is preferred to the circle, the ovoid to the oval, contrary to the preference of Hutcheson for the circle.

19. *Ibid.*, v, ed. cit., p. 24.

20. *Ibid.*, p. 25.

21. *Ibid.*, p. 26.

22. *Ibid.*, xii, ed. cit., p. 95.

23. *Ibid.*, xiv, ed. cit., pp. 114–15.

24. Wilson O. Clough considers that reference of beauty to physiological causes contributed to breakdown of the classical system of objective reason and "left open a way for subjective and individualistic claims" ("Reason and Genius," *PQ*, XXIII [January, 1944], 36). Such an inference contrasts nicely with Hogarth's own title declaration—*Written with a View of Fixing the Fluctuating Ideas of Taste*. Presupposed by Hogarth is the likeness, not the difference, of men's senses, and that to refer beauty to such causes was to *remove* it from the realm of subjective judgment.

25. Hogarth, *Analysis*, vi, ed. cit., p. 29.

26. *Ibid.*, xi, ed. cit., pp. 87–88.

27. *Ibid.*, vi, ed. cit., p. 31.

28. Hogarth's print, "The Country Dance," lends itself neatly to analysis in terms of mechanical associations, for instance; cf. Henri Bergson's theory of the comic in *Le Rire, essai sur la signification du comique* (Paris: F. Alcan, 1900).

29. Hogarth, *Analysis*, vii, ed. cit., p. 38.

30. See, for instance, Winckelmann's "Instructions for the Connoisseur," in Henry Fusseli's translation of his *Reflections on the Painting and Sculpture of the Greeks* . . . (2d ed.; London, 1767): "The line which beauty describes is elliptical, both uniform and various: 'tis not to be described by a circle, and from every point changes its direction. . . . 'Tis not in the power of Algebra to determine which line, more or less elliptic, forms the divers parts of the system into beauty—but the ancients knew it . . ." (p. 259). It remains doubtful whether this elliptical line has a reverse curve, however.

31. Burke (ed.), *Analysis*, p. xlviii.

32. Hogarth, *Analysis* (1753 ed.), viii, p. 40.

33. *Ibid.*, ix, ed. cit., p. 49.

34. Hogarth, British Museum Additional MS 27, 991, f. 19. The table following is taken from Egerton MS 3011, f. 18b. Both extracts are printed also by Burke, the table with slight differences in the transcription.

35. Hogarth, *Analysis*, Preface, ed. cit., p. iv.

36. *Ibid.*, xi, ed. cit., p. 68.

37. *Ibid.*, p. 69.

38. *Ibid.*, p. 76.

39. A letter to the Rev. Herbert Mayo, who had suggested an application of Hogarth's theory to sound, reads as follows:

"Leicester Fields 4th Aprill 1761

"Sr.

An answer to the favour of your letter after so much time past since the receipt of it, must seem somewhat unpolite, particularly as the subject of yours is so genteel a complement to me, the only excuse I can make for the delay, is my endeavouring to add something of my own in confirmation of what you have so well advanced on the Rules of Beauty being applicable to sounds, but I found it better to drop my own opinion of the matter and send you one of that great Master of Harmony, Mr. Handel, who once, as I was told, describing Mrs. Woffington the actresses manner of speaking, sometimes in, and sometimes out of tune, did it by notes very similar to those you have placed on the lines you have so obligingly communicated to me, which I am sure you will think much better authority than any I can pretend to give you of my own.

I am Sr. your much
obliged humble servant
Wm. Hogarth

"P.S.

I intend as soon as possible to publish a supplement to my Analysis in which perhaps I shall make some use of your observation together with what else may occur to me on the subject."

This letter is found as an unsigned item in *The Living Age*, CCCXIX (8th series, Vol. XXXII; December 22, 1923), 579–80. It may be conjectured from Hogarth's reply that Mayo argued partly on the basis of the visual notation representing the sound.

40. There is an apparent inconsistency in Hogarth's organization. At the start of Chapter xi he distinguishes the two general ideas of form explained above, and subsequently divides the second into two aspects—"general measurements" (as height to breadth, &c.) which can be described by straight orthogonal lines, and "such appearances of dimensions as are too intricately varied to admit of a description by lines" (*Analysis*, xi, ed. cit., p. 74). Accordingly, his discussion of both aspects is based on fitness as well as variety, and all is in order. But farther on (p. 89) Hogarth reviews his procedure and identifies the first aspect of the second "general idea"—the measurement of contents by orthogonal lines—with the first general idea, "on surface," limiting the second and more extensive idea

of form, arising from fitness for movement, to the nicer proportions. This is, no doubt, a careless confusion rather than an inconsistency in thought.

41. Hogarth, *Analysis*, xvii, ed. cit., p. 142.

42. See the letter to Mayo, *supra*, p. 333.

43. J. Burke, *Hogarth and Reynolds*, p. 11.

44. The observations of Holmes and Hubbard are to be found in the *Journal of the Royal Society of Arts*, LXXX, No. 4139 (March 18, 1932), 438–59.

Chapter 5

1. *An Essay on Taste, by Alexander Gerard . . . with Three Dissertations on the Same Subject by Mr. De Voltaire, Mr. D'Alembert, F. R. S., Mr. De Montesquieu*, London, 1759. My references are to this edition, except for those to Part iv in the 1780 (third) edition.

Gerard wrote his *Essay* before Burke published the *Sublime and Beautiful* in April of 1757; publication of Gerard's book in May, 1759, came so shortly after the second edition of Burke's (January, 1759) containing the "Introductory Essay on Taste," that Gerard very probably had not seen this "Essay"—if, indeed, he had seen the treatise itself.

For an account of the circumstances of composition of Gerard's two books, see Margaret Lee Wiley, "Gerard and the Scots Societies," in *The University of Texas Publication: Studies in English*, No. 4026 (Austin: University of Texas, 1940), pp. 132–36; and see James McCosh, *The Scottish Philosophy* (New York: Scribner, 1890), pp. 227–29 and 467–73 for information on Gerard and the Aberdeen Philosophical Society.

2. *An Essay on Taste. To Which Is Now Added Part Fourth, Of the Standard of Taste: with Observations Concerning the Imitative Nature of Poetry. By Alexander Gerard, D.D. Professor of Divinity in King's College, Aberdeen. The Third Edition*, Edinburgh and London, 1780. This edition omits the French authors. Despite the length and importance of the additions (almost a third of the whole), they have been entirely ignored by modern commentators on Gerard.

3. *An Essay on Genius, by Alexander Gerard, D.D. . . . .* (London and Edinburgh, 1774), Advertisement, p. iii.

4. Gerard, *Essay on Taste*, Introduction, ed. cit., pp. 1–2.

5. *Ibid.*, iii. 1, ed. cit., pp. 162–63n.

6. *Ibid.*, p. 160.

7. *Ibid.*, pp. 164–65. McKenzie (*Critical Responsiveness*, pp. 136–37) sees Gerard's principle as an anticipation of the theory of empathy; Gerard, however, works wholly with ideas and impressions, and does not introduce the physiological responses which are emphasized in the theory of empathy. The systematic context is that of Hume, not Lipps.

8. Gerard, *Essay on Taste*, iii. 1, ed. cit., pp. 169–70. Note the resemblance to Hume, *Treatise*, ii. 1. 11.

9. Gerard, *Essay on Taste*, iii. 1, ed. cit., p. 172.

10. *Ibid.*, iii. 6, ed. cit., p. 205.

11. *Ibid.*, pp. 201–2.

12. The analysis of the faculties is carried out chiefly in the *Essay on Genius*; for memory, see ii. 9 and iii. 3.

13. For the philosophical relations, see *Essay on Genius*, ii. 10; for the natural relations, *ibid.*, ii. 1. Gerard's analysis differs in some particulars from Hume's. His philosophical relations are resemblance, contrariety, degree of quality, proportion in quantity, identity, time-and-place, coexistence, causation, the uniformity of nature; he finds identity, universal causation, and the uniformity of nature to be inexplicable intuitions, whereas Hume analyzes all of these; and Hume would consider coexistence only a modification of causation. Gerard divides his natural relations into simple—not dependent on additional habits of the imagination—and compounded. The simple principles are resemblance, contrariety (which for Hume is merely a species of resemblance), and vicinity; the complex relations are coexistence (involving a notion of substance and identity), cause-and-effect (involving a notion of power and necessary connection), and order (which includes conception of design)—all which for Hume are causation.

14. Gerard, *Essay on Taste*, iii. 1, ed. cit., p. 170; compare with Hume, *Treatise*, iii. 3. 2.

15. Gerard, *Essay on Genius*, ii. 3, ed. cit., pp. 147–84.

16. Gerard, *Essay on Taste*, i. 1, ed. cit., pp. 3–11.

17. *Ibid.*, p. 8.

18. *Ibid.*, i. 2, ed. cit., p. 13.

19. *Ibid.*, p. 14. In a footnote, Gerard criticizes Longinus for "resolving the sensation of sublimity into the *last* of these principles [self-glorification], without investigating the others, of which *it* is but a consequence . . ."; doubtless he would criticize Burke for resolving it entirely into the *first*.

20. Gerard acknowledges in a note that "most of the species of sublimity are explained, nearly from the principles here assigned" in Baillie's essay (*ibid.*, p. 13).

21. Hume, *Treatise*, ii. 3. 8, ed. cit., II, 209. See all of ii. 3. 7, 8.

22. Gerard, *Essay on Taste*, i. 2, ed. cit., pp. 17–18.

23. *Ibid.*, p. 17.

24. *Ibid.*, p. 18.

25. *Ibid.*, p. 19.

26. *Ibid.*, p. 23.

27. Dr. [John] Baillie, *An Essay on the Sublime*, ed. Samuel Holt Monk (Augustan Reprint Society Publication No. 43; Los Angeles, 1953), p. 32.

28. *Ibid.*, p. 31.

29. Gerard, *Essay on Taste*, i. 2, ed. cit., p. 19.

30. Baillie, *Essay on the Sublime*, p. 33.

31. Gerard, *Essay on Taste*, i. 3, ed. cit., p. 31.

32. *Ibid.*, p. 47. Gerard illustrates the last of these three modes by citing the imitation of a beautiful original. But this seems an error; Gerard is pointing out that an imitation of something beautiful may itself exhibit beauty (unlike representations of grandeur, which are not grand in themselves), but there is no question in such imitations of necessarily suggesting ideas from other senses.

33. "So great," says Gerard, "is the power of variety in producing beauty, that an ingenious artist, who has lately *analyzed* it, not altogether without reason, resolves almost the whole of it into that principle. . . . He holds uniformity no further necessary, than it is requisite to convey the idea of rest or motion, without possibility of falling. But here he goes too far. It were easy to point out instances,

where uniformity is studied, though it cannot have any degree of this effect: and he acknowledges that beauty resides only in a *composed* variety; which necessarily implies a mixture of uniformity" (*ibid.*, pp. 34–35n). Gerard overlooks that what he terms "uniformity" includes also what Hogarth terms "simplicity," and that Hogarth concedes the value of regularity in forms merely decorative.

34. *Ibid.*, p. 47.
35. *Ibid.*, p. 42.
36. *Ibid.*, p. 43.
37. Monk, *The Sublime*, p. 110.
38. *Ibid.*
39. Gerard, *Essay on Taste*, i. 4, ed. cit., pp. 49–50.
40. *Ibid.*, pp. 54–55.
41. *Ibid.* (3d ed.), Appendix, pp. 283–84.
42. *Ibid.* (1st ed.), i. 5, p. 64.
43. *Ibid.*, ii. 7, ed. cit., p. 148.
44. *Ibid.*, ii. 1, ed. cit., p. 89.
45. *Ibid.*, ii. 2, ed. cit., p. 96.
46. *Ibid.*, ii. 3, ed. cit., pp. 104–5.
47. *Ibid.*, i. 7, ed. cit., pp. 77–78.
48. Marjorie Grene, "Gerard's *Essay on Taste*," MP, XLI (August, 1943), 45.
49. *Ibid.*, p. 58.
50. McKenzie (*Critical Responsiveness*, pp. 268, 296–97) is also unaware of the fourth part of the *Essay on Taste*.
51. Gerard, *Essay on Taste* (3d ed.), iv. 1, ed. cit., p. 200.
52. *Ibid.*, iv. 2, ed. cit., p. 216.
53. *Ibid.*, iv. 5, ed. cit., p. 251.
54. See especially the final chapter of Lord Kames's *Elements of Criticism* (and *infra*, pp. 119–20) and the Introduction to Richard Payne Knight's *An Analytical Inquiry into the Principles of Taste* (and *infra*, pp. 254–55).
55. Gerard, *Essay on Taste*, iii. 3, ed. cit., pp. 182–83.
56. *Ibid.*, p. 185n.
57. *Ibid.*, p. 184.
58. John Stuart Mill, *A System of Logic, Ratiocinative and Inductive*, Book VI, Chaps. 9 and 10 ("Of the Physical, or Concrete Deductive Method" and "Of the Inverse Deductive, or Historical Method").
59. Gerard, *Essay on Taste*, iii. 6, ed. cit., pp. 207–8.
60. The *Essay on Genius* is, as a whole, not closely enough related to the present study to admit of its being treated here. The general plan of the book can perhaps be grasped by noting that genius itself is an efficient cause, and that the three parts of the treatise, "Of the Nature of Genius," "Of the General Sources of the Varieties of Genius," and "Of the Kinds of Genius," deal with the faculties involved in genius (material cause), the modifications and compoundings of these faculties (formal cause), and the ends which marshal these combinations and modifications into distinct species of genius (final cause).

Chapter 6

1. Richard Payne Knight, *An Analytical Inquiry into the Principles of Taste,* iii. 1. 59 (3d ed.; London, 1806), p. 374.

2. James Boswell's *Life of Samuel Johnson,* ed. Alexander Napier (London: George Bell & Sons, 1884), I, 485.

3. Sir Joshua Reynolds, Discourse viii, *The Literary Works of Sir Joshua Reynolds, Kt.,* ed. Edmond Malone (5th ed.; London, 1819), I, 282n.

4. Hume to Adam Smith, April 12, 1759, in *The Letters of David Hume,* ed. J. Y. T. Greig (Oxford: Clarendon Press, 1932), I, 303.

5. The satire on Lord Bolingbroke, *A Vindication of Natural Society* (London, 1756) preceded it from the press; Burke appears to have intended publication of the *Sublime and Beautiful* early in 1756, but put it off in order to write and publish the *Vindication.*

6. Theodore McGinnes Moore, "The Background of Edmund Burke's Theory of the Sublime (1660–1759)" (Unpublished Ph.D. dissertation, Cornell University, 1933), pp. 2–20. The differences of the first and second editions of the *Sublime and Beautiful* are related to the reviews of the first edition by Herbert Wichelns, "Burke's Essay on the Sublime and Its Reviewers," *JEGP,* XXI (1922), 645–61.

7. Burke, *Sublime and Beautiful* (1st ed., 1757), Preface, pp. vi–vii, quoted by Wichelns, "Burke's Essay on the Sublime and Its Reviewers," *JEGP,* XXI (1922), 645.

8. Burke himself uses the term "efficient cause" loosely: "when I speak of cause, and efficient cause, I only mean certain affections of the mind, that cause certain changes in the body; or certain powers and properties in bodies, that work a change in the mind" (*Sublime and Beautiful* [text of the second edition], iv. 1, in *The Works of the Right Honourable Edmund Burke* [London: Oxford, 1906], I, 175). He does not distinguish explicitly the object from the principles by which the object acts, and accordingly remarks that certain proportions are alleged to be "the efficient cause of beauty" (*ibid.,* iii. 4, in *Works,* I, 144)—where in strict accuracy he should say "material cause."

9. Monk (*The Sublime,* p. 98) sees Burke as an advance towards subjectivism: "although he cannot, by the very nature of his reasoning, refer beauty and sublimity to the perceiving mind alone, as Kant was to do and as Hume had already done, he does, perforce, concentrate most of his attention on the effect rather than on the qualities of objects."

10. Burke, *Sublime and Beautiful,* iii. 2, in *Works,* I, 141.

11. McKenzie, *Critical Responsiveness,* pp. 88–89.

12. Burke, *Sublime and Beautiful,* Introduction, in *Works,* I, 66.

13. *Ibid.,* p. 67.

14. *Ibid.,* p. 68.

15. *Ibid.,* p. 78. Gerard (*Essay on Taste* [3d ed.], iv. 3, ed. cit., pp. 220–24) gives a clear précis of Burke's argument, but considers that Burke is trying to explain away diversities of sentiment, and that he minimizes the transformations imagination effects with the data of sense in presenting images "which the senses could not possibly exhibit, and which give pleasure or disgust on totally different

principles." It is certainly true that Burke's argument is sketchy in dealing with imagination and judgment.

16. Burke, *Sublime and Beautiful*, i. 1, in *Works*, I, 84.

17. *Ibid.*, i. 4, in *Works*, I, 88.

18. *Ibid.*, i. 7, in *Works*, I, 91.

19. Cf. *supra*, pp. 74–75 for discussion of Baillie's and Gerard's views on this topic, and *infra*, pp. 272–73 for an account of Richard Payne Knight's critique of the terrific sublime.

20. Burke, *Sublime and Beautiful*, i. 7, in *Works*, I, 91–92.

21. *Ibid.*, i. 17, in *Works*, I, 102.

22. *Ibid.*, iv. 7, in *Works*, I, 181.

23. Hutcheson, it might be remarked, had tried to show that horrid objects affect us unpleasantly only through fear for ourselves or compassion for others when reason or association makes us apprehend danger; when the fear is removed by reasoning or experience, such objects may become pleasing. Hutcheson's analysis agrees with Burke's in finding agreeable objects which might be but are not now fearful; it contrasts with Burke's in that Hutcheson is not concerned with differentiating two modes of agreeableness, and considers that the fear, once dispelled practically, has no longer any influence whatever. (See *Inquiry*, i. 6, p. 67.)

24. Burke, *Sublime and Beautiful*, i. 8, in *Works*, I, 92.

25. *Ibid.*, i. 14, in *Works*, I, 98.

26. For Hutcheson, see *supra*, pp. 33–34; for Kames, *infra*, pp. 115–16.

27. Burke, *Sublime and Beautiful*, i. 15, in *Works*, I, 99.

28. Knight, *Analytical Inquiry*, iii. 1. 1–13, ed. cit., pp. 318–30 and throughout iii. 1.

29. Burke, *Sublime and Beautiful*, i. 17, in *Works*, I, 102–3.

30. *Ibid.*, ii. 1, in *Works*, I, 108.

31. Samuel Johnson's *A Dictionary of the English Language* . . . (London, 1755) gives evidence of the connection of all these feelings with fear. "Astonishment" is defined as "Amazement; confusion of mind from fear or wonder"; "amazement" as "Such a confused apprehension as does not leave reason its full force; extreme fear; horrour"; "awe" as "Reverential fear"; &c. Johnson is unilluminating on "sublimity" itself. He gives three meanings: (1) "Height of place; local elevation"; (2) "Height of nature; excellence"; (3) "Loftiness of style or sentiment." To the phrase, "the sublime," he assigns only the meaning, "The grand or lofty stile," remarking that "*The sublime* is a Gallicism, but now naturalized." There are no changes in any of these definitions in later editions.

32. See Burke, *Sublime and Beautiful*, ii. 2, in *Works*, I, 109, the passage beginning "Indeed terror is in all cases whatsoever, either more openly or latently, the ruling principle of the sublime," and continuing to the end of the section. This passage was added in the second edition, but the same etymological point was made in the first more briefly (*ibid.*, iv. 7, in *Works*, I, 181).

33. *Ibid.*, ii [4], in *Works*, I, 112 and 114.

34. *Ibid.*, ii. 6, in *Works*, I, 121.

35. *Ibid.*, ii. 5, in *Works*, I, 115.

36. *Ibid.*, iv. 2, in *Works*, I, 176.

37. *Ibid.*, iv. 3, in *Works*, I, 177.

38. *Ibid.*, iv. 6, in *Works*, I, 180.

39. *Ibid.*, iv. 7, in *Works*, I, 181.

40. Knight, *Analytical Inquiry*, i. 5. 4, 5, ed. cit., pp. 59–60.

41. Burke, *Sublime and Beautiful*, iv. 24, in *Works*, I, 201.

42. See Goldsmith's review, *Monthly Review*, XVI (May, 1757), 480; Burke's reply, beginning "Some who allow darkness to be a cause of the sublime . . . ," was added to the middle of iv. 16.

43. Cf. *infra*, pp. 204–8.

44. Burke, *Sublime and Beautiful*, iii. 1, in *Works*, I, 138.

45. It is here that Burke lays down the four rules of reasoning cited *supra*. Much of this discussion, including the rules, was added in the second edition; Wichelns ("Burke's Essay on the Sublime and Its Reviewers," *JEGP*, XXI [1922], 656–58) suggests that Burke was answering the strictures of Arthur Murphy in the *Literary Magazine*, II, 187, and those of the reviewer in the *Critical Review*, III, 366–67.

46. This is the very answer which Uvedale Price was later to give to Reynolds' *Idler* papers—see "An Introductory Essay on Beauty; with Remarks on the Ideas of Sir Joshua Reynolds and Mr. Burke, upon That Subject," prefixed to *A Dialogue on the Distinct Characters of the Picturesque and the Beautiful . . .* , in *Essays on the Picturesque* (London, 1810), III, 229–32.

47. Burke, *Sublime and Beautiful*, iii. 8, in *Works*, I, 156–57. Burke illustrates his argument with the instance of a watch: the case, polished and engraved, is beautiful; the mechanism is fit. Blair uses the same illustration (borrowed, very probably from Burke, like so many points in Blair), but makes both excellences into varieties of beauty (Hugh Blair, *Lectures on Rhetoric and Belles Lettres*, v, I, 111).

48. Burke, *Sublime and Beautiful*, iii. 11, in *Works*, I, 159.

49. *Ibid.*, iii. 10, in *Works*, I, 158.

50. *Ibid.*, iii. 12, in *Works*, I, 160.

51. William Gilpin, *Three Essays: On Picturesque Beauty; on Picturesque Travel; and On Sketching Landscape . . .* (2d ed.; London, 1794), p. 6n.

52. Aristotle *Eth. Nic.* iv. 3. 1123^{b}6. See also *Rhet.* i. 5. 1361^{a}1–8 and *Poet.* vii. 1450^{b}34–51^{a}5. Thomas Twining's comments are in his *Aristotle's Treatise on Poetry, Translated: with Notes . . .* (London, 1789), pp. 263–65, note 61. Price ("Introductory Essay on Beauty," *Essays on the Picturesque*, III, 192) may possibly be using Twining.

53. Dugald Stewart, *Philosophical Essays* (Edinburgh, 1810), ii. 1. 1. 5, pp. 275–76n.

54. Knight, *Analytical Inquiry*, ii. 2. 107–8, ed. cit., pp. 231–33; see i. 5. 4, 16 (ed. cit., pp. 59, 68) for discussion of beauty so far as it depends on the sense of sight purely.

55. Burke was followed by Price in this use of "fine"; and he himself followed usage in some measure. Johnson's *Dictionary* (1755) gives "11. Applied to person, it means beautiful with dignity," and "13. Showy; splendid." Burke's "specious" harks back to the Latin *speciosus*, "splendid," "imposing." The closest Johnson comes is "1. Showy; pleasing to the view."

56. Cf. *infra*, pp. 257–58.

57. Burke, *Sublime and Beautiful*, iii. 23, in *Works*, I, 168. Burke did not have the sanction of contemporary usage for this employment of "elegant." John-

son defines it "1. Pleasing with minuter beauties," and for "Elegance, Elegancy," he gives "Beauty of art; rather soothing than striking; beauty without grandeur," none of which definitions implies regularity. Johnson's definitions correspond, incidentally, to the sense Reynolds gives the term "elegant" when he contrasts it with the sublime.

58.　It does not appear to me conformable to usage to term warmth "beautiful." Softness, though of itself tactile, has visual signs and is appreciated as a visual beauty; smoothness and gradual variation are both visual and tactile; but warmth has no connection with sight (or hearing) and therefore none with what is usually felt to be beautiful, being only a pleasing organic sensation having a vague analogy —like sweetness of taste—with the beautiful.

59.　Burke, *Sublime and Beautiful*, iii. 25, in *Works*, I, 171.

60.　*Ibid.*, iv. 19, in *Works*, I, 195.

61.　*Ibid.*, iv. 24, in *Works*, I, 202.

62.　*Ibid.*, iii. 27, in *Works*, I, 172–73; this passage was added in the second edition.

63.　McKenzie, *Critical Responsiveness*, p. 246.

64.　Howard, "Burke among the Forerunners of Lessing," *PMLA*, XXII (1907), 614.

65.　Burke, *Sublime and Beautiful*, v. 2, in *Works*, I, 207.

66.　*Ibid.*, p. 210.

67.　*Ibid.*, v. 5, in *Works*, I, 214—from a passage added in the second edition.

68.　Hume, *Treatise*, i. 1. 7.

69.　McKenzie, *Critical Responsiveness*, p. 249.

70.　Howard, "Burke among the Forerunners of Lessing," *PMLA*, XXII (1907), 614.

71.　Donald Cross Bryant, *Edmund Burke and His Literary Friends* ("Washington University Studies—New Series; Language and Literature"—No. 9 [St. Louis, 1939]), p. 234, quoting from Sir James Prior, *Life of Edmond Malone* . . . (London, 1860), p. 154.

72.　Bryant, *Burke and His Literary Friends*, pp. 95–96, based on James Prior, *The Life of Oliver Goldsmith* (2 vols. in one; London, 1837), II, 428, and other sources.

73.　Howard, "Burke among the Forerunners of Lessing," *PMLA*, XXII (1907), 610, quoting from *G. E. Lessing's sämtliche Schriften*, eds. K. Lachmann and Franz Muncker (3d ed., 22 vols.; Stuttgart and Leipzig: G. J. Göschen'sche Verlagshandlung, 1886–1910), XVII (Leipzig, 1904), 138.

Chapter 7

1.　The first six editions, those of bibliographical significance, are dated 1762, 1763, 1765, 1769, 1774, and 1785; there was also an unauthorized Dublin edition in 1772. See the (incomplete) list of editions in Helen Whitcomb Randall's *The Critical Theory of Lord Kames* ("Smith College Studies in Modern Languages," XXII, Nos. 1–4 [Northampton, Mass.: Smith College, 1944, as of 1940–41]), 137–39.

2.　Bosanquet, *History of Aesthetic*, pp. 202–6.

3. [Lord Kames], *Essays on the Principles of Morality and Natural Religion*, ii. 4 (Edinburgh, 1751), p. 276. Gordon McKenzie finds this position inconsistent with the professedly empirical character of Kames's philosophy; see his "Lord Kames and the Mechanist Tradition," *University of California Publications in English*, XIV (1942; Berkeley: University of California Press, 1943), 107–8. I consider, however, that the common sense and intuitive senses of the Scottish school are quite consistent with empiricism; I see in the criticism of Kames no "mixture of contradictory elements," and my own strictures turn on other matters.

4. [Kames], *Essays*, ii. 1, ed. cit., p. 227.

5. *Ibid.*, ii. 2; and compare *Elements of Criticism*, ii. 1. 1 (2d ed.; Edinburgh, 1763), I, 66. My references to the *Elements* are to this second edition unless otherwise specified.

6. Kames, *Elements*, ii. 1. 6 (7 in 4th and later eds.), ed. cit., I, 110. For "substance" and "body" see definition 4 of the Appendix (III, 428–29) and *Essays*, ii. 3, especially (ed. cit.,) pp. 244 ff.

7. [Kames], *Essays*, ii. 3, ed. cit., p. 260.

8. Kames, *Elements* (3d ed.), Appendix, definition 14, II, 505–8.

9. *Ibid.* (2d ed.), xviii. 2, II, 304–5.

10. This quotation is found in the fifth and later editions only, in definition 15 of the Appendix to the *Elements*.

11. [Kames], *Essays*, ii. 4, ed. cit., p. 285.

12. *Ibid.*, ii. 6, ed. cit., p. 307.

13. *Ibid.*, ii. 7, ed. cit., p. 373.

14. Kames, *Elements*, Introduction, ed. cit., I, 1 ff. and Appendix, definition 13, ed. cit., III, 432–33; see also *Essays*, ii. 3, especially (ed. cit.) p. 243.

15. Kames, *Elements*, Introduction, ed. cit., I, 5.

16. *Ibid.*, p. 14.

17. *Ibid.*, Dedication, ed. cit., I, iv.

18. *Ibid.*, iii, ed. cit., I, 252.

19. *Ibid.*, Introduction, ed. cit., I, 16.

20. *Ibid.*, p. 18.

21. *Ibid.*, pp. 17–18.

22. Randall, *Lord Kames*, pp. 23–27.

23. Kames, *Elements*, ii. 1. 1, ed. cit., I, 52 ff. In interpreting the distinction between passion and emotion as a reflection of the difference between a practical and an aesthetic attitude towards objects, Monk (*The Sublime*, p. 113) reads into Kames's distinction a difference which is not there; practical attitudes give rise to both passions and emotions, and aesthetic contemplation likewise can arouse passions as well as emotions.

24. Kames, *Elements*, ii. 1. 3 (4 in 4th and later eds.), ed. cit., I, 73–79. Hutcheson had already noted the sympathetic emotion of virtue in the *Essay on the Passions*, iii. 3. 3, ed. cit., p. 69.

25. Kames, *Elements*, ii. 2, ed. cit., I, 135.

26. *Ibid.*, p. 137. Hutcheson (*Inquiry into Beauty and Virtue*, ii. 2. 8, ed. cit., pp. 140–43) had made a similar point about virtue; virtue may be either painful or pleasant in direct feeling, but all virtue is pleasant ("agreeable," as Kames

would say) in retrospective survey. The observation is only incidental for Hutcheson, but it serves to illustrate the naturalness of such a distinction in the British psychologies.

27. Kames, *Elements*, ii. 3, ed. cit., I, 145.

28. Compare Kames's confident assertion that "the distinction between primary and secondary qualities in matter, seems now fully established" (*Elements*, iii, ed. cit., I, 270); again, Kames's refutation of Hume's doctrine of impressions depends upon taking "impression" in an anatomical sense at which Hume would have scoffed.

29. *Ibid.*, ii. 6, ed. cit., I, 227.

30. *Ibid.*, xi, ed. cit., II, 36–37.

31. *Ibid.*, viii, ed. cit., I, 379–83. The development of this principle illustrates rather amusingly two of Kames's crotchets. There is first the claim of originality, that this principle "lies still in obscurity, not having been unfolded by any writer, though its effects are extensive"; and then the final cause is pointed out—not only pointed out, but the rather startling claim is made that "the final cause of this principle is an additional proof of its existence."

32. *Ibid.*, iii, ed. cit., I, 252.

33. *Ibid.*, pp. 252–53.

34. *Ibid.*, p. 254.

35. *Ibid.*, xiv, ed. cit., II, 103.

36. *Ibid.*, iii, ed. cit., I, 259.

37. *Ibid.*, ix, ed. cit., I, 422–23.

38. *Ibid.*, iv, ed. cit., I, 275.

39. *Ibid.*, pp. 276–77. Note the resemblance of the emotions to their causes.

40. *Ibid.*, pp. 314–15. Hume could have brought this controversy neatly under the contrariety of sympathy and comparison.

41. *Ibid.*, vi, ed. cit., I, 334.

42. It is true, to be sure, that the picturesque has connections with the ludicrous, as in the genre painting of the Dutch school, and that the sublime may be connected with the ludicrous in the mock-heroic. Beauty has never, I think, any but an accidental connection with the ludicrous.

43. This distinction of primary and secondary relations is first made in a footnote added to the third edition.

44. Kames, *Elements*, x, ed. cit., II, 8.

45. *Ibid.*, xi, ed. cit., II, 30.

46. *Ibid.* (3d ed.), I, 348.

47. This explication of the plan of the book corresponds pretty closely with that given by Randall (*Lord Kames*, p. 23, n. 2). The chief difference is in placing the chapter on the external language of passion (xv); clearly, this chapter belongs with the following chapters on sentiment and passionate language, for all three deal with the expression of passion.

Randall's account of the *Elements* seems to me good, and especially in the treatment of organization and procedure. Murray W. Bundy, however, gives her book (and Lord Kames's) an excoriating review in "Lord Kames and the Maggots in Amber," *JEGP*, XLV (April, 1946), 199–208; the basis of Bundy's attack is an antipathy to British empiricism which prevents him from following Kames's arguments or grasping his conclusions. Gordon McKenzie also fails to see the force of Kames's organization, urging that the theory of emotion is not of much relevance to criticism, and that "each chapter is essentially a fresh start from a familiar point of view rather than a consequence of the material already presented" (*Critical Responsiveness*, p. 143).

48. Kames, *Elements* (3d ed.), xv, I, 431. This remark, though added only in the third and subsequent editions, merely elaborates the doctrine of the earliest editions.

49. *Ibid.*, (2d ed.), xvi, II, 153.

50. *Ibid.*, xxi, ed. cit., III, 235.

51. *Ibid.*, p. 237.

52. *Ibid.*, xxii, ed. cit., III, 245n.

53. *Ibid.*, p. 247.

54. *Ibid.*, p. 249.

55. Kames makes an effort to show that Aristotle's pity-and-fear correspond to his own notions. Randall, though not quite accepting this preposterous claim, does consider that Kames's treatment of tragedy is "remarkably faithful to Aristotle in letter and in spirit," and points out that Butcher's interpretation of Aristotle runs pretty close to Kames's (*Lord Kames*, pp. 52–54). But it must be emphasized that Kames's discussion of tragedy depends directly from his analysis of the passions, faculties, and virtues; Aristotle's treatment is more self-contained and centers about the four causes—object, manner, and means of imitation, and catharsis.

56. It was in this chapter on architecture and gardening that Kames inserted some notions on ornament supplied by Mrs. Montagu—the "maggots in amber," as she playfully dubbed the insertions. Murray W. Bundy takes Mrs. Montagu's rather conventional remarks stressing the influence of historical and religious associations on our notions of beauty in ornaments and the interpretation of ornaments as signs of moral traits or other affecting circumstances, as penetrating "to the heart of the aesthetic problem of the century: she has appealed from the rational to the imaginative comprehension of beauty." Bundy alleges that Lord Kames reduces all beauty to utility, congruity, and propriety, thereby making all "beauty, intrinsic as well as relative, essentially a matter of the understanding" ("Lord Kames and the Maggots in Amber," *JEGP*, XLV [April, 1946], 203, 207). Yet Kames's greatest concern was to assert the prerogatives of direct perception against the overweening claims of ratiocinative analysis! Bundy is led to describe Mrs. Montagu's sprightly reply to Kames's revision of her remarks as ironically devastating criticism, and to insinuate that Kames's eventual acknowledgement of her contribution in the fifth edition must have been dictated by her outraged protests. The reader can judge for himself by reading the exchange of letters reproduced by Randall (*Lord Kames*, pp. 94 ff.).

57. McKenzie, "Lord Kames and the Mechanist Tradition," *University of California Publications in English*, XIV, 105–6.

58. McKenzie, *Critical Responsiveness*, pp. 295–96. See also Monk, *The Sublime*, pp. 132–33 and 237–38; but these opinions are found very widely.

59. Kames, *Elements*, xxv, ed. cit., III, 406–8.

60. *Ibid.*, p. 426.

61. *Ibid.*, pp. 418–19.

Chapter 8

1. See Robert Morell Schmitz, *Hugh Blair* (Morningside Heights, N.Y.: King's Crown Press, 1948) for details of Blair's life and works.

2. Letter to Thomas Percy, 31 Jan. 1772, cited by Schmitz (*Hugh Blair*, p. 66, n. 19) from a MS of the Historical Society of Pennsylvania.

3. Schmitz, *Hugh Blair*, p. 66.

4. Blair, *Lectures on Rhetoric and Belles Lettres*, v (4th ed.; London and Edinburgh, 1790), I, 119–20n. Blair apparently added the footnote references when preparing for publication—see the Preface, where he speaks of "remembering" the books he had consulted in preparation of the lectures.

5. The first edition of the *Lectures* was published in 1783; the first edition of the *Dissertation* (London, 1763) was followed by a second (1765) containing important additions. Schmitz (*Hugh Blair*, pp. 42–60, 88–90, 127–28) gives an account of Blair's part in the publication and criticism of the Ossianic poems; he is somewhat inclined to minimize the scholarship supporting the semi-authenticity of Ossian.

6. See Schmitz, *Hugh Blair*, pp. 143–45, and T. E. Jessop, *A Bibliography of David Hume and the Scottish Philosophy*, pp. 101–2, for the bibliography.

7. Blair, *Lectures*, i, ed. cit., I, 15.

8. *Ibid.*, p. 4.

9. *Ibid.*, p. 18.

10. *Ibid.*, ii, ed. cit., p. 20.

11. *Ibid.*, p. 21.

12. *Ibid.*, p. 34.

13. *Ibid.*, p. 38.

14. *Ibid.*, p. 39.

15. *Ibid.*, pp. 39–40.

16. *Ibid.*, iii, ed. cit., p. 56.

17. *Ibid.*, pp. 56–57.

18. *Ibid.*, p. 59.

19. *Ibid.*, pp. 61–62.

20. *Ibid.*, p. 65.

21. *Ibid.*, p. 67.

22. Blair, *A Critical Dissertation on the Poems of Ossian, the Son of Fingal*, appended to *The Poems of Ossian* . . . (London, 1790), II, 425.

23. Blair, *Lectures*, iii, ed. cit., I, 69–70.

24. *Ibid.*, p. 70.

25. *Ibid.*

26. *Ibid.*

27. *Ibid.*, p. 71.

28. *Ibid.*, iv, ed. cit., I, p. 74. Richardson uses "sublime" to mean "the most excellent of what is excellent, as the excellent is the best of what is good"; for literature this formula becomes "the greatest and most noble thoughts, images or sentiments, conveyed to us in the best chosen words" whether these words be plain and pointed or florid and heroic; for painting, the formula is "the greatest and most beautiful ideas conveyed to us the most advantageously." See Jonathan

Richardson, *An Essay on the Theory of Painting*, in *The Works of Mr. Jonathan Richardson* . . . (London, 1773), pp. 124 and 136. This chapter "Of the Sublime" appeared first in full in the second edition of the *Essay*, 1725. Much of what is generally treated of as the sublime is handled by Richardson under other heads, however; see especially his treatment of "Grace and Greatness" (pp. 93–123).

29. Blair, *Lectures*, iv, ed. cit., I, 75.
30. *Ibid.*, p. 73.
31. *Ibid.*, pp. 75–76.
32. Blair, *Dissertation*, in *Poems of Ossian*, II, 424.
33. Blair, *Lectures*, iv, ed. cit., I, 93–94.
34. Blair, *Dissertation*, in *Poems of Ossian*, II, 324.
35. *Ibid.*, p. 426. It is interesting to note that Johnson does not sanction the use of "pathetic" to refer to compassion and tenderness in his *Dictionary*; the only sense admitted for "pathetical, pathetick" is "Affecting the passions; passionate; moving." There is no change in this definition through the successive editions, even though Johnson himself used the word to mean "compassionate and tender."
36. Blair, *Lectures*, iv, ed. cit., I, 76.
37. Blair, *Dissertation*, in *Poems of Ossian*, II, 283–84.
38. Blair, *Lectures*, v, ed. cit., I, 101.
39. *Ibid.*, p. 102.
40. *Ibid.*, p. 104.
41. *Ibid.*, p. 105.
42. *Ibid.*, p. 108.
43. *Ibid.*, pp. 108–9.
44. *Ibid.*, p. 110.
45. *Ibid.*, pp. 113–14.
46. *Ibid.*, p. 118.

Chapter 9

1. The discourses were delivered to the Royal Academy, of which Reynolds was first president, on ceremonial occasions from 1769 to 1790; they were published individually, the first seven were published together in 1778, and the entire fifteen were edited by Edmond Malone, together with the other literary works of Reynolds, in 1797.
2. This chapter is adapted from my article, "General and Particular in the *Discourses* of Sir Joshua Reynolds: A Study in Method," *JAAC*, XI (March, 1953), 231–47, which may be consulted for somewhat fuller treatment both of Reynolds and of the pertinent scholarship.
3. Roger Fry (ed.), *Discourses Delivered to the Students of the Royal Academy by Sir Joshua Reynolds, Kt.* (London: Seeley and Co., 1905), pp. 40 and 179.
4. Michael Macklem, "Reynolds and the Ambiguities of Neo-Classical Criticism," *PQ*, XXXI (October, 1952), 383–98.
5. E[lbert] N. S. Thompson, "The *Discourses* of Sir Joshua Reynolds," *PMLA*, XXXII (1917), 365.
6. Reynolds, *The Literary Works of Sir Joshua Reynolds, Kt.*, ed. Edmond

Malone (5th ed.; London, 1819), Discourse xv, II, 217. I shall refer to this edition (pagination of all the Malone editions but the first is almost identical) as simply *Works*.

7. Joseph Burke, *Hogarth and Reynolds: A Contrast in English Art Theory* (The William Henry Charlton Memorial Lecture, November, 1941; London: Oxford, 1943), pp. 23–24.

8. Wilson O. Clough, "Reason and Genius," *PQ*, XXIII (January, 1944), 46–50. Reynolds, like Hogarth, Hume, and Burke, is made to contribute to the development of subjectivism in taste, in express contradiction to his announced intention.

9. Fry (ed.), *Discourses*, p. 44. Bellori's *Idea of a Painter* (translated in Dryden's preface to his translation of DuFresnoy's *Art of Painting* [pp. v–xiii of the second edition, 1716]) is repeatedly cited in this connection. Frederick Whiley Hilles, on the other hand, finds Count Algarotti's *Essay on Painting* (Englished in 1764) to be the original of Reynolds' theory: see *The Literary Career of Sir Joshua Reynolds* (Cambridge University Press, 1936), p. 121. Burke makes the same suggestion. In general, art scholars look for Reynolds' sources in Renaissance and eighteenth-century art critics, while literary scholars search in Johnson and Edmund Burke; but almost all agree in tracing the inheritance back to Plato and/or Aristotle.

10. Louis Bredvold, "The Tendency toward Platonism in Neo-Classical Esthetics," *ELH*, I (September, 1934), 115.

11. Macklem, "Reynolds and the Ambiguities of Neo-Classical Criticism," *PQ*, XXXI (October, 1952), 385–86.

12. Hoyt Trowbridge, "Platonism and Sir Joshua Reynolds," *ES*, XXI (February, 1939), 1.

13. The *Discourses* are neatly analyzed in terms of the problems to which they are addressed by Elder Olson in his Introduction to *Longinus*, *"On the Sublime"* . . . *and Sir Joshua Reynolds*, *"Discourses on Art"* . . . (Chicago: Packard, 1945). I take this analysis for granted here.

14. The distinctive traits of Aristotelian and Platonic thought, as I here understand them, are set forth in Richard P. McKeon's "The Philosophic Bases of Art and Criticism," *MP*, XLI (November, 1943), 65–87 and (February, 1944), 129–71. See McKeon's comment on Reynolds, pp. 155–56, n. 3.

15. Reynolds, *Works*, Discourse vii, I, 204. Note that this passage from the seventh discourse (like the thirteenth discourse) refers taste to human nature.

16. *Ibid.*, Discourse xiii, II, 135–36. Again, rules are "not to be determined by narrow principles of nature, separated from . . . [the] effect on the human mind" (*ibid.*, Discourse viii, I, 281).

17. See the second chapter ("Likeness Generalized: Aristotle and Sir Joshua Reynolds") of her *Retreat from Likeness in the Theory of Painting* (2d ed.; New York: Columbia University Press, 1949).

18. Reynolds, *Works*, Discourse vii, I, 224–25. Even on the conventional theme of the moral influence of art, Reynolds' statements are cast in characteristic terms:

"The Art which we profess has beauty for its object; this it is our business to discover and to express; the beauty of which we are in quest is general and intellectual; it is an idea that subsists only in the mind; the sight never beheld it, nor has the hand expressed it: it is an idea residing in the breast of the artist, which he is always labouring to impart, and which he dies at last without imparting; but which he is yet so far able to communicate as to raise the thoughts, and extend the views of the spectator; and which, by a succession of art, may be so far diffused, that its effects may extend themselves imperceptibly into publick benefits, and be among the means of bestowing on whole nations refinement of taste: which, if it does not lead directly to purity of manners, obviates at least their greatest depravation, by disentangling the mind from appetite, and conducting the thought through successive stages of excellence, till that contemplation of universal rectitude and harmony which began by Taste, may, as it is exalted and refined, conclude in Virtue" (*ibid.*, Discourse ix, II, 7–8).

19. *Ibid.*, Discourse vii, I, 200. Observe that the three examples correspond to the three modes of truth specified.

20. "The terms beauty, or nature, which are general ideas," Reynolds declares, "are but different modes of expressing the same thing . . ." (*ibid.*, p. 204). Or again, "there is but one presiding principle, which regulates and gives stability to every art. The works, whether of poets, painters, moralists, or historians, which are built upon general nature, live forever . . ." (*ibid.*, Discourse iv, I, 112).

21. For a study of the senses in which this term may be used, see Richard P. McKeon, "Literary Criticism and the Concepts of Imitation in Antiquity," *MP*, XXXIV (August, 1936), 1–35.

22. Reynolds, *Works*, Discourse ii, I, 32.

23. *Ibid.*, Discourse vi, I, 175.

24. *Ibid.*, Discourse ii, I, 35. The direct source of the passage appears to have been *The Painting of the Ancients* of Franciscus Junius (see Hilles, *Literary Career*, p. 127).

25. Reynolds, *Works*, Discourse vi, I, 181–82.

26. *Ibid.*, Discourse iii, I, 53.

27. *Ibid.*, p. 52 and Discourse xiii, II, 121. Once again the discourses, both early and late, appeal to the mind; there is no shift in orientation.

28. *Ibid.*, Discourse i, I, 9.

29. *Ibid.*, Discourse xiii, II, 142.

30. *Idler* No. 82 (November 10, 1759).

31. Sir Uvedale Price, "An Introductory Essay on Beauty; with Remarks on the Ideas of Sir Joshua Reynolds and Mr. Burke, upon That Subject," prefixed to his *A Dialogue on the Distinct Characters of the Picturesque and the Beautiful . . .* (Hereford, 1801); see *infra*, pp. 206–7.

Richard Payne Knight, *An Analytical Inquiry into the Principles of Taste* (3d ed.; London, 1806), i. 5. 23.

Dugald Stewart, *Philosophical Essays* (Edinburgh, 1810), ii. 1. 1. 7; and cf. *infra*, pp. 294–95.

32. See Fry's Introduction to the third discourse (*Discourses* [ed. Fry], pp. 39–47).

33. On the question of method here mooted, see Paul Goodman, "Neo-Classicism, Platonism, and Romanticism," *Journal of Philosophy*, XXXI, No. 6 (March 15, 1934), 148–63.

34. The letter is in Frederick Whiley Hilles, *Letters of Sir Joshua Reynolds* (Cambridge University Press, 1929), pp. 90–93.

35. Reynolds, *Works*, Discourse viii, I, 276.

36. *Ibid.*, Discourse iv, I, 92; the numerous similar passages are trivial, since Reynolds does not regard this as a major distinction. Johnson's *Dictionary* (1755) supports Reynolds' sense of "elegance"; "elegant" is defined, "1. Pleasing with minuter beauties," and "Elegance, Elegancy" is defined as "Beauty of art; rather soothing than striking; beauty without grandeur."

37. Reynolds, *Works*, Discourse xv, II, 204–5.

38. *Ibid.*, Discourse v, I, 124 and ff.

39. *Ibid.*, Discourse viii, I, 282n.

40. Thompson, "The *Discourses* of Sir Joshua Reynolds," *PMLA*, XXXII (1917), 358; Donald Cross Bryant, *Edmund Burke and His Literary Friends* ("Washington University Studies—New Series; Language and Literature"—No. 9; St. Louis, 1939) pp. 53–54. Chapter iii of Bryant treats of Burke's relations with Reynolds; Bryant merely follows Thompson on this aesthetic point.

41. Edmund Burke, "On Taste," *Sublime and Beautiful*, in *Works*, I, 67; Reynolds, *Works*, Discourse vii, II, 199.

42. Hilles (*Literary Career*, chap. vii) gives neither Johnson nor Burke much credit for aid in composing the discourses. The revisions with which Johnson and Malone touched up the first printed editions of the individual discourses are analyzed in an exhaustive collation of texts by Lauder Greenway, *Alterations in the Discourses of Sir Joshua Reynolds* (New York: Privately printed, 1936); Greenway's conclusion is that the revisions concerned only minutiae of style— Reynolds, in short, wrote his own discourses.

43. Reynolds, *Works*, Discourse xi, II, 45.

44. *Ibid.*, Discourse xv, II, 206–7.

45. *Ibid.*, Discourse xiii, II, 111.

46. *Ibid.*, p. 112.

47. *Ibid.*, Discourse iii, I, 55.

48. *Ibid.*, Discourse vi, I, 156.

49. *Ibid.*, Discourse xi, II, 43.

50. *Ibid.*, Discourse vi, I, 186.

51. *Ibid.*, p. 145.

52. *Ibid.*, Discourse xv, II, 188–89.

53. *Ibid.*, Discourse vi, I, 172.

54. *Ibid.*, p. 155.

55. *Ibid.*, Discourse viii, I, 264. The arts "in their highest province, are not addressed to the gross senses; but to the desires of the mind, to that spark of divinity which we have within, impatient of being circumscribed and pent up by the world which is about us" (*ibid.*, Discourse xiii, II, 142–43). It is patent that in Reynolds' thought, wish-fulfillment is apprehension of the Ideal; the distinction of wish-fulfilling idealization of the actual from the transcendent Ideal (which Macklem stresses in "Reynolds and the Ambiguities of Neo-Classical Criticism," *PQ*, XXXI [October, 1952], 383–98) involves no real opposition.

56. Reynolds, *Works*, Discourse vii, I, 201.

57. *Ibid.*, Discourse ii, I, 26–27.

58. *Ibid.*, Discourse xiii, II, 113–18.

59. *Ibid.*, Discourse v, I, 128–29.

60. Reynolds speaks of "whatever partakes of fancy or caprice, or goes under

the denomination of Picturesque" (*ibid.*, Discourse x, II, 37); throughout the tenth discourse the picturesque serves to set off effects inappropriate to sculpture, which above all other media requires a chaste gravity—the grand style. I postpone discussion of Reynolds' views on the picturesque, however, until I treat his correspondence with Gilpin (*infra*, pp. 199–201).

61. Reynolds, *Works*, Discourse xiii, II, 127.

62. *Ibid.*, Discourse v, I, 132.

63. The painter "must sometimes deviate from vulgar and strict historical truth, in pursuing the grandeur of his design" (*ibid.*, Discourse iv, I, 85). Thus, Gothic architecture, "though not so ancient as the Grecian, is more so to our imagination, with which the Artist is more concerned than with absolute [i.e., historical] truth" (*ibid.*, Discourse xiii, II, 138).

64. *Ibid.*, Discourse i, I, 8.

Chapter 10

1. Reid observes of Kames's *Elements of Criticism* that "in that Appendix, most of the words [i.e., philosophical terms] are explained on which I have been making observations; and the explication I have given, I think, agrees, for the most part, with his" (*Essays on the Intellectual Powers of Man*, i. 1, in *The Works of Thomas Reid . . .* , ed. Sir William Hamilton [8th ed.; Edinburgh: Maclachlan and Stewart, 1880], I, 230a). Methodologically, Gerard and Alison are, on the whole, closer to Hume.

2. The early work, *An Inquiry into the Human Mind on the Principles of Common Sense* (Edinburgh, 1764) does not treat of aesthetic taste or its objects. Reid's psychology is completed in the *Essays on the Active Powers of Man* (Edinburgh, 1788), which again does not touch upon taste.

3. Monk, *The Sublime*, p. 147.

4. David O. Robbins, "The Aesthetics of Thomas Reid," *JAAC*, No. 5 (Spring, 1942), p. 38. Robbins' point of view is clear in the remark that "in the last few decades of the eighteenth century, when English aesthetics had run stale after its promising start in Addison and Shaftesbury, Reid stands out by contrast and in his own right as an original thinker" (*ibid.*, p. 30).

5. Reid, *Intellectual Powers*, viii. 1, in *Works*, I, 490a.

6. *Ibid.*

7. *Ibid.*, p. 490a–b.

8. *Ibid.*, p. 490b.

9. Reid, *An Inquiry into the Human Mind on the Principles of Common Sense*, vii, in *Works*, I, 205b–206a, editor's note. Reid does do Locke at least the justice to say that his doctrine on secondary qualities "is not so much an error in judgment as an abuse of words" (*Intellectual Powers*, viii. 4, in *Works*, I, 499b).

10. Reid, *Intellectual Powers*, viii. 1, in *Works*, I, 491b.

11. *Ibid.*, p. 492a.

12. *Ibid.*, i. 1, in *Works*, I, 224b. Reid himself is obliged, however, to explain away some of the implications of the language used by all men; and in any case, the "just foundation in nature" can certainly not be taken as guaranteeing the validity of a distinction. Even Stewart criticizes Reid for, in assuming

too unqualifiedly that language is the express image of thought, often laying "greater stress on the structure of speech, than . . . it can always bear in a philosophical argument" (*Philosophical Essays*, i. 5. 1, in *Works*, V, 154).

13. Reid, *Intellectual Powers*, viii. 2, in *Works*, I, 493a.

14. *Ibid.*

15. *Ibid.*, viii. 3, p. 494b.

16. *Ibid.*, p. 498a.

17. *Ibid.*, p. 495b.

18. *Ibid.*, p. 498a.

19. *Ibid.*, p. 497b.

20. Robbins, "The Aesthetics of Thomas Reid," *JAAC*, No. 5 (Spring, 1942), pp. 37–38.

21. Reid, *Intellectual Powers*, viii. 3, in *Works*, I, 496a.

22. *Ibid.*

23. *Ibid.*, p. 498a.

24. *Ibid.*, viii. 4, in *Works*, I, 498b.

25. *Ibid.*, p. 502a–b.

26. *Ibid.*, p. 498b.

27. *Ibid.*, p. 501b.

28. *Ibid.*, p. 502b.

29. *Ibid.*, viii. 3, in *Works*, I, 503a.

30. Letter to Alison of February 3, 1790, in *Works*, I, 89b.

31. Reid, *Intellectual Powers*, viii. 4, in *Works*, I, 503b.

32. *Ibid.*, p. 505b. Reid is not at all points consistent in appreciation of the beauty of contrivance. He notes that poisonous animals and plants are disagreeable to the eye, a generalization which appears to me (despite the authority of Linnaeus) false—but true or false, it cannot be made consistent with Reid's system, for the poisonousness of such animals and plants often exhibits the nicest adaptation to the ends of the species.

33. Stewart, *Philosophical Essays*, i. 5. 2, in *Works*, V, 161.

34. Reid, *Intellectual Powers*, viii. 4, in *Works*, I, 507b. Grace is of two sorts, one majestical (grand) the other familiar (beautiful).

Chapter 11

1. *Monthly Review*, III (Enlarged Series; 1790), 361–73; IV (1791), 8–19. See also the *New Annual Register* (1790), p. 203.

2. Letter to Alison of February 3, 1790, in Hamilton's edition of Reid's *Works* (8th ed.; Edinburgh, 1880), I, 89. This is the letter discussed *supra*, p. 155.

3. Stewart, *Elements*, i. 5. 2. 2, in *Works*, ed. Hamilton (Edinburgh, 1877), II, 321; *Philosophical Essays*, *pluries*, in *Works*, V.

4. *The Letters of Robert Burns*, ed. Francis H. Allen (Boston: Houghton, 1927), III, 9–10. William Knight (*The Philosophy of the Beautiful; Being Outlines of the History of Aesthetics* [New York: Scribner, 1891], p. 213) detects a "delicate irony" in this letter; but Knight takes little stock in the "degenerate teaching" of the associationists, and is perhaps inclined to see such irony too easily.

5. Jeffrey reviewed the *Essays* in the *Edinburgh Review* for May of 1811 (XVIII, 1–46), and subsequently expanded the review into the article "Beauty" for the *Encyclopaedia Britannica* supplement of 1816. His advocacy was like that of most enthusiastic disciples—it altered the doctrine while spreading it.

6. Bosanquet, *A History of Aesthetic*, p. 441. But of course Alison and the other philosophical critics were much concerned with distinguishing the relevant from the accidental in association; Bosanquet errs gravely in applying his system to Alison, for Alison was treating the very problems which Bosanquet regards as central, employing throughout the very contrary (form and expression) on which Bosanquet's history is based. Bosanquet applies his principles rigidly and without insight except to the schools from which he sprang.

7. Archibald Alison, *Essays on the Nature and Principles of Taste* (4th ed.; Edinburgh, 1815), Introduction, I, xiv.

8. *Ibid.*, p. xi.

9. *Ibid.*, p. xxiii. This important point in the outline is omitted in the first edition.

10. *Ibid.*, p. xiv.

11. *Ibid.*, p. xxv.

12. *Ibid.*, p. xiv.

13. *Ibid.*, pp. xviii–xxi; this discussion was added in the second edition. Alison's distinction between these two classes of theorists is weak, for it presupposes that philosophers avoid postulating special and appropriated faculties; Hutcheson and Kames fall, in these terms, with the artists and amateurs.

14. *Ibid.*, i. Conclusion. 4, ed. cit., I, 172.

15. *Ibid.*, ii. 1, ed. cit., I, 69.

16. I see no objection to analyzing the argument of Alison in the terms of J. S. Mill's canons of induction, for questions of logic are independent of history. But in any case, Mill's canons bear a close relation to Hume's rules for judging of causes and effects, and with Hume Alison was familiar.

17. Alison, *Essays*, i. 1. 1, ed. cit., I, 5–6.

18. *Ibid.*, i. 1. 2. 1, ed. cit., I, 11.

19. *Ibid.*, i. 1. 2. 2, ed. cit., I, 13–14.

20. *Ibid.*, i. 1. 3. 2, ed. cit., I, 43. Alison also uses "picturesque" in the ordinary sense of "fit for painting"—see *ibid.*, ii. 6. 5. 2, ed. cit., II, 411.

21. *Ibid.*, i. 2. 1. 2, ed. cit., I, 78.

22. *Ibid.*, i. 2. 2, ed. cit., I, 81.

23. *Ibid.*, i. 2. 2. 4, ed. cit., I, 119.

24. *Ibid.*, i. 2. 3. 4, ed. cit., I, 157.

25. *Ibid.*, i. Conclusion. 3, ed. cit., I, 161.

26. *Ibid.*, i. Conclusion. 4, ed. cit., I, 172.

27. *Ibid.*, ii. 1, ed. cit., I, 176–77.

28. James McCosh, *The Scottish Philosophy* (New York: Scribner, 1890), p. 311. When McCosh tells us that certain colors, proportions, and sounds—all reducible to mathematical ratios—are inherently pleasing, and that other beauties land us in the moral good; that, in short, "beauty is a gorgeous robe spread over certain portions of the true and the good (*ibid.* [article on Stewart], p. 297), it is clear that we can expect no very sympathetic insight into a literal and associational theory.

29. Alison, *Essays*, ii. 6. 6, ed. cit., II, 415–16.

30. *Ibid.*, ii. 1, ed. cit., I, 189.

31. See Reid's letter to Alison, *supra*, p. 155.

32. Alison, *Essays*, ii. 6. 6, ed. cit., II, 417.

33. See Monk, *The Sublime*, pp. 148–53; McKenzie, *Critical Responsiveness*, pp. 46, 71; Martin Kallich, "The Meaning of Archibald Alison's *Essays on Taste*," *PQ*, XXVII (October, 1948), 315.

34. Alison does not employ resemblance, contiguity, and cause-and-effect as the categories of all spontaneous association; nor does he employ the terms "idea" and "impression" as Hume does. He speaks of "association in the proper sense"—i.e., accidental association—in contradistinction to "experience," another usage foreign to Hume. In addition to these differences in terminology, Hume would (as I think) see no impossibility in the production of emotions by material properties, nor would he emphasize that qualities of matter may resemble those of mind, or the sensations from the former the emotions raised by the latter.

35. Alison, *Essays*, ii. 6. 6, ed. cit., II, 416.

36. There is so little in common between Alison and the "Platonists" that it is difficult to point up differences. Among the moderns, Hutcheson and Reid are treated above; Shaftesbury and Spence need not be examined here; a few words on Akenside may be ventured. Akenside is often regarded, as by Reid (*Intellectual Powers*, viii. 4, in *Works*, I, 503a) and by Stewart (*Philosophy of the Active and Moral Powers of Man*, ii. 5. 2, in *Works*, VI, 309), as having asserted that matter is beautiful only as the expression of mind when he cried,

> "Mind, mind alone (bear witness, earth and heaven!)
> The living fountains in itself contains
> Of beauteous and sublime . . ."

(*The Pleasures of Imagination* [London, 1744], Bk. I, ll. 481–83). But the context of this enigmatic utterance suggests that the meaning may be merely this: that all beauty and sublimity have their origin in the mind of God and their highest expression in the mind of man—which is not at all equivalent to Alison's position that particular material qualities are beautiful or sublime only as signs of particular mental qualities.

37. Alison, *Essays* (1st ed.), Conclusion, p. 411.

38. *Ibid.*, pp. 411–12.

39. *Ibid.*, p. 412.

40. *Ibid.*, p. 413. The original is in large and small capitals.

41. Alison, *Essays*, ii. 6. 6 (4th ed., following the 2d), II, 423. The original is in small capitals.

42. *Ibid.*, pp. 417–23 (condensed). An earlier and not wholly identical account is found in ii. 1, ed. cit., I, 179–87. In this first list, Alison suggests that the *analogy* of mental and material properties may be of two kinds—either the analogy of inanimate matter with mind through the resemblance of material properties to qualities which the body assumes in response to mental dispositions, or the original and unanalyzable resemblance of certain sensations and emotions (as of the sensation of gradual descent and the emotion of decay, or of silence and tranquillity, &c.). The differences between the two lists are easily accounted

for: the early list is of the causes of association between matter and mind, the later of the classes of such associations.

43. Alison, *Essays*, ii. 2. 1, ed. cit., I, 252.

44. *Ibid.*, ii. 3, ed. cit., I, 290.

45. *Ibid.*, ii. 3. 1, ed. cit., I, 299.

46. *Ibid.*, ii. 4. 1. 2, ed. cit., I, 329.

47. *Ibid.*, p. 375.

48. *Ibid.*, ii. 4. 1. 3. 1, ed. cit., II, 5.

49. A great part of the beauty of composition is of course *relative* rather than natural beauty—a beauty of design.

50. Hogarth, *Analysis of Beauty*, chap. viii.

51. Alison, *Essays*, ii. 4. 1. 3. 2, ed. cit., II, 37–38 (condensed).

52. McKenzie declares (*Critical Responsiveness*, p. 162) that the "importance of Alison's perception that because literature is primarily emotional, literary form is in the most real sense a structure of emotions rather than of ideas, personalities, and events can hardly be overstated." Nonetheless, it is precisely a psychology of emotion that is most imperatively required to complete Alison's system.

53. Alison, *Essays*, ii. 4. 2. 2. 2, ed. cit., II, 135–36.

54. *Ibid.*, ii. 4. 2. 2. 4, ed. cit., II, 189.

55. *Ibid.*, pp. 190–91.

56. Monk, *The Sublime*, p. 154.

57. Christopher Hussey, *The Picturesque: Studies in a Point of View* (London: Putnam, 1927), p. 15. Setting aside the inaccuracies of Hussey's account, I must remark the unhappy moral position in which he places us— that of theologians conspiring to suppress what is known to be true for the sake of what is groundless but indispensable.

58. Kallich, "The Meaning of Archibald Alison's *Essays on Taste*," PQ, XXVIII (October, 1948), 319 ff.

59. McKenzie, *Critical Responsiveness*, p. 165.

60. Alison, *Essays*, ii. 6. 4. 1, ed. cit., II, 367.

61. *Ibid.*, Introduction, ed. cit., I, xv.

62. *Ibid.*, ii. 4. 3, ed. cit., II, 202; my italics.

63. *Ibid.*, ii. 5. 1, ed. cit., II, 212–13.

64. *Ibid.*, ii. 6. 2. 3, ed. cit., II, 297.

65. *Ibid.*, ii. 6. 2. 1, ed. cit., II, 226.

66. *Ibid.*, ii. 6. 2. 2, ed. cit., II, 247–48.

67. *Ibid.*, ii. 6. 3. 2, ed. cit., II, 327–28.

68. *Ibid.*, ii. 2. 2. 2, ed. cit., I, 258–60.

69. *Ibid.*, ii. 4. 2. 1. 1, ed. cit., II, 60.

70. *Ibid.*, ii. 5. 1, ed. cit., II, 207.

71. *Ibid.*, ii. 6. 4, ed. cit., II, 358.

72. *Ibid.*, ii. 6. 5, ed. cit., II, 380.

73. *Ibid.*, ii. 6. 5. 2, ed. cit., II, 387.

74. *Ibid.*, ii. 6. 6, ed. cit., II, 424.

75. *Ibid.*, pp. 436–38.

76. *Ibid.*, p. 442.

77. *Ibid.*, ii. 6. 2. 3, ed. cit., II, 268.

78. *Ibid.*, p. 294.

Chapter 12

1. John Britton, *Picturesque Antiquities of the English Cities* (London: Dean and Son, *ca.* 1830), p. [v].

2. [William Aglionby], *Painting Illustrated in Three Diallogues . . . Together with the Lives of the Most Eminent Painters . . .* (London, 1685), p. 24.

3. See Act IV, scene 2 of *The Tender Husband*. It is of interest to note that as late as 1783 William Mason uses "picturesque" to refer to the allegorical manner of the grand style, a usage quite anomalous at that late date. The twenty-third axiom he isolates in DuFresnoy's *De Arte Graphica* ("Of Picturesque Ornament") reads, in his translation,

> "Each nobler symbol classic Sages use,
> To mark a virtue, or adorn a Muse,
> Ensigns of war, of peace, or Rites divine,
> These in thy work with dignity may shine."

See Mason's *DuFresnoy* in *The Literary Works of Sir Joshua Reynolds*, ed. Malone (5th ed.; London, 1819), III, 51. Applied to allegorical painting, "picturesque" can mean "vivid" as representation of idea, "pictorial" as composition.

For Pope, see the letter to Caryll of December 21, 1712 (*The Works of Alexander Pope*, eds. Croker and Elwin, VI [London: J. Murray, 1871], 178); the sense I judge to be (*OED* to the contrary) "graphic," not "fit for painting." The passages in the *Iliad* too (final note to Book X, first note to Book XVI) use "picturesque" to mean "as distinctly conceived and presented as a picture."

4. Johnson's definitions are:

(1) *graphically:* "In a picturesque manner; with good description or delineation."

(2) *Love* [as noun]: "11. Picturesque representation of love.

> The lovely babe was born with ev'ry grace:
> Such was his form as painters, when they show
> Their utmost art, on naked *loves* bestow.
>
> *Dryden.*"

(3) *prospect* [as noun]: "5. View delineated; a picturesque representation of a landscape."

Note that in the second definition, "picturesque" is again used to refer to allegorical painting. The example given from Reynolds to illustrate the third definition does not, unhappily, support it, for Reynolds clearly refers to a real scene, not to an imitation. What is of chief interest in this definition, however, is the literal use of "picturesque" to mean "in a picture," a use which does not often recur.

The first two of these definitions appeared in the first edition of the *Dictionary* (1755), the third in the sixth (1785).

5. See the references to Carel van Mander's *Het Schilder-Boeck . . .* (second

edition of the first part, Amsterdam, 1618) and to Gérard de Lairesse's *Het groot Schilderboek* (2d ed.; Haarlem, 1740) in *Woordenboek der Nederlandsche Taal* (14th Deel; 's Gravenhage and Leiden, 1936).

6. Joachim von Sandrart, *L'Academie Todesca della Architectura Scultura et Pictura: oder Teutsche Academie der edlen Bau- Bild- und Mahlerey-Künste* . . . (Nürnberg and Frankfurt, 1675), sec. 259 of chap. xxii of part one of the third book of the First Part, as reprinted in A. R. Peltzer's *Joachim von Sandrarts Academie* . . . (Munich: G. Hirth, 1925), p. 203. The passage contains another Dutch word, "alludien" (Dutch "aloud"—"very old"), not glossed by Peltzer. "Schilderachtig" is not given in any German dictionary; its place is later taken by "malerisch."

7. Painters, Hogarth assures us in the first MS draft of *The Analysis of Beauty* (before 1753), regard asymmetrical adornments as "Pictoresque" (Egerton MS 3011 f. 60b, quoted from *The Analysis of Beauty*, ed. Burke, p. 174); Richard Polwhele finds the sonnet especially adapted to "the more pictoresque Objects of still Life" ("Advertisement" to his anonymous *Pictures from Nature. In Twelve Sonnets* . . . [London, 1785]); the same form is used regularly by Nathan Drake. I take it that it reflects Price's view of the etymology, of which more hereafter.

"Picteresque" occurs in *An Essay on Harmony, as It Relates Chiefly to Situation, and Buildings* (1739), as cited in Manwaring, *Italian Landscape*, p. 134.

Dr. John Langhorne, in a note to the first of Collins' "Persian Eclogues," uses a form which implies the contrary etymology: "The characteristics of modesty and chastity are extremely happy and *peinturesque*. . ." (*The Poetical Works of William Collins* [London: William Pickering, 1830], p. 107—Langhorne's edition was first published in 1765).

The only writer known to me who uses the form "picturesk" is William Marshall, author of *A Review of The Landscape, A Didactic Poem* . . . (London, 1795) and of *Planting and Rural Ornament* (rev. ed., 2 vols.; London, 1796).

8. Blair, *Lectures*, xxxix, ed. cit., III, 121; the discussion is of pastoral poetry. See also Blair's treatment of Picturesque Description (*Lectures*, xl, ed. cit., III, 159 ff.).

9. *The Expedition of Humphry Clinker*, in *The Works of Tobias Smollett* (New York: George D. Sproul, 1902), XII, 188–89.

10. Edmond Malone (ed.), *Literary Works of Reynolds*, I, xxi.

11. Johnson lists "pictorial" in his *Dictionary* (1755), assigning the meaning, "produced by a painter." Citing an instance from Sir Thomas Browne, he remarks, "A word not adopted by other writers, but elegant and useful."

12. Robert S. Bridges, "Pictorial. Picturesque. Romantic. Grotesque. Classical.," in *SPE Tract No. XV* (Oxford: Clarendon Press, 1923), p. 16.

13. *Ibid.*, p. 19.

14. Hussey, *The Picturesque*, pp. 4–5.

15. *Ibid.*, p. 17.

16. Wylie Sypher, "Baroque Afterpiece: The Picturesque," *Gazette des Beaux-Arts*, XXVII (January, 1945), p. 46.

17. *Ibid.*, p. 56.

Chapter 13

1. For biographical, bibliographical, and historical information about Gilpin and his writings, consult William D. Templeman's *The Life and Work of William Gilpin (1724–1804), Master of the Picturesque and Vicar of Boldre* ("Illinois Studies in Language and Literature," Vol. XXIV, Nos. 3 and 4; Urbana: University of Illinois Press, 1939).

2. *A Dialogue upon the Gardens of the Right Honourable The Lord Viscount Cobham, at Stow in Buckinghamshire.* Printed for B. Seeley, Buckingham, sold by J. and J. Rivington, London, 1748 (later eds., 1749 and 1751). The evidence for Gilpin's authorship of this small work is in Templeman's *Gilpin,* pp. 33–35 (external) and 117–28 (internal), in which latter place an extensive précis is given.

3. *An Essay upon Prints; Containing Remarks upon the Principles of Picturesque Beauty, the Different Kinds of Prints, and the Characters of the Most Noted Masters* . . . (London, 1768). The first edition and the second (also 1768) are anonymous; the third (1781), fourth (1792), and fifth (1802) carry the author's name.

4. *Ibid.* (1st ed.), p. 2. The succeeding definition is of "*Picturesque grace:* an agreeable form given, in a picture, to a clownish figure" (*ibid.,* p. 3).

5. London, 1792. There was a second edition in 1794, and a third was included in *Five Essays, on Picturesque Subjects; with a Poem on Landscape Painting* (London, 1808), which includes also the second edition of *Two Essays: One, On the Author's Mode of Executing Rough Sketches; the Other, On the Principles on Which They Are Composed* . . . (London, 1804).

6. Two volumes; London, 1791; further editions appeared in 1794 and 1808, in 1834 (edited by Sir Thomas Dick Lauder), and in 1879 and 1887 (edited by Francis George Heath).

7. Consult Templeman for details of the bibliography.

8. Gilpin, *Three Essays* (2d ed.), i, p. [3]—the opening sentence.

9. *Ibid.,* [Dedication], ed. cit., p. ii.

10. *Ibid.,* i, ed. cit., p. 4. Gilpin declines the inquiry into "the *general sources of beauty,* either in nature, or in representation," as leading "into a nice, and scientific discussion, in which it is not our purpose to engage" (*ibid.*).

11. *Ibid.*

12. *Ibid.,* p. 6. Gilpin doubts Burke's doctrine that smoothness is the most considerable source of beauty, and he argues vigorously against Burke's notion of the diminutiveness of beauty, contending that there is "a beauty, between which and diminutives there is no relation; but which, on the contrary, excludes them: and in the description of figures, possessed of that species of beauty, we seek for terms, which recommend them more to our *admiration* than our *love*" (*ibid.,* pp. 5–6n).

13. *Ibid.,* pp. 6–7.

14. Quoted by Hussey, *The Picturesque,* p. 119.

15. Gilpin, *Three Essays,* i, ed. cit., p. 17.

16. *Ibid.,* p. 21.

17. *Ibid.,* p. 19.

18. *Ibid.*

19. *Ibid.*, p. 26. Templeman gives an extensive précis of the earlier parts of Gilpin's essay (*Gilpin*, pp. 134–40); but he wholly ignores this section, which is of the most considerable philosophic importance, and which leads (as I think) to the further evolution of picturesque theory.

20. Gilpin, *Three Essays*, i, ed. cit., pp. 26–27.

21. *Ibid.*, p. 28. Hutcheson's principle is fitted to an analogizing system and (as Gilpin indicates) does not readily admit discrimination of *kinds* of beauty.

22. *Ibid.*, p. 30.

23. *Ibid.*, p. 33.

24. The subject of picturesque travel has been handled by Elizabeth Wheeler Manwaring, *Italian Landscape in Eighteenth Century England* (New York: Oxford, 1925), pp. 167–200, and by Hussey, *The Picturesque*, pp. 83–127. Monk treats of "sublime travel" in *The Sublime*, pp. 203–32, and makes many observations pertinent to the present subject.

25. Gilpin, *Three Essays* (letter to Reynolds), p. 36.

26. *Ibid.*, ii, ed. cit., p. 43.

27. Gilpin, *Forest Scenery* (3d ed.; London, 1808), II, 168–69.

28. Gilpin, *Three Essays*, ii, ed. cit., p. 43.

29. Gilpin, *Forest Scenery*, II, 175. "To make an object truely picturesque, it should be marked strongly with some peculiar character," remarks Gilpin in explaining the unpicturesqueness of the mule (*ibid.*, II, 271).

30. Gilpin, *Three Essays*, ii, ed. cit., p. 46.

31. *Ibid.*, pp. 49–50.

32. Templeman (*Gilpin*, p. 142) suggests that this formation of general ideas enables the picturesque traveler to set up his own standards of beauty, and connects it with an alleged striving for individual standards of taste in the later eighteenth century; but surely it would be more natural to see general ideas and typical forms as *opposed* to personal and idiosyncratic taste.

33. Gilpin, *Three Essays*, ii, ed. cit., pp. 51–52.

34. *Ibid.*, pp. 57–58—the concluding sentence of the essay. A rough sketch, "which the imagination *only* can translate," is more apt to raise this enthusiasm than a finished work of art.

35. *Ibid.*, iii, ed. cit., p. 87.

36. For an account of this transaction, see William D. Templeman, "Sir Joshua Reynolds on the Picturesque," *MLN*, XLVII (November, 1932), 446–48. Taylor prints the letter, but terms it a "paper" and appears to think that it was written after the 1791 letter to Gilpin; see Charles Leslie and Tom Taylor, *Life and Times of Sir Joshua Reynolds* . . . (London: J. Murray, 1865), II, 606–8.

37. Leslie and Taylor, *Reynolds*, II, 606.

38. *Ibid.*, pp. 606–7.

39. Gilpin, *Three Essays*, i, ed. cit., p. 27.

40. Leslie and Taylor, *Reynolds*, II, 608.

41. Gilpin, *Three Essays*, pp. 34–35. Gilpin prints Reynolds' reply and his own note of thanks on pp. 34–37.

42. *Ibid.*, pp. 35–36.

43. In the tenth discourse (1780), Reynolds uses the picturesque to set off

effects inappropriate to sculpture, a medium which can tolerate only the grand style. It is noteworthy that Gilpin recognizes no essential difference between painting and sculpture in the scope of their imitations. He grants that it is more difficult for sculpture to exhibit animated action or the passions, but considers that when this effect is nonetheless achieved such statues will be preferred (*Three Essays*, i, p. 13). This position is in interesting contrast with the remark of Uvedale Price only two years later, that the picturesque may be given definition *in extenso* as that which painting can, and sculpture can not, represent.

44. Gilpin, *Forest Scenery*, II, 234.

Chapter 14

1. The picturesque works are:

An Essay on the Picturesque, As Compared with the Sublime and the Beautiful, and on the Use of Studying Pictures, for the Purpose of Improving Real Landscape ([Vol. I]; London, 1794). 2d ed., 1796.

A Letter to H. Repton, Esq., on the Application of the Practice As Well As the Principles of Landscape-Painting to Landscape-Gardening. Intended As a Supplement to the "Essay on the Picturesque," to Which Is Prefixed Mr. Repton's Letter to Mr. Price (London, 1795). 2d ed., Hereford, 1798.

An Essay on the Picturesque . . . Vol. II (London, 1798). This volume consists of three essays: "An Essay on Artificial Water, &c.," "An Essay on the Decorations near the House," "An Essay on Architecture and Buildings, As Connected with Scenery."

A Dialogue on the Distinct Characters of the Picturesque and the Beautiful, in Answer to the Objections of Mr. Knight. Prefaced by an Introductory Essay on Beauty; with Remarks on the Ideas of Sir Joshua Reynolds & Mr. Burke upon That Subject (Hereford, 1801).

All these were gathered together with a few additions and alterations into *Essays on the Picturesque, As Compared with the Sublime and the Beautiful; and, on the Use of Studying Pictures, for the Purpose of Improving Real Landscape* (3 vols.; London, 1810). The works included in this 1810 edition are found again in *Sir Uvedale Price on the Picturesque: with an Essay on the Origin of Taste, and Much Original Matter, by Sir Thomas Dick Lauder, Bart. . . .* (Edinburgh and London, 1842).

I have used the 1810 edition, which I refer to as "*Works*"; the 1794 volume, as it appears in the *Works*, I refer to simply as "*Essay*."

2. Uvedale Price, *Essay*, i. 3, in *Works*, I, 37.

3. *Ibid.*, p. 40.

4. Price, *Works*, II, vi–vii.

5. Price, *Essay*, i. 3, in *Works*, I, 46–47.

6. *Ibid.*, i. 4, in *Works*, I, 88–89.

7. *Ibid.*, pp. 92–93.

8. *Ibid.*, i. 9, in *Works*, I, 221. The case is analogous in ethics; envy and revenge, for instance, are both modes of ill-will, and are most easily differentiated by pointing to their different causes.

9. Price, *Dialogue* ("Introductory Essay on Beauty"), in *Works*, III, 203.

10. Price, *Essay*, i. 9, in *Works*, I, 212–13.

11. Reynolds declares that if a critic pretends to measure beauty by "a particular gradation of magnitude, undulation of a curve, or direction of a line, or whatever other conceit of his imagination he shall fix on as a criterion of form, he will be continually contradicting himself, and find at last that the great mother of nature will not be subjected to such narrow rules" (*Idler*, No. 82 [November 10, 1759]).

12. Price, *Dialogue* ("Introductory Essay on Beauty"), in *Works*, III, 213–14.

13. *Ibid.*, pp. 237–38. Payne Knight also makes the observation that Reynolds and Burke pointed to different aspects of the beautiful, and that their difference was merely verbal: "It will readily appear that these two great critics differ so widely merely from attaching different meanings to the word beauty; which, the one confines to the *sensible*, and the other to the *intellectual* qualities of things; both equally departing from that general use of the term, which is the only just criterion of propriety in speech" (*Analytical Inquiry*, i. 5. 23, p. 75).

14. Price, *Dialogue* ("Introductory Essay on Beauty"), in *Works*, III, 239.

15. Price, "On Architecture and Buildings," in *Works*, II, 247.

16. Jean-Jacques Mayoux urges that Payne Knight's *The Landscape* for the first time considered beauty to be in the perceiver rather than in the object perceived, and he finds Price to be "un esprit peu clair et tout engagé dans les idées reçues," ideas like the notion that beauty exists objectively; see *Richard Payne Knight et le pittoresque: Essai sur une phase esthétique* (Thèse pour le doctorate ès-lettres présentée . . . [à l'] Université de Paris; Paris: Les Presses Modernes, 1932), p. 82. For Hussey, too, Price attempted to establish an objectivism, but the effort was "sophistry, as objectivism must always be" (*The Picturesque*, p. 78).

17. Price, "On Architecture and Buildings," in *Works*, II, 247.

18. *Ibid.*, pp. 213–14 and 365–66.

19. Burke mentions one trait of the picturesque in remarking on the cruciform plan of churches, and finds it distasteful: "there is nothing more prejudicial to the grandeur of buildings than to abound in angles: a fault obvious in many; and owing to an inordinate thirst for variety, which, whenever it prevails, is sure to leave very little true taste" (*Sublime and Beautiful*, ii. 9, in *Works*, I, 126).

20. Price, *Essay*, i. 3, in *Works*, I, 44; the etymology and its implications are drawn out at length, *ibid.*, i. 9, *Works*, I, 211 ff. Neither of these passages was present in the 1794 edition.

21. Price, *Works*, II, xiii–xiv and xv–xvi.

22. Price, *Essay*, i. 3, in *Works*, I, 49.

23. Intricacy Price defines as "*that disposition of objects, which, by a partial and uncertain concealment, excites and nourishes curiosity*" (*ibid.*, i. 2, in *Works*, I, 22). And "variety, of which the true end is to relieve the eye, not to perplex it, does not consist in the diversity of separate objects, but in that of their effects when combined together; in diversity of composition, and of character" (*ibid.*, ii. 2, in *Works*, I, 286).

24. Price's mention of Salvator as picturesque, though accompanied by the remark that his work "has a savage grandeur, often in the highest degree sublime" (*ibid.*, i. 3, in *Works*, I, 67), has misled some commentators into making Salvator a type of the picturesque (see Miss Manwaring, *Italian Landscape*, p.

55). Salvator is here employed to distinguish beautiful from picturesque because he stands on the sublime side of picturesqueness, farthest from beauty. Ordinarily, in landscape, Claude is beautiful, Salvator sublime, and Gaspar "Poussin" (Dughet) picturesque; in history and portrait, the great Romans and Florentines are sublime, Correggio and Guido beautiful, Tintoretto and Veronese picturesque.

25. Price, *Essay*, i. 4, in *Works*, I, 69. This association became a commonplace. Britton, about 1830, writes, "With all due deference to the high authority of Gilpin . . . I cannot approve of his compound term 'Picturesque Beauty.' The words are of dissimilar import, and excite different ideas. Whilst one designates objects that are rough, rugged, broken, ruinous; the other applies to such as are smooth, clean, fresh, regular, perfect. One may be said to designate old; the other young, or new" (*Picturesque Antiquities of the English Cities*, p. [v]).

26. Price, *Essay*, i. 3, in *Works*, I, 51–52 and i. 4, *Works*, I, 78–83.

27. Burke, *Sublime and Beautiful*, iii. 2–5 on proportion, and (especially) iii. 23 on elegance and speciousness.

28. Price, *Essay*, i. 3, in *Works*, I, 65.

29. *Ibid.*, i. 6, in *Works*, I, 127.

30. Rubens is a curious exception: eminently picturesque in other particulars, his paintings employ freshly beautiful colors.

31. Burke, *Sublime and Beautiful*, iii. 15.

32. Price, *Essay*, i. 9, in *Works*, I, 188.

33. *Ibid.*, p. 189.

34. *Ibid.*, p. 203.

35. It tells against any *literal* identification of beauty and picturesqueness, at any rate. Mayoux, who is given to finding divided souls in writers, says that "comme les préromantiques, Price est une âme partagée. Écoutons le proclamer avec insistence que le laid peut fort souvent être pittoresque. S'il était romantique, peut-être oserait-il proclamer que *le beau c'est le laid*, et l'harmonie serait rétablie dans son âme, avec l'unité de plaisir esthétique" (*Richard Payne Knight et le pittoresque*, pp. 69–70). Mayoux's beauty is not the specific beauty of the writers of the eighteenth century.

36. Isabel W. Chase gives a plausible account of the development of picturesque landscaping: "First comes the recognition that a garden-scene, as well as a scene in nature, may resemble a picture, or may even perhaps be reminiscent of some particular landscape painting. Second comes the comprehension that a scene in a garden contains many of the characteristics which, in nature, the seeing eye of a painter would notice. Third comes the realization that an original scene may be composed in a garden out of the simple elements of landscape—trees, shrubs, flowers, grass, rocks, and water—as a painter would compose a picture upon a canvas" (*Horace Walpole: Gardenist* [Princeton: Princeton University Press for University of Cincinnati, 1943], pp. 127–28).

37. Price, *Essay*, i. 1, in *Works*, p. 3.

38. *Ibid.*, pp. 12–13.

39. *Ibid.*, p. 14.

40. Price, "On Artificial Water," in *Works*, II, 98.

41. Price, *Essay*, i. 2, in *Works*, I, 29–30.

42. Letter to Gilpin, via Mason, of 1776; in Leslie and Taylor's *Reynolds*, II, 607.

43. Here as in other passages of the *Essay* Price leads a reaction towards the old style. Mayoux overlooks this evidence in declaring that "Knight fut le premier qui osât regretter le style, autour de la maison, des vieux *jardins italiens*," that "Price ne s'en aperçut, qu'après Knight" that the Italianate style was truly picturesque (*Knight*, pp. 76–77). Of course Price and Knight had shared their tastes for years before either published, and it is academic to discuss which was the originator.

44. Price, *Essay*, ii. 1, in *Works*, I, 238.

45. Not only Repton (of whom below), but George Mason in *An Essay on Design in Gardening* (2d ed.; London, 1795) and William Windham, statesman and friend of Payne Knight, in a "Letter to Humphry Repton" (printed, without the author's name, in an Appendix to Repton's *Sketches and Hints on Landscape Gardening* [London, (1795)]), argue with Price on this point. All of them imagine Price to be supporting a more radical position than he really is.

46. Price, "On Artificial Water," in *Works*, II, 18–19.

47. *Ibid.*, pp. 103–4.

48. Price, "On Decorations near the House," in *Works*, II, 131–32.

49. Mr. Hussey and M. Mayoux enter with much subtlety upon the question whether the picturesque improver is to concern himself with the view from the outside in or that from the inside out; Hussey (*The Picturesque*, p. 181) traces a change in Knight's views on this subject, a change which Mayoux shows to be imaginary. Price disposes of the alternative altogether by observing that "whatever constitutes a good fore-ground to the view *from* the house, will, generally speaking, have equally a good effect from every other point" ("On Architecture and Buildings," *Works*, II, 269–70).

50. Price, "On Architecture and Buildings," in *Works*, II, 206.

51. *Ibid.*, p. 247.

52. *Ibid.*, pp. 287–88. This use of painting is by no means an eccentricity of Price's; the pages of the *Journal of the Warburg and Courtauld Institutes*, *The Burlington Magazine*, *The Architectural Review*, and other journals of art and aesthetics offer many studies of architecture as it appears in painting.

53. Price, "On Architecture and Buildings," in *Works*, II, 304.

54. Sir Thomas Dick Lauder, in editing this passage, remarks that "if the roof of a cottage be well formed, and well projected, so as to throw a deep shadow over the wall beneath it, I do not conceive that it will be necessary to thatch it, in order to add to the picturesque effect, at the risk of diminishing the comfort of the poor inmates" (*Price on the Picturesque*, p. 398). Lauder seems tempted to the opposite view, and ends by suggesting a compromise, a tile roof covered with thatch—a species of fakery with which Price would have had little sympathy. Price, Knight, and Gilpin are all warmly humanitarian; when Hussey insists upon the inhuman objectivity of the picturesque viewpoint, his judgment is simply a consequence of his presuppositions about the route along which aesthetic sensitivity must develop.

55. Price, *Essay*, Appendix, in *Works*, I, 347–48 (note to p. 42 of 1794 ed.).

56. *Ibid.*, pp. 349–50 (note to p. 44 of 1794 ed.). It is remarkable that Gil-

pin's notion is a naïve anticipation of the sophisticated and "metaphysical" theory of R. Payne Knight, of which below.

57. *Ibid.*, p. 356 (note to p. 55 of 1794 ed.).

58. *Ibid.*, p. 360 (note to p. 59 of 1794 ed.).

59. Bosanquet, *A History of Aesthetic*, p. 3.

60. Templeman, *Gilpin*, p. 252.

61. Mayoux, *Knight*, pp. 64 and 66. "Tout d'abord," stresses Mayoux, "remarquons que Price achève l'abaissement du *Beau*, commencé par Burke, de telle sort que l'emploi du mot par lui devient . . . entièrement viole, et manifeste une espèce de psittacisme" (*ibid.*, p. 70).

62. *Ibid.*, p. 67.

Chapter 15

1. Humphry Repton (1752–1818) was a prolific writer. His published works consist largely of extracts and illustrations drawn from the reports, "Red Books" as he called them, which he prepared for the estates on which he was consulted. The major works are these:

A Letter to Uvedale Price, Esq. (London, 1794). This letter was reprinted as a footnote to the Appendix of *Sketches and Hints.*

Sketches and Hints on Landscape Gardening. Collected from Designs and Observations Now in the Possession of the Different Noblemen and Gentlemen, for Whose Use They Were Originally Made. The Whole Tending to Establish Fixed Principles in the Art of Laying Out Ground (London, [1795]).

Observations on the Theory and Practice of Landscape Gardening. Including Some Remarks on Grecian and Gothic Architecture, Collected from Various Manuscripts, in the Possession of the Different Noblemen and Gentlemen, for Whose Use They Were Originally Written; the Whole Tending to Establish Fixed Principles in the Respective Arts (London, 1803). 2d ed.; London, 1805.

An Inquiry into the Changes of Taste in Landscape Gardening. To Which Are Added, Some Observations on Its Theory and Practice, Including a Defence of the Art (London, 1806).

Designs for the Pavilion at Brighton: Humbly Inscribed to His Royal Highness the Prince of Wales. By H. Repton, Esq. with the Assistance of His Sons, John Adey Repton, F.S.A. and G[eorge] S[tanley] Repton, Architects (London, 1808). This work includes *An Inquiry into the Changes in Architecture, as It Relates to Palaces and Houses in England; Including the Castle and Abbey Gothic, the Mixed Style of Gothic, the Grecian and Modern Styles: with Some Remarks on the Introduction of Indian Architecture.*

Fragments on the Theory and Practice of Landscape Gardening. Including Some Remarks on Grecian and Gothic Architecture, Collected from Various Manuscripts in Possession of the Different Noblemen and Gentlemen, for Whose Use They Were Originally Written; the Whole Tending to Establish Fixed Principles in the Respective Arts. By H. Repton, Esq. Assisted by His Son, J[ohn] Adey Repton, F.A.S. (London, 1816).

All of my references are taken from the following edition of Repton's *Works: The Landscape Gardening and Landscape Architecture of the Late Humphry Repton, Esq. Being His Entire Works on These Subjects. A New Edition: with an Historical and Scientific Introduction, a Systematic Analysis, a Biographical Notice, Notes, and a Copious Alphabetical Index.* By J[ohn] C[laudius] Loudon, F.L.S. . . . (London, 1840).

2. Repton, *Designs*, in *Works*, p. 376, and *Sketches and Hints*, vii, in *Works*, p. 90.

3. Repton, *Letter to Price*, in *Works*, p. 105.

4. Repton attributes this phrase to Price; *Sketches and Hints*, Appendix, in *Works*, p. 104.

5. *Ibid.*, p. 105.

6. Repton, *Letter to Price*, in *Works*, p. 106.

7. In the Advertisement to the *Inquiry into the Changes of Taste in Landscape Gardening* (1806), Repton declines to publish a new edition of *Sketches and Hints*, of which, he says, two hundred and fifty copies were "published by Messrs. Boydells in 1794" (*Works*, p. 323). And in the concluding pages of *Fragments*, his last work, Repton reviews his life as an improver and recollects the time "when I first appeared before the public, in 1794, in a work which has long been out of print" (*ibid.*, p. 604)—quoting from *Sketches*. The Advertisement to *Theory and Practice*, on the other hand, speaks of the lapse of "seven years" since the *Sketches*; supposing this to have been written in 1802 (the dedication to the King is dated December 31, 1802), we are just able to get *Sketches* into 1795.

8. In the letter to Price so dated, Repton mentions adding to his "great work, which has long been all printed & only waits the colouring of some plates to be published" one "Appendix on Mr. Knight's attack & another on yours including my printed Letter in which I had softened some passages before I had the pleasure of seeing your last work [the *Letter to Repton*]."

9. Repton, *Works*, p. 127.

10. Repton, *Sketches and Hints*, Appendix, in *Works*, pp. 111–14.

11. Repton, *Theory and Practice*, Preface, in *Works*, p. 125.

12. *Ibid.*, i, in *Works*, p. 133.

13. *Ibid.*, vii, in *Works*, p. 207.

14. Repton, *Fragments*, xxxiii, in *Works*, pp. 572–76.

15. Repton, *Theory and Practice*, iii, in *Works*, p. 162.

16. Repton, *Sketches and Hints*, vi, in *Works*, pp. 84–85.

17. Nikolaus Pevsner, "The Genesis of the Picturesque," *The Architectural Review*, XCVI (November, 1944), 146.

18. See the report on Endsleigh, *Fragments*, xxxiv, in *Works*, p. 589. Price and Knight, incidentally, both attack pseudo-rivers.

19. Repton, *Theory and Practice*, Preface, in *Works*, p. 129.

20. *Ibid.*, x, in *Works*, p. 234.

21. *Ibid.*, pp. 234–37.

22. Repton, *Fragments*, xxvii, in *Works*, pp. 525–36. Even some of the early reports manifest a leaning in this direction; the very early work at Bulstrode (*Theory and Practice*, v, in *Works*, pp. 187–92) shows a tendency towards compartmentalization of the gardens.

23. Repton does not attribute the idea of a winter garden to Lord Kames; he does frequently refer to Kames, however, and I think that the influence of Kames's remarks on gardening has not been sufficiently remarked.

24. For an account of the gardenesque, see Loudon's introduction to his *Works of Repton*, p. viii; Loudon is not just in denying to Repton credit for originating this style which Loudon himself developed so much more fully. See also (besides the standard histories of gardening) H. F. Clark, "Parks and Pelargoniums," *The Architectural Review*, XCIX (February, 1946), 49–56; Clark attributes the gardenesque style to Repton's influence.

25. See Repton, *Designs*, in *Works*, pp. 365–66.

26. Repton, *Fragments*, xxvii, in *Works*, p. 530.

27. *Ibid.*, viii and xxxiv, in *Works*, pp. 433 and 595. The smell and taste interest themselves in the flowers and fruits.

28. *Ibid.*, xxvii, in *Works*, p. 525.

29. Repton, *Designs*, in *Works*, p. 365.

30. Price, *Letter to Repton*, in *Works*, III, 58–59 (*et sparsim*).

31. Repton, *Theory and Practice*, ix, in *Works*, p. 222. The French author is René Louis Girardin, Viscomte de Ermenonville, whose *De la composition des paysages* . . . (Paris, 1777) had been Englished in 1783.

32. Repton, *Sketches and Hints*, vii, in *Works*, p. 96; the list is repeated in *Inquiry*, iii, in *Works*, pp. 355–56.

33. Repton, *Sketches and Hints*, vii, in *Works*, p. 98.

34. Repton, *Theory and Practice*, ix, in *Works*, p. 228n.

35. Repton, *Sketches and Hints*, Introduction, in *Works*, pp. 29 and 30.

36. Repton, *Fragments*, xv, in *Works*, p. 467.

37. Repton, *Designs*, in *Works*, p. 365.

38. Repton, *Fragments*, vi, in *Works*, p. 427.

39. Repton, *Designs*, in *Works*, p. 362n.

40. Repton, *Fragments*, xxxiv, in *Works*, pp. 589–92.

41. Repton, *Sketches and Hints*, Appendix, in *Works*, p. 113.

42. See (one instance of many) *Sketches and Hints*, ii, in *Works*, pp. 56–57. It was this idea which Repton thinks Price stole from him; see *ibid.*, Appendix, in *Works*, pp. 105–6.

43. Repton, *Theory and Practice*, xii, in *Works*, p. 277; see also *Sketches and Hints*, ii, in *Works*, p. 56.

44. Repton, *Designs*, in *Works*, p. 385; similar remarks are found throughout this book.

45. Repton, *Fragments*, xiii, in *Works*, pp. 457–59; *Theory and Practice*, xii, in *Works*, pp. 277–78.

46. Repton, *Sketches and Hints*, v, in Works, p. 82.

47. Repton, *Fragments*, xxxiii, in *Works*, p. 575.

48. *Ibid.*, xxxvi, in *Works*, p. 603.

Chapter 16

1. Repton, *Letter to Price*, in Price, *Works*, III, 3. (Price reprints Repton's *Letter* as prolegomenon to his own, and I quote from this edition.)

2. Price, *Letter to Repton*, in *Works*, III, 146–49.

3. *Ibid.*, pp. 62–63.

4. Repton, *Letter to Price*, in Price, *Works*, III, 4n. In a conciliatory (manuscript) letter to Price, dated February 5, 1795 (bound in with the Newberry

Library copy of Price's *Essay*, &c.), Repton mentions that he had "softened some passages" in his printed *Letter* before including it as a footnote to *Sketches and Hints*. Comparison of the softened version with the original (as reprinted by Price), however, reveals only two trifling changes. A sarcastic reference is deleted from the passage here quoted from, and one other little sarcasm is omitted.

5. Price, *Letter to Repton*, in *Works*, III, 32–33.

6. Repton himself later speaks of time, neglect, and accident producing unexpected beauties in planting (*Inquiry*, i, in *Works*, p. 335n; repeated in *Fragments*, xxviii, in *Works*, p. 557). A controversial spirit informs the *Letter to Price* and causes Repton to exaggerate his position—though he doubtless did become in later years more sensible to the limitations of Brown.

7. Repton, *Letter to Price*, in Price, *Works*, III, 6.

8. Price, *Letter to Repton*, in *Works*, III, 49–50.

9. Burke himself seems to have favored Repton in this controversy, if we may believe Mrs. Crewe's report, "Extracts from Mr. Burke's Table-Talk at Crewe Hall. Written down by Mrs. Crewe," in the Philobiblon Society *Miscellanies*, VII, 42–43 (quoted, mediately, by Templeman, *Gilpin*, pp. 255–56). Burke "spoke often with great respect of Mr. Repton, & considered him as having much more comprehensive correct & even pure Views of these subjects, than his late Antagonists, & he often declared that much as he had thought & had amused himself with these, he felt unequal to enter the lists against Mr. Repton." He "admired many parts" of Price and Knight, but thought that "like most System-mongers they had pursued their Theories to a dangerous length." Repton, incidentally, had improved Crewe Hall.

10. Repton, *Letter to Price*, in Price, *Works*, III, 7.

11. Price, *Letter to Repton*, in *Works*, III, 89.

12. *Ibid.*, p. 72.

13. Repton, *Letter to Price*, in Price, *Works*, III, 10.

14. Price, *Letter to Repton*, in *Works*, III, 104; *Essay on the Picturesque*, in *Works*, I, 338.

15. Nikolaus Pevsner, "Genesis of the Picturesque," *The Architectural Review*, XCVI (November, 1944), 146.

16. I. de Wolfe, "Townscape: A Plea for an English Visual Philosophy Founded on the True Rock of Sir Uvedale Price," *The Architectural Review*, CVI (December, 1949), 354–74.

17. Price, *Letter to Repton*, in *Works*, III, 106.

18. *Ibid.*, p. 107. Price here repeats the advice of his *Essay*, that lower growths, especially of spinous plants, should be mixed with the young trees, which would at the same time protect the trees and vary and soften the summits and outlines of the plantation. Repton often repeats this idea in his Red Books, and may well have borrowed it from Price.

19. Repton, *Fragments*, x, in *Works*, p. 444, and xi, p. 452. It must be noted that even in *Theory and Practice* the sixth of Repton's objections to modern gardening asserted that Repton had never advised a belt, and the seventh spoke of "that ugly deformity called a *Clump*" (Preface, in *Works*, p. 128).

20. Repton, *Letter to Price*, in Price, *Works*, III, 19.

21. *Ibid.*, pp. 20–21.

22. Price, *Letter to Repton*, in *Works*, III, 130.

23. Lines 238–49 of "On Landscape Painting, A Poem," in Gilpin's *Three Essays*. Gilpin's travel books are full of scenes too extensive for the pencil, "views, which may rather be called *amusing*, than *picturesque*" (*Forest Scenery*, iii. 7, ed. cit., II, 131). Gilpin acknowledges that nine persons in ten prefer amusing views to those pleasing to the picturesque eye. ("Amusing" means, I presume, "absorbing," and the amusing may verge on the lower degrees of sublimity.)

24. Price, *Letter to Repton*, in *Works*, III, 151.

25. MS letter of December 24, 1794, bound in Newberry Library copy of Price's *Essay*.

26. Repton, *Theory and Practice*, ix, in *Works*, p. 229. Christopher Hussey, himself a practicing landscapist, declares that "Price's later essays are admirable practical guides to gardening. . ." (*The Picturesque*, p. 175); Repton's judgment is biased. Curiously, in his letter to Price of February 5, 1795 (bound in Newberry Library copy of Price's *Essay*), Repton stresses that "we perfectly agree concerning artificial water," and devotes a paragraph to detailing circumstances in which his plans regarding water have agreed with Price's views.

27. Repton, *Sketches and Hints*, Appendix, in *Works*, p. 116. Repton does not identify the author of the letter, but that the letter was Windham's was well known; Dugald Stewart refers it to him in the third edition of his *Philosophical Essays*, 1818.

28. MS letter, Repton to Robson, December 24, 1794 (bound in Newberry Library copy of Price's *Essay*). The copious marginalia Repton entered in his presentation copy of Price's *Essay* do not show Repton as altogether charmed, however; many of the marginalia are symbols referred to this key on the back of the flyleaf:

Marks explained	
Y	I assent to the position
N.	I do not allow it
?	doubtful if so—
R—	Ridiculous
G.	Good description &c.
C.	contemptuous allusions
O—	obscure in Stile.
V.	Verbose or affected Stile
P.	Pointed either at me or personally Some one else

29. Price, *Letter to Repton*, in *Works*, III, 175 ff.

30. MS letter, Repton to Price, of February 5, 1795.

31. Repton, *Sketches and Hints*, Appendix, in *Works*, p. 111.

32. Repton, *Fragments*, v, in *Works*, p. 424.

33. *Ibid.*, xi, in *Works*, p. 447.

34. *Ibid.*, x, in *Works*, p. 440.

Chapter 17

1. Knight's writings include (among other works):
The journal of a voyage to Sicily with Philip Hackert and Charles Gore,

April–June, 1777; the original is lost, but the journal was translated by Goethe as "Tagebuch einer Reise nach Sicilien" in his *Philip Hackert. Biographische Skizze* . . . (Tübingen, 1811); portions are retranslated by Brian Miller in Nikolaus Pevsner's "Richard Payne Knight," *Art Bulletin*, XXXI (December, 1949), 293–320.

An Account of the Remains of the Worship of Priapus, Lately Existing at Isernia in the Kingdom of Naples, etc.; to Which Is Added a Discourse on the Worship of Priapus, and Its Connection with the Mystic Theology of the Ancients (London, 1786).

An Analytical Essay on the Greek Alphabet (London, 1791).

The Landscape, a Didactic Poem in Three Books. Addressed to Uvedale Price, Esq. (London, 1794); 2d ed., 1795. My references, unless otherwise stated, are to the first edition.

The Progress of Civil Society. A Didactic Poem in Six Books (London, 1796).

Introduction to Vol. I of *Specimens of Ancient Sculpture*, "Preliminary Dissertation on the Rise, Progress and Decline of Antient Sculpture" (London: Published by the Dilettanti, 1809).

An Analytical Inquiry into the Principles of Taste (London, 1805); 2d ed., 1805; 3d, 1806; 4th, 1808. My references are to the third edition.

Alfred; a Romance in Rhyme (London, 1823); a didactic poem on education.

This list, although incomplete, shows the scope of Knight's taste and thought, and suggests that he deserves to occupy a more conspicuous place in histories of English thought and literature than he has hitherto been granted.

2.   Mayoux, writing of the picturesque controversy, declares: "Knight est à mon sens, l'esprit le plus vigoureux et le plus critique qui s'y soit jeté. Il représente le momente de conscience claire du mouvement. L'attitude pittoresque en lui se rattache d'une manière qu'il m'a paru intéressant de marquer, à une personnalité originale, et à une conception complexe, mais non confuse, du beau et du sentiment artistique . . ." (*Richard Payne Knight et le pittoresque*, p. 6).

3.   Repton, *Sketches and Hints*, vii, in *Works*, pp. 101–2n. Nikolaus Pevsner sees Hearne's engraving of the picturesque scene as the most striking sign of the revival of Elizabethan and Jacobean architecture ("Good King James Gothic," *The Architectural Review*, CVII [February, 1950], 117–22).

4.   Repton, *Sketches and Hints*, vii, in *Works*, p. 95.

5.   [John Matthews], *A Sketch from The Landscape, a Didactic Poem. Addressed to R. P. Knight Esqr. With Notes, Illustrations, and a Postscript* (London, 1794), pp. 13–14.

6.   *Ibid.*, pp. 20–22.

7.   *Ibid.*, pp. 5 and 7.

8.   *Ibid.*, pp. 7–8.

9.   The formal system was at least "negatively good," says Knight, in that it was confined within narrow bounds. "Those who think, on the contrary, that it was *positively bad;*" rejoins Matthews in a postscript, "who look up with reverence to the memory of Brown, as the great destroyer of an unnatural and absurd system, will feel with indignation an injury offered to his ashes. This sentiment produced the present hasty Sketch. . . ." In Knight are revived the wit and verse of Pope, in Matthews his taste.

10. This taste is illustrated by a plate of an Etruscan cup of the most ordinary manufacture but exhibiting nice correspondence of lines; this plate earned for Knight Walpole's epithet, "The Knight of the Brazen Milk-Pot." Matthews pretends to contrast with the old Grecian forms the modern chamber pot of his title page vignette, "So lumpy, round, without expression!"

11. Translated in Pevsner, "Richard Payne Knight," *Art Bulletin*, XXXI (December, 1949), 312.

12. The note to *The Landscape* is most readily available in Price's works, where it is reprinted as prolegomenon to the *Dialogue on the Distinct Characters of the Picturesque and the Beautiful* . . . ; the quotation is in Price, *Works*, III, 249–51.

13. Knight, *Analytical Inquiry*, Introduction, ed. cit., p. 9.

14. *Ibid.*, ed. cit., p. 11. This distinction of figurative (employing the idea of one thing to illustrate another) and transitive (following common elements of meaning linking words together) is a hint from which Dugald Stewart constructs an entire aesthetics.

15. *Ibid.*, ed. cit., pp. 12–13.

16. *Ibid.*, ed. cit., p. 18.

17. *Ibid.*, i. 3. 11, ed. cit., p. 40.

18. *Ibid.*, i. 1. 4, ed. cit., p. 20.

19. *Ibid.*, i. 1. 6, ed. cit., pp. 23–24.

20. *Ibid.*, i. 3. 12–13, ed. cit., pp. 41–42.

21. *Ibid.*, i. 5. 9, ed. cit., p. 63.

22. *Ibid.*, i. 5. 11, ed. cit., p. 65.

23. *Ibid.*, i. 5. 16, ed. cit., p. 68.

24. *Ibid.*, i. 5. 17, ed. cit., p. 69.

25. *Ibid.*, i. 5. 35, ed. cit., p. 96.

26. *Ibid.*, i. 5. 22, ed. cit., p. 74. "Who shall ever understand the English language," cries Knight, "if new and uncouth words ["picturesqueness"] are thus to deprive those sanctioned by long usage of their authorized and established meaning?" (*ibid.*, i. 5. 17, ed. cit., p. 68n).

27. *Ibid.*, ii. 1. 15, ed. cit., p. 110.

28. *Ibid.*, ii. 1. 27, ed. cit., pp. 119–20. The pleasure from light or didactic verse, which does not sustain such enthusiasm, "arises from the charms of neatness, point, and emphasis; all of which are improved and invigorated by the regularity of a metrical style . . ." (*ibid.*, ii. 1. 34, ed. cit., p. 130).

29. The Huntington Library has a copy of the *Analytical Inquiry* with annotations by Coleridge and Wordsworth which have been elaborately edited by Edna Aston Shearer in "Wordsworth and Coleridge Marginalia in a Copy of Richard Payne Knight's *Analytical Inquiry into the Principles of Taste*," *HLQ*, I (October, 1937), 63–99. The marginalia deal mostly with Knight's opinions on Milton, with his conception of poetic belief, and with the problem of fear in the sublime; many are in Coleridge's inimitably venomous style, epithets like "Booby," "Prater," "Rogue," &c. being heaped upon Knight. As to Milton, Coleridge justifies some of the labored lines cited by Knight as echoing the sense—which, though plausible, does not affect Knight's observation on the effect of the versification as such.

30. Knight, *Analytical Inquiry*, ii. 1. 37, ed. cit., p. 133.

31. *Ibid.*, ii. 2. 15, ed. cit., p. 146.

32. *Ibid.*, ii. 2. 19, ed. cit., p. 149.

33. *Ibid.*, ii. 2. 20–21, ed. cit., pp. 150–51. Knight notes (ii. 2. 27, ed. cit., pp. 154–55) the "late" application of the word "picturesque" to literature, signifying clear and vivid narration or description which paints to the imagination. In English, of course, this use was almost coeval with the sense "pictorial," and far older than the sense which Knight assigns the term. Early English use of the term in the sense "pictorial" usually referred to painting in a style appealing to imagination and intellect without the sensual appeal to vision which Knight stresses.

34. *Ibid.*, ii. 2. 24, ed. cit., pp. 152–53.

35. *Ibid.*, ii. 2. 28, ed. cit., p. 157.

36. *Ibid.*, ii. 2. 29, ed. cit., p. 158.

37. Knight constructed Downton Castle with an irregular Gothic exterior and a Grecian interior. Repton generously declares that "after the literary controversy between Mr. Knight and me, I should be sorry to be misunderstood as casting any reflection on the castle character of Downton; for although, perhaps, some may think that its outline was directed by the eye of a painter, rather than that of an antiquary, yet its general effect must gratify the good taste of both . . ." (*Fragments*, x, in *Works*, p. 441). Pevsner ("Richard Payne Knight," *Art Bulletin*, XXXI [December, 1949], 293–320) shows by photographs how Downton imitates buildings in Claude.

38. See *Inquiry*, i, in *Works*, p. 330; *Fragments*, xxvi, xxviii, and xxxiii, in *Works*, pp. 522, 546, 575, and 579. In the third of these passages, Repton speaks of the "absurdities of circuitous approaches, so aptly ridiculed by a modern poet"!

39. Repton, *Inquiry*, iii, in *Works*, pp. 352–53.

40. Knight, *Analytical Inquiry*, ii. 2. 94n, ed. cit., p. 220.

41. *Ibid.*, ii. 2. 54, ed. cit., p. 182.

42. *Ibid.*, pp. 181–82.

43. *Ibid.*, ii. 2. 101, ed. cit., p. 225.

44. *Ibid.*, ii. 2. 55, ed. cit., p. 184. It must be said in fairness to Hogarth that he criticized Rubens' lines as *too* undulating, as gross and clumsy.

45. *Ibid.*, ii. 2. 65, ed. cit., p. 192.

46. *Ibid.*, ii. 2. 68, ed. cit., p. 194.

47. *Ibid.*, ii. 2. 74, ed. cit., pp. 196–97. Mayoux and Hussey agree that Price was an "objectivist"—a view which I have examined above. Sir Thomas Dick Lauder observes more reasonably that Price confined himself to the popular view which contents itself with enumerating the objective properties that excite the emotions of sublimity, &c., in us, without penetrating into the deeper inquiry, why the mind is thus affected (*Sir Uvedale Price on the Picturesque*, p. 1).

48. Knight, *Analytical Inquiry*, ii. 2. 80, ed. cit., p. 204.

49. *Ibid.*, ii. 2. 86, ed. cit., p. 211.

50. *Ibid.*, ii. 2. 109, ed. cit., p. 234. I have been avoiding mention of the digressions on government, morals, love, &c., with which Knight enlivens his book; but I include this fragment as a sample of his style, both in content and in language reminiscent of Gibbon. Knight subscribes to a sentimental ethics, "for without some mixture of passion, sentiment, or affection, beneficence it-

self is but a cold virtue; and philosophers and divines, who have laboured to subject them all to the dominion of reason, or sink them in the more brilliant illuminations of faith, have only succeeded in suppressing the mild and seductive, together with some few of the sordid and selfish passions; while all those of a sour and sanguinary cast have acquired additional force and acrimony from that pride and confidence, which the triumph over the others naturally inspired. The censor Cato, the saint Bernard, and the reformer Calvin, were equally insensible to the blandishments of love, the allurements of pleasure, and the vanity of wealth; and so, likewise, were the monsters Marat and Robespierre: but all equally sacrificed every generous and finer feeling of humanity, which none are naturally without, to an abstract principle or opinion; which, by narrowing their understandings, hardened their hearts, and left them under the unrestrained guidance of all the atrocious and sanguinary passions, which party violence could stimulate or excite" (*ibid.*, ii. 2. 112, ed cit., pp. 236–37).

51. *Ibid.*, ii. 2. 127, ed. cit., p. 253.

52. *Ibid.*, ii. 3. 1, ed. cit., p. 262.

53. *Ibid.*, ii. 3. 6, ed. cit., p. 265.

54. *Ibid.*, ii. 3. 8, ed. cit., p. 266. Identity is not really, it appears to me, a subject of demonstrative proof by number; identity is recognized intuitively rather than proved in the last analysis. But this correction does not affect Knight's inferences.

55. *Ibid.*, ii. 3. 16, ed. cit., p. 273.

56. Knight credits Johnson with discovery of our awareness of imitation in the drama, and with the rejection of the unities; he does not, here or elsewhere, seem familiar with Lord Kames, whose destructive analysis of stage illusion and the unities preceded Johnson's.

57. If the one action of the *Iliad*, Knight observes wittily, were really the arousal and allaying of Achilles' wrath, "the mighty and all-accomplished hero would have been introduced, with so much pomp of poetry, merely to wrangle with his prince, weep for his mistress, and carve a supper for three of his friends" (*ibid.*, ii. 3. 22, ed. cit., p. 276).

58. *Ibid.*, ii. 3. 23, ed. cit., p. 277.

59. *Ibid.*, ii. 3. 46, ed. cit., pp. 301–2.

60. *Ibid.*, ii. 3. 49n, ed. cit., p. 305.

61. *Ibid.*, iii. 1. 1, ed. cit., p. 318.

62. *Ibid.*, iii. 1. 7, ed. cit., p. 323.

63. *Ibid.*, iii. 1. 11, ed. cit., p. 327. Knight's position might be criticized in view of modern theories of sadistic pleasure; but even so, sadistic pleasure is not an aesthetic pleasure operating sympathetically.

64. *Ibid.*, ii. 1. 15, ed. cit., p. 332. This passage evoked from Coleridge a lengthy and confused note filling the margins of four pages, a note exposing the errors of Knight and outlining his own idea of poetic belief. The curious thing is that Coleridge attacks Knight with violence while asserting much the same thing in other terms. (Shearer, "Wordsworth and Coleridge Marginalia," *HLQ*, I [October, 1937], 79–81.)

65. Knight, *Analytical Inquiry*, iii. 1. 19, ed. cit., pp. 335–36.

66. *Ibid.*, iii. 1. 21, ed. cit., p. 337.

67. *Ibid.*, iii. 1. 26, ed. cit., p. 342.

68. *Ibid.*, iii. 1. 28, ed. cit., p. 346.

69. As Mayoux suggests (*Richard Payne Knight*, p. 114), "cette notion de *sympathie* avec les passions profondes ne se substitue pas sans intention chez Knight à la terreur et à la pitié aristotéliciennes; il s'agit d'atteindre cette perversion de la notion prétendue esthétique de *terreur* que Burke a mise à la base de sa sublimité."

70. Knight, *Analytical Inquiry*, iii. 1. 41, ed. cit., p. 358.

71. The sublime may operate on the nervous system, that is, by stretching the nervous fibres. With characteristically venomous wit, Knight observes that "this *stretching* power of ideas of terror, no pathologist has, I believe, discovered or even surmised, though the *laxative* power of terror itself is so well known, as to have been celebrated even by poets; with more, indeed, of the accuracy of philosophy than the delicacy of poetry" (*ibid.*, iii. 1. 63, ed. cit., p. 378).

72. *Ibid.*, iii. 1. 51, ed. cit., pp. 367–68.

73. Burke, *Sublime and Beautiful*, i. 7, in *Works*, I, 91–92.

74. Knight, *Analytical Inquiry*, iii. 1. 61, ed. cit., p. 376.

75. *Ibid.*, iii. 1. 51, ed. cit., pp. 367–68. Curiously, in *The Landscape* Knight had admitted a role to terror; the sublime, he sings, is not the monstrous

> "But nature's common works, by genius dress'd   160
> With art selected, and with taste express'd;
> Where sympathy with terror is combin'd,
> To move, to melt, and elevate the mind."

76. Knight, *Analytical Inquiry*, ii. 3. 46, ed. cit., p. 302.

77. *Ibid.*, iii. 1. 59, ed. cit., p. 374.

78. *Ibid.*, iii. 1. 81, ed. cit., p. 391.

79. Monk finds treatment of the sublime "the least important part of Knight's book," and sees in this inferiority a deeper meaning: "The eighteenth century had set itself a task that was beyond its powers. It was not imaginatively equipped to deal with ultimates in art, and it failed" (*The Sublime*, pp. 161 and 163). This evaluation accords with the Kantian bias of Monk's study.

80. Knight, *Analytical Inquiry*, iii. 2. 1, ed. cit., p. 413.

81. *Ibid.*, iii. 2. 13, ed. cit., pp. 423–24.

82. *Ibid.*, iii. 2. 14, ed. cit., p. 425.

83. *Ibid.*, iii. 3. 2, ed. cit., pp. 429–30.

84. *Ibid.*, iii. 3. 9, ed. cit., p. 438.

85. *Ibid.*, iii. 3. 25, ed. cit., p. 454.

86. *Ibid.*, iii. 3. 40, ed. cit., pp. 472–73.

87. *Ibid.*, iii. 3. 32, ed. cit., p. 461.

Chapter 18

1. Knight, note to *The Landscape*, in Price, *Works*, III, 251. (Price reprints Knight's note intact before breaking it up for his *Dialogue*.) Mayoux sums up Knight's view neatly: "Un phénomène de dissociation (et de culture spécialisée) est au fond de la beauté pittoresque simple; des phénomènes d'association sont audessous du pittoresque romantique et des mille espèces de beauté

transmises par la vue, mais autres que la primitive beauté de sensation: telle est sur ce point et sous sa première form la conception de Knight" (*Richard Payne Knight*, p. 80). The term "pittoresque romantique" is of course only Mayoux's, who considers the picturesque as a prelude to romanticism.

2. Hussey (*The Picturesque*, pp. 69–78) gives an entertaining running summary of the *Dialogue*; but I take it up here from a different point of view.

3. Price, *Works*, III, 266.

4. *Ibid.*, p. 270.

5. *Ibid.*, pp. 272–73. It is of course not really the case that Price and Knight agree so entirely on "general principles."

6. *Ibid.*, pp. 325–26.

7. *Ibid.*, p. 329.

8. *Ibid.*, p. 314.

9. Nikolaus Pevsner argues that the *Dialogue* shows the difference between Knight and Price to be merely a matter of words. Price "insists on the necessity of the term Picturesque in addition to Burke's Sublime and Beautiful. Time has indeed proved its usefulness, if not its necessity. Regarding the latter, which would be the logical justification of Price's system, Knight, the more analytical thinker of the two, could not be confuted, once he had gathered his objections into a more coherent form [in the *Analytical Inquiry*]" ("Richard Payne Knight," *Art Bulletin*, XXXI [December, 1949], 305).

10. Gilpin had arrived at a similar paradox by different reasoning and for different purposes; cf. *supra*, p. 195.

11. Price, *Works*, III, 372–73. We have come full circle—Seymour said the same thing at the beginning of the outing.

12. *Ibid.*, p. 375.

13. Knight, *Analytical Inquiry*, ii. 2. 81, p. 208.

14. Price, *Works*, III, 399–400.

Chapter 19

1. Monk, *The Sublime*, p. 6.

2. Of even greater importance than the positive advance of metaphysical psychology was the "satisfactory refutation of that sceptical philosophy, which had struck at the root of all knowledge and all belief," in which work Reid, Stewart assures us, was signally successful. "The rubbish being now removed, and the foundations laid, it is time to begin the superstructure": Dugald Stewart, *Elements of the Philosophy of the Human Mind* (Part I, Introduction, Part i), in *The Collected Works of Dugald Stewart, Esq., F.R.S.S.*, ed. Sir William Hamilton ([2d ed.]; Edinburgh: T. & T. Clark, 1877), II, 56.

3. Volume I of the *Elements* was published in London, 1792; Volume II in Edinburgh, 1814; Volume III in London, 1827. The *Philosophical Essays* appeared at Edinburgh, 1810, with further editions in 1816 and 1818.

4. The *Active and Moral Powers* appeared in two volumes at Edinburgh, 1828; the *Lectures* as Vols. VIII and IX of Hamilton's edition of the *Works*. A brief conspectus of the entire system is afforded by Stewart's textbook, *Outlines of Moral Philosophy* (Edinburgh, 1793); in the *Works* this is divided by subject among Vols. I, VI, and VIII.

5. Stewart, *Elements*, Preface, Vol. III, in *Works*, IV, [1].

6. Stewart, *Essays*, i. 5. 2, in *Works*, V, 163.

7. *Ibid.*, p. 161.

8. *Ibid.*, i. 5. 3, in *Works*, V, 176.

9. Even such minor pronouncements as those of Joseph Warton, William Windham, and Whately are mentioned. Missing from the list of British writers are Harris, Spence, Webb, Usher, John Stedman (for his anonymous *Laelius and Hortensia* . . . [Edinburgh, 1782]), and the author, whether William Greenfield or Edward Mangin, of *Essays on the Sources of the Pleasures Received from Literary Compositions* (though this work, published London, 1809, may not have come into Stewart's hands).

10. Stewart, *Essays*, ii. 1. 1. 1, in *Works*, V, 191–92. Stewart himself, incidentally, speaks of the "beautiful result" of researches on conjunctions—a strange locution (*ibid.*, 1. 5. 2, in *Works*, V, 166).

11. *Ibid.*, ii. 1. 1. 1, in *Works*, V, 193–94.

12. *Ibid.*, pp. 195–96.

13. *Ibid.*, ii. 2. 5, in *Works*, V, 322. For the clue from Knight which Stewart has seized, see the *Analytical Inquiry*, Introduction, secs. 7 and 8.

14. [Francis Jeffrey], *Edinburgh Review*, XVII (November, 1810), 199.

15. Stewart, *Essays*, ii. 1. 1. 2, in *Works*, V, 204.

16. *Ibid.*, ii. 4. 1, in *Works*, V, 386.

17. *Ibid.*, ii. 1. 1. 2, in *Works*, V, 207.

18. *Ibid.*, ii. 1. 1. 3, in *Works*, V, 217.

19. Stewart, *Elements*, Introduction, Part i, in *Works*, II, 52–53; and *Essays*, Preliminary Dissertation, chap. i, in *Works*, V, 6–7, as well as Part I, Essay iv ("On the Metaphysical Theories of Hartley, Priestley, and Darwin").

20. Stewart appears to consider that brilliant reflection is organically pleasing (pleasing also in some circumstances as a sign of art). This is a point difficult to support. One recalls the equally plausible argument of Payne Knight, that a blended variety of mellow tints is organically pleasing, and brilliant reflections harshly irritating to the eye.

21. Stewart, *Essays*, ii. 1. 1. 4, in *Works*, V, 224–25.

22. *Ibid.*, ii. 1. 1. 5, in *Works*, V, 230. Stewart considers that the primitive meaning of "picturesque" is "graphic"; I believe that he is mistaken, that the primitive meaning is that which Price supposes, "after the manner of painters."

23. *Ibid.*, Note X (referring to *Essays*, ii. 1. 1. 5, in *Works*, V, 233), in *Works*, V, 439.

24. *Ibid.*, ii. 1. 1. 5, in *Works*, V, 236.

25. *Ibid.*, ii. 1. 1. 6, in *Works*, V, 249.

26. I should put the case this way: the properties perceived by touch, excepting temperature and pressure (which are not deemed "beautiful"), are through experience judged of by sight; odors and tastes are not *seen*, and hence are not beautiful.

27. Stewart, *Essays*, ii. 1. 1. 6, in *Works*, V, 251.

28. *Ibid.*

29. *Ibid.*, pp. 252–53.

30. *Ibid.*, p. 248. There is here a double transition, from physical beauty to the expression of moral qualities in the countenance, and from this expres-

sion to the qualities themselves; when we apprehend them through the voice, and judge the sound beautiful, there is a third transition.

31. *Ibid.*, p. 253.

32. *Ibid.*, ii. 1. 1. 7, in *Works*, V, 260. Stewart balances this criticism by acknowledging that "great praise is due to those who have so happily illustrated the process by which taste is guided in the study of *ideal beauty;* a process which Reynolds must be allowed to have traced and described with admirable sagacity, even by such as think the most lightly of the metaphysical doctrine which he has blended with his statement of the fact."

33. Stewart, *Elements*, i. 5. 1. 1, in *Works*, II, 259–60. Fancy is not a faculty but an acquired habit of perception.

34. *Ibid.*, i. 3, in *Works*, II, 144.

35. *Ibid.*, i. 4. 1, in *Works*, II, 162.

36. *Ibid.*, i. 7. 1, in *Works*, II, 435.

37. *Ibid.*, p. [431]; and see pp. 435–36 for the analysis of imagination.

38. Stewart, *Essays*, ii. 1. Introduction, in *Works*, V, 190.

39. *Ibid.*, ii. 1. 2, in *Works*, V, 263–64.

40. *Ibid.*, pp. 265–66.

41. *Ibid.*, ii. 2. 1, in *Works*, V, 277.

42. *Ibid.*, pp. 278–79.

43. *Ibid.*, p. 279.

44. *Ibid.*, Note AA (referring to *Essays*, ii. 2. 1, in *Works*, V, 281), in *Works*, V, 442–43.

45. *Ibid.*, ii. 2. 2, in *Works*, V, 296–97.

46. *Ibid.*, ii. 2. 3, in *Works*, V, 301.

47. *Ibid.*, p. 303.

48. *Ibid.*, p. 305. Stewart criticizes Knight's position that the pathetic is always sublime. "In this assertion," Stewart writes, "he has certainly lost sight entirely of the meaning in which the words Sublime and Pathetic are commonly understood in our language; a standard of judgment, upon questions of this sort, from which there lies no appeal to the arbitrary definition of any theorist; not even to the authority of Longinus himself" (*ibid.*, Note KK [referring to *Essays*, ii. 2. 4, in *Works*, V, 320], in *Works*, V, 450).

49. Longinus *De Sublimitate* 7, quoted by Stewart (Stewart's italics), *Essays*, ii. 2. 4, in *Works*, V, 318.

50. Stewart, *Essays*, ii. 2. 4, in *Works*, V, 318.

51. *Ibid.*, ii. 3. 1, in *Works*, V, 337.

52. See Stewart, *Elements*, i. 2, in *Works*, II, 120–43, and *Elements*, iii. 1, in *Works*, IV, 185–249 *passim*. See also *Essays*, ii. 3. 1, in *Works*, V, 330–36.

53. Stewart, *Essays*, ii. 3. 2, in *Works*, V, 341.

54. *Ibid.*, ii. 3. 3, in *Works*, V, 357.

55. *Ibid.*, p. 361.

56. *Ibid.*

57. *Ibid.*, pp. 361–62.

58. *Ibid.*, ii. 3. 4, in *Works*, V, 382–83.

59. *Ibid.*, p. 370.

60. *Ibid.*, ii. 4. 2, in *Works*, V, 406.

61. *Ibid.*, pp. 399–400.

Retrospect

1. R. S. Crane, "On Writing the History of English Criticism, 1650–1800," *University of Toronto Quarterly*, XXII (July, 1953), 385.

2. *The Spectator*, No. 29 (April 3, 1711), I, 109.

3. Crane, "English Neoclassical Criticism: An Outline Sketch," in *Critics and Criticism, Ancient and Modern* (Chicago: University of Chicago Press, 1952), p. 383.

4. *Ibid.*, pp. 382–84.

5. Blair, *Lectures*, ii, ed. cit., I, 40.

6. The method which I have called "analytic and genetic" appears to be similar to the "logistic" method which Richard P. McKeon describes in his intricate "Philosophy and Method," *JP*, XLVIII, No. 22 (October 25, 1951), 653–82.

BIBLIOGRAPHY OF WORKS CITED

[Addison, Joseph]. *The Guardian*, in *The Works of the Right Honourable Joseph Addison*. . . . Vol. IV. "Bohn's Standard Library"; London: G. Bell, 1888.

————. *The Spectator*. Edited by G. Gregory Smith. 8 vols. London: Dent, 1897–98.

Aglionby, William. *Painting Illustrated in Three Diallogues. Containing Some Choice Observations upon the Art. Together with the Lives of the Most Eminent Painters, from Cimabue, to the Time of Raphael and Michael Angelo.* London, 1685.

[Akenside, Mark]. *The Pleasures of Imagination.* London, 1744.

Akenside, Mark. *The Pleasures of Imagination.* Revised edition, in *The Poems of Mark Akenside.* Edited by Jeremiah Dyson. London, 1772.

Aldridge, Alfred Owen. "A French Critic of Hutcheson's Aesthetics," *Modern Philology*, XLV (February, 1948), 169–84.

Alison, Archibald. *Essays on the Nature and Principles of Taste.* Edinburgh, 1790.

————. *Essays on the Nature and Principles of Taste.* 4th ed. 2 vols. Edinburgh, 1815.

Baillie, Dr. [John]. *An Essay on the Sublime.* London, 1747. As reprinted by The Augustan Reprint Society, with Introduction by Samuel H. Monk, Los Angeles, 1953.

Birkhoff, George David. *Aesthetic Measure.* Cambridge, Mass.: Harvard University Press, 1933.

Blair, Hugh. *A Critical Dissertation on the Poems of Ossian, the Son of Fingal*, appended to *The Poems of Ossian* . . . . 2 vols. London, 1790.

————. *Lectures on Rhetoric and Belles Lettres.* 4th ed. 3 vols. London, 1790.

Blanshard, Frances. *Retreat from Likeness in the Theory of Painting.* 2d ed. New York: Columbia University Press, 1949.

Bosanquet, Bernard. *A History of Aesthetic.* London: Swan, Sonnenschein & Co., 1892.

Boswell, James. *Life of Samuel Johnson.* Edited by Alexander Napier. Vol. I. London: G. Bell, 1884.

Bowen, Marjorie (pseudonym of G. M. V. Long). *William Hogarth, the Cockney's Mirror.* 2d ed. New York: D. Appleton Century Co., 1937.

Bredvold, Louis. "The Tendency toward Platonism in Neo-Classical Esthetics," *English Literary History*, I (September, 1934), 91–119.

Brett, R. L. "The Aesthetic Sense and Taste in the Literary Criticism of the Early Eighteenth Century," *The Review of English Studies*, XX (July, 1944), 199–213.

Bridges, Robert S. "Pictorial. Picturesque. Romantic. Grotesque. Classical." in *SPE [Society for Pure English] Tract No. XV*, pp. 15–21. Oxford: Clarendon Press, 1923.

Britton, John. *Picturesque Antiquities of the English Cities*. London: Dean and Son, [*ca.* 1830].

Brown, Stuart Gerry. "Observations on Hume's Theory of Taste," *English Studies*, XX (October, 1938), 193–98.

Brunius, Teddy. *David Hume on Criticism.* "*Figura*, Studies Edited by the Institute of Art History, University of Uppsala," No. 2. Stockholm: Almqvist and Wiksell, 1952.

Bryant, Donald Cross. *Edmund Burke and His Literary Friends.* "Washington University Studies—New Series; Language and Literature"—No. 9. St. Louis, 1939.

Bundy, Murray W. "Lord Kames and the Maggots in Amber," *The Journal of English and Germanic Philology*, XLV (April, 1946), 199–208.

Burke, Edmund. *A Philosophical Inquiry into the Origin of Our Ideas of the Sublime and Beautiful: with an Introductory Discourse Concerning Taste, and Several Other Additions*, in *The Works of the Right Honourable Edmund Burke*. Vol. I. "The World's Classics"; London: Oxford, 1925.

Burke, J[oseph] T. A. "A Classical Aspect of Hogarth's Theory of Art," *Journal of the Warburg and Courtauld Institutes*, VI (1943), 151–53.

Burke, Joseph. *Hogarth and Reynolds: A Contrast in English Art Theory.* The William Henry Charlton Memorial Lecture, November, 1941. London: Oxford, 1943.

———. *William Hogarth: The Analysis of Beauty, with the Rejected Passages from the Manuscript Drafts and Autobiographical Notes*. Oxford: Clarendon Press, 1955.

Burns, Robert. *The Letters of Robert Burns.* Edited by Francis H. Allen. Vol. III. Boston: Houghton, 1927.

Chase, Isabel Wakelin. *Horace Walpole: Gardenist*. Princeton: Princeton University Press for the University of Cincinnati, 1943.

Clark, H. F. "Parks and Pelargoniums," *The Architectural Review*, XCIX (February, 1946), 49–56.

Clough, Wilson O. "Reason and Genius—An Eighteenth Century Dilemma (Hogarth, Hume, Burke, Reynolds)," *Philological Quarterly*, XXIII (January, 1944), 33–54.

Crane, R[onald] S. "English Neoclassical Criticism: An Outline Sketch," in *Critics and Criticism, Ancient and Modern*, pp. 372–88. Chicago: University of Chicago Press, 1952.

Crane, Ronald S. "History versus Criticism in the University Study of Literature," *The English Journal* (College Edition), XXIV (October, 1935), 645–67.

———. "Interpretation of Texts and the History of Ideas," *College English*, II (May, 1941), 755–65.

Crane, R[onald] S. "On Writing the History of English Criticism, 1650–1800," *University of Toronto Quarterly*, XXII (July, 1953), 376–91.

De Wolfe, I. "Townscape: A Plea for an English Visual Philosophy Founded on the True Rock of Sir Uvedale Price," *The Architectural Review*, CVI (December, 1949), 354–74.

Gerard, Alexander. *An Essay on Genius*. London, 1774.

———. *An Essay on Taste. With Three Dissertations on the Same Subject, by Voltaire, D'Alembert, and Montesquieu*. London, 1759.

———. *An Essay on Taste. To Which Is Now Added Part Fourth, of the Standard of Taste: with Observations Concerning the Imitative Nature of Poetry*. 3d ed. Edinburgh, 1780.

[Gilpin, William]. *A Dialogue upon the Gardens of the Right Honourable the Lord Viscount Cobham, at Stow in Buckinghamshire*. Printed for B. Seeley, Buckingham, sold by J. and J. Rivington, London, 1748.

———. *An Essay upon Prints; Containing Remarks upon the Principles of Picturesque Beauty, the Different Kinds of Prints, and the Characters of the Most Noted Masters . . . .* London, 1768.

Gilpin, William. *Remarks on Forest Scenery, and Other Woodland Views, Relative Chiefly to Picturesque Beauty. Illustrated by the Scenes of New Forest in Hampshire*. 3d ed. 2 vols. London, 1808.

———. *Three Essays: On Picturesque Beauty; On Picturesque Travel; and On Sketching Landscape: to Which Is Added a Poem, On Landscape Painting*. 2d ed. London, 1794.

Goodman, Paul. "Neo-Classicism, Platonism, and Romanticism," *The Journal of Philosophy*, XXXI, No. 6 (March 15, 1934), 148–63.

Greenway, Lauder. *Alterations in the Discourses of Sir Joshua Reynolds*. New York: Privately printed, 1936.

Grene, Marjorie. "Gerard's *Essay on Taste*," *Modern Philology*, XLI (August, 1943), 45–58.

Hamm, Victor L. "Addison and the Pleasures of the Imagination," *Modern Language Notes*, LII (November, 1937), 498–500.

Hathaway, Baxter Levering. "The Lucretian 'Return upon Ourselves' in Eighteenth-Century Theories of Tragedy," *Publications of the Modern Language Association*, LXII (September, 1947), 672–89.

Hilles, Frederick Whiley. *Letters of Sir Joshua Reynolds*. Cambridge: Cambridge University Press, 1929.

———. *The Literary Career of Sir Joshua Reynolds*. Cambridge: Cambridge University Press, 1936.

Hipple, Walter J. "The Aesthetics of Dugald Stewart: Culmination of a Tradition," *The Journal of Aesthetics and Art Criticism*, XIV (September, 1955), 77–96.

———. "General and Particular in the *Discourses* of Sir Joshua Reynolds: A Study in Method," *The Journal of Aesthetics and Art Criticism*, XI (March, 1953), 231–47.

———. "The Logic of Hume's Essay 'Of Tragedy,'" *The Philosophical Quarterly*, VI (January, 1956), 43–52.

Hogarth, William. *The Analysis of Beauty, Written with a View of Fixing the Fluctuating Ideas of Taste*. London, 1753.

Howard, William Guild. "Burke among the Forerunners of Lessing," *Publications of the Modern Language Association*, XXII (1907), 608–32.

Hume, David. *An Enquiry Concerning the Principles of Morals*. LaSalle, Ill.: Open Court, 1946.

————. *Essays Moral, Political, and Literary*. Edited by T. H. Green and T. H. Grose. 2 vols. London: Longmans, 1875.

————. *The Letters of David Hume*. Edited by J. Y. T. Greig. 2 vols. Oxford: Clarendon Press, 1932.

————. *A Treatise of Human Nature* . . . . Edited by T. H. Green and T. H. Grose. 2 vols. New edition. London: Longmans, 1882.

Hussey, Christopher. *The Picturesque: Studies in a Point of View*. London: Putnam, 1927.

[Hutcheson, Francis]. *An Essay on the Nature and Conduct of the Passions and Affections. With Illustrations of the Moral Sense. By the Author of the Inquiry into the Original of Our Ideas of Beauty and Virtue*. London, 1728.

————. *An Inquiry into the Original of Our Ideas of Beauty and Virtue; in Two Treatises. In Which the Principles of the Late Earl of Shaftsbury Are Explain'd and Defended, Against the Author of the "Fable of the Bees" and the Ideas of Moral Good and Evil Are Establish'd, According to the Sentiments of the Antient Moralists. With an Attempt to Introduce a Mathematical Calculation in Subjects of Morality*. London, 1725.

[Jeffrey, Francis, Lord]. "*Essays on the Nature and Principles of Taste. By Archibald Alison* . . . ," *The Edinburgh Review*, XVIII (May, 1811), [1]–46.

————. "*Philosophical Essays. By* Dugald Stewart . . . ," *The Edinburgh Review*, XVII (November, 1810), 167–211.

Jessop, T. E. *A Bibliography of David Hume and of Scottish Philosophy from Francis Hutcheson to Lord Balfour*. London: A. Brown & Sons, 1938.

Johnson, Samuel. *A Dictionary of the English Language* . . . . 2 vols. London, 1755.

————. *A Dictionary of the English Language* . . . . 6th ed. London, 1785.

Journal of the Royal Society of Arts, LXXX, No. 4139 (March 18, 1932), 438–59.

Kallich, Martin. "The Association of Ideas and Critical Theory: Hobbes, Locke, and Addison," *English Literary History*, XII (December, 1945), 290–315.

————. "The Meaning of Archibald Alison's *Essays on Taste*," *Philological Quarterly*, XXVII (October, 1948), 314–24.

Kames, Henry Home, Lord. *Elements of Criticism*. 3 vols. 2d ed. Edinburgh, 1763.

————. *Elements of Criticism*. 2 vols. 3d ed. Edinburgh, 1765.

[Kames, Henry Home, Lord]. *Essays on the Principles of Morality and Natural Religion*. Edinburgh, 1751.

Knight, Richard Payne. *An Analytical Inquiry into the Principles of Taste*. 3d ed. London, 1806.

Knight, R[ichard] P[ayne]. *The Landscape, a Didactic Poem in Three Books. Addressed to Uvedale Price, Esq*. London, 1794.

Langhorne, Dr. John (ed.). *The Poetical Works of William Collins*. London: William Pickering, 1830.

Lauder, Sir Thomas Dick (ed.). *Sir Uvedale Price on the Picturesque: with an*

Essay on the Origin of Taste, and Much Original Matter, by Sir Thomas Dick Lauder, Bart. . . . Edinburgh: Caldwell, Lloyd, & Co., 1842.

Leslie, Charles, and Taylor, Tom. *Life and Times of Sir Joshua Reynolds* . . . . 2 vols. London: J. Murray, 1865.

The Living Age, CCCXIX (8th series, Vol. XXXII; December 22, 1923), 579–80. Item: Hogarth's letter to the Rev. Mayo.

Longinus. *Longinus, "On the Sublime": An English Translation by Benedict Einarson . . . and Sir Joshua Reynolds, "Discourses on Art." With an Introduction by Elder Olson.* . . . Chicago: Packard, 1945.

Macklem, Michael. "Reynolds and the Ambiguities of Neo-Classical Criticism," *Philological Quarterly*, XXXI (October, 1952), 383–98.

Manwaring, Elizabeth Wheeler. *Italian Landscape in Eighteenth Century England.* New York: Oxford, 1925.

[Matthews, John]. *A Sketch from The Landscape, a Didactic Poem. Addressed to R. P. Knight, Esqr. With Notes, Illustrations, and a Postscript.* London, 1794.

Mayoux, J[ean] J[acques]. *Richard Payne Knight et le pittoresque: Essai sur une phase esthétique.* Thèse pour le doctorate ès-lettres presentée . . . [à l'] Université de Paris—Faculté des Lettres. Paris: Les Presses Modernes, 1932.

McCosh, James. *The Scottish Philosophy, Biographical, Expository, Critical, from Hutcheson to Hamilton.* New York: Scribner, 1890.

McKenzie, Gordon. *Critical Responsiveness: A Study of the Psychological Current in Later Eighteenth-Century Criticism.* "University of California Publications in English," Vol. XX (1949). Berkeley: University of California Press, 1949.

———. "Lord Kames and the Mechanist Tradition," *University of California Publications in English*, XIV (1942; Berkeley: University of California Press, 1943), 107–8.

McKeon, Richard P. "Literary Criticism and the Concepts of Imitation in Antiquity," *Modern Philology*, XXXIV (August, 1936), 1–35.

———. "The Philosophic Bases of Art and Criticism," *Modern Philology*, XLI (November, 1943), 65–87 and (February, 1944), 129–71.

———. "Philosophy and Method," *The Journal of Philosophy*, XLVIII, No. 22 (October 25, 1951), 653–82.

Mill, John Stuart. *A System of Logic, Ratiocinative and Inductive.* 9th ed. 2 vols. London: Longmans, Green, Reader, & Dyer, 1873.

Monk, Samuel H. *The Sublime: A Study of Critical Theories in XVIII-Century England.* New York: Modern Language Association, 1935.

Moore, Theodore McGinnes. "The Background of Edmund Burke's Theory of the Sublime (1660–1759)." Unpublished Ph.D. dissertation, Cornell University, 1933.

Olson, Elder (ed.). *Longinus, "On the Sublime": An English Translation by Benedict Einarson . . . and Sir Joshua Reynolds Discourses on Art. With an Introduction by Elder Olson* . . . . Chicago: Packard, 1945.

Pevsner, Nikolaus. "The Genesis of the Picturesque," *The Architectural Review*, XCVI (November, 1944), 139–46.

———. "Good King James Gothic," *The Architectural Review*, CVII (February, 1950), 117–22.

———. "Humphry Repton: A Florilegium," *The Architectural Review*, CIII (February, 1948), 53–59.

————. "Richard Payne Knight," *The Art Bulletin*, XXXI (December, 1949), 293–320.

Polwhele, Richard. *Pictures from Nature. In Twelve Sonnets* . . . . London, 1785.

Pope, Alexander. *The Works of Alexander Pope.* Edited by Croker and Elwin. 10 vols. London: J. Murray, 1871.

Price, Uvedale. *An Essay on the Picturesque, As Compared with the Sublime and the Beautiful; and, on the Use of Studying Pictures, for the Purpose of Improving Real Landscape.* London, 1794. Bound with Price's *A Letter to H. Repton, Esq.* . . . (London, 1795), Humphry Repton's *A Letter to Uvedale Price, Esq.* (London, 1794), manuscript letters, &c.; in Newberry Library, Chicago.

————. *Essays on the Picturesque, As Compared with the Sublime and the Beautiful; and, on the Use of Studying Pictures, for the Purpose of Improving Real Landscape.* 3 vols. London, 1810.

————. *Sir Uvedale Price on the Picturesque* . . . . Edited by Sir Thomas Dick Lauder (q.v.). Edinburgh, 1842.

Quennell, Peter. *Hogarth's Progress.* New York: Viking Press, Inc., 1955.

Randall, Helen Whitcomb. *The Critical Theory of Lord Kames.* "Smith College Studies in Modern Languages," Vol. XXII, Nos. 1–4 (October, 1940–July, 1941). Northampton, Mass.: Departments of Modern Languages of Smith College, 1944.

Read, Stanley E. *A Bibliography of Hogarth Books and Studies, 1900–1940; with an Introductory Essay on Trends in Hogarth Criticism, 1764–1940.* Chicago: De Paul University, 1941.

————. "Some Observations on William Hogarth's *Analysis of Beauty:* A Bibliographical Study," *The Huntington Library Quarterly*, V (April, 1942), 360–73.

Reid, Thomas. *The Works of Thomas Reid, D.D.* . . . Edited by Sir William Hamilton, Bart. 8th ed. 2 vols. Edinburgh: Maclachlan and Stewart, 1880.

Repton, Humphry. *The Art of Landscape Gardening. Including His "Sketches and Hints on Landscape Gardening" and "Theory and Practice of Landscape Gardening."* Edited by John Nolen. Boston: Houghton, 1907.

————. *The Landscape Gardening and Landscape Architecture of the Late Humphry Repton, Esq. Being His Entire Works on These Subjects* . . . . Edited by J[ohn] C[laudius] Loudon. London: Published by the editor, 1840.

Reynolds, Sir Joshua. *The Literary Works of Sir Joshua Reynolds, Kt.* Edited by Edmond Malone. 5th ed. 3 vols. London, 1819.

Richardson, Jonathan. *The Works of Mr. Jonathan Richardson* . . . . Edited by his son, J. Richardson. London, 1773.

Robbins, David O. "The Aesthetics of Thomas Reid," *The Journal of Aesthetics and Art Criticism*, No. 5 (Spring, 1942), pp. 30–41.

Sandrart, Joachim von. *Joachim von Sandrarts Academie der Bau-, Bild- und Mahlerey-Künste von 1675. Leben der berühmten Maler, Bildhauer, und Baumeister.* Herausgegeben und kommentiert von Dr. A. R. Peltzer. München: G. Hirth's Verlag, 1925.

Schmitz, Robert Morell. *Hugh Blair.* Morningside Heights, N.Y.: King's Crown Press, 1948.

Scott, William Robert. *Francis Hutcheson.* Cambridge: Cambridge University Press, 1900.

Shearer, Edna Aston. "Wordsworth and Coleridge Marginalia in a Copy of Richard Payne Knight's *Analytical Inquiry into the Principles of Taste,*" *The Huntington Library Quarterly,* I (October, 1937), 63–99.

Smollett, Tobias. *The Expedition of Humphry Clinker,* in *The Works of Tobias Smollett,* Vols. XI and XII. New York: George D. Sproul, 1902.

Steele, Sir Richard. *The Tender Husband; or, The Accomplish'd Fools. A Comedy.* London, 1705.

Stewart, Dugald. *The Collected Works of Dugald Stewart, Esq., F.R.S.S.* Edited by Sir William Hamilton, Bart. [2d ed.] 11 vols. Edinburgh: T. & T. Clark, 1877.

————. *Philosophical Essays.* Edinburgh, 1810.

Swabey, William Curtis. "Benevolence and Virtue," *The Philosophical Review,* LII (September, 1943), 452–67.

Sypher, Wylie. "Baroque Afterpiece: The Picturesque," *Gazette des Beaux-Arts,* XXVII (January, 1945), 39–58.

Templeman, William D. *The Life and Work of William Gilpin . . . .* "Illinois Studies in Language and Literature," Vol. XXIV, Nos. 3 and 4. Urbana: University of Illinois Press, 1939.

————. "Sir Joshua Reynolds on the Picturesque," *Modern Language Notes,* XLVII (November, 1932), 446–48.

Thompson, E[lbert] N. S. "The Discourses of Sir Joshua Reynolds," *Publications of the Modern Language Association,* XXXII (1917), 339–66.

Thorpe, Clarence DeWitt. "Addison and Hutcheson on the Imagination," *English Literary History,* II (November, 1935), 215–34.

————. "Addison's Contribution to Criticism," in *The Seventeenth Century: Studies in the History of English Thought and Literature from Bacon to Pope, by Richard Foster Jones and Others Writing in His Honor,* pp. 316–29. Stanford, Cal.: Stanford University Press, 1951.

————. "Addison's Theory of the Imagination as 'Perceptive Response,' " *Papers of the Michigan Academy of Science, Arts, and Letters,* XXI (1935; Ann Arbor: University of Michigan Press, 1936), 511–30.

Trowbridge, Hoyt. "Platonism and Sir Joshua Reynolds," *English Studies,* XXI (February, 1939), 1–7.

Tuveson, Ernest. "Space, Deity, and the 'Natural Sublime,' " *Modern Language Quarterly,* XII (March, 1951), 20–38.

Twining, Thomas. *Aristotle's Treatise on Poetry, Translated: with Notes on the Translation, and on the Original; and Two Dissertations, on Poetical, and Musical, Imitation.* London, 1789.

Warton, Joseph. *The Adventurer,* No. 80 (August 11, 1753).

Wasserman, Earl R. "The Pleasures of Tragedy," *English Literary History,* XIV (December, 1947), 283–307.

Webb, Daniel. *An Inquiry into the Beauties of Painting; and into the Merits of the Most Celebrated Painters, Ancient and Modern.* Dublin, 1764.

Wichelns, Herbert A. "Burke's Essay on the Sublime and Its Reviewers," *The Journal of English and Germanic Philology,* XXI (1922), 645–61.

Wilenski, R. H. *English Painting.* London: Faber, 1933.

Wiley, Margaret Lee. "Gerard and the Scots Societies," in *The University of Texas Publication: Studies in English*, No. 4026 (Austin: University of Texas, 1940), pp. 132–36.

Winckelmann, Abbé Johann Joachim. *Reflections on the Painting and Sculpture of the Greeks: with Instructions for the Connoisseur, and An Essay on Grace in Works of Art*. Translated by Henry Fusseli. 2d ed. London, 1767.

INDEX

Addison, Joseph: on taste, 7, 305; role in tradition, 9, 313; on novelty, 18–19, 70, 87, 112, 151, 197, 311, 316; on gardens, 21, 312; and Alison, 180; and Blair, 24, 125; and Burke, 19; and Hutcheson, 15, 34; and Kames, 109; and Locke, 15, 324; and Longinus, 16–17; and Reid, 151; mentioned, 83, 287, 317, 318, 320, 326

Aglionby, William: on the picturesque, 185, 186

Akenside, Mark: on novelty, 16, 151, 311; on beauty of matter (and Reid), 155; (and Alison), 169, 352; (and Stewart), 287

Algarotti, Count, 346

Alison, Archibald: on taste, 7, 305; method, 8, 306–7, 308; role in tradition, 316–17; and Addison, 7, 180; and Akenside, 169, 352; and Gerard, 74; and Hartley, 168–69; and Hogarth, 55, 62, 172–73; and Hume, 29, 37, 158, 169, 174, 351, 352; and Hutcheson, 169, 173; and Jeffrey, 158, 290; and Kames, 168, 172, 178, 180; and Knight, 158, 259, 270; and Lauder, 159; and Mill's methods, 161–78 *passim;* and Plato, 169–70; and Reid, 153, 155, 157, 158, 168, 169, 170; and Reynolds, 175; and Smith, 176; and Spence, 169; and Stewart, 158, 287, 289–90, 294, 299; mentioned, 29, 76, 81, 99, 119, 185, 196, 312, 313, 314, 318, 319, 320

Angelico, Fra, 61

Aristotle: on beauty of size, 94; and Gerard, on probability, 78; criticized by Kames, 101; and Kames, on tragedy, 117–18, 343; and Knight, on tragedy, 269, 272, 371; and Reynolds, 135–36, 137; and Stewart, 296

Association: Addison, 23–24; Alison, 29, 161, 164, 170, 172; Burke, 90–91, 96–97, 240; Gerard, 72–73; Hogarth, 62, 64–65; Hutcheson, 29; Kames, 29, 109; Knight, 259–70 *passim;* Price, 206–8, 239–40; Repton, 235–37; Reynolds, 141; Stewart, 289–302 *passim;* general, 8, 309, 313–19 *passim*

Bacon, Francis: inductive method (and Gerard), 81

Baillie, John: on the sublime, 71–74, 89

Beattie, James: Reynolds and, 141; mentioned, 9, 70, 149, 287

Bellori, 346

Bergson, Henri, 342

Berkeley, Bishop: Kames and, 100, 101; and Knight, 255; and Reid, 149, 150; and Stewart, 286

Birkhoff, George, 28

Blair, Hugh: role in tradition, 9, 315–16, 317; on tragedy, 50; on the picturesque, 186; and Addison, 24, 125; and Burke, 124, 127, 339; and Gerard, 124, 125, 127, 132; and Hogarth, 130; and Hutcheson, 130–31; and Kames, 124, 126; and Knight, 128; and Longinus, 128; and Stewart, 287, 297

Bosanquet, Bernard, 99, 159, 222, 331, 351

Botticelli, 61

Britton, John: on the picturesque, 185, 360

Brown, John: Alison and, 158; mentioned, 9

Brown, Lancelot (Capability): Kames and, 119; and Knight, 250, 282; and Matthews, 250, 367; and Price, 215–16, 239, 241, 242, 282; and Repton, 224, 229, 239, 242, 244, 365

Buffier, Claude, 287, 295

385